formula one

THE 1999 SEASON

This edition published in 1999 by
Michael O'Mara Books Limited
9 Lion Yard, Tremadoc Road
London SW4 7NQ

ISBN 1-85479-463-9

Book created by Mixing
Written by Chuck Penfold
Edited by W.E.D. Hilber
Printed in Germany
Photography: Ferdi and Bodo Kraeling
Copyright © 1999 Mixing

formula one

THE 1999 SEASON

Formula One World Championship 1999 – The Races

His star burned out after his pit stop: Heinz-Harald Frentzen led the way in his home Grand Prix at the Nurburgring - until a technical failure forced him to retire.

From waterboy to championship contender: It was a very good year for Northern Ireland's Eddie Irvine.

Right: The start of the first ever Malaysian Grand Prix.

Above: One of the most fateful moments of the 1999 Grand Prix Season. David Coulthard collides with team-mate Mika Hakkinen in the first curve at Spa-Francorchamps. Right: A season to forget for Ferrari's Michael Schumacher.

Features

Below: After 98 days on the sidelines Michael Schumacher made his comeback at the Malaysian Grand Prix.

Above: The most pleasant surprise of the season. Heinz-Harald Frentzen established himself in the elite class of Formula One drivers.

Above left: Pedro Diniz walked away virtually unscathed from his horrific crash at the Nurburgring. Above: A man of the future. Ralf Schumacher repeatedly displayed outstanding driving skill in the inferior Williams-Supertec. Left: It was the most difficult season of defending champion Mika Hakkinen's career.

Speed in the City

"The Monaco Grand Prix is akin to flying a helicopter in your living room." The Formula One drivers like McLaren´s David Coulthard zip along at speeds of up to 280 kph, often just millimetres from the barriers. One this is for certain, the last true city course on the Grand Prix circuit is utterly unforgiving.

The Next Superstar

Ralf Schumacher hasn't only emerged from his older brother's shadow, he's driven his inferior Williams-Supertec into the limelight. He missed winning his home race at the Nurburgring by the skin of his teeth. No matter, Frank Williams extended his contract to 2003.

Dreams of a Third Title

It could have been his year. In Monaco Michael Schumacher drove to an impressive victory but his hopes of a third drivers championship were dashed by his high-speed crash at Silverstone. The German superstar will take those same hopes into the 2000 season.

Back With A Vengeance

Heinz-Harald Frentzen looked better than ever in 1999. Trading cockpits with Ralf Schumacher really paid off. For a time it even looked as if the Jordan driver might have an outside shot at the drivers championship. With victories at Magny-Cours and Monza he returned to the ranks of the very best drivers.

A Rocky Road

A difficult title defence: it was without a doubt McLaren driver Mika Hakkinen´s most difficult season of his Formula One career - even with Michael Schumacher on the sidelines. The Finn was plagued by the fact that McLaren doesn't have a team order combined with his own mistakes and technical failure such as this blown tyre at Hockenheim.

A Fourth Groove

Evolution instead of revolution. Following last year's radical change to the Formula One of the narrow lanes Grand Prix cars returned to the track this season looking almost identical to the way they looked when they left last autumn in Japan. The only visible change was the addition of a fourth groove on the treads of their front tyres. But this was enough to cause quite a stir. The 1.4 centimetres less of tyre contacting the road proved devastating for some veteran drivers.

The new front tyres with four grooves even led to some veteran drivers to retire.

The extra groove was actually designed to a have a significant positive impact. The world motor-racing authority FIA ordered it added to the front tyres in the interest of safety. But it's most immediate effect seemed to be to throw team orders out of whack. Several high-profile drivers had trouble adjusting. Veteran stars like Englishman Damon Hill, Alessandro Zanardi and Olivier Panis eventually ran out of excuses for their disappointing results. Hill looked bad beside his younger team-mate Heinz-Harald Frentzen, so bad in fact that his frustration over the new tyres eventually drove him to retire from driving. "These tyres are for the Kart generation", complained the former world champion. "They're used to skidding into curves."

According to treaded tyre advocate and FIA President Max Mosley, the less the tyre surface actually contacts the road, the slower drivers are forced to take the corners. As if that weren't enough of a penalty for full-blooded Formula

One drivers who like to speed around the curves as fast as possible, the fact that there was only one tyre supplier this season made matters much worse. Without the pressure of competition Bridgestone changed its development goal from making its tyres faster, to making them more durable.

The combination of these two changes meant that most drivers found that the adjustment from three to four grooves was even more difficult than the adjustment from slicks to treads. While aerodynamic aids ensured sufficient adhesion in fast curves, the drivers were surprised by the reduced grip at lower speeds. The secret to success obviously lies in a sensitive foot on the gas and a fluid driving style, in other words the way Heinz-Harald Frentzen drives. Rubens Barrichello is another driver who made the adjustment well. His secret is completing braking before actually entering the curve, and only then beginning to steer into it. But drivers who are used to slamming

their cars into the curves, like Champ Car master Zanardi for example lose traction on their front tyres. This not only costs valuable time, but also shortens the life of the tyre. But the Italian Williams driver was unrepentant, explaining: "If it works for Ralf Schumacher, I've got to be able to do it do."

What aggravated both the drivers and the engineers even more than the lack of traction was something that hadn't been expected: The new tyres wear out faster than the old ones. That's because the tyres don't wear evenly across the five points at which they make contact with the road. The old slicks with one wide point of contact were much better in this respect. The frustrated Hill put the chances of solving this problem at 1000 to one.

This fourth groove didn't arrive without affecting the design of Formula One racers either. Again it was McLaren head designer Adrian Newey who was the first to recognise the sign of the times. While the rest of the constructors imitated the design they'd used the previous year trying to compensate for the lower traction on the front axle by moving some of the weight of the car forward, Newey was again a step ahead. The current design guru remembered that one of the most important factors is the balance of the car. So he moved the cockpit back 15 centimetres and made the tank shorter but taller, concentrating the weight of the car in the middle. It obviously had the desired effect.

Former world champion Damon Hill simply couldn´t adjust to four grooves.

Only a sensitive foot on the gas and brake pedal will do: Formula One cars under the current regulations.

FIA-President Max Mosley: Introducing measures designed to improve safety for both drivers and fans.

Compared to the controversy which developed over the unpopular grooves, the rest of the rule changes introduced this season were far less spectacular. The Formula One super brains concentrated themselves on plugging up the few remaining minor loopholes in the regulations. In the off season the engineers at Ferrari, Sauber and BAR had been tinkering around with rear wings, putting them through high speed tests looking to get more speed out of a narrower surface on the straightaways but which would at the same time maintain the downward air pressure and thus traction on the curves. After Michael Schumacher crashed during a test run, and Jacques Villeneuve did the same in the first race of the season, both because these aerodynamic aids had broken, the Formula One police put an end to such experiments. They demanded that any new such additions must first pass a FIA test, standing up to 100 kilograms of pressure without bending. However the engineers decided to give up on the idea entirely in the interest of the safety of the drivers.

Finally in an effort to save the multi-million circus which is the Formula One, from a cost explosion FIA decided to limit the number of test driving days to 50. It was a radical limit which simply didn't work. While the rich teams went out and tested their cars to their heart's delight - at additional expense of course - the less affluent teams reluctantly acted in accordance with the decree issued in Geneva, simply because they didn't have the money to do otherwise.

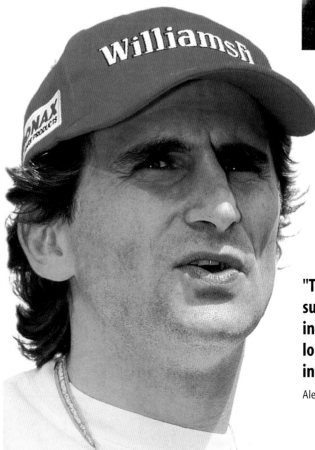

"These tyres do not suit my natural driving style. I can no longer slam my car into the curves."

Alessandro Zanardi of Williams

1st Race in the World Championship 1999, Albert Park Circuit, Melbourne (AUS), 7th March 1999

Same proc

It all started just as it had one year earlier. During the entire weekend in Melbourne the silver arrows of McLaren-Mercedes dominated qualifying. Nobody came even close, not even Ferrari's Michael Schumacher. But the Australian Grand Prix was proof that success in qualifying is no guarantee of success in the race itself. Ferrari's number two driver, Northern Ireland's Eddie Irvine took the chequered flag for his first ever Formula One victory.

On top »down under«: In the land of the kangaroos Eddie Irvine sprang to the top of the podium for the first time.

Off and running into a news season: Mika Hakkinen won the sprint out of the gate but not the race.

An impressive debut: Ralf Schumacher made it to the podium in his very first race for Williams.

Many British Formula One fans who subscribe to the theory that he who starts from the pole position almost always wins, likely stayed in bed, believing they already knew the outcome of the race. After all, the McLarens demonstrated their superiority qualifying 1.3 seconds per lap ahead of their closest competition. But those who did manage to get up in the wee hours of that Sunday morning were rewarded with and exciting and incident-packed race.

The early laps though resembled a video replay of the previous year's Australian Grand Prix. Starting from the first row, Mika Hakkinen and David Coulthard left the competition behind. They quickly sped out to a lead of almost 2 seconds per round, and they looked to be in a completely different class from all the others. The question on the minds of many motor racing fans was whether the two Mercedes drivers would manage to yet again lap the rest.

Their superiority was no coincidence. Yet again the team from Woking had proved its uncanny instinct regarding the difficult conditions »down under«. Beginning with the training laps, all of the teams were faced with problems with their cars´ front tyres - and the slippery street course in Melbourne provides precious little traction. Only the McLarens - development partners with Bridgestone - appeared unaffected by such problems, and completed record lap times.

Above: Hard Luck - Ferrari had problems getting off the mark.
Middle: Zanardi´s excursion onto the lawn. Below: Non-finisher -
Coulthard´s gearbox packed in.
Right: Out of the points - Schumacher plays catch-up

Talent pays off: Toranosuke Takagi finished seventh.

Reason to celebrate: Pedro de la Rosa finished his first Grand Prix in the points.

But the impressiveness of the way the silver arrows had marked their return from the winter break was more than matched by the unceremonious manner in which they bowed out of the race. On the 14th lap Coulthard parked his car in the garage, following a loss hydraulic pressure. Eight laps later his Finnish team-mate was force out by a throttle linkage failure in his car.

The team had elected to run the calculated risk of going with the new McLaren MP/14, despite the fact that it had never been tested over the full length of a Grand Prix race. Before the season's first race, McLaren had seriously considered using a modified version of the car they used in the 1998 season. But for team boss Ron Dennis, this was out of the question. »Even if we didn't cross the finish line, now we know where we stand in comparison with the other teams. Besides, I'd rather take a fast car and make it reliable, than take a reliable, but slow car fast.« McLaren's Scottish player remained optimistic. »We know at least that we went out leading, and that's important,« said Coulthard. »I think the car is capable of going quicker, which bodes well for Brazil.«

Ferrari and former world champion Michael Schumacher also experienced an emotional roller coaster ride on this first Grand Prix weekend of the season. Despite Eddie Irvine's victory it had already become clear that in technical terms Ferrari were bound to be up against it once again. Just like in the last race of the previous season - at Suzuka - Schumacher was forced to start from the back of the field after stalling his Ferrari before the second warm-up lap.

No luck at all: Rubens Barrichello

Some lesser drivers might have been discouraged to the point of writing off the race. Not Michael Schumacher. The German set out on one of those missions he's so famous for - chasing the pack, and gradually passing numerous opponents. Badoer, Panis, Zonta, Alesi, Zanardi, Diniz, and a few others followed the German from their rear view mirrors into their field of sight - in front of them. By the 22nd lap the former world champion had clawed his way into fourth place. But it was all for nought. Five laps later the right rear tyre on his car gave up the ghost - another tribute of sorts to Suzuka 1998.

Despite such setbacks, the man from Kerpen, a small town near Cologne, famous for its Gothic cathedral still managed to just kept on improving on the day's fastest lap time, with the fastest 1.2 seconds faster than the best the McLaren's could do, while they were still in the race that is. During his pit stop on lap 38 his Ferrari crew replaced his steering wheel and corrected the car's gear trouble. However in the end the Prussian star was able to do no better than eighth. »The McLarens' lead caught me by surprise, but I won't get concerned unless two races down the road we haven't been able to solve the problem. The car is reliable and is full of potential. We'll get some more speed out of it too«, said Schumacher afterwards. To him giving up is a foreign concept.

But while it wasn't a great day for the German, it could have been worse, he could have been Rubens Barrichello. It took a whole series of misfortunes to prevent the Stewart-Ford team from getting its first ever win on the Formula One circuit. It was clear even before the race that not everything was going according to plan for the Scottish team. Despite this the Brazilian driver in his Stewart SF-3 managed to qualify in what for him was a sensational fourth. Starting from the second row, it looked like anything might be possible on the Sunday of the race. But as other drivers were taking their start positions following the warm up laps, the Stewart pit team were scrambling to extinguish fires in both of their cars that were supposed to race. The cause

Above: more bad luck - Gene's GP debut. Below: Pure fun - a F1 Fan.

Perfection: World champion Mika Hakkinen was untouchable in qualifying.

Complete commitment: Michael Schumacher even did his best when rally-cross driving was called for.

Zanardi was battling just to keep up with the rest of the pack. In qualifying the returnee to the Formula One circuit was almost a second slower than his team-mate. On Sunday things went from bad to worse. Zanardi´s race ended with a crash on lap 20, who at the time was running in a disappointing 13th position. The fact that his best lap was more than 3 and a half seconds slower than that of his German team-mate likely did nothing to improve his downcast demeanour.

But there was one pleasant surprise down under. His name: Pedro Diniz. The son of a rich Brazilian businessman proved that he has what it takes to make it on the Formula One circuit without having to pay his way in. Although he was forced to use the reserve car in qualifying, (which is tailored to Jean Alesi), the Sauber driver started from 14th in the grid - two positions ahead of his team-mate. At one point during the race he'd even clawed his way up to fourth, before being forced out with gearbox trouble.

Same procedure as last year? Not quite. Fortunately Formula One motor racing is always full of surprises. And so far no clear trend is apparent. For that we'll have to wait for the Brazilian Grand Prix - at least.

was faulty oil valves, which meant that for Johnny Herbert the Australian Grand Prix was over before it began. But »Rubinho« climbed into the reserve car and tore out of the pits to give chase to the rest of the field. That was, until trouble developed with his fuel pump, forcing him back into the pits for repairs. As if that weren't enough, then he was assessed a stop and go penalty for overtaking during a safety car lap. This set him back further. A frustrated Barrichello told reporters afterwards, »I could have won this race«. But it wasn't all bad news. With his 5th place finish the Brazilian, who at 26 is already a Formula One veteran earned two important points for Stewart, and even recorded the day's second fastest lap.

Irvine proved that he can win.

Ferrari's number two Eddie Irvine left Australia at the other end of the emotional spectrum. One can only imagine how the 33 year-old bon vivant celebrated his first ever Formula One victory. For three long years he'd toiled as Michael Schumacher´s waterboy. Now in Melbourne this happy go lucky Northern Irishman had proved once and for all that he had what it takes to win. All this having only had part of one day to test the new Ferrari prior to the race. All of the other test laps had been driven by his team-mate. Despite this Irvine climbed into the cockpit of what to him was still an almost completely foreign car and drove an intelligent and flawless race. It was Irvine's first win in the 82nd Grand Prix race of his career. After spraying champagne all over pit lane, he finally spoke to reporters. »It's great, everyone slags me off because I go out and have fun and stuff like that,« he said. »So the young drivers coming up at least know you can win in Formula One and still have a good time.«

But it wasn't a doddle. Heinz-Harald Frentzen made an outstanding debut for the Jordan Mugen Honda team, and kept the pressure up on Irvine throughout the race. They even made a pit stop on lap 34, entering and leaving the pits as if driving in formation. The German found himself within striking distance, just waiting to make his move. But it wasn't to be Frentzen´s day. A defective sensor prevented the Honda V-10 engine from optimal performance. Instead of making a run at winning the race, Frentzen soon found himself having to fight off the challenge of the »other« Schumacher, Michael's brother Ralf. The Williams driver had his first chance to pass his compatriot on lap 18. In the confusion caused by Hakkinen´s troubled Mercedes, Schumacher slipped past the Jordan driver. But the counter attack came on the very next curve. Frentzen was back in second.

Heinz-Harald´s team-mate on the other hand could hardly contain his disappointment. In his 100th Formula One race, the former world champion didn't get very far. In qualifying Frentzen was just 4 tenths of a second better. But in the race itself, the Englishman didn't even make it to the second curve. »I had a brilliant start, but then I was knocked out by a competitor who apparently couldn't find the brake pedal.«

The two Williams drivers were also world's apart. While Ralf Schumacher came in a respectable third, two time Champ Car champion Alessandro

Above: Pure joy - Heinz-Harald Frentzen´s move to Jordan paid off right away.
Below: The most possible points - Eddie Irvine was the hero of the day.

Statistics

🇦🇺 **1st Race of the World Championship 1999, Albert Park Circuit, Melbourne (AUS), 7th March 1999**

Course length:	5,303 km
Distance of race:	57 (= 302,213 km)
Start time:	2.00 UTC
Weather on day of race:	warm, sunny
Attendance:	118 000
1998 Results:	1. Mika Hakkinen (FIN, McLaren-Mercedes MP4/13), 1 h 31'45"996
	2. David Coulthard (GB, McLaren-Mercedes MP4/13), +0"702 s
	3. Heinz-Harald Frentzen (D, Williams-Mecachrome FW20), −1 Lap
Pole position 1998:	Mika Hakkinen (McLaren-Mercedes MP4/13), 1'30"010 m
Fastest Lap 1998:	Mika Hakkinen (McLaren-Mercedes MP4/13), 1'31"649 m
Fastest pit stop 1998:	Mika Hakkinen (McLaren-Mercedes MP4/13), 11"242 s

Not a lot of grip on the track, but a great atmosphere

"For a city course Melbourne is great. The Albert Park Circuit has the feel of a real racetrack. As far as atmosphere is concerned Australia's one of the best races of the season. Here everyone battles to get enough traction. The car constantly understeers because the track is slippery and the asphalt is often very hot."

Eddie Irvine

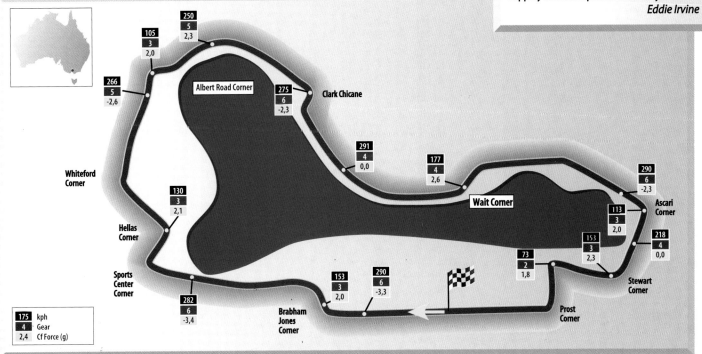

175 kph / 4 Gear / 2,4 Cf Force (g)

Results

	Driver	Team	Pit stops	Laps	Time (hours)	Average speed	Behind 1st	prev. driver
1.	Eddie Irvine	Ferrari	1	57	1 h 35'01"659	190,852	–	–
2.	Heinz-Harald Frentzen	Jordan-Mugen-Honda	1	57	1 h 35'02"686	190,818	1"026 s	5"986 s
3.	Ralf Schumacher	Williams-Supertec	1	57	1 h 35'08"671	190,618	7"012 s	5"986 s
4.	Giancarlo Fisichella	Benetton-Playlife	2	57	1 h 35'35"077	189,740	33"418 s	26"406 s
5.	Rubens Barrichello	Stewart-Ford	3	57	1 h 35'56"357	189,038	54"697 s	21"279 s
6.	Pedro de la Rosa	TWR-Arrows	2	57	1 h 36'25"976	188,071	1'24"316 m	29"619 s
7.	Toranosuke Takagi	TWR-Arrows	1	57	1 h 36'27"947	188,007	1'26"288 m	1"972 s
8.	Michael Schumacher	Ferrari	3	56	1 h 35'16"505	187,017	1 lap	1 lap

Driver	Team	Pit stops	in lap	Reason f. retiring	Position before retiring
Ricardo Zonta	BAR-Supertec	3	48	gearbox trouble	8
Luca Badoer	Minardi-Ford	2	42	gearbox trouble	9
Alexander Wurz	Benetton-Playlife	1	28	rear wheel suspension	10
Pedro Diniz	Sauber-Petronas	1	27	gearbox trouble	4
Marc Gené	Minardi-Ford	1	25	collision with Trulli	12
Jarno Trulli	Prost-Peugeot	1	25	collision with Gené	13
Olivier Panis	Prost-Peugeot	0	23	wheel mount	9
Mika Hakkinen	McLaren-Mercedes	1	21	engine trouble	16
Alessandro Zanardi	Williams-Supertec	1	20	crash	13
David Coulthard	McLaren-Mercedes	0	13	engine trouble	2
Jacques Villeneuve	BAR-Supertec	0	13	broken rear wing	8
Damon Hill	Jordan-Mugen-Honda	0	0	collision with Trulli	9
Jean Alesi	Sauber-Petronas	0	0	gearbox trouble	16
Johnny Herbert	Stewart-Ford	0	didn´t restart	engine overheated	–

Australian GP

1st Race of the World Championship 1999, Albert Park Circuit, Melbourne (AUS), 7th March 1999

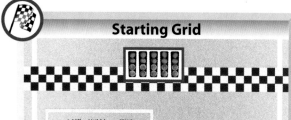

Starting Grid

1 Mika Häkkinen (FIN)
McLaren-Mercedes MP4/14
1'30"462 m (293,7 km/h) [1]

2 David Coulthard (GB)
McLaren-Mercedes MP4/14
1'30"946 m (291,3 km/h)

3 Michael Schumacher (D)
Ferrari F399
1'31"781 m (285,1 km/h)

16 Rubens Barrichello (BR)
Stewart-Ford SF3
1'32"148 m (286,4 km/h)

8 Heinz-Harald Frentzen (D)
Jordan-Mugen-Honda 199
1'32"276 m (288,1 km/h)

4 Eddie Irvine (GB)
Ferrari F399
1'32"289 m (288,0 km/h)

9 Giancarlo Fisichella (I)
Benetton-Playlife B199
1'32"540 m (285,0 km/h)

6 Ralf Schumacher (D)
Williams-Supertec FW21
1'32"691 m (284,5 km/h)

7 Damon Hill (GB)
Jordan-Mugen-Honda 199
1'32"695 m (286,7 km/h)

10 Alexander Wurz (A)
Benetton-Playlife B199
1'32"789 m (285,2 km/h)

22 Jacques Villeneuve (CDN)
BAR-Supertec 01
1'32"888 m (284,2 km/h)

19 Jarno Trulli (I)
Prost-Peugeot AP02
1'32"971 m (281,0 km/h)

17 Johnny Herbert (GB)
Stewart-Ford SF3
1'32"991 m (286,0 km/h)

12 Pedro Diniz (BR)
Sauber-Petronas C18
1'33"374 m (283,6 km/h)

5 Alessandro Zanardi (I)
Williams-Supertec FW21
1'33"549 m (283,9 km/h)

11 Jean Alesi (F)
Sauber-Petronas C18
1'33"910 m (283,8 km/h)

15 Toranosuke Takagi (J)
TWR-Arrows A20
1'34"182 m (280,5 km/h)

14 Pedro de la Rosa (E)
TWR-Arrows A20
1'34"244 m (281,9 km/h)

23 Ricardo Zonta (BR)
BAR-Supertec 01
1'34"412 m (283,8 km/h)

18 Olivier Panis (F)
Prost-Peugeot AP02
1'35"068 m (281,3 km/h)

20 Luca Badoer (I)
Minardi-Ford-Zetec-R M01
1'35"316 m (281,2 km/h)

21 Marc Gené (E) [2]
Minardi-Ford-Zetec-R M01
1'37"013 m (275,2 km/h)

107-percent time   1'36"794 m

Best Laps

In Training on Friday (m)			
1. Häkkinen	1'30"324	12. Wurz	1'33"110
2. Coulthard	1'30"969	13. Trulli	1'33"252
3. Herbert	1'32"569	14. Alesi	1'33"305
4. Hill	1'32"661	15. R. Schumacher	1'33"323
5. Villeneuve	1'32"717	16. Panis	1'34"129
6. M. Schumacher	1'32"722	17. de la Rosa	1'34"194
7. Barrichello	1'32"828	18. Takagi	1'34"386
8. Frentzen	1'32"876	19. Zanardi	1'35"444
9. Fisichella	1'32"975	20. Badoer	1'35"839
10. Irvine	1'32"994	21. Gené	1'36"848
11. Diniz	1'32"999	22. Zonta	1'48"227

In the Race on Sunday (m)			
1. M. Schumacher	1'32"112	12. Trulli	1'34"980
2. Barrichello	1'32"894	13. de la Rosa	1'35"220
3. Häkkinen	1'33"309	14. Takagi	1'35"877
4. Frentzen	1'33"378	15. Panis	1'35"910
5. R. Schumacher	1'33"407	16. Wurz	1'36"068
6. Irvine	1'33"560	17. Badoer	1'37"073
7. Coulthard	1'33"603	18. Zanardi	1'37"146
8. Fisichella	1'33"657	19. Gené	1'37"454
9. Diniz	1'34"748	20. Hill	1'37"491
10. Zonta	1'34"756	21. Alesi	–
11. Villeneuve	1'34"771	22. Herbert	–

Total Pit Stop Times

Lap	Time (s)	Lap	Time (s)	Lap	Time (s)
13 Zanardi	23"512	27 Wurz	27"315	38 M. Schumacher	46"248
15 Diniz	24"711	27 M. Schumacher	41"287	40 de la Rosa	23"293
15 Zonta	34"918	31 Barrichello	26"345	46 Zonta	28"728
15 Badoer	46"637	31 Zonta	29"441		
18 Fisichella	37"052	32 Takagi	27"046		
18 Häkkinen	47"557	32 Barrichello	26"335		
22 Trulli	23"752	33 R. Schumacher	24"890		
22 Barrichello	25"027	33 Badoer	27"282		
22 de la Rosa	23"919	34 Irvine	24"474		
23 Gené	27"215	34 Frentzen	24"630		
23 Trulli	28"602	37 Fisichella	25"520		

The Race Lap by Lap

Pre-start: A nightmare scenario for Stewart - both cars go up in flames in the starting grid. The start is abandoned. Barrichello switches to the reserve car. Herbert is out. **Start:** Just like at the '98 season finale in Japan - Michael Schumacher has trouble getting it into gear, and has to line up in 20th. Häkkinen gets off the mark first ahead of Coulthard, Irvine, Frentzen, Ralf Schumacher and Fisichella. Trulli pushes Hill before the first curve. **Lap 3:** Häkkinen followed by Coulthard, Irvine, Frentzen, R. Schumacher, Fisichella and Trulli. M. Schumacher is 15th. **Lap 14:** The rear wing breaks on Villeneuve's BAR, the Canadian is out. The safety-car is sent out. Coulthard gives up in at the pits. **Lap 18:** The end of the amber light phase - Häkkinen can't accelerate and makes a 30 second pitstop. Trulli and Fisichella make contact at the end of the straightaway. The order: Irvine ahead of Frentzen, Trulli, R. Schumacher. **Lap 21:** Zanardi ends his comeback in the guiderail. The safety-car returns. M. Schumacher is up to sixth. **Lap 22:** Häkkinen retires to the pits. **Lap26:** Gené and Trulli collide and are eliminated. **Lap 27:** Deja-vu number two for M. Schumacher - tyre problems, just like in Japan. Following a change of tyres he returns in 11th and last place. **Lap 28:** Wurz is out due to rear axle trouble. **Lap 31:** Barrichello was doing just fine in fourth place - until a 10 second penalty for overtaking during an amber light phase. **Lap 34:** Irvine and Frentzen enter the pits simultaneously. Eddie maintains his lead. **Lap 37:** Pitstop for M. Schumacher. **Lap 38:** M. Schumacher returns to the pits. **Lap 43:** Barrichello is back up to fifth. **Lap 49:** BAR's debut ends with gearbox trouble for Zonta. **Lap 57:** R. Schumacher challenges Frentzen, who's trying to catch Irvine, that's how they finish.

Standings

Driver	Points	Team	Points
1. Eddie Irvine	10	1. Ferrari	10
2. Heinz-Harald Frentzen	6	2. Jordan-Mugen-Honda	6
3. Ralf Schumacher	4	3. Williams-Supertec	4
4. Giancarlo Fisichella	3	4. Benetton-Playlife	3
5. Rubens Barrichello	2	5. Stewart-Ford	2
6. Pedro de la Rosa	1	6. TWR-Arrows	1

The crucial seconds: A Grand Prix race starts when the ten red lights are extinguished.

When to Hit the Accelerator

'"When the flag drops, the nonsense stops": the old master Jack Brabham was always relieved when the flag finally dropped, meaning he had nothing left to do but concentrate on driving as fast as he could. But times have changed: the regulations regarding the correct starting procedure are among the most complicated in the Formula One rule book.

Safety-cars: Overtake them and you´ll be penalised.

It´s all down to big brother: Races are started by computers.

Safety first: When the safety-car´s yellow lights are extinguished overtaking is allowed on the following lap.

Red flag: When cars block the track the start is abandoned and the offenders are banished to the back of the grid.

The opening race of the season in Australia: Michael Schumacher´s championship aspirations get off to a bad start. In the warm-up lap the Ferrari driver can't get into gear and almost the whole field overtakes him before the German driver finally gets his Ferrari into motion. Following Schumacher´s blunder, what ensued was an animated conversation via radio with the Ferrari team in the pits. Nobody was sure whether Schumacher was still allowed to take his place in the second row of the starting grid, a right he'd earned by qualifying third. Before the team's experts had finished thumbing through the rule book, the previous season's championship runner-up took matters into his own hands. In order to avoid any possible penalty, he took up a different starting position, all the way at the back of the pack. But according to the rules Schumacher did actually still have the right to start from the position in which he'd qualified, because he had managed to get his car into gear before his last opponent had passed him in the warm-up. Not

Hard luck for Michael Schumacher: After stalling his Ferrari on the warm-up lap the German wound up starting from the very last row of the grid.

If the traffic light´s red, it´s already too late: Those who don´t make it into the starting grid in time have to wait in the pits.

Procedures following the illegal start of a race:

Failure to arrive in the starting grid	Start from the pits if the last in the starting grid overtakes you.
Stalling one´s engine on the warm-up lap	a) If the last opponent doesn´t overtake you - start from your qualifying position. Must be completed before the pole sitter is standing still. b) If you drop back to last in the warm-up, you start from the last row. c) If you only get going after the red light, the car is removed from the track, you may start from the pits. *Unnecessary overtaking in the warm-up lap: 10 second penalty.*
Causing the abandonment of a start	After five minutes a new warm-up lap, refuelling forbidden, the race is shortened by one lap. *The driver who caused the abandonment starts from the last row.*
Stalling one´s engine at the start of the race	The car is pushed off. If in the process the driver gets the car started again, he can follow the pack. The same is true if the mechanics successfully repair the car. *False start: 10 second stop-and go penalty.*
Abandonment on the first lap	The race is considered not to have started. The procedure starts again with a warm-up lap and drivers may switch to a reserve car. They cannot refuel. Should a driver have been forced back to last due to an offence, he may start from his qualifying position. *The additional lap is subtracted from the total distance of the race.*
Start or restart behind the safety-car	Last lap without the yellow light, and after the finish line has been passed, overtaking is allowed. *Doing so beforehand means a 10 second penalty.*

knowing details like this cost championship points.

Mastering the rules is a job for specialists. The Formula One rule book has become so large and so complicated that these days every team has its own rules expert, who does nothing but study the regulations. There are certainly enough details to trip up the drivers and their teams. For example had Schumacher fallen back to the very last place in warm-up, then he would have been banished to last place. If a driver doesn't manage to get his car going at all in the warm-up lap, or if he only does so after the lights have turned red, then he's sent not just to the back of the starting grid - he´s banished all the way into the pits. There he has to wait until all the rest of the field has taken off, and wait for the light, that turns red 15 minutes before the start of the race, to turn green again.

One thing that is clear is the intention of these regulations. The idea is to make whoever causes a start to be abandoned, start from the last row - even if it's a driver with a shot at the title, as was the case in the dramatic last race of the season in Japan last year, when Michael Schumacher´s car stalled waiting for the starting signal. The only hope in such cases is that the race officials stop the race before the end of the first lap. Then the race is considered not to have started in the first place. Each and every qualifier lines up his original place in the grid all over again, and the countdown begins afresh from the five minute mark. If the first start ends with an accident and the officials abandon the race, even the drivers involved in the crash can start again, using the reserve cars. Before this generous regulation was introduced, drivers were at the mercy of the officials. When in 1976 local hero James Hunt illegally drove his T-car back into the starting grid for the restart at Brands Hatch, the British officials turned a blind eye.

The human element, with all of its capacity for error is becoming less and less of a factor. The Formula One supremos are increasingly relying on technology to get the job done. A false start is no longer determined by the judgement of an official. Instead transmitters register even the most subtle movement of any car in the starting grid. If the race officials discover a car in motion before the red light has gone out, the offending driver is waved into the pits for a 10 second penalty.

The same fate hangs over the head of any driver who for whatever reason chooses to ignore the starting procedures following a safety-car phase. No driver may overtake another until the end of the lap in which the yellow lights on the safety car have been extinguished and it has turned off into the pits, and this only after the driver in question has passed the starting/finish line. It sounds simple, but that's only the case if all of the drivers put their toe down immediately after the re-start. In Melbourne for example Mika Hakkinen developed gear-box trouble precisely when the safety-car´s yellow lights were extinguished and it turned into pit row. This caused considerable confusion among the rest of the pack. Instead of speeding past the troubled Finn, the rest of the pack was forced to crawl along behind him for several hundred metres until they reached the chequered line.

A Breakthrough fo

A silver arrow in seventh heaven: Mika Hakkinen was unstoppable at Interlagos.

Teutonic trio: Mercedes driver Mika Hakkinen shared the victory podium with Michael Schumacher (left) and Heinz-Harald Frentzen (right).

The second race of the season made one thing clear: 1999 too would be a season of duels, Mika Hakkinen versus Michael Schumacher, and McLaren-Mercedes versus Ferrari. But the real star of the weekend drove his way into the hearts of 100 thousand fans. Driving in his home country Stewart driver Rubens Barrichello surprised even himself by holding the lead for 23 laps.

r Stewart

Brazilian GP

Ready, set, go! Soon after the start of the Brazilian Grand Prix Mika Hakkinen jumped out into the lead ahead of Rubens Barrichello.

Above: No land in sight - Zanardi was eliminated by gearbox trouble. Middle: Hero of the masses - Rubens Barrichello leading the way at his home Grand Prix. Below: Bad luck - Ricardo Zonta crashed in training and injured his foot.

In Formula One terms, Brazil has seen better days. When national hero Ayrton Senna lost his life at Imola in 1994, millions of people living in Brazil's slums or "favelas" were robbed of a dream. Senna was loved not just for his driving skill, but also for the fact that he put much of his considerable personal financial means to work to help the impoverished of his homeland. His compatriots continue to benefit from his generosity even now, five years after his death, as the Ayrton Senna Foundation supports numerous charitable undertakings. Since his death though, Brazil has been waiting in vain for a new Formula One hero. This could soon change.

The atmosphere in the stands of the Autodromo Carlos Pace in Sao Paolo was reminiscent of Senna´s glory days. La ola, the wave, samba dancing, in short mass hysteria - all because a Brazilian driver was once again out in front in the Brazilian Grand Prix. Rubens Barrichello, in his 7th Formula One season, competing in his 99th Grand Prix, despite being only 26 years old. "When I suddenly found myself in the lead, I just concentrated on the job at hand, and did my best. I didn't even notice the cheers of the fans", said the Stewart-Ford driver. "If you're in it to win, you don't have time to indulge in emotions."

For a full 23 laps the whole country watched as he led the pack. For 19 more, millions of Brazilians hoped for at least a place on the podium. The unreliability of the Ford 10 cylinder engine under the hood reared its ugly head, and forced him to retire. But by then "Rubinho" had long since proved that he too belonged in the class of the very best drivers. Paul Stewart, the son of former champion Jackie Stewart and the Stewart team's deputy chairman admitted that reliability remained a problem. "Nonetheless, we come away from the weekend knowing that the car has the pace. It's always easier to find reliability than speed, so we can take heart from our performance."

From then on, the two main protagonists from the ´98 season took centre stage at the Autodromo Carlos Pace: Mika Hakkinen and Michael Schumacher. They also appeared to have slipped back into their same roles, on the one hand the cool Finn with the superior car who had again dominated qualifying, on the other, the determined German, who this time was unable to conceal his frustration at the poor performance of his Ferrari. Schumacher trailed Hakkinen by a whole second - a minor catastrophe. The facial

"We've failed to reach our goal", complained Michael Schumacher.

expressions in the Ferrari pits following the race revealed the team's deep disappointment. "We have failed to reach our goal", said Schumacher, "to be competitive from the first race on."

Two silver arrows started in the front row with Schumacher all the way behind Rubens Barrichello in fourth.

McLaren number one: when the red lights went out David Coulthard´s silver arrow stayed put. By the time the Scot really got going, he'd given everyone else a two lap head start. On the 22nd lap he was put out of his misery, forced to retire due to gearbox trouble.

McLaren number two: Mika Hakkinen easily got off to the best start, and pulled away to a two second lead ahead of Barrichello and Schumacher, before the hand of fate toyed with him, too. As he was exiting the "Curva del Sol" his gearbox gave up the ghost. Hakkinen was powerless to prevent Rubinho and Schumacher from overtaking him. "Everything was going great, my lead on Rubens was increasing, and then suddenly it wouldn't go into 5th gear. That's it, game over I thought to myself. But I tried again

"Game over", thought Mika Hakkinen.

and to my surprise it was working again." These few seconds seemed like an eternity to Mercedes boss Norbert Haug. "I thought it was all a bad dream, one of them doesn't even get off the finish line properly, and the other gets knocked out..."

Mika Hakkinen then went to work. Beginning from third place he started to chase the two who'd just passed him. It wasn't long before he had Michael Schumacher and his Ferrari in his sights. He chased the two-time world champion lap after lap around the grid. "I wasn't very happy. A few times I had opportunities to pass, but the risk was too high. So I decided to wait until Michael had to refuel."

His patience paid off. When the German headed to the pits on lap 38, the Finn shot out into the lead. Then the Finn had just 4 laps to build up the best lead he could on his Ferrari rival. He wasn't bothered a bit when the winner of the Australian Grand Prix, Northern Irishman Eddie Irvine appeared. When he returned to the track with his Mercedes freshly topped up with fuel, Schumacher was in second - to stay. There was nothing left that could get in the way of Hakkinen´s first win of the season.

But the lads in the Ferrari pits weren't about

Six points: Michael Schumacher had to make do with second place.

Far left: Off-road - debutante Stephane Sarrazin first rumbled over the grass, then wrote off his Minardi. Left: A good performance - Ralf Schumacher.

Far left: Bad show: David Coulthard botched the start and failed to finish. Left: Good show - Jean Alesi fought his way through the field, but didn't get to the finish line either.

to hang their heads. The members of the grand old team had been pleasantly surprised by how competitive they'd been in Brazil. Literally overnight their engineers had altered the wing, making it easier for Schumacher to overtake his competitors. However the German driver admitted, "we still don't have the raw speed to beat McLaren without a little help from elsewhere."

It was a good day for the Germans - first place for McLaren´s car maker, Mercedes, second for Michael Schumacher, and third for

Left: Eddie Jordan's dream comes true - Heinz-Harald Frentzen (right) made it to the podium again.

Frentzen has the smile wiped off his face.

another German driver Heinz-Harald Frentzen. Just as he had in Melbourne, Frentzen drove an outstanding race. The Jordan driver started from 8th in the grid and at the end of the race was rewarded with a place on the podium. "Our strategy worked perfectly", smiled the 31 year old afterwards. But it wasn't all smooth sailing. Twice Frentzen had his third place finish seriously come under threat. Practically without warning his racer stopped on the last lap due to an acute lack of fuel - during his one and only pit

stop his crew hadn't put enough fuel in his car's tank. "I'm just glad that I had a few very fast laps towards the end so that Hakkinen wasn't able to lap me", said the relieved undertaker's son. Then his smile disappeared for a few anxious moments - as he learned that he could be facing disqualification. There was so little fuel left in the tank, that the Jordan technicians had great difficulty draining the small amount needed for the obligatory post-race analysis.

Ralf Schumacher ended the Brazilian Grand Prix in fourth place, in the points once again, well ahead of his team-mate Alex Zanardi. Fol-

lowing Australia, the Italian, for whom Williams had had high expectations, experienced his second debacle in a row. He was one second behind the younger Schumacher in qualifying, and two seconds slower per lap in the race itself - a very disappointing result indeed. But his entire team, Williams, wasn't in the form of past years either. The former perennial champions had sunk to the middle of the pack, and there appeared little to do but hope for better things in the coming season in their new partnership with BMW.

Finally, Jean Alesi offered proof that in this part of the world too, the Formula One has a lot of excitement to offer. The charismatic, and sometimes unpredictable Italian-Frenchman found himself all the way at the back of the pack, after spinning out on just the second lap. No reason to give up though, instead incentive for the Sauber driver to aggresively pursue all of his opponents peering at him through their rearview mirrors. And chase he did, overtaking the likes of Quebec´s Jacques Villeneuve, Alex Zanardi, and Ralf Schumacher as if each of them was standing still. He recorded the fourth fastest lap of the day, only to fall victim to something beyond his control - a gearbox problem on the 21st lap. By then he'd managed to climb all the way to fifth. Just as in the case of Brazilian driver Rubens Barrichello, it was a great effort that went unrewarded.

In demand: Michael Schumacher autographs.

Statistics

Course length:	4,292 km
Distance of race:	72 (= 309,024 km)
Start time:	18.00 UTC
Weather on day of race:	cloudy, warm, windy
Attendance:	119 000
1998 Results:	1. Mika Hakkinen (FIN, McLaren-Mercedes MP4/13), 1 h 37'11"747
	2. David Coulthard (GB, McLaren-Mercedes MP4/13), +1"102 s
	3. Michael Schumacher (D, Ferrari F300), +1'00"550 m
Pole position 1998:	Mika Hakkinen (McLaren-Mercedes MP4/13), 1'17"092 m
Fastest Lap 1998:	Mika Hakkinen (McLaren-Mercedes MP4/13), 1'19"337 m
Fastest pit stop 1998:	Jacques Villeneuve (Williams-Mecachrome FW 20), 33"185 s

Here engine power and good physical condition count most

"Interlagos is a fantastic track which demands the best of both car and driver. You can't have enough power for the uphill curve which leads into the finish line straightaway. The narrow in field is a really fun challenge, and driving counter clockwise forces you to use different muscles."

Mika Hakkinen

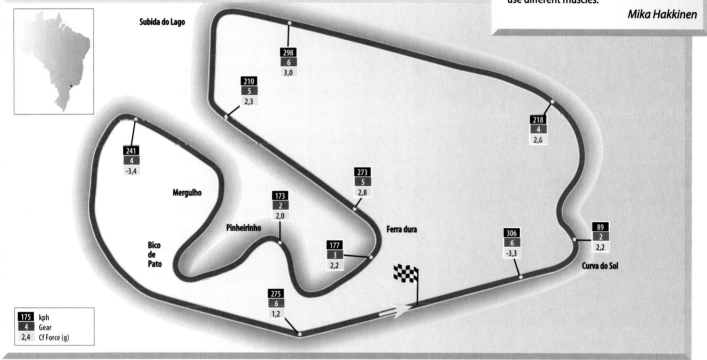

175	kph
4	Gear
2,4	Cf Force (g)

Results

Driver	Team	Pit stops	Laps	Time (hours)	Average speed	Behind 1st	prev. driver
1. Mika Hakkinen	McLaren-Mercedes	1	72	1 h 36'03"785	192,994	–	–
2. Michael Schumacher	Ferrari	1	72	1 h 36'08"710	192,829	4"925 s	–
3. Heinz-Harald Frentzen[1]	Jordan-Mugen-Honda	1	71	1 h 35'56"877	190,542	retirement	–
4. Ralf Schumacher	Williams-Supertec	1	71	1 h 36'22"860	189,685	1 lap	25"983 s
5. Eddie Irvine	Ferrari	2	71	1 h 36'23"103	189,677	1 lap	0"243 s
6. Olivier Panis	Prost-Peugeot	3	71	1 h 37'13"368	188,043	1 lap	50"265 s
7. Alexander Wurz	Benetton-Playlife	1	70	1 h 36'12"021	187,365	2 laps	1 lap
8. Toranosuke Takagi	TWR-Arrows	1	69	1 h 37'10"072	184,750	3 laps	1 lap
9. Marc Gené	Minardi-Ford	2	69	1 h 37'02"116	183,099	3 laps	52"044 s

Driver	Team	Pit stops	in lap	Reason f. retiring	Position before retiring
Pedro de la Rosa	TWR-Arrows	1	53	hydraulics	8
Jacques Villeneuve	BAR-Supertec	1	50	hydraulics	9
Alessandro Zanardi	Williams-Supertec	2	44	gearbox	12
Rubens Barrichello	Stewart-Ford	1	43	engine	3
Pedro Diniz	Sauber-Petronas	0	43	collission with Takagi	7
Giancarlo Fisichella	Benetton-Playlife	0	39	clutch	6
Stéphane Sarrazin	Minardi-Ford	0	32	crash	11
Jean Alesi	Sauber-Petronas	1	28	gearbox	9
David Coulthard	McLaren-Mercedes	1	23	gearbox	18
Jarno Trulli	Prost-Peugeot	1	22	gearbox	18
Johnny Herbert	Stewart-Ford	0	16	hydraulics	19
Damon Hill	Jordan-Mugen-Honda	0	11	crash	20

1) Didn't complete race, but counted due to distance driven

Brazilian GP

2nd Race of the World Championship1999,
Autodromo Carlos Pace, Interlagos (BR), 11th April 1999

Starting Grid

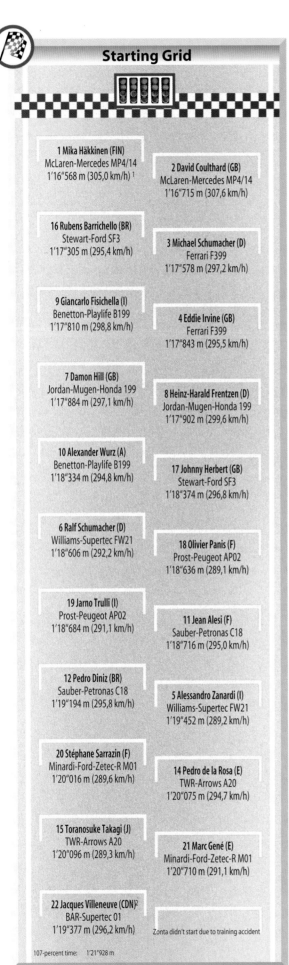

1 Mika Häkkinen (FIN)
McLaren-Mercedes MP4/14
1'16"568 m (305,0 km/h) [1]

2 David Coulthard (GB)
McLaren-Mercedes MP4/14
1'16"715 m (307,6 km/h)

16 Rubens Barrichello (BR)
Stewart-Ford SF3
1'17"305 m (295,4 km/h)

3 Michael Schumacher (D)
Ferrari F399
1'17"578 m (297,2 km/h)

9 Giancarlo Fisichella (I)
Benetton-Playlife B199
1'17"810 m (298,8 km/h)

4 Eddie Irvine (GB)
Ferrari F399
1'17"843 m (295,5 km/h)

7 Damon Hill (GB)
Jordan-Mugen-Honda 199
1'17"884 m (297,1 km/h)

8 Heinz-Harald Frentzen (D)
Jordan-Mugen-Honda 199
1'17"902 m (299,6 km/h)

10 Alexander Wurz (A)
Benetton-Playlife B199
1'18"334 m (294,8 km/h)

17 Johnny Herbert (GB)
Stewart-Ford SF3
1'18"374 m (296,8 km/h)

6 Ralf Schumacher (D)
Williams-Supertec FW21
1'18"606 m (292,2 km/h)

18 Olivier Panis (F)
Prost-Peugeot AP02
1'18"636 m (289,1 km/h)

19 Jarno Trulli (I)
Prost-Peugeot AP02
1'18"684 m (291,1 km/h)

11 Jean Alesi (F)
Sauber-Petronas C18
1'18"716 m (295,0 km/h)

12 Pedro Diniz (BR)
Sauber-Petronas C18
1'19"194 m (295,8 km/h)

5 Alessandro Zanardi (I)
Williams-Supertec FW21
1'19"452 m (289,2 km/h)

20 Stéphane Sarrazin (F)
Minardi-Ford-Zetec-R M01
1'20"016 m (289,6 km/h)

14 Pedro de la Rosa (E)
TWR-Arrows A20
1'20"075 m (294,7 km/h)

15 Toranosuke Takagi (J)
TWR-Arrows A20
1'20"096 m (289,3 km/h)

21 Marc Gené (E)
Minardi-Ford-Zetec-R M01
1'20"710 m (291,1 km/h)

22 Jacques Villeneuve (CDN)[2]
BAR-Supertec 01
1'19"377 m (296,2 km/h)

Zonta didn't start due to training accident

107-percent time: 1'21"928 m

1.) Lap time (top speed in qualifying); 2.) Relegated to back of starting grid due to illegal fuel.

Best Laps

In Training on Friday (m)			
1. Häkkinen	1'18"881	12. Alesi	1'20"824
2. Coulthard	1'19"352	13. Herbert	1'20"934
3. M. Schumacher	1'19"621	14. Zonta	1'21"116
4. Irvine	1'19"772	15. Diniz	1'21"323
5. Fisichella	1'20"309	16. Zanardi	1'21"773
6. Barrichello	1'20"338	17. Gené	1'21"897
7. Trulli	1'20"359	18. Takagi	1'22"355
8. Frentzen	1'20"431	19. de la Rosa	1'22"494
9. Panis	1'20"562	20. Sarrazin	1'22"578
10. R. Schumacher	1'20"671	21. Hill	1'32"229
11. Wurz	1'20"779	22. Villeneuve	1'36"568

In the Race on Sunday (m)			
1. Häkkinen	1'18"448	12. Fisichella	1'20"484
2. M. Schumacher	1'18"616	13. Villeneuve	1'20"727
3. Irvine	1'18"816	14. Diniz	1'20"833
4. Alesi	1'18"897	15. Trulli	1'20"969
5. Frentzen	1'19"009	16. Hill	1'21"140
6. Coulthard	1'19"310	17. Sarrazin	1'21"225
7. Panis	1'19"386	18. Zanardi	1'21"473
8. R. Schumacher	1'19"395	19. Takagi	1'21"598
9. Barrichello	1'19"477	20. de la Rosa	1'21"698
10. Wurz	1'20"145	21. Gené	1'21"731
11. Herbert	1'20"324		–

Total Pit Stop Times

Lap	Time (s)	Lap	Time (s)	Lap	Time (s)
11 Zanardi	34"893	40 de la Rosa	32"772		
12 Panis	34"096	42 Häkkinen	30"983		
20 Trulli	47"618	41 Wurz	32"543		
22 Coulthard	33"328	41 Takagi	32"359		
26 Alesi	46"641	42 Zanardi	42"514		
27 Barrichello	31"245	43 Villeneuve	35"085		
27 Panis	37"500	45 Frentzen	30"780		
34 Gené	35"674	47 Panis	31"159		
35 R. Schumacher	33"386	50 Gené	40"903		
38 M. Schumacher	32"552	55 Irvine	32"791		
40 Irvine	33"656				

The Race Lap by Lap

Start: Coulthard stands still and is pushed into the pits. Hakkinen leads ahead of Barrichello, M. Schumacher, and Irvine. **Lap 3:** With his car repaired Coulthard storms out of the pits just as leader Hakkinen passes. **Lap 4:** Hakkinen can´t accelerate, Barrichello goes into the lead. M. Schumacher moves into second. Hakkinens problem disappears as quickly as it appeared. He holds down third. **Lap 11:** Coulthard is three laps back but as fast as the leader Barrichello, lets M. Schumacher and Hakkinen past. Behind them: Irvine ahead of Fisichella, Frentzen and Wurz. **Lap 15:** Alesi, who started in 14th overtakes Herbert and is up to seventh. **Lap 19:** Alesi overtakes Frentzen. **Lap 21:** Fisichella is Alesi´s next victim, Alesi is fifth. **Lap 22:** Trulli is out due to gearbox trouble. **Lap 25:** Alesi has Irvine in his sights, who turns into the pits. **Lap 27:** Barrichello, cheered on by the fans stops to refuel and returns to the track in fourth. **Lap 32:** Badoer replacement Sar-

razin´s Minardi crashes out of the race. **Lap 36:** Barrichello seizes third from Irvine. The first pitstop for the seventh-placed R.Schumacher. **Lap 38:** A defective clutch forces Fisichella to retire. **Lap 42:** Hakkinen returns to the track as the leader following a pitstop that was five seconds shorter than M. Schumacher´s. **Lap 43:** Barrichello´s outstanding performance is over due to engine trouble. **Lap 45:** Frentzen´s only pitstop, he´s now fourth. **Lap 56:** An unplanned pitstop for Irvine, Frentzen inheirits third, R. Schumacher is in fourth. **Lap 71:** Frentzen runs out of fuel, but at the same time Hakkinen gets the chequered flag. HHF finishes third.

Standings

Driver	Points	Team	Points
1. Eddie Irvine	12	1. Ferrari	18
2. Mika Häkkinen	10	2. McLaren-Mercedes	10
3. Heinz-Harald Frentzen	10	3. Jordan-Mugen-Honda	10
4. Ralf Schumacher	7	4. Williams-Supertec	7
5. Michael Schumacher	6	5. Benetton-Playlife	3
6. Giancarlo Fisichella	3	6. Stewart-Ford	2
7. Rubens Barrichello	2	7. TWR-Arrows	1
8. Pedro de la Rosa	1	8. Prost-Peugeot	1
9. Olivier Panis	1		

When he was 22 he was tipped as a rising star. But the death of his idol, Ayrton Senna plunged the young Brazilian into crisis. Now Rubens Barrichello is back - stronger, more mature, and faster than ever. He's just on the verge of breaking into the elite of Formula One drivers. In the coming season he'll be joining one of the sport's top teams, replacing Eddie Irvine as Michael Schumacher´s team-mate at Ferrari.

The Young
Veteran

R ubens Barrichello´s best season so far on the Formula One circuit got off to a catastrophic start. In the starting grid of the Australian Grand Prix in Melbourne, his Stewart-Ford caught fire. Team-mate Johnny Herbert's car did as well, and for the same reason - oil was dripping onto their cars´ exhaust pipes. Barrichello began the race from pit row, way behind the rest of the pack. But during the course of the race he recorded the second fastest lap of the day and finished an impressive fifth. One race later at his home Grand Prix, the Brazilian even led for much of the way. There's no doubt: Rubens is back.

Things had got quiet around the South American once touted as a super young talent, who'd left home at the tender age of 18 back in 1990 to compete in the Opel Lotus Euroseries and one year later, win the hotly contested Formula 3 championship - against none other than David Coulthard. As a 20 year-old Rubens made his

debut on the Formula One circuit, earning two of the young Jordan team's three points that year. Barrichello, who even then looked older than he really is, appeared to be on his way up, with nothing to get in his way. Back home in Brazil, where the hearts of Formula One fans still belonged to his idol, Ayrton Senna, Barrichello was being talked up as the South American superstar's natural successor.

But the 1994 season turned out to be Senna´s last. On that fateful end of April, early May weekend when both the three time world champion and Austrian driver Roland Ratzenberger lost their lives at Imola, it was Barrichello who was the first to crash. In the Friday training session the Jordan driver flew off the track in the "Variante Bassa" chicane, with only the edge of the fence preventing him from flying into the stands.

"My problems started after Senna´s death", "Rubinho" says in retrospect. "I was always looking for him. He'd been there to help me." It was

the beginning of a difficult period for the then 22 year-old Barrichello. He was overcome by the self-imposed pressure to replace the beloved Senna in the hearts of his compatriots. He tried too hard, trying to get more out of his Jordan-Hart than it was actually capable of. Motor racing experts describe this as "overdriving". Not just that but the one time Kart world champion was having a lot of difficulty adjusting from a right foot to a left foot brake pedal. "The video footage of the races showed us that for six or seven races I was still stepping on the brakes well into the straight-aways."

Even if 1994, when he finished 6th in the drivers standings, was a great year for Rubens on paper, even taking the pole position for Jordan during the chaotic qualifying sessions at Spa-Francorchamps, Barrichello felt uneasy and overwhelmed. Little things were niggling away at him, like the fact that he had signed an option sheet to join McLaren for the 1995 season - an

Close but no cigar: At the Nurburgring Johnny Herbert, not Rubens brought Stewart their first win.

Gave Barrichello the support he needed: former world champion Jackie Stewart.

Keeping the favourites on their toes: In his Stewart-Ford SF3 Rubens Barrichello was always one of the fastest pursuers of the McLarens and the Ferraris. He just missed winning his home Grand Prix in Brazil.

incredible opportunity. But at the second last race of the season Ron Dennis told him the bad news. McLaren had decided to go with Mika Hakkinen instead. "It's hard to say what went wrong", says Barrichello even today. "At the beginning they were so enthusiastic about signing me, and then there was silence. I'm still convinced today that Ron highly respects my driving ability."

Going into the next season Rubens consoled himself with the fact that the Jordan team had signed a big name to produce their cars. But the Peugeot 10 cylinder engines turned out to be a big disappointment. They didn't have a lot of guts and they were too heavy. In fact the entire cars were prone to trouble. After five disappointing Grand Prix races the quiet Brazilian finally solved his braking problems and his luck turned. He finished that year's controversial Canadian Grand Prix in a surprising second place. "After I'd beaten my team-mate Eddie Irvine in qualifying

again in Montreal, I did it again in Magny Cours and in Silverstone. Formula One racing is to a large extent a mental game." But at the end of the season Eddie Irvine moved to Ferrari to play understudy to Michael Schumacher. Barrichello stayed put.

In his fourth year at Jordan the straight-forward Brazilian - "I've always hated politics" - seemed to finally have established himself as the team's number one. At the start of the season he consistently out-performed team-mate Martin Brundle. "The season started really well. Martin even asked me to tell him my secret: the veteran asking me, the kid! But later he got faster than me. It was only then that I noticed that we weren't driving identical cars. My team had let me down...."

Barrichello reacted by signing for Jackie Stewart's new team in 1996. "That was really my first year in Formula One", he recollects today. "I started from scratch all over again, with the

dark clouds behind me. I knew more about life. I was no longer trying to win for Ayrton. First and foremost, I wanted to win for myself - and then for Brazil." Rubens bloomed in the Ford machine, finishing a surprising second in Monaco. In particular it seemed to be the support of three time world champion Jackie Stewart that really made the difference. "I feel like a new man, I'm happier and faster than I was before." When Frank Williams made him an offer for the 1999 season, Rubens declined, despite the fact that the past season had seen a lot of technical problems for Stewart. "I had the feeling that I still owed Stewart one", he explained.

However the South American also happened to know that the team had made some big changes for the new season. Their new car - the SF3 - was promising right from the very start, and no longer was Ford merely supporting Stewart, the American concern bought the entire team. The Zetec 10 cylinder had been improved significantly as well, ever since Ford had bought engine maker Cosworth back from Audi. Barrichello turned out to have made the right decision. While he narrowly missed his first Grand Prix win in Brazil, team-mate Johnny Herbert turned the trick at the Nurburgring. "I wish I could have won this one for Jackie Stewart", lamented Rubens.

Had he managed it, it would have been a parting gift since the now 27 year-old veteran has signed on with Ferrari for 2000. He'll be trading cockpits with Eddie Irvine who'll take Barrichello's place at the Stewart team which beginning next season will be known as Jaguar. "It's the chance of a lifetime", smiles Rubens when he thinks about the chance to race alongside one of the best. "Michael Schumacher is in the same class as Ayrton. He's the best, and now I'll find out where I stand."

San Marino GP

**3rd Race of the World Championship 1999, Autodromo Enzo
e Dino Ferrari, Imola (I), 2nd May 1999**

Despite the spring-like weather in Imola,

the McLaren drivers were in for a chilly

reception. Ferrari had closed the technical

gap between themselves and Mercedes

much quicker than expected. Not just that,

but Imola is Ferrari's home turf. And the

technical improvements bore quick fruit.

Michael Schumacher was to send the Ferrari

faithfull the "Tifosi" into fits of ecstasy.

Dark sunglasses can't hide the bitter truth: At Imola McLaren driver Mika
Hakkinen threw away his chance at victory.

Red

Ecstasy

San Marino GP

For the past 16 years they'd been reduced to worshipping Ferrari gods of the past: French-Canadian Gilles Villeneuve, the late father of Jacques, remembered for his daring style and masterful command of the vehicle, Jean Alesi, who never had the luck with him at Imola, Austrian Gerhard Berger who scarcely escaped death in a fire here in 1989. But even more so, they continue to cherish their fond memories the last Ferrari drivers who did manage to win their home Grand Prix: Didier Pironi (1982) and Patrick Tambay (1983). But now the ghosts can be laid to rest. Michael Schumacher graced the Tifosi with their first Ferrari victory at Imola in 16 years - an event which deeply moved the usually cool German superstar.

Following the dominance of McLaren-Mercedes in Melbourne and Interlagos, the Ferrari team boss considered the fact that they'd reduced McLaren´s edge in qualifying from 1.6 to 0.2 seconds a success. "If in Interlagos anyone had predicted that we'd be so close behind, I wouldn't have believed them." Actually it may have had something to do with psychology. Michael Schumacher´s facial expression in the first two races of the season indicated that he was beginning to seriously think about leaving Ferrari. But in Imola, Ferrari had obviously considerably closed the mechanical gap, and Schumacher, apparently filled with fresh hope, re-emerged as the motivated, competitive driver all of his fans love.

Ferrari also had the track going for them. The stop and go course at Imola isn't as unforgiving of aerodynamics deficiencies as are Melbourne and Interlagos with all their fast curves. In addition, Ferrari managed to get their Bridgestones up to proper running temperature for the first time. A new front wing in V shape was another piece in the puzzle of success. It all allowed Michael Schumacher to be a serious threat to take the pole position for the first time this season.

The pole sitter, Hakkinen, though remained cool. The red lights had scarcely been extinguished before the champion was off and running, with team-mate Coulthard, Schumacher and Irvine struggling to keep up. He stretched out his lead over the first seven laps to 5.4 seconds. He planned to make two pit stops, so he had to open up as big a lead as possible. Coulthard, who only planned to make one, was just 3.3 seconds ahead of "Schumi". This is where Ross Brawn comes in. On the evening before the race, Ferrari's technical director and his star driver had gone over the scenario. The first pit stop, at about the half-way point of the race was cast in stone. But for the next one, Brawn, the strategic super-brain of the Formula One, had thought up two possibilities. If Schumacher was ahead, they would completely fill his fuel tank. This would weigh the car down and prevent him from achieving optimal lap times, but Schumacher would still be able to defend the lead. If the German though didn't have the lead, plan B would come into force. "We had to devise a flexible strategy", explained Michael Schumacher later.

Above: Hard luck - Ralf Schumacher was fourth until being forced out. Middle: Damon Hill finished fifth due to Frentzen´s misfortune. Right: A rare oasis of peace and quiet.

A joyful homecoming: Giancarlo Fisichella secured two points.

Dithering: Coulthard overtook too carefully to have a chance at victory.

"A bad mistake", grimaced Mika Hakkinen.

The problem named Hakkinen, who couldn't have been beat by any strategy in the world on this day, took care of itself on lap 17. The Finnish driver made a very rare error, making contact with the wall coming out of a curve. A skid, a spin-out, and the end of the race, just like that. The world champion came to a stop in a cloud of dust directly in front of the McLaren-Mercedes director's stand.

David Coulthard, of whom that can't always be said, inherited the lead, but was tormented by the image of the aggressive Michael Schumacher in his rear-view mirror. Ferrari's number one had been encouraged by the misfortune of his Finnish rival, and set about attacking Coulthard. But before Schumacher could overtake the Scotsman master tactician Ross Brawn had to reach into his bag of tricks again. He instantly assessed the situation and put his plan into action. The pit stop at the half-way point of the race was extremely short. Schumacher left with his fuel tank only half full. Coulthard´s though was filled to the brim, when he pulled into the pit four laps later. He spent just three seconds longer in the pits

Above left: A matter of millimetres - parking the team lorries requires precise steering and steady nerves.
Middle: Comeback number one - at Imola Mika Salo replaced the injured BAR driver Ricardo Zonta.
Left: Ford's progress - the Stewarts were faster than ever.

than his Ferrari competitor, but it turned out to be three seconds too many. As Coulthard returned to the track, Schumacher cruised by, and took over first.

But by using a pit-stop to seize the lead, Ferrari had only completed half of the job. They knew that Coulthard, with a full tank, would be able to run the rest of the race non-stop. Now the job of these "Red Barons", with a much lighter vehicle, was to build up enough of a lead so that Schumacher could safely make his second pit-stop. On paper what they aimed to do was next to impossible - building up a lead of a full 25 seconds in just 14 laps. That's even no simple task, even with less weight on board. But Schumacher made the impossible possible. Just as he'd done one year earlier in Hungary, Schumacher took off as if he was in qualifying, cutting through the ranks of his opponents like a knife through very warm butter. Under such circumstances as these, near misses are unavoidable. This time it was Pedro Diniz who found himself with his heart in his mouth. As Torped(r)o was rounding the Tamburello curve, he narrowly missed the Ferrari star by the skin of his teeth.

"DC" on the other hand seemed to be dithering. Instead of getting down to the job of chasing the leader, he just hung back. A potential Grand Prix winner approaches his job with a different attitude. His frustration was complete after a dual with Oliver Panis. He'd hardly got by the Frenchman, who'd been battling Fisichella for several laps, before he wound up on the grass. Panis sneaked by, and the Scotsman was back to where he started.

The result: Schumacher put even more space

between himself and Coulthard, then slipped into the pits for a few litres of petrol for the final few laps, and the push for the chequered flag. "This was a must-win race for us", said Coulthard after the race, "and the reason we lost had nothing to do with me or the team."

But the excitement in the stands was unsurpassed. The Ferrari fans had waited a decade and half to see one of their own win at Imola, and that's just what "Michele nazionale" did. Not only did he win on Ferrari's home turf, but in so doing, Michael Schumacher went top of the table in the season standings. The red flag with Ferrari's trademark horse was prancing through the stands, and the fans broke into a chorus of victory songs that they never wanted to end. They celebrated one of the most interesting victories in years in a mood reminiscent of carnival in Rio or a ´70´s love-in. The only damper on the festivities was that Ferrari's number two, Eddie Irvine had been running in a solid third when he was forced to retire with only 15 laps remaining. It was the first Ferrari engine failure since the 1998 Australian Grand Prix. But by the time "Schumi" crossed the finish line that had been forgotten.

By all but Heinz-Harald Frentzen that is. "When I came over the hill at Piratella, there was nothing but oil and water, and nobody had come out to wave the oil flag." The unavoidable skid cost Frentzen what would have been a sure third place finish. "Everyone must have been suffering from shock, thinking that it was Michael's engine that had virtually self-destructed."

In the end it was Rubens Barrichello who took what should have been Frentzen´s place on

the post-race podium. The Brazilian though was pensive. "In 1994 my life changed forever, and I hope it's taken a new turn today. I dedicate this result to Ayrton Senna - this means a lot to me." Since the black Imola weekend of 1994 when Barrichello too experienced a few scary seconds, before Senna and Roland Ratzenberger both died in crashes, Imola has no longer been a temple to speed. Instead it represents a change in thinking about the safety of drivers and spectators, which has played a central role in Formula One rule changes in recent years.

"Nobody waved the oil flag."

Heinz-Harald Frentzen

The driver who probably had the shortest moment of joy about a championship point was Alex Zanardi. The Italian had hardly had a chance to realise that sixth-placed Johnny Herbert had been forced to retire due to engine trouble, when he skidded out on the oil left behind by Herbert's misfortune. The former Lotus team-mates made their way back to the pits together on foot, and exchanged thoughts about a shared superstition. "Before the race we didn't wish each other luck, because when we have neither of us has finished," explained Zinardi.

Instead it was Jean Alesi who picked up the single point for finishing sixth. The amateur wine-grower, whose "Chateauneuf du Pape" had just won a gold medal, gave his Swiss Sauber

Above: Gunning for victory - Michael Schumacher. Below: Contemplative - Heinz-Harald Frentzen´s powers of concentration didn't do him any good.

team a reason to celebrate their 100th Grand Prix and for a short time at least, forget their technical stagnation.

For the BAR team the optimism of training was short-lived. "I´d have to think quite a ways back to put my finger on a so perfect qualification lap", smiled Jacques Villeneuve after qualifying. Their fifth place in the grid rubbed salt into the wounds of Benetton and Williams, who until then could blame their troubles on their Supertec engines - the same ones that BAR use.

Left: Ecstasy - the Tifosi had good reason to celebrate at Imola. Michael Schumacher (right) presented them with the first Ferrari victory at home in 16 years.

Statistics

Course length:	4,93 km
Distance of race:	62 (= 305,66 km)
Start time:	13.00 UTC
Weather on day of race:	cloudless, warm
Attendance:	90 000
1998 Results:	1. David Coulthard (GB, McLaren-Mercedes MP4/13), 1 h 34'24"59_
	2. Michael Schumacher (D, Ferrari F300), +4"554 s
	3. Eddie Irvine (GB, Ferrari F300), +51"776 s
Pole position 1998:	David Coulthard (McLaren-Mercedes MP4/13), 1'25"973 m
Fastest Lap 1998:	Michael Schumacher (Ferrari F300), 1'29"345 m
Fastest pit stop 1998:	Michael Schumacher (Ferrari F300), 23"299 s

This course is demanding on the brakes

"Driving here is something special. The Tifosi are really unique in the way they cheer on their beloved Ferraris. The track is located in a hilly area, and gives the impression of being a combination city/country course. Since it was update though Imola has lost some of its rhythmic symmetry."

Michael Schumacher

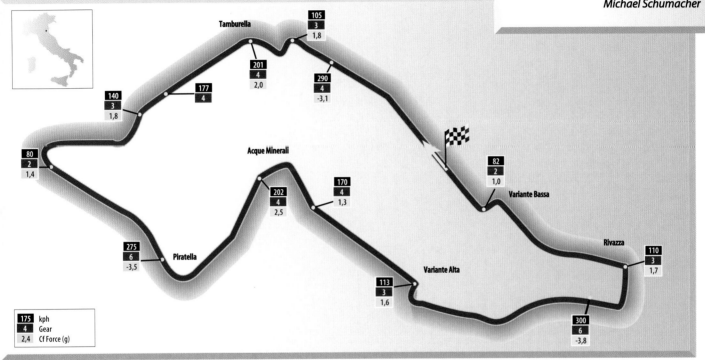

Results

Driver	Team	Pit stops	Laps	Time (hours)	Average speed	Behind 1st	prev. driver
1. Michael Schumacher	Ferrari	2	62	1 h 33'44"792	195,481	–	–
2. David Coulthard	McLaren-Mercedes	1	62	1 h 33'49"057	195,333	4"265 s	–
3. Rubens Barrichello	Stewart-Ford	2	61	1 h 33'46"721	192,259	1 lap	1 lap
4. Damon Hill	Jordan-Mugen-Honda	2	61	1 h 33'47"629	192,288	1 lap	0"908 s
5. Giancarlo Fisichella	Benetton-Playlife	2	61	1 h 34'27"002	190,893	1 lap	39"373 s
6. Jean Alesi	Sauber-Petronas	3	61	1 h 34'33"056	190,689	1 lap	6"054 s
7. Mika Salo [1]	BAR-Supertec	2	59	1 h 32'08"096	189,268	retirement	–
8. Luca Badoer	Minardi-Ford	2	59	1 h 33'53"344	185,732	3 laps	1'45"248
9. Marc Gené	Minardi-Ford	2	59	1 h 34'16"112	184,985	3 laps	22"768 s
10. Johnny Herbert [1]	Stewart-Ford	1	58	1 h 29'37"619	191,264	retirement	–
11. Alessandro Zanardi [1]	Williams-Supertec	2	58	1 h 29'45"043	191,001	retirement	–

Driver	Team	Pit stops	in lap	Reason f. retiring	Position before retiring
Pedro Diniz	Sauber-Petronas	3	50	crash	12
Olivier Panis	Prost-Peugeot	2	49	engine	10
Eddie Irvine	Ferrari	1	47	engine	3
Heinz-Harald Frentzen	Jordan-Mugen-Honda	1	47	crash	4
Toranosuke Takagi	TWR-Arrows	2	30	spun out	15
Ralf Schumacher	Williams-Supertec	1	29	electrical	4
Mika Hakkinen	McLaren-Mercedes	0	18	crash	1
Pedro de la Rosa	TWR-Arrows	0	6	collission	17
Alexander Wurz	Benetton-Playlife	0	6	collission	18
Jarno Trulli	Prost-Peugeot	0	1	crash	14
Jacques Villeneuve	BAR-Supertec	0	–	gearbox	5

1) Didn´t complete race, but counted due to distance driven.

San Marino GP

3rd Race of the World Championship 1999,
Autodromo Enzo e Dino Ferrari, Imola (I), 2nd May 1999

Starting Grid

1 Mika Häkkinen (FIN)
McLaren-Mercedes MP4/14-5
1'26"362 m (302,1 km/h) [1]

2 David Coulthard (GB)
McLaren-Mercedes MP4/14-4
1'26"384 m (303,2 km/h)

3 Michael Schumacher (D)
Ferrari F399/193
1'26"538 m (299,0 km/h)

4 Eddie Irvine (GB)
Ferrari F399/191
1'26"993 m (298,0 km/h)

22 Jacques Villeneuve (CDN)
BAR-Supertec 01/3
1'27"313 m (291,8 km/h)

16 Rubens Barrichello (BR)
Stewart-Ford SF3/4
1'27"409 m (297,1 km/h)

8 Heinz-Harald Frentzen (D)
Jordan-Mugen-Honda 199/5
1'27"613 m (299,8 km/h)

7 Damon Hill (GB)
Jordan-Mugen-Honda 199/4
1'27"708 m (294,1 km/h)

6 Ralf Schumacher (D)
Williams-Supertec FW21/4
1'27"770 m (290,6 km/h)

5 Alessandro Zanardi (I)
Williams-Supertec FW21/5
1'28"142 m (290,2 km/h)

18 Olivier Panis (F)
Prost-Peugeot AP02/3
1'28"205 m (295,0 km/h)

17 Johnny Herbert (GB)
Stewart-Ford SF3/5
1'28"246 m (294,9 km/h)

11 Jean Alesi (F)
Sauber-Petronas C18/1
1'28"253 m (295,6 km/h)

19 Jarno Trulli (I)
Prost-Peugeot AP02/2
1'28"403 m (290,2 km/h)

12 Pedro Diniz (BR)
Sauber-Petronas C18/3
1'28"559 m (293,0 km/h)

9 Giancarlo Fisichella (I)
Benetton-Playlife B199/4
1'28"750 m (293,0 km/h)

10 Alexander Wurz (A)
Benetton-Playlife B199/5
1'28"765 m (289,9 km/h)

14 Pedro de la Rosa (E)
TWR-Arrows A20/4
1'29"293 m (293,0 km/h)

23 Mika Salo (FIN)
BAR-Supertec 01/5
1'29"461 m (289,6 km/h)

15 Toranosuke Takagi (J)
TWR-Arrows A20/2
1'29"656 m (290,9 km/h)

21 Marc Gené (E)
Minardi-Ford-Zetec-R M01/4
1'30"035 m (289,4 km/h)

20 Luca Badoer (I)
Minardi-Ford-Zetec-R M01/1
1'30"945 m (289,2 km/h)

107-percent time: 1'32"407 m

1.) Lap time (top speed in qualifying).

Best Laps

In Training on Friday (m)

1. Häkkinen	1'28"467	12. Panis	1'30"408
2. Coulthard	1'28"605	13. Diniz	1'30"482
3. Irvine	1'29"046	14. Salo	1'30"569
4. Hill	1'29"452	15. Wurz	1'30"830
5. M. Schumacher	1'29"534	16. Fisichella	1'30"854
6. Zanardi	1'29"641	17. Frentzen	1'30"991
7. R. Schumacher	1'29"630	18. Herbert	1'31"046
8. Villeneuve	1'29"765	19. de la Rosa	1'31"257
9. Barrichello	1'29"792	20. Badoer	1'31"547
10. Trulli	1'29"808	21. Takagi	1'31"557
11. Alesi	1'30"182	22. Gené	1'33"529

In the Race on Sunday (m)

1. M. Schumacher	1'28"547	12. Diniz	1'30"908
2. Häkkinen	1'29"145	13. Fisichella	1'30"977
3. Coulthard	1'29"199	14. Salo	1'31"007
4. Irvine	1'29"726	15. Herbert	1'31"238
5. Panis	1'30"081	16. Takagi	1'31"587
6. Hill	1'30"140	17. Badoer	1'32"851
7. Frentzen	1'30"229	18. Gené	1'33"175
8. Zanardi	1'30"254	19. de la Rosa	1'33"328
9. Alesi	1'30"442	20. Wurz	1'33"337
10. Barrichello	1'30"564		–
11. R. Schumacher	1'30"737		–

Total Pit Stop Times

Lap	Time (s)	Lap	Time (s)	Lap	Time (s)
15 Alesi	27"592	29 Irvine	25"237	41 Gené	25"865
17 Takagi	44"670	29 Hill	25"640	42 Badoer	26"644
21 Badoer	26"696	29 Zanardi	25"406	43 Barrichello	25"868
24 Barrichello	26"368	30 Alesi	25"879	45 M. Schumacher	24"541
23 Takagi	26"934	31 M. Schumacher	23"922	45 Alesi	25"330
23 Gené	28"102	31 Herbert	30"613	45 Salo	26"048
24 Salo	27"599	35 Coulthard	26"216	46 Zanardi	25"293
25 Diniz	29"834	35 Fisichella	28"793	49 Hill	24"360
26 Panis	25"605	35 Diniz	189"684		
27 Frentzen	25"181	40 Diniz	26"956		
28 R. Schumacher	26"007	41 Panis	55"569		

The Race Lap by Lap

Start: Hakkinen gets off to a good start, Villeneuve can't get it into gear and is lucky not to be rear-ended. **Lap 12:** Hakkinen is 8.9 seconds ahead of Coulthard who's followed by M. Schumacher, Irvine, Barrichello, Frentzen, R. Schumacher, Hill, and Alesi. **Lap 17:** The Finn leads by 15 points but loses control of his Mercedes and crashes into the wall across from the pits. M. Schumacher begins to close the ground on second place Coulthard. The rest of the order remains unchanged. **Lap 30:** Ralf Schumacher´s Williams gives up due to an electrical failure. His brother is driving record laps and goes to the pits for the shortest stop of the day. **Lap 32:** Tora Takagi receives a 10 second penalty for overtaking under a blue flag. **Lap 35:** Pit stop for leader Coulthard. When he returns to the track after 26.2 seconds M. Schumacher has overtaken him and is in the lead. **Lap 36:** Diniz lurches from side to side in Tamburello and just misses Coulthard. **Lap 39:**

Fisichella and Panis are in such a heated battle for sixth place that they don't let Coulthard overtake them. **Lap 42:** First "Fisico", then on orders from his team Panis let Coulthard overtake. He makes a braking error, hits the grass and is stuck behind them again. **Lap 45:** M. Schumacher makes his second pit stop. Because Coulthard is again stuck in traffic the Ferrari driver maintains his lead. **Lap 47:** Eddie Irvine is unchallenged in third, but has to retire due to engine trouble. Behind him Frentzen skids on the resulting oil and goes off the track. **Lap 49:** Coulthard is closing the ground on M. Schumacher, but Schumacher defends his lead. **Lap 59:** Engine trouble for Herbert, Zanardi slides off the track. **Lap 62:** Schumacher wins at Ferrari's home track.

Standings

Driver/Points

1. Michael Schumacher	16	Jean Alesi	1
2. Eddie Irvine	12		
3. Mika Häkkinen	10		
Heinz-Harald Frentzen	10		
5. Ralf Schumacher	7		
6. David Coulthard	6		
Rubens Barrichello	6		
8. Giancarlo Fisichella	5		
9. Damon Hill	3		
10. Pedro de la Rosa	1		
Olívier Panis	1		

Team

	Points
1. Ferrari	28
2. McLaren-Mercedes	16
3. Jordan-Mugen-Honda	13
4. Williams-Supertec	7
5. Stewart-Ford	6
6. Benetton-Playlife	5
7. TWR-Arrows	1
8. Prost-Peugeot	1
9. Sauber-Petronas	1

Men in red: Ferrari at Imola - on this day red was Italy's only national colour.

45

The Career Te

The worst thing that can happen to a Formula One driver is to wind up as two time world champion Michael Schumacher´s team-mate. That's been known to spell the end of a number of promising Formula One careers. Just like Niki Lauda, Ayrton Senna and Alain Prost before him, the German knows how to use his outstanding talent, political acumen and psychological tricks to get his entire team focused on his personal success.

Two Grand Prix wins weren´t good enough: At Benetton Johnny Herbert had little to smile about.

The list of his victims is quite impressive: Andrea de Cesaris, Nelson Piquet, Martin Brundle, Riccardo Patrese, Jos Verstappen, J.J. Lehto and even Johnny Herbert - all of them were subject to the same fate - they were members of the same team as Michael Schumacher. The result was always the same, either it turned out to be the end of their career, or their career suffered a significant setback.

There's an old saying in motor sport: the most bitter rival of any driver is his own team-mate. For Michael Schumacher this rule of thumb doesn't seem to apply. For the most successful German Formula One driver of all time, it's long gone without saying that he's the dominant member of a two time driving team. He's who everyone else measures himself against. He's determined to beat the fastest drivers in the sport. He lives to beat a Villeneuve driving for Williams-Renault or a Hakkinen driving for McLaren-Mercedes. Beating the best in an inferior car is what satisfies him most. How his team-mate does means nothing to him.

Big names dot the list of team-mates he's brought down. Top drivers have retired, promising youngsters have been branded forever as failures, because they looked average next to Michael Schumacher. Long before Eddie Irvine, his team-mate of four years first spoke of the "Schumacher steamroller", Johnny Herbert put it this way: "He inhales the air very air his team-mate is trying to breathe." The current Stewart driver says Schumacher´s greatest asset is his unwavering self-confidence, bordering on Teutonic arrogance. "He's the sort of driver every team boss dreams of. With that sort of support anybody would do well."

What Herbert's forgetting though is that everybody starts from scratch. Nobody rolled out the red carpet for the unknown German, whose way into the Jordan cockpit was made easier by a financial injection from Mercedes. The Rhinelander has earned everything he's achieved.

In his debut he embarrassed veteran Andrea de Cesaris on Spa-Francorchamps, the most difficult course on the Formula One circuit. Benetton team boss Flavio Briatore didn't hesitate for a second in signing up the diamond in the rough for his young English-Italian team. That gave the young German the chance to learn the Formula One craft next to a three-time world champion in the form of Nelson Piquet. At least that was the plan. Things transpired quite differently: the young German wound up giving the Brazilian playboy a few lessons in driving. After Schumacher had bettered his team-mate in qualifying for four out of five races and finished in the points three times, the Piquet era had come to an end. The young German had arrived.

With Piquet gone, in 1992 Briatore signed Englishman Martin Brundle, a driver who had held his own with none other than Ayrton Senna in the Formula 3. For Benetton Brundle did very well indeed, earning the team several world championship points. But in the end, the winner of the team-internal dual was Michael Schumacher with his first Grand Prix victory and a sensational third place in the drivers standings. Brundle had been relieved of his reputation as a young gun and in the sporting manner of an English gentleman admitted without a trace of envy, "He's the best. A lot of drivers can be fast in a flawless car, but he gets the most out of a car in the most unfavourable of conditions." Williams team boss Frank Williams was just as complementary. "Michael is always a threat, even if you were to put him in a push car."

The Formula One patriarch knows of what he speaks. Driving a superior Williams-Renault in 1992 Riccardo Patrese finished second in the drivers standings. One year later he was Schumacher´s next victim. The German made the Italian look average at best. That's partly due to the fact that Patrese was the first driver to be subjected to a "Schumacher model". Teamed up with technicians Ross Brawn and Rory Byrne,

Schumacher´s first victim: Three time Formula One champion Nelson Piquet called it a career.

From "young gun" to "also-ran": Britain´s Martin Brundle .

minator

The gaze of a man with an iron will to win: Michael Schumacher´s team-mates are not allowed to get in his way.

The sole survivor: Eddie Irvine is the first Formula One driver to be able to continue his career as a number one driver, after playing second fiddle to Michael Schumacher.

„I need Schumacher",
admitted Eddie Irvine.

who were later to follow him to Ferrari, Schumacher had the B193 practically tailor-made for him. Patrese didn´t share his team-mate's fondness for the Kart-like handling and extreme oversteering. With this car Schumacher was even able to finish ahead of Williams´ Alain Prost several times. His team-mate though performed miserably, and that spelled the end of his Formula One career. Not just that, but the Italian is still mystified by the German's remarkable fitness which allows him to be at his best in the cockpit. In 1994 the transformation of the Benetton team into Schumacher´s team was complete. The German had arrived as motor sport's newest superstar. While he secured the world championship against England's Damon Hill of Williams, his team-mates were having their problems. Benetton´s perennial driver J.J. Lehto had a late start to the season due to a serious accident in a test run. When he did finally get back into the cockpit, he looked no better than his replacement, Jos Verstappen who had just switched from Formula 3 to Formula One. Both were obviously no match for Schumacher´s speed and mental toughness. Lehto, who'd once been considered a major talent, never really got his feet back under the table in the Formula One, and Verstappen was relegated to driving for lesser teams. Finally it was Johnny Herbert's turn in the last two Grand Prix races of 1994, and the Englishman made no mistake, offering himself up as the number two for the coming season. Herbert

	Year	Races	Training	Points	Victories
Andrea de Cesaris	1991	1	0:1	0:0	0:0
Nelson Piquet	1991	5	1:4	4,5:4	0:0
Martin Brundle	1992	16	0:16	38:53	0:1
Riccardo Patrese	1993	16	0:16	20:52	0:1
Jos Verstappen	1994	8	0:8	8:50	0:5
JJ Lehto	1994	4	0:4	1:36	0:3
Johnny Herbert	1994 / '95	19	1:18	49:112	2:9
Eddie Irvine	1996 – '99	58	4:54	114:255	1:16

made the most of his opportunity promptly winning both races. But it wasn't quite as impressive as it first sounds. In both cases his countryman, Damon Hill had inadvertently helped him along his way, having knocked off his arch-rival (and himself) in his eagerness to cross the finish line first. Schumacher won a record nine races that season for his first drivers championship. Despite the Englishman's brave effort, Herbert was simply outclassed.

Schumacher then moved to a team plagued by a chronic lack of success in the previous few years: Ferrari. While Jean Alesi and Gerhard Berger, his predecessors at Marinello and successors at Benetton rejected the cars tailored to Schumacher´s liking as "undriveable" and crashed them almost in the dozens, Schumacher was driving record-setting laps at Fiorano. Although the Ferrari F310 was brought into the

world as an aerodynamic miscarriage, the defending world champion pushed it to three wins that season. The fact that Eddie Irvine, his new team-mate did better than him in the first qualifying of the season left Schumacher simply amused. It was to remain an extremely rare occasion.

In the 126 Grand Prix races of Schumacher´s career a team-mate has only qualified better a total of six times.

Ferrari put it's whole team at Schumacher´s disposal, even, on his request, signing on Brawn and Byrne his old technicians at Benetton. Irvine, as the "second man" became the first team-mate to successfully adapt to Schumacher´s style. In training he approached Schumacher bit by bit, but in the races themselves he proved still to be second best.

The months which followed Schumacher´s injury at Silverstone proved that without him

A familiar pose. Michael Schumacher celebra tes while his subordinates cheer him on. Only Northern Ireland's Eddie Irvine has been able to get Ferrari to focus on the number two driver, and that only due to a serious injury to the bold German.

A short and uneventful career. Jos Verstappen made the jump directly from Formula 3 to Bennetton and failed miserably.

A rare sight: Michael Schumacher rarely gives advice to team-mates, like former understudy Johnny Herbert.

Ferrari lacks direction. Such a strong personality is simply irreplaceable as a motivator. Eddie Irvine, who at first enjoyed his new but temporary role as Ferrari's number one wasn't able to step into that role. With the Italian team clearly in stagnation the Northern Irishman was eventually forced to admit, "I need Schumacher". What he meant was that first and foremost, he missed Schumacher´s work in constantly developing the cars from a technical point of view. No other driver can push the Ferrari to its limit while at the same time providing such detailed information about how the car is performing, thus giving them valuable clues as to how to improve the cars. Eddie Irvine though is the only driver who's survived alongside Schumacher, and has been able to continue driving for a top team. His advice for Rubens Barrichello, his successor at Ferrari: "You have to be smart - smart and unemotional."

One-Two

for **Ferrari**

Would the little ball in Monaco's street roulette fall on red once again? Ferrari wasn't content to rely on luck, and so put their faith in this race in devising the best strategy, and letting their gifted driver, now at the top of the table take care of the rest.

Hard work pays off: Michael Schumacher went for broke and catapulted himself out into first off the start. The German had perfected this manoeuvre in training.

Speed is - in Monaco at least - pure sorcery: Mika Hakkinen between the guard-rails.

Celebrating Mika Hakkinen´s pole position like a victory: Mercedes sporting director Norbert Haug (left), development board member Dieter Zetsche (middle) and private car sales manager Juergen Hubbert (right).

here's nothing closer to a roman chariot race", was how one commentator in the motor racing periodical "Autocar" described the course at the time of the first Monaco Grand Prix in 1929. Seventy years later the fascination with this race remains just as strong. As the modern day gladiators accelerate their cars to speeds of up to 290 kph, through narrow streets where the speed limit would normally be just 30 kph, the spectators are closer to the action than on any other course. Here it's the driver that makes the difference, technical superiority plays a secondary role. So it was the perfect stage for the new points leader, Michael Schumacher to show off his stuff, and defend his lead at the top of the standings, because he, more than any other driver is master of this labyrinth of curves.

Still on a high after his performance at Imola, Schumacher wasted no time in setting out to prove who's boss in this principality (apart from Prince Rainier of course). The German was so dominant manoeuvring his racer through the narrow passages between the walls and guard-rails, that there never seemed to be any serious doubt that it would be he who would lock up the pole position this time around - this despite a crash on Saturday morning, which had his mechanics working overtime to put things right. But Hakkinen surprised everybody, just seconds ahead of

the chequered flag, the Finn catapulted himself into pole position, with an average speed of 150 kph - incredible for this course through the streets of Monte Carlo. Shortly before that Schumacher had broken off his last qualifying lap, apparently convinced that his time was unassailable. Coulthard and Hakkinen sped onwards, despite the yellow flag, in accordance with the rules by

Eddie Irvine improved his team's lead to 2:0.

the way, since the rule book states that drivers only have to take their feet off the gas when the flag is actually waved. Mercedes sporting director Norbert Haug celebrated this last second coup clapping shoulders with such force, that McLaren director Ron Dennis almost collapsed.

But after the start of the race it was the others who were celebrating. For it wasn't the silver arrows that shot out into the lead, but instead, it was the two Ferraris. In an all-or-nothing duel of acceleration ahead of the "Ste. Devote" curve, Schumacher edged out Hakkinen, while Irvine had similar success against Coulthard. "Even I was surprised that Mika didn't have a better start", said the German after the race. "Then on the straight-away I was faster. When we brushed each other, Mika gave way, otherwise there would have been an accident." The Finn though wasn't nearly as impressed by this manoeuvre, "after we made contact I couldn't steer precisely".

The "Scuderia Ferrari" had their number one driver to thank once again. It was he who was responsible for putting them out in front. Schumacher doesn't exactly have a reputation for laziness when it comes to training, and the two time world champion had put in overtime yet again. While the rest of the field spent the Friday which was training-free sunning themselves on the decks of some of the impressive yachts in the harbour, or making public relations appearances, Schumacher flew to Fiorano for simulated starts at the in-house racetrack. Having collected all the data he needed, he flew back to the Cote d'Azur on the same day.

"I was too ambitious", admitted Damon Hill.

While the red and silver four, Schumacher out in front followed by Hakkinen, Irvine and Coulthard surged away from the pack, the rest were making their way through the first curve, without the usual trouble that it presents. Lap after lap the bright racers sped without incident through Monte Carlo, which is such an interesting course that it's fascinating even when no-one is trying to pass. Anyone who tries to do so here treads a fine line between "determination" and "desperation". After starting from 17th in the grid, Englishman Damon Hill topped off his

A Scotsman's misery: David Coulthard failed to finish for the third time in four races.

Steady Eddie: Eddie Irvine made it a perfect one-two victory for Ferrari in Monaco.

Unwise gamble: Jean Alesi's risk ended in a duel with the guard-rail - the guard-rail won.

Tunnel vision: the cars shoot though the Grand Hotel underpass at speeds of up to 270 kph. Damon Hill is no exception.

Busy beaver: point collector Heinz-Harald Frentzen finished fourth at Monte Carlo.

weekend with a move which falls into the latter category. Ahead of the tricky exit from the tunnel he tried to slip into a gap which didn't exist, with predicable result. "The accident was my fault", admitted the former world champion afterwards. "I was simply too ambitious." An annoyed Ralf Schumacher, who'd been sent into a spin and banished to last place by Hill's foolhardy move was diplomatic. "I saw him coming, but I didn't think he'd really try it."

His brother meanwhile was buzzing along a half second ahead of Hakkinen. both Ferraris had started the race with just a little fuel in their tanks, and were making full use of the edge this gave them in terms of weight. Eddie Irvine was continuing to put more space between himself and David Coulthard in their "duel of the deputies". Then Coulthard's car began to belch

A great performance in front of the crowd. Giancarlo Fisichella and Alexander Wurz.

His most loyal fans: When Michael Schumacher (right) puts his toe down daughter Gina-Maria and wife Corinna cheer him on.

smoke. Lap after lap the handsome Scot spread a cloud of smoky fog behind him, Was his a new marketing move by West, the team sponsors, or was this a mechanical problem? The answer came on lap 37. David parked his Mercedes in the garage. A gearbox problem had forced him to retire for the third time in just four races.

That's a "success" rate that BAR driver Jacques Villeneuve could only dream off. After qualifying in a respectable eighth place - even when he was in championship form he qualified no higher in Monaco, a course he hates, once again he failed to make it to the finish line. This time it was an oil leak that prevented him from finishing a race for the first time with his new team. But it wasn't all bad news for BAR. In Monaco British American Racing team boss

Left: mutual congratulations - Team-mates Michael Schumacher and Eddie Irvine. right: More light than darkness - Alex Zanardi in Monaco.

Craig Pollock made an announcement that made BAR the envy of several other teams. He announced that he had signed Honda to produced the engines for BAR, beginning next season.

On lap 37 Toranosuke Tagagi also left the race, but in a most spectacular manner. Instead of attacking his opponents from behind, the "Tiger" set up a trap. When his engine blew up it left a long trail of oil behind him. The first victim was the reigning world champion, who instead of turning in the direction of the Grand Hotel carried on straight ahead into the emergency exit. "The rear wheels began to swing out of line with the front wheels, and had I tried to turn I would have wound up in the guard-rail", explained Hakkinen. It was to cost him 18 seconds, and a sure second place finish.

That's because when it was clear that Schumacher no longer needed the help of super-brain Ross Brawn, the latter reached into his bag of tricks to help Eddie Irvine. What he pulled out was the tactic that, had he needed it would have helped Schumacher overtake Hakkinen. The first pit stop was deliberately short, with Irvine's tank

Ready for transport? Arrows on the hook (left), some fringe benefits of the yachts in the harbour (right).

"Had I given way I would have flown straight into the guard-rail", explained Mika Hakkinen.

being only partially filled. The lighter car would allow him to achieve a series of extremely fast laps, to create enough of a lead to safely make a second pit stop. That's the theory behind what in practice worked even better due to Hakkinen´s spot of bad luck. The first ever one-two win for Ferrari on this Mediterranean track was sealed.

"Super Frentzen" exclaimed Eddie Jordan.

Behind them it was a cool Heinz-Harald Frentzen who turned 32 during the week. The German waited until Barrichello headed to the pits before sprinting though a couple of laps and into fourth. "Our goal was to win the race against Stewart-Ford. That's what we did," Frentzen said proudly. Eddie Jordan's comment: "Super-Frentzen".

In training Frentzen had lost the battle of prestige after one of his fingers got caught in the gearshift behind the steering wheel. That's why Barrichello qualified as the best of the rest in his 100th Grand Prix race. On race day though the Stewart team was to learn yet another costly lesson. Suspension failure in both cars cost the Scottish team what would have been their well deserved first world championship points. Despite this "Rubinho" and team-mate Johnny Herbert were able to prove through the data, that it was a material weakness, not driver error that had caused the suspension system to fail.

Ralf Schumacher ended his weekend to forget in the guard-rail in front of the Grand Hotel. But instead of probing him about his apparent lack of concentration the media appeared more interested in grilling him about his affair with Jordan pit girl Katie Price. Ralf´s team-mate Alex Zanardi meanwhile was comparing himself with the comic character Mr Bean, even if he did make it over the finish line. "Believe it or not, the seat broke. This car definitely needs to be improved", he said

The winner though didn't have any such problems, nor did he have any difficulty keeping both feet firmly on the ground. The champagne had hardly been uncorked, when Schumacher warned: "we won't know where we really stand until Barcelona. The 16 points we earned today will prove to be vital later on." Schumacher didn't want to hear anything of the fact that with his 16th victory for Ferrari he had surpassed the great Niki Lauda and become the greatest Ferrari driver of all time. This was possibly due to the fact that he still had his sights set on equalling a couple of the Austrian's other exploits - two world championships in a Ferrari cockpit.

"We'll need these points later", warned Michael Schumacher.

One of a kind: even in the modern era the Monaco Grand Prix course remains a fascinating anachronism.

Statistics

Course length:	3,367 km
Distance of race:	78 (= 262,626 km)
Start time:	13.00 UTC
Weather on day of race:	cloudless, warm
Attendance:	130 000
1998 Results:	1. Mika Hakkinen (FIN, McLaren-Mercedes MP4/13), 1 h 51'23"59!
	2. Giancarlo Fisichella (I, Benetton-Playlife B198), +11"475 s
	3. Eddie Irvine (GB, Ferrari F300), +41"378 s
Pole position 1998:	Mika Hakkinen (McLaren-Mercedes MP4/13), 1'19"798 m
Fastest Lap 1998:	Mika Hakkinen (McLaren-Mercedes MP4/13), 1'21"973 m
Fastest pit stop 1998:	Michael Schumacher (D, Ferrari F300), 24"328 s

Overtaking on this guard-rail canal is virtually impossible.

"Monaco is one of a kind. The face of the whole city changes on Grand Prix weekend. It's always exciting to travel so close alongside the guard-rails. The key points are the blind curves at the casino and the tunnel. Overtaking is virtually impossible. Sometimes you can if you want to risk it at the Loews hairpin."

Michael Schumacher

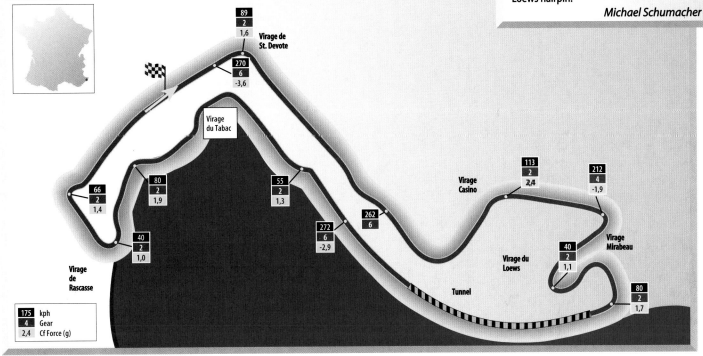

Results

Driver	Team	Pit stops	Laps	Time (hours)	Average speed	Behind 1st	prev. driver
1. Michael Schumacher	Ferrari	1	78	1 h 49'31"812	143,864	–	–
2. Eddie Irvine	Ferrari	2	78	1 h 50'02"288	143,200	30"476 s	–
3. Mika Hakkinen	McLaren-Mercedes	1	78	1 h 50'09"295	143,049	37"483 s	7"007 s
4. Heinz-Harald Frentzen	Jordan-Mugen-Honda	1	78	1 h 50'25"821	142,892	54"009 s	16"526 s
5. Giancarlo Fisichella	Benetton-Playlife	1	77	1 h 49'32"705	142,001	1 lap	1 lap
6. Alexander Wurz	Benetton-Playlife	1	77	1 h 49'47"799	141,675	1 lap	16"054 s
7. Jarno Trulli	Prost-Peugeot	2	77	1 h 50'05"845	141,288	1 lap	18"046 s
8. Alessandro Zanardi	Wiliams-Supertec	1	76	1 h 49'49"514	139,799	2 laps	1 lap
9. Rubens Barrichello [1]	Stewart-Ford	1	71	1 h 40'57"711	142,067	retirement	

Driver	Team	Pit stops	in lap	Reason f. retiring	Position before retiring
Ralf Schumacher	Williams-Supertec	1	55	crash	10
Jean Alesi	Sauber-Petronas	2	51	crash	11
Pedro Diniz	Sauber-Petronas	0	50	crash	8
Olivier Panis	Prost-Peugeot	1	41	engine	12
David Coulthard	McLaren-Mercedes	0	37	gearbox	4
Mika Salo	BAR-Supertec	0	37	crash	11
Toranosuke Takagi	TWR-Arrows	0	37	engine	15
Jacques Villeneuve	BAR-Supertec	0	33	hydraulics	8
Johnny Herbert	Stewart-Ford	0	33	suspension	11
Pedro de la Rosa	TWR-Arrows	0	31	gearbox	19
Marc Gené	Minardi-Ford	0	25	crash	19
Luca Badoer	Minardi-Ford	0	11	gearbox	18
Damon Hill	Jordan-Mugen-Honda	0	4	crash	17

1) Didn´t complete race, but counted due to distance driven.

Monaco GP

**4th Race of the World Championship 1999,
Monte Carlo (MC), 16th May 1999**

Starting Grid

1 Mika Häkkinen (FIN)
McLaren-Mercedes MP4/14-5
1'20"547 m (284,4 km/h) [1]

3 Michael Schumacher (D)
Ferrari F399/193
1'20"611 m (284,2 km/h)

2 David Coulthard (GB)
McLaren-Mercedes MP4/14-4
1'20"956 m (288,0 km/h)

4 Eddie Irvine (GB)
Ferrari F399/191
1'21"011 m (279,5 km/h)

16 Rubens Barrichello (BR)
Stewart-Ford SF3/4
1'21"350 m (281,5 km/h)

8 Heinz-Harald Frentzen (D)
Jordan-Mugen-Honda 199/5
1'21"556 m (280,0 km/h)

19 Jarno Trulli (I)
Prost-Peugeot AP02/2
1'21"769 m (276,4 km/h)

22 Jacques Villeneuve (CDN)
BAR-Supertec 01/3
1'21"827 m (280,0 km/h)

9 Giancarlo Fisichella (I)
Benetton-Playlife B199/6
1'21"938 m (280,2 km/h)

10 Alexander Wurz (A)
Benetton-Playlife B199/5
1'21"968 m (278,4 km/h)

5 Alessandro Zanardi (I)
Williams-Supertec FW21/5
1'22"152 m (280,9 km/h)

23 Mika Salo (FIN)
BAR-Supertec 01/3
1'22"241 m (278,9 km/h)

17 Johnny Herbert (GB)
Stewart-Ford SF3/5
1'22"248 m (282,1 km/h)

11 Jean Alesi (F)
Sauber-Petronas C18/5
1'22"354 m (279,2 km/h)

12 Pedro Diniz (BR)
Sauber-Petronas C18/4
1'22"659 m (278,9 km/h)

6 Ralf Schumacher (D)
Williams-Supertec FW21/4
1'22"719 m (281,3 km/h)

7 Damon Hill (GB)
Jordan-Mugen-Honda 199/4
1'22"832 m (281,9 km/h)

18 Olivier Panis (F)
Prost-Peugeot AP02/3
1'22"916 m (279,0 km/h)

15 Toranosuke Takagi (J)
TWR-Arrows A20/2
1'23"290 m (274,6 km/h)

20 Luca Badoer (I)
Minardi-Ford-Zetec-R M01/1
1'23"765 m (277,7 km/h)

14 Pedro de la Rosa (E)
TWR-Arrows A20/4
1'24"260 m (289,4 km/h)

21 Marc Gené (E)
Minardi-Ford-Zetec-R M01/4
1'24"914 m (289,4 km/h)

107-percent time: 1'26"185 m

[1].) Lap time (top speed in qualifying).

58

Best Laps

In Training on Friday (m)			
1. M. Schumacher	1'22"718	12. Trulli	1'23"958
2. Häkkinen	1'22"854	13. Zanardi	1'24"065
3. Panis	1'23"318	14. Wurz	1'24"263
4. Irvine	1'23"396	15. Alesi	1'24"492
5. Fisichella	1'23"458	16. R. Schumacher	1'24"906
6. Coulthard	1'23"503	17. Diniz	1'25"094
7. Barrichello	1'23"545	18. de la Rosa	1'26"148
8. Salo	1'23"793	19. Frentzen	1'26"336
9. Villeneuve	1'23"862	20. Takagi	1'27"618
10. Herbert	1'23"865	21. Gené	1'27"687
11. Hill	1'23"874	22. Badoer	1'28"316

In the Race on Sunday (m)			
1. Häkkinen	1'22"259	12. Villeneuve	1'23"537
2. M. Schumacher	1'22"288	13. Barrichello	1'23"583
3. Frentzen	1'22"471	14. Trulli	1'23"646
4. Irvine	1'22"572	15. Panis	1'24"480
5. Diniz	1'22"637	16. Salo	1'24"787
6. R. Schumacher	1'22"837	17. Herbert	1'24"919
7. Coulthard	1'22"883	18. Takagi	1'26"482
8. Wurz	1'23"236	19. Gené	1'26"864
9. Zanardi	1'23"294	20. de la Rosa	1'26"914
10. Alesi	1'23"417	21. Badoer	1'28"691
11. Fisichella	1'23"473	22. Hill	1'28"848

Total Pit Stop Times

Lap	Time (s)	Lap	Time (s)	Lap	Time (s)
23 Trulli	24"101	52 R. Schumacher	25"357		
27 Panis	23"976	56 Irvine	23"332		
37 Irvine	23"387	57 Frentzen	24"073		
42 M. Schumacher	26"745				
43 Fisichella	27"197				
44 Wurz	26"866				
50 Häkkinen	26"172				
50 Barrichello	25"866				
50 Alesi	34"261				
50 Zanardi	25"839				
52 Trulli	23"525				

The Race Lap by Lap

Start: M. Schumacher gets off to a brilliant start, edging past pole sitter Hakkinen before the first curve. Irvine overtakes Coulthard in the same fashion. **Lap 4:** Hill begins a too ambitious overtaking attempt causing both himself and R. Schumacher to crash. Ralf continues in last place. Hill is out. The McLaren-Ferrari combination continue to lead followed by Barrichello, Frentzen, Trulli, and Fisichella. **Lap 18:** Coulthard's fastest lap, but is soon slowed down by gearbox trouble. **Lap 31:** M. Schumacher's lead over Hakkinen is up to 16 seconds, and the Finn is now only 1.2 seconds ahead of Irvine. **Lap 33:** Herbert's right rear wheel breaks off in front of the Casino, Villeneuve retires due to engine trouble. **Lap 37:** Short fuelling stop for Irvine. Coulthard parks his Mercedes in the pits. **Lap 39:** Takagi's engine blows, Hakkinen skids on the oil and takes the Mirabeau emergency exit. Thanks to his reverse gear he returns to the track and soldiers on. Irvine is just behind him, despite his pit stop. **Lap 50:** Hakkinen goes to the pits, Irvine is second. **Lap 56:** Irvine's second pit stop, he remains ahead of Hakkinen. **Lap 57:** Frentzen's only pit stop, therefore he needs very little fuel. He returns to the track ahead of Barrichello to move into fourth. **Lap 67:** Hakkinen drives the fastest lap but Irvine is still 7.5 seconds ahead of him. **Lap 72:** Fifth placed Barrichello has a suspension failure and spins out into the guard-rail. Fisichella inherits the points. **Lap 78:** M. Schumacher wins at Monaco for the fourth time, 30 seconds ahead of team-mate Irvine. Reigning world champion Hakkinen is third.

Standings

Driver/Points			
1. Michael Schumacher	26	Jean Alesi	1
2. Eddie Irvine	18	Alexander Wurz	1
3. Mika Häkkinen	14		
4. Heinz-Harald Frentzen	13		
5. Ralf Schumacher	7		
Giancarlo Fisichella	7		
7. David Coulthard	6		
Rubens Barrichello	6		
9. Damon Hill	3		
10. Pedro de la Rosa	1		
Olivier Panis	1		

Team	Points
1. Ferrari	44
2. McLaren-Mercedes	20
3. Jordan-Mugen-Honda	16
4. Benetton-Playlife	8
5. Williams-Supertec	7
6. Stewart-Ford	6
7. TWR-Arrows	1
Prost-Peugeot	1
Sauber-Petronas	1

Ralf Schumacher feels at home on the
narrow streets of Monaco.

Spending to the Max

Formula One is a world of extremes: In no other motor sport is more money spent on technical and logistical support just to ensure that motor cars can drive in circles. Seen over the course of an average season a team's parts and labour costs make painfully clear that this is no sport for just any average Joe.

Expensive cosmetics: A new nose for a Ferrari costs about £4000, minus the wings.

Prepared by hand: A team like Jordan goes through more than 4,000 Bridgestone tyres.

Disposable parts: A Formula One ca rear view mirrors tossed in the dust after each and ev race.

T he sum of £700,000 is an incredible amount of money for any mortal. A working man or woman on a wage of about £1400 a month would have to work roughly 41 years and 8 months to earn that much. But this princely sum isn't nearly enough for a Formula One team to be competitive for even a single season. A team like Jordan spend that much for a season's hotel and travel costs alone. In the world's most expensive sport the rules of the real world simply don't apply.

In fact in Formula One motor racing no cost is too high and no effort is spared to reach the ultimate goal - success on the racetrack. This of course begins with the high technology that goes into the design and production of the cars themselves. Lighter, stronger, faster: Every individual

part is pushed to the edge of it's limitations. This naturally results in incredible wear and tear on the moving parts. Jordan will go through about 85 Mugen-Honda ten cylinder engines this season alone, even if the cost per unit is practically incalculable due to the high cost of research and development that go into them. The costs for these triumphs of engineering - made up of 3,200 individual parts, are much higher than the budget for hotel and travel costs for a single season. The ultra-compact gearbox, which most of the teams have managed to develop and adapt for their own means costs an estimated £600 thousand alone.

Staggering figures? There's no doubt about that. When it comes to the annual costs of laundering the overalls worn by the mechanics in the

pits for example that's almost enough to open up your own launderette: £13,000 annually. But it's also the little things that can quickly run up a Formula One team's costs. Take the brake linings for example. They only cost £100 a piece, but a team typically goes through a thousand of them in a single season.

Many parts are only used in one Formula One race - they're replaced after every race whether they need to be or not, for fear of possible mechanical failure. This isn't just true of the nuts and bolts, but also of things like the rear view mirror and the cogs in the gearbox.

In addition to the 16 Grand Prix races per season, ambitious teams will spend about 125 days a year on testing the cars over about 15,000 kilometres of track. In Ferrari's case, those fig-

A short life: The extremely expensive high tech steering wheel is seldom used for more than three races.

Wear and tear: Sauber-Petronas go through more than 80 of the former Ferrari ten cylinder engines in a single season.

No ordinary brakes: The brake linings alone cost £100 apiece.

Roll on down the highway: Every Formula One team owns at least three specially-outfitted trucks and a double-decker coach.

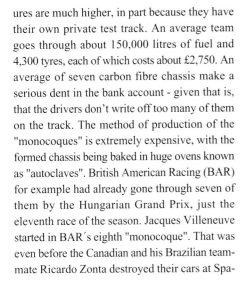

ures are much higher, in part because they have their own private test track. An average team goes through about 150,000 litres of fuel and 4,300 tyres, each of which costs about £2,750. An average of seven carbon fibre chassis make a serious dent in the bank account - given that is, that the drivers don't write off too many of them on the track. The method of production of the "monocoques" is extremely expensive, with the formed chassis being baked in huge ovens known as "autoclaves". British American Racing (BAR) for example had already gone through seven of them by the Hungarian Grand Prix, just the eleventh race of the season. Jacques Villeneuve started in BAR´s eighth "monocoque". That was even before the Canadian and his Brazilian team-mate Ricardo Zonta destroyed their cars at Spa-

Francorchamps. The noses alone - without the accompanying front wings cost a whopping £4,200 each.

But it's not just the technology which gobbles up huge amounts of sterling. When the teams have to travel overseas about 18 tonnes of equipment has to be loaded into specially-chartered freight jumbo jets. Meanwhile the teams´ 500 horsepower lorries - teams generally have about three of them - travel about 18,000 kilometres between races, test tracks, and their home bases throughout Europe during the course of an average season. Then come the 38 tonne trucks parked at the track by any given team's engine maker, and the double-decker team coaches complete with hospitality tents. During a typical Formula One season the Jordan will typically use

its hospitality facilities to entertain about 1,500 guests of sponsor Benson & Hedges. By entertaining they don't simply mean pulling a few cans of lager out of the refridgerator and slapping a few spam sandwiches together - it means lashing out on a buffet with about 73 kilograms of elegantly laid out ham and some 800 bottles of fine wine.

Appearances obviously count for a lot, and not just when it comes to the grub at the hospitality tents. The cars have to look classy too, that's why they get an average of 60 new paint jobs per season, and almost 9,000 sponsors stickers are pressed on to the cars with tender loving care. Then all that's required is about 400 cans of polish and a good helping of elbow grease.

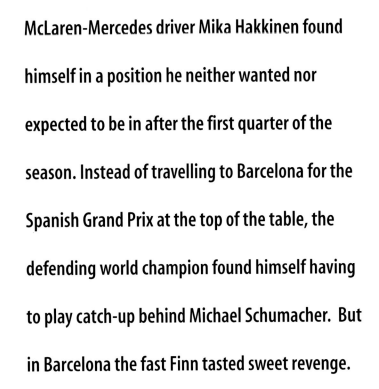

Silver Arrows
on the Horizon

McLaren-Mercedes driver Mika Hakkinen found

himself in a position he neither wanted nor

expected to be in after the first quarter of the

season. Instead of travelling to Barcelona for the

Spanish Grand Prix at the top of the table, the

defending world champion found himself having

to play catch-up behind Michael Schumacher. But

in Barcelona the fast Finn tasted sweet revenge.

Their opponents in their sights: Mika
Hakkinen and Michael Schumacher continued their battle for the title in Spain.

Where the Finn loves to win: In Spain Mika Hakkinen got his revenge after being humiliated in the previous two races.

Whatever Ferrari's strategy was, it failed miserably...

The McLaren drivers approached the Spanish Grand Prix as if it were a race which would decide their ultimate destiny. The season hadn't begun well for David Coulthard and Mika Hakkinen, both of whom had been plagued by various problems. The Ferrari drivers had already made three appearances on the highest podium step, while only once had the Finnish defending champion managed the like. "If the Ferraris beat us here, we can as good as write off any chance at the world championship", predicted McLaren's number one driver ahead of the race. Despite being technically superior, the runaway favourites were clearly on the defensive.

But despite two spectacular victories in a row, Michael Schumacher knew that it wouldn't be easy for him and his Northern Irish teammate on the "Circuit de Catalunya". The flat track is as good as tailor-made for McLaren-Mercedes, who incidently had spent the better part of their winter testing programme at the Spanish course. Not just that, but since the opportunities to overtake on this track are about as plentiful as icebergs in sunny Spain, everyone knew that qualifying on the Iberian penninsula would take on more impor-

tance than anywhere else, with the possible exception of the narrow streets of Monte Carlo.

In the last training session though it became apparent that an upset could be in the making. Until the 59th minute it looked as if a Ferrari would come out on top in one hour qualifying session. What was most surprising was that the driver on his way to an apparent upset wasn't Michael Schumacher but Ferrari's number two, Eddie Irvine. But that didn't phase Mika Hakkinen. In literally the last second the Finn completed a perfect lap to claim first - if only by the skin of his teeth. He nipped Irvine by all of 0.133 of a second, who himself finished just 25 thousandths of a second ahead of David Coulthard. Michael Schumacher, who certainly wasn't amused by finishing second best to his teammate completed the second row of the starting grid, while Sauber driver Jean Alesi, and a still determined Jacques Villeneuve somewhat surprisingly took their places in the third row.

Villeneuve's season so far couldn't have been much worse: not one finish in four Grand Prix starts. Villeneuve's new BAR team, formed by his former coach and manager Craig Pollock, and experienced racecar designer Adrian Reynard

had high hopes going into the season, but by now, the reality of the Formula One circuit had dragged all of them back down to earth. Instead of winning their first Grand Prix early in their first season, as they had said they expected to, the BAR team were instead notable for their spectacular series of technical problems and bad luck. There was no question: the emotional Villeneuve was on the verge of reacting the way he often does in such situations - by doing something radical.

This much was clear: the start of this race would be of prime importance. It would be the best, or maybe even only opportunity to make up for ground lost in qualifying, or put more space between oneself, and one's opponents. Whatever Ferrari's strategy had been, it failed miserably. McLaren's silver arrows catapulted themselves out ahead of the pack into the first right-hand curve. If that wasn't enough, Eddie Irvine held up his German teammate. "I had a good start, but then David and Eddie got in my way, so much so that I had to apply the brakes", recounted Schumacher later. While the two Ferrari drivers were cruising towards the first bend, another took advantage of what he recognised as a golden opportunity. Jacques Villeneuve cooly manoeu-

The agony of defeat: In Spain too Alex Zanardi failed to live up to the hopes of his Williams team.

Blowing in the wind: A gust sent Eddie Irvine's Ferrari off the track in Friday's open training session.

A solid second: David Coulthard wasn't to be had.

Bringing up the rear: Fisichella only managed to place 13th in qualifying.

Frustration: Rubens Barrichello was disqualified.

vered the two "reds" to the outside of the curve and slipped into first - first among the non-McLarens that is. For Schumacher, the current standings leader, things could have hardly been worse.

The son of Ferrari legend Gilles Villeneuve though was looking great. "My car felt really good today", explained the French-Canadian who grew up in Switzerland. "It was surprisingly easy to keep Michael at bay behind me." Schumacher was left with no other choice but to stay close to Villeneuve and be patient. "On the first lap I could have gone after him in the fifth curve", explained the fourth-placed Ferrari driver. "But that would have been very risky. So I decided to wait and see."

Unfortunately, almost all of his Formula One colleagues followed this maxim as well. It certainly didn't turn into the breath-taking race full of incidents that all motor racing fans crave. The 22 cars drove the 4.728 kilometre course in practically the same order they began until the first pit stops. At the front of the pack Mika Hakkinen steadily opened up his lead over Scotsman David Coulthard. Behind them Villeneuve continued to stay ahead of the two Ferraris, and even increased

Hopes dashed: For a while in Spain - Jacques Villeneuve looked to have a chance of making it to the podium - but he again failed to finish.

Above: As hard as the Ferrari mechanics worked to try to overtake Coulthard in the pits, it wasn't enough. Below: Local hero Pedro de la Rosa stops to refuel.

Royal guest: King Juan Carlos visits Heinz-Harald Frentzen and Eddie Jordan.

the space between himself and Schumacher, followed by Irvine. Behind them was a surprising Jarno Trulli, who had gunned his Prost-Peugeot through the first few metres to improve from ninth to sixth, with Sauber driver Jean Alesi, Ralf Schumacher of Williams, Jordan's Heinz-Harald Frentzen, and Stewart driver Rubens Barrichello in tow. To be precise, in the first 22 of a total of 65 laps there were just two changes of position. Alex Wurz shot off the track in the fifth, allowing Riccardo Zonta's replacement, Mika Salo to move into 16th. Eleven laps later Giancarlo Fisichella ran into problems with his Benetton, and Alex Zanardi, who once again proved to be a disappointment, improved from 15th to 14th - not exactly where one is used to seeing Williams drivers.

Eddie Irvine was the first to head to the pits, on lap 22. Two laps later Villeneuve and Michael Schumacher did the same. That was bad news for the BAR driver: the Ferrari mechanics had Schumi out of the pits fast enough for him to take over third, 18 seconds behind David Coulthard. For Schumacher, this was no time to savour this minor success. For him, this was time to get down to the matter at hand. As he'd so often done before, he set out on a string of extremely fast laps, making up ground all the way. On several laps he made good a full second on the leaders. By lap 42 the Scottish McLaren-Mercedes was in his sights. "Things were going very well", smiled

the Ferrari superstar later. But then he was held up by "an Arrows driver. That disappointed me", complained the German, "after that I had no chance. I lost a lot of time there." Two laps later his Scottish competitor also stopped for fuel, but too quickly for Schumacher, banishing Ferrari's number one to third for the balance of the race.

Out in front, Mika Hakkinen probably had little idea of what was going on some distance behind him. Ralf Schumacher finished in fifth after a similarly uneventful race, but behind him there was a heated battle for the final world championship point. Trulli, Barrichello, and Jordan driver Damon Hill were all determined to cross the finish line in sixth. It wasn't decided until all of them were lapped. Hill took advantage of the opportunity presented, when Barrichello got out of the way to let Schumacher past. The Englishman slipped in behind the German and left the Brazilian in his wake. However the former world champion wasn't able to successfully challenge Jarno Trulli. The Italian secured his team its second world championship point of the season.

A couple of footnotes: Heinz-Harald Frentzen was forced to retire on lap 35 due to driveshaft trouble. Jacques Villeneuve, who was so impressive in the first third of the race maintained his consistency. The charismatic former champion was forced out by gearbox trouble, making it a perfect record - five 1999 Formula One starts, five non-finishes.

Champagne dance: Mika Hakkinen celebrating his second victory of the season.

Statistics

Course length:	4,728 km
Distance of race:	65 (= 307,32 km)
Start time:	13.00 UTC
Weather on day of race:	warm, overcast
Attendance:	81 000
1998 Results:	1. Mika Hakkinen (FIN, McLaren-Mercedes MP4/13), 1 h 33'37"621
	2. David Coulthard (GB, McLaren-Mercedes MP4/13), + 9"439 s
	3. Michael Schumacher (D, Ferrari F300), + 47"094 s
Pole position 1998:	Mika Hakkinen (McLaren-Mercedes MP4/13), 1'20"262 m
Fastest Lap 1998:	Mika Hakkinen (McLaren-Mercedes MP4/13), 1'24"275 m
Fastest pit stop 1998:	David Coulthard (McLaren-Mercedes MP4/13), 25"165 s

The teams know all there is to know about this course

"This course on the edge of Barcelona is very technically demanding. The long and fast curves put a lot of pressure on the front tyres so the correct balance is of particular importance. As one of the most used test tracks, all of the teams know it very well. The challenge is to take that knowledge and put it to good use on the day."

Mika Hakkinen

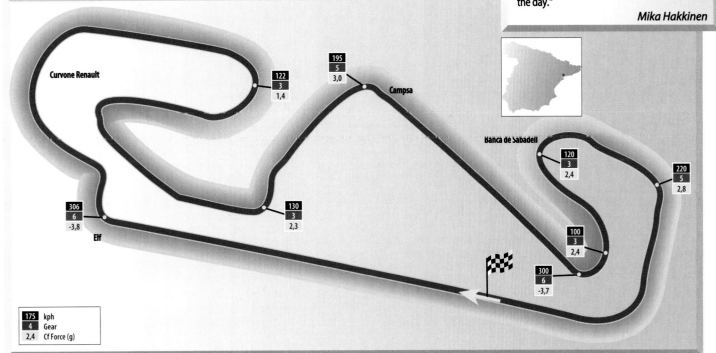

175	kph
4	Gear
2,4	Cf Force (g)

Results

Driver	Team	Pit stops	Laps	Time (hours)	Average speed	Behind 1st	prev. driver
1. Mika Hakkinen	McLaren-Mercedes	2	65	1 h 34'13"665	195,608	–	–
2. David Coulthard	McLaren-Mercedes	2	65	1 h 34'19"903	195,393	6"238 s	–
3. Michael Schumacher	Ferrari	1	65	1 h 34'24"510	195,234	10"845 s	4"607 s
4. Eddie Irvine	Ferrari	2	65	1 h 34'43"847	194,569	30"182 s	19"337 s
5. Ralf Schumacher	Williams-Supertec	2	65	1 h 35'40"873	192,637	1'27"208 m	57"026 s
6. Jarno Trulli	Prost-Peugeot	2	64	1 h 34'24"028	192,245	1 lap	1 lap
7. Damon Hill	Jordan-Mugen-Honda	2	64	1 h 34'25"044	192,211	1 lap	1"016 s
8. Mika Salo	BAR-Supertec	2	64	1 h 35'21"065	190,329	1 lap	56"021 s
9. Giancarlo Fisichella	Benetton-Playlife	3	64	1 h 35'22"704	190,274	1 lap	6"844 s
10. Alexander Wurz	Benetton-Playlife	3	64	1 h 35'29"548	190,047	1 lap	1 lap
11. Pedro de la Rosa	TWR-Arrows	3	63	1 h 34'41"268	188,666	2 laps	1 lap
12. Toranosuke Takagi	TWR-Arrows	2	62	1 h 34'38"929	185,746	3 laps	

Driver	Team	Pit stops	in lap	Reason f. retiring	Position before retiring
Luca Badoer	Minardi-Ford	2	51	spun out	14
Jacques Villeneuve	BAR-Supertec	1	41	gearbox	5
Pedro Diniz	Sauber-Petronas	1	41	power transmission	9
Johnny Herbert	Stewart-Ford	1	41	power transmission	11
Heinz-Harald Frentzen	Jordan-Mugen-Honda	1	36	drive shaft	8
Jean Alesi	Sauber-Petronas	1	28	electrical	9
Alessandro Zanardi	Williams-Supertec	0	25	gearbox	13
Olivier Panis	Prost-Peugeot	0	25	gearbox	21
Luca Badoer	Minardi-Ford	0	0	engine failure	22
Rubens Barrichello [1]	Stewart-Ford	2	64	disqualified	8

1) Finished in eight but disqualified due to a rule infraction

Spanish GP

Starting Grid

1 Mika Häkkinen (FIN)
McLaren-Mercedes MP4/14-5
1'22"088 m (319,3 km/h) [1]

4 Eddie Irvine (GB)
Ferrari F399/191
1'22"219 m (307,1 km/h)

2 David Coulthard (GB)
McLaren-Mercedes MP4/14-4
1'22"244 m (314,1 km/h)

3 Michael Schumacher (D)
Ferrari F399/193
1'22"277 m (308,1 km/h)

11 Jean Alesi (F)
Sauber-Petronas C18/5
1'22"388 m (306,2 km/h)

22 Jacques Villeneuve (CDN)
BAR-Supertec 01/3
1'22"703 m (306,2 km/h)

16 Rubens Barrichello (BR)
Stewart-Ford SF3/4
1'22"920 m (308,9 km/h)

8 Heinz-Harald Frentzen (D)
Jordan-Mugen-Honda 199/6
1'22"938 m (305,7 km/h)

19 Jarno Trulli (I)
Prost-Peugeot AP02/6
1'23"194 m (301,4 km/h)

6 Ralf Schumacher (D)
Williams-Supertec FW21/4
1'23"303 m (303,2 km/h)

7 Damon Hill (GB)
Jordan-Mugen-Honda 199/4
1'23"317 m (305,2 km/h)

12 Pedro Diniz (BR)
Sauber-Petronas C18/6
1'23"331 m (306,0 km/h)

9 Giancarlo Fisichella (I)
Benetton-Playlife B199/6
1'23"333 m (304,3 km/h)

17 Johnny Herbert (GB)
Stewart-Ford SF3/5
1'23"505 m (309,5 km/h)

18 Olivier Panis (F)
Prost-Peugeot AP02/5
1'23"559 m (301,0 km/h)

23 Mika Salo (FIN)
BAR-Supertec 01/5
1'23"683 m (300,0 km/h)

5 Alessandro Zanardi (I)
Williams-Supertec FW21/5
1'23"703 m (306,2 km/h)

10 Alexander Wurz (A)
Benetton-Playlife B199/5
1'23"824 m (305,9 km/h)

14 Pedro de la Rosa (E)
TWR-Arrows A20/4
1'24"619 m (299,6 km/h)

15 Toranosuke Takagi (J)
TWR-Arrows A20/2
1'25"280 m (299,8 km/h)

21 Marc Gené (E)
Minardi-Ford-Zetec-R M01/4
1'25"672 m (298,0 km/h)

20 Luca Badoer (I)
Minardi-Ford-Zetec-R M01/1
1'25"833 m (298,6 km/h)

107-percent time: 1'27"834 m

Best Laps

In Training on Friday (m)

1.	Irvine	1'23"577	12. Diniz	1'24"823
2.	Frentzen	1'23"790	13. Trulli	1'24"957
3.	M. Schumacher	1'23"895	14. Panis	1'25"140
4.	**Häkkinen**	**1'23"982**	15. Fisichella	1'25"448
5.	Zanardi	1'24"312	16. Herbert	1'25"667
6.	Hill	1'24"318	17. Wurz	1'25"901
7.	Coulthard	1'24"339	18. Salo	1'25"990
8.	Barrichello	1'24"347	19. de la Rosa	1'26"595
9.	Villeneuve	1'24"458	20. Takagi	1'27"296
10.	R. Schumacher	1'24"559	21. Badoer	1'27"314
11.	Alesi	1'24"571	22. Gené	1'27"506

In the Race on Sunday (m)

1.	M. Schumacher	1'24"982	12. Frentzen	1'26"894
2.	**Häkkinen**	**1'25"209**	13. Salo	1'27"004
3.	Irvine	1'25"343	14. Wurz	1'27"029
4.	Coulthard	1'25"487	15. Fisichella	1'27"098
5.	Barrichello	1'26"006	16. Panis	1'27"175
6.	Diniz	1'26"315	17. Zanardi	1'27"248
7.	Hill	1'26"348	18. de la Rosa	1'27"409
8.	Trulli	1'26"505	19. Herbert	1'27"442
9.	R. Schumacher	1'26"520	20. Takagi	1'29"184
10.	Alesi	1'26"542	21. Badoer	1'29"632
11.	Villeneuve	1'26"675		

Total Pit Stop Times

Lap	Time (s)	Lap	Time (s)	Lap	Time (s)	Lap	Time (s)
17 de la Rosa	31"482	25 Hill	27"178	40 Badoer	32"096	50 Hill	25"455
18 Herbert	29"669	26 Coulthard	30"416	41 Takagi	26"149	50 Salo	26"161
19 Wurz	29"812	26 Alesi	26"643	42 Trulli	29"493		
19 Badoer	26"609	26 Frentzen	26"344	43 M. Schumacher	26"125		
21 Fisichella	25"310	26 Barrichello	26"947	43 Barrichello	27"605		
21 Salo	29"344	27 R. Schumacher	26"764	44 **Häkkinen**	**26"307**		
22 Irvine	25"800	27 Diniz	25"445	44 R. Schumacher	25"374		
23 **Häkkinen**	**25"955**	31 de la Rosa	27"442	45 Coulthard	25"650		
23 Trulli	26"086	33 Wurz	24"678	46 de la Rosa	30"970		
23 Takagi	28"299	35 Fisichella	26"312	48 Fisichella	25"009		
24 Villeneuve	27"891	41 Irvine	26"549	49 Wurz	25"587		

The Race Lap by Lap

Start: Hakkinen gets off the mark well, as usual. M. Schumacher is held up by Irvine who gets off to a very bad start. Despite a lacklustre start Coulthard maintains second. Villeneuve profits from Irvine's involuntary blockade and is in third ahead of M. Schumacher. Panis and Gené remain standing at the start, the Frenchman continues from the back, the Spaniard's race is over. **Lap 10:** Hakkinen leads ahead of Coulthard and Villeneuve, who has the much faster M. Schumacher chomping at his heels. They're followed by Irvine, Trulli, Alesi, R. Schumacher, and Frentzen. **Lap 22:** Irvine is the first to make a pit stop, and drops back to tenth. **Lap 23:** Hakkinen makes a pit stop, Coulthard leads. **Lap 24:** Villeneuve and M. Schumacher both head to the pits. Ferrari is faster, the German seizes third from the French-Canadian. **Lap 26:** Coulthard's pit stop takes longer than usual as David stops to late and the mechanics have to drag the fuelling system

to him. But he maintains second, Schumacher's getting his revenge for being stuck behind Villeneuve. **Lap 36:** Frentzen is forced out by an acceleration problem. **Lap 41:** Irvine's second refuelling stop. **Lap 43:** M. Schumacher refuels again. His team's quick works raises hope of second. **Lap 45:** Coulthard turns off to refuel. Although M. Schumacher has made up some ground on the Scot, the McLaren team sends Coulthard back out still ahead of the German. **Lap 50:** The first four positions are carved in stone. Behind the two McLarens and the Ferrari are Hill, R. Schumacher, and Trulli. **Lap 55:** Hakkinen is held up trying to overtake. Coulthard and Schumacher edge closer. **Lap 62:** Hill overtakes Barrichello in spectacular fashion along the outer edge of the track. **Lap 65:** Hakkinen wins.

Standings

Driver/Points

1. Michael Schumacher	30
2. Mika Häkkinen	24
3. Eddie Irvine	21
4. Heinz-Harald Frentzen	13
5. David Coulthard	12
6. Ralf Schumacher	9
7. Giancarlo Fisichella	7
8. Rubens Barrichello	6
9. Damon Hill	3
10. Pedro de la Rosa	1
Olivier Panis	1
Jean Alesi	1
Alexander Wurz	1
Jarno Trulli	1

Team

	Points
1. Ferrari	51
2. McLaren-Mercedes	36
3. Jordan-Mugen-Honda	16
4. Williams-Supertec	9
5. Benetton-Playlife	8
6. Stewart-Ford	6
7. Prost-Peugeot	2
8. TWR-Arrows	1
Sauber-Petronas	1

1.) Lap time (top speed in qualifying).

Benetton-Renault's Austrian Alexander Wurz could do no better than tenth.

The Up-And-Comer

Finally out from the shadow of his older brother. Following his third season on the Formula One circuit

one thing is clear: No longer does anybody doubt the outstanding talent of Ralf Schumacher. At the

Nurburgring he once again narrowly missed getting his first Grand Prix victory.

There are some people who hand out praise as willingly as they would likely admit their own guilt. Frank Williams and Patrick Head, the owners of the most successful Formula One team of the 1990´s are two good examples. But lately the two of them have been speaking in most glowing terms about their youngest driver. "He reminds me in many ways of Nigel Mansell", admits Williams, who's known to be a big fan of the British former world champion. "He's very talented, has incredible concentration, and he's a hard worker - he's gone far beyond our expectations of him." No, for once the lavish praise is not for superstar Michael Schumacher - although he without a doubt is someone Williams would love to have on his team, but it's not far off: it's Michael's brother Ralf of whom Williams is singing the praises now.

The younger Schumacher´s completed his apprenticeship in the big time extremely quickly. After two years working for Eddie Jordan, Ralf, still a very young 24 years old, has developed into a very poised driver. Not only did Schumacher cross the finish line in eleven of the first 15 races of the 1999 season, but only once did he fail to finish in the points. In other words all of the 33 points that put Williams in fifth place in the constructors championship were driven home by him. Team-mate Alex Zanardi - signed by Williams as the supposed overachiever from the American Champ Car Series has yet to earn a single point. The Italian's return to Formula One has been a difficult one to say the least. He simply hasn't been able to come to grips with the difficult handling Williams complete with treaded Formula One tyres.

Lesser Drivers Couldn't Have Stood Up to the Pressure

Williams, the former perennial champions who won the constructors world championship every year from 1992 to 1997, are in a slump. Since Renault officially pulled out, the team from Grove in Oxfordshire has had to make do with the ten cylinder engine produced by Supertec, who´ve been producing near enough the same old Renault engine with hardly any improvements. In the world of Formula One motor racing standing still means in fact going in reverse. As a result the British team has found a new

On the same wavelength: Schumacher and the Williams team.

Faster than the car is capable of: Ralf Schumacher in action.

At the top of his game: Like his brother Ralf never seems to have an off-day.

engine producer, and they're hoping that beginning in the 2000 season BMW can help them return to their former glory. But Williams and Head aren't just putting their hopes in a German car maker - they've signed their German driver to a contract which runs until 2003.

Not everybody would have predicted Ralf Schumacher´s incredibly quick development as a Formula One driver. When he made the jump from Japan's Formula 3000 championship to the Formula One circuit in 1997 he had to put up with a lot of criticism in the media. As the younger brother of Michael Schumacher his each and every move was put under the microscope, with everything he did, in particular his mistakes were played up - particularly in the German tabloids. Not every man of his age could have stood up to such pressures. But Ralf Schumacher could, in part because he'd been dealing with being compared to his older brother since he first hit adolescence.

The Same Iron Will

But it hasn't always been easy living in the shadow of a brother's who's six years older and a motor racing superstar. In that sort of situation it's easy to look substandard in comparison. But particularly since entering the Formula One circuit the younger Schumacher´s character has developed very quickly - quicker than almost anyone could have expected. "He's matured in an extraordinarily short period of time", says former world champion Damon Hill. "When I think back to his reputation in his first Formula One season..." Then something else occurs to the Englishman who's known not to be Michael Schumacher´s biggest fan: "He's also developing the same iron will that sets Michael apart."

Arrogance? "More like shyness", Frank Williams was surprised to find out before his new employee´s first season at Williams. Gary Anderson, Jordan's former technical director adds: "I think his arrogance is simply meant to cover up his shyness and the fact that he's still a bit unsure of himself." It's a funny old world: The younger Schumacher traded cockpits with the sensitive Heinz-Harald Frentzen, who never felt at home in the emotionally cool Williams team camp. Now he seems to have found a home at Jordan and may be seeing his career finally take off. "In his two years at Jordan Ralf had to find out where his

limits are", explains Frank Williams. "But he's done a great job for us. He's grown up fast and he's extremely professional for a 24 year-old." Something else has impressed the team boss too: "Just like his brother he doesn't seem to have off days - he's always fast off the mark and this is very important for the further development of the car."

While the physically challenged team boss has a reputation for being distant and lacking a sense of humour, Ralf Schumacher, unlike Frentzen seems to be on the same wavelength as Frank Williams. This may have to do in part with the young German's discipline, which he demands of himself but also expects from others. In terms of fitness for example, he's almost his brother's equal, despite his stockier body type. It's also rumoured that the first thing he reported to his boss about his first Williams test drive was that the session had got underway late. From then on the chemistry was right. "It's always easier when you get the season off to a good start", admits Ralf Schumacher. "But I enjoy the open atmosphere around this team."

So what does Ralf Schumacher see as the differences? "You can't really compare Jordan with Williams", says the young German. "Williams is bigger and has a bigger budget to work with. What Eddie Jordan and his team achieved last year and this year as well is really impressive. But Williams has more potential: the technical department alone has much more knowledge and experience."

Like the rest of the Williams team, Ralf Schumacher is hoping for big things from the new BMW engine. "The Supertec is very reliable and handles well, but it's simply not powerful enough", is how he assesses the team's current dilemma - even if the French engine supplier made significant improvements in the second half of the season. "I hope that the BMW ten cylinder will be a good one right from the start - even though the odd problem will be inevitable. BMW started work on the car very early and the coming season will start for us in February, so we won't be short of time for development work. BMW is very optimistic, and they have some very good people."

What are Ralf´s hopes for next season? "If the car is as good as we hope it will be, we think we can be competitive by halfway through the season, even if that may sound a little overly optimistic at the moment."

The man pulling the strings: Ralf´s manager Wilhelm Weber.

Enthused about the younger Schumacher: Frank Williams believes Ralf is on the verge of super stardom.

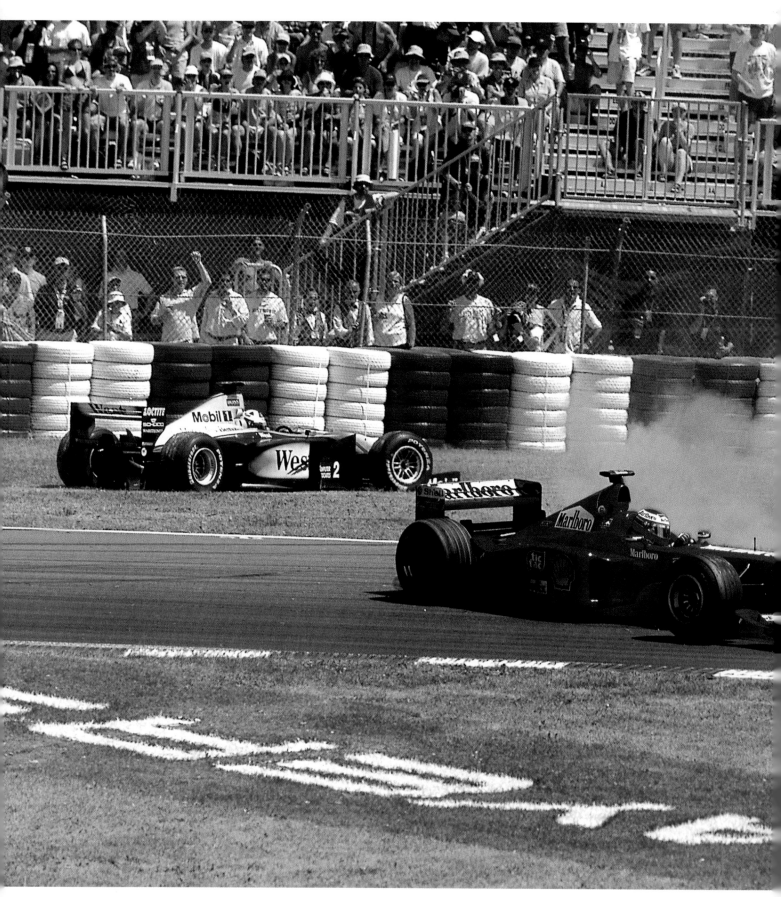

Schumacher´s Ar

David Coulthard left the track in an attempt to overtake Eddie Irvine.

Michael Schumacher had good reason to grimmace, after what looked like a certain victory slipped through his fingers.

There was no shortage of action at this edition of the Canadian Grand Prix. While Michael Schumacher was frustrated by what he describes as his "one mistake every year", the rest of the field was involved in an exciting race. In the end the only really satisfied driver though was Mika Hakkinen.

nual Mistake

Flawless: Mika Hakkinen took full advantage when opportunity knocked.

No complaints: Ralf Schumacher crossed the finish line in fourth.

The third Mercedes: The safety-car.

There's a particular curve on the "Circuit Gilles Villeneuve" that since this season's Canadian Grand Prix, a certain former world champion would rather not be reminded of. "Turn 15" is the name of the disaster-ridden stretch of track which caused such a stir, and it's also the portion of the course where incidents occured which forced the safety-car into action on three occasions. But it's not the only possible trap for Formula One drivers. The "Senna Hairpin" curve at the end of the straightaway following the starting line is where more spectacular mishaps occur off the start, than anywhere else on the Formula One circuit. That's the way is was last season, and this season was to be no different.

Jean Alesi, the southern Frenchman with Sicilian blood was beside himself with rage. "Trulli is an idiot", complained the Sauber driver minutes after the start of the race. The Italian with the Finnish-sounding name had unceremoniously forced both Alesi and Rubens Barrichello from the course at non other than that "Senna Hairpin". What annoyed the hotblooded Frenchman even more, was that one year earlier Trulli

had forced him from the track at exactly the same place. The Prost driver though felt himself unjustly accused: "Frentzen got off to a bad start and was increasingly drifting towards my side. I had to evade him and wound up on the grass. Jean should take it easy and put his brain back into gear..."

"Jean should put his brain into gear"

But another daring manoeuvre at the same spot was more successful. Michael Schumacher, who for the first time this season had managed to edge out arch-rival Mika Hakkinen for the pole position, didn't get out of the starting blocks nearly as well as the defending champion. But Schumacher swung over and cut off the McLaren-Mercedes. Schumacher then found himself out in front, ahead of Hakkinen and Eddie Irvine. However in actual fact it was a Mercedes which had taken the lead - the safety car driven by Formula 3,000 ace Oliver Gavin.

Shortly afterwards the race officials gave the green light again, and once again Schumacher got down to the job of building up his lead. But not for long: Gavin was out on the track again on lap four. Ricardo Zonta was the first victim of "Turn 15" in the 1999 edition of the Canadian Grand Prix. The reigning GT world champion had lost control of his BAR-Suptertec on the narrow and extremely slippery right-left chicane and crashed into the wall. It wasn't until lap eight that Gavin was able to again park his Mercedes CLK 55 at the end of the pit lane.

The race started for a third time with Schumacher ahead of Hakkinen and Irvine, followed by David Coulthard, Giancarlo Fisichella, Heinz-Harald Frentzen, Johnny Herbert, Ralf Schumacher, Pedro Diniz and Jacques Villeneuve. One again Ferrari's number one set out to put as much space as possible between himself and Mika Hakkinen. But the "Circuit Gilles Villeneuve", which lies on one of Montreal's islands in the middle of the St Lawrence River, hadn't yet claimed its last victim. On lap 15 it was Damon Hill's turn. For no apparent reason the Englishman massaged the same wall off Turn 15 that

A stranger on friendly turf: Giancarlo Fisichella has always done well in Canada. This time he finished second.

Unhappy homecoming: Jacques Villeneuve again failed to finish.

A taste of success: Johnny Herbert earned his first points of the season.

had already ended the race for Zonta. "My mistake", admitted the 1996 world champion, "Unfortunately it´s not the wall´s fault. I lost control of the car."

For the time being Michael Schumacher was in luck. This time the safety car didn´t appear, because Hill was able to steer what was left of his car off of the track without outside assistance. But while the standings leader was continually increasing his lead on the defending champion, it was all for nought. He too fell victim to Turn 15, and he made no excuses. "I lost control of the car at the last chicane because I went off the racing line and got on the dirt and I ended up in the wall." The two time champion continued, "It was a shame because the car was working perfectly. I usually make one mistake a year and I hope this is the last one for this season."

Mika Hakkinen was the chief beneficiary of Schumacher´s "annual mistake". The Finn took over the lead, unchallenged by either Ferrari´s Northern Irishman or his Scottish teammate. He defended that lead through his one pitstop on lap 37 and right through to the finish line. After the race, Hakkinen told reporters he wasn´t sur-

prised that Schumacher was knocked out. "We were pushing our cars to the very limit in the first half of the race, and I knew it was just a matter of time until one of us would make a mistake or fall victim to a technical problem."

"It was the other guy."

Despite Mika´s 7 second lead on Eddie Irvine, there was no danger of being bored by the Canadian Grand Prix. Ralf Schumacher was the next protagonist. On lap 33 the younger of the two Schumacher brothers, who´s firmly established himself as Williams´ number one, briefly left the track, allowing the surprising Sauber driver Pedro Diniz to take over sixth place. What made matters worse was that now he was being challenged by Jacques Villeneuve. The fact that in technical terms, the Quebecois´ BAR-Supertec car is no match for the Williams racer doesn´t faze a non-conformist like Villeneuve. The 1997 world champion drove like a man posessed, gun-

ning for his German competitor - until lap 35, when he too failed to meet the challenge of Turn 15.

Villeneuve hit the wall hard, and while he was able to climb uninjured out of his cockpit, the impact of the crash had strewn pieces of what had been his BAR-Supertec all over the track. Pace car driver Oliver Gavin once again swung into action and set the pace for a full five laps. Just as in the American Champ Car Series, the majority of the drivers used this opportunity to make their only stop in the pits.

The green light had hardly been given when second place Eddie Irvine had his problems with Turn 15. The Northern Irishman´s Ferrari drifted perilously close to the wall, avoiding a crash by the narrowist of margins. That was the only invitation David Coulthard needed. The handsome Scott used his momentum to challenge "Crazy Eddie" at the end of the start/finish line straightaway. Irvine bravely fought off the challenge, but at a cost. The two cars made contact, sending both off the track. The Ferrari was the first to return, having dropped back to eighth, but set out on an exciting bid to recover lost ground.

Left: Helpless - the Ferrari mechanics watch in horror as the fastest qualifier - their own Michael Schumacher - crashes.

Canadian GP

Left: Reason to celebrate - Mika Hakkinen´s victory in Canada put him on top of the drivers standings. Below: Hard luck at home - Villeneuve hit the wall.

Coulthard returned to the track in ninth, but only after a quick stop in the pits to make sure his Mercedes was still in satisfactory shape. Coulthard later fended off Irvine´s accusations. "I think Eddie expected me to become invisible... but there was nowhere to go. I don´t think it was deliberate."

At the same time Giancarlo Fisichella had moved into second place - but not for long. The young Roman lost a lot of time following Olivier Panis, who´s known to be extremely uncooperative when it comes to being lapped by faster competitors. The Frenchman was no different this time. By the time Fisichella had finally found a way around the Benetton driver, Heinz-Harald Frentzen was there to use his opportunity to the full, and slip past Fisischella and into second.

But the Jordan driver didn´t have much of a chance to chase Hakkinen either. Four laps before the end of the race, Frentzen was hit with a spot of bad luck that had cost him an almost certain win at the 1997 Australian Grand Prix - a brake disk disintegrated on him - causing him to go crashing into the wall. Fortunately the German wasn´t seriously injured, although he was knocked unconcious. He was taken to Sacre Coeur hospital for observation.

Gavin was sent out onto the track for the fouth and final time making the 1999 Canadian the first ever Formula One race to end with the drivers crossing the finish line under a yellow flag. Mika Hakkinen crossed the line first ahead of Fisichella, Irvine, and Ralf Schumacher That gave him 34 world championship points and put him top of the table for the first time this season.

The second city course after Monaco: Montreal's track is laid out on an island in the St Lawrence River.

Statistics

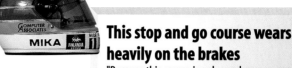
Course length: 4,421 km

Distance of race: 69 (= 305,049 km)

Start time: 18.00 UTC

Weather on day of race: cloudless, sunny, light wind

Attendance: 104 000

1998 Results:
1. Michael Schumacher (D, Ferrari F300), 1 h 40'57"355
2. Giancarlo Fisichella (I, Benetton-Playlife B198), +16"662 s
3. Eddie Irvine (GB, Ferrari F300), +1'00"059 m

Pole position 1998: David Coulthard (GB, McLaren-Mercedes MP4/13), 1'18"213 m

Fastest Lap 1998: Michael Schumacher (Ferrari F300), 1'19"379 m

Fastest pit stop 1998: Eddie Irvine (Ferrari F300), 23"516 s

This stop and go course wears heavily on the brakes

"Because this course is only used once a year it's always dirty, offering little in the way of traction. It's often not until Saturday's qualifying that you get enough grip. With its long straight-aways it reminds me a bit of Monza, and it's just about as hard on the brakes. When the braking-balance is right it's relatively easy to overtake opponents."

Mika Hakkinen

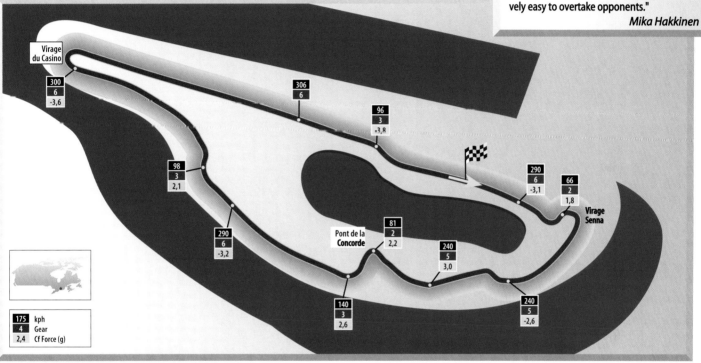

Results

Driver	Team	Pit stops	Laps	Time (hours)	Average speed	Behind 1st	prev. driver
1. Mika Hakkinen	McLaren-Mercedes	1	69	1 h 41'35"727	180,155	–	–
2. Giancarlo Fisichella	Benetton-Playlife	1	69	1 h 41'36"509	180,132	1"015 s	–
3. Eddie Irvine	Ferrari	1	69	1 h 41'37"524	180,102	1"796 s	1"015 s
4. Ralf Schumacher	Williams-Supertec	1	69	1 h 41'38"119	180,084	2"391 s	0"595 s
5. Johnny Herbert	Stewart-Ford	2	69	1 h 41'38"532	180,072	2"804 s	0"413 s
6. Pedro Diniz	Sauber-Petronas	1	69	1 h 41'39"438	180,045	3"710 s	0"906 s
7. David Coulthard	McLaren-Mercedes	3	69	1 h 41'40"731	180,007	5"003 s	1"293 s
8. Marc Gené	Minardi-Ford	1	68	1 h 41'39"918	177,422	1 lap	1 lap
9. Olivier Panis	Prost-Peugeot	2	68	1 h 41'40"658	177,400	1 lap	0"740 s
10. Luca Badoer	Minardi-Ford	2	67	1 h 41'38"062	174,866	2 laps	1 lap
11. Heinz-Harald Frentzen [1]	Jordan-Mugen-Honda	1	65	1 h 34'50"784	181,787	retirement	retirement

Driver	Team	Pit stops	in lap	Reason f. retiring	Position before retiring
Alessandro Zanardi	Williams-Supertec	2	51	gearbox	8
Toranosuke Takagi	TWR-Arrows	1	42	power transmission	9
Jacques Villeneuve	BAR-Supertec	0	35	crash	8
Michael Schumacher	Ferrari	0	30	crash	1
Pedro de la Rosa	TWR-Arrows	0	23	power transmission	11
Damon Hill	Jordan-Mugen-Honda	0	15	crash	11
Rubens Barrichello	Stewart-Ford	1	15	collision damage	18
Ricardo Zonta	BAR-Supertec	0	3	crash	13
Jean Alesi	Sauber-Petronas	0	1	collission	8
Jarno Trulli	Prost-Peugeot	0	1	collission	9
Alexander Wurz	Benetton-Playlife	0	1	drive shaft	22

1) Didn´t complete race but counted due to distance driven

6th Race of the World Championship 1999, Circuit Gilles Villeneuve, Montreal (CDN), 13th June 1999

Starting Grid

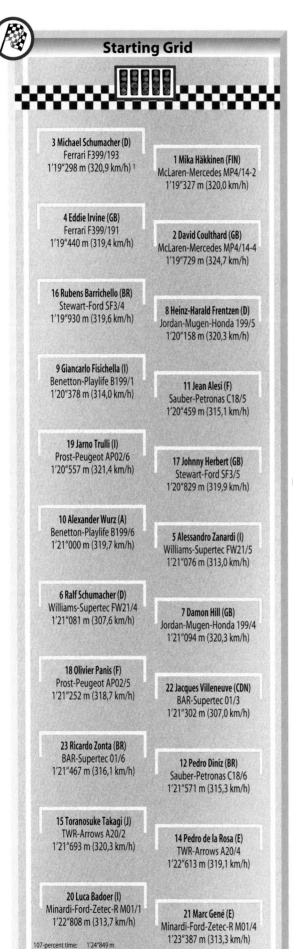

3 Michael Schumacher (D)
Ferrari F399/193
1'19"298 m (320,9 km/h) [1]

1 Mika Häkkinen (FIN)
McLaren-Mercedes MP4/14-2
1'19"327 m (320,0 km/h)

4 Eddie Irvine (GB)
Ferrari F399/191
1'19"440 m (319,4 km/h)

2 David Coulthard (GB)
McLaren-Mercedes MP4/14-4
1'19"729 m (324,7 km/h)

16 Rubens Barrichello (BR)
Stewart-Ford SF3/4
1'19"930 m (319,6 km/h)

8 Heinz-Harald Frentzen (D)
Jordan-Mugen-Honda 199/5
1'20"158 m (320,3 km/h)

9 Giancarlo Fisichella (I)
Benetton-Playlife B199/1
1'20"378 m (314,0 km/h)

11 Jean Alesi (F)
Sauber-Petronas C18/5
1'20"459 m (315,1 km/h)

19 Jarno Trulli (I)
Prost-Peugeot AP02/6
1'20"557 m (321,4 km/h)

17 Johnny Herbert (GB)
Stewart-Ford SF3/5
1'20"829 m (319,9 km/h)

10 Alexander Wurz (A)
Benetton-Playlife B199/6
1'21"000 m (319,7 km/h)

5 Alessandro Zanardi (I)
Williams-Supertec FW21/5
1'21"076 m (313,0 km/h)

6 Ralf Schumacher (D)
Williams-Supertec FW21/4
1'21"081 m (307,6 km/h)

7 Damon Hill (GB)
Jordan-Mugen-Honda 199/4
1'21"094 m (320,3 km/h)

18 Olivier Panis (F)
Prost-Peugeot AP02/5
1'21"252 m (318,7 km/h)

22 Jacques Villeneuve (CDN)
BAR-Supertec 01/3
1'21"302 m (307,0 km/h)

23 Ricardo Zonta (BR)
BAR-Supertec 01/6
1'21"467 m (316,1 km/h)

12 Pedro Diniz (BR)
Sauber-Petronas C18/6
1'21"571 m (315,3 km/h)

15 Toranosuke Takagi (J)
TWR-Arrows A20/2
1'21"693 m (320,3 km/h)

14 Pedro de la Rosa (E)
TWR-Arrows A20/4
1'22"613 m (319,1 km/h)

20 Luca Badoer (I)
Minardi-Ford-Zetec-R M01/1
1'22"808 m (313,7 km/h)

21 Marc Gené (E)
Minardi-Ford-Zetec-R M01/4
1'23"387 m (313,3 km/h)

107-percent time: 1'24"849 m

Best Laps

In Training on Friday (m)			
1. Coulthard	1'20"614	12. Panis	1'22"027
2. Barrichello	1'21"012	13. Frentzen	1'22"156
3. Herbert	1'21"059	14. Trulli	1'22"228
4. Häkkinen	1'21"244	15. Takagi	1'22"323
5. Fisichella	1'21"530	16. de la Rosa	1'22"469
6. Irvine	1'21"534	17. Alesi	1'22"472
7. M. Schumacher	1'21"560	18. Zanardi	1'22"535
8. Hill	1'21"709	19. Badoer	1'22"691
9. R. Schumacher	1'21"845	20. Villeneuve	1'22"898
10. Wurz	1'21"950	21. Zonta	1'23"256
11. Diniz	1'21"984	22. Gené	1'26"279

In the Race on Sunday (m)			
1. Irvine	1'20"382	12. Takagi	1'22"792
2. M. Schumacher	1'20"709	13. Gené	1'22"888
3. Coulthard	1'20"961	14. de la Rosa	1'23"380
4. Häkkinen	1'21"047	15. Badoer	1'23"394
5. Frentzen	1'21"284	16. Zanardi	1'23"442
6. Fisichella	1'21"345	17. Barrichello	1'23"785
7. Diniz	1'21"864	18. Hill	1'23"953
8. R. Schumacher	1'22"002	19. Zonta	2'03"039
9. Herbert	1'22"078		
10. Panis	1'22"100		
11. Villeneuve	1'22"283		

Total Pit Stop Times

Lap	Time (s)	Lap	Time (s)	Lap	Time (s)
1 Barrichello	178"079	36 Panis	25"716		
24 Herbert	26"526	36 Gené	39"525		
28 Takagi	26"514	37 Zanardi	28"150		
36 Fisichella	26"762	38 Coulthard	27"916		
36 Frentzen	25"746	41 Coulthard	30"812		
36 Diniz	28"924	46 Badoer [2]	27"260		
36 R. Schumacher	28"450	48 Zanardi [2]	26"890		
36 Herbert	32"728	49 Coulthard [2]	28"305		
36 Badoer	29"452	49 Panis [2]	27"530		
37 Häkkinen	26"079				
37 Irvine	29"317				

The Race Lap by Lap

Start: M. Schumacher slips past Hakkinen ahead of the first curve. Trulli is pushed onto the grass, can't brake and winds up in the path of Alesi and Barrichello. Trulli and Alesi are done, the Brazilian and his patched up car last another 15 laps. **Lap 1:** As a result of the accident the safety-car is out. **Lap 2:** Ahe race is on, M. Schumacher is out in front of Hakkinen, Irvine, Fisichella and Coulthard. **Lap 3:** Coulthard overtakes Fisichella. Zonta crashes his BAR into the wall at the end of the last curve causing another safety-car phase. **Lap 8:** Following the restart M. Schumacher distances himself from his pursuers once again. **Lap 15:** Hill hits the infamous wall and parks his car alongside the track. **Lap 29:** Now it's Schumacher's turn. He brakes late enters the curve wrong and smashes his Ferrari into the wall of shame. Hakkinen inherits the lead. **Lap 35:** Villeneuve doesn't want to be left out and becomes the fourth former world champion to hit the concrete.

The ensuing safety-car phase is opportunity for all those left to make pit stops. **Lap 41:** Hakkinen is quickest in the restart. Behind him Coulthard his trying to overtake Irvine for second. But he fails, Irvine spins out and Coulthard heads to the pits for a nose job. Fisichella is second ahead of Frentzen. **Lap 43:** Frentzen laps the Italian who's held up trying to lap others. **Lap 55:** Irvine is making up lost ground. In his most spectacular move he squeezes straight through the curve and overtakes Herbert. Three laps later its R. Schumacher's turn. **Lap 66:** Frentzen, in second place has a brake disk break up and crashes into a pile of tyres. **Lap 69:** The safety-car returns, the race ends under yellow.

Standings

Driver/Points			
1. Mika Häkkinen	34	Panis	1
2. Michael Schumacher	30	Alesi	1
3. Eddie Irvine	25	Wurz	1
4. Heinz-Harald Frentzen	13	Trulli	1
Giancarlo Fisichella	13	Diniz	1
6. David Coulthard	12		
Ralf Schumacher	12		
8. Rubens Barrichello	6		
9. Damon Hill	3		
10. Johnny Herbert	2		
11. de la Rosa	1		

Team	Points
1. Ferrari	55
2. McLaren-Mercedes	46
3. Jordan-Mugen-Honda	16
4. Benetton-Playlife	14
5. Williams-Supertec	12
6. Stewart-Ford	8
7. Prost-Peugeot	2
Sauber-Petronas	2
9. TWR-Arrows	1

1) Lap time (top speed in qualifying); 2) Ten second stop and go penalty.

A Thinking Mar

The thinker: Former nuclear physicist Ross Brawn (left) reacts almost instantly to changing situations. Michael Schumacher puts his tactics into action.

Takes responsibility: Ferrari team boss Jean Todt always stands behind Ross Brawn's often daring decisions.

s Sport

The driver drives, his team does the thinking. In Formula One motor racing it's not just about coupling the best driver with the fastest car. Having a clever strategist back in the team directors box who can react with the right tactic at the right moment is one key to success in the world´s fastest sport.

The brain behind Williams´ successes: Team owner and technical director Patrick Head. Even as Grand Prix races are in progress he looks out for the right strategy for his drivers.

Technical Dialogue: Every time they enter the pits the driver reports metre by metre on how the car is performing on the track.

Formula One races are decided in the head - as far as strategy goes at least, there's no disputing this statement. One two or three pit stops, a full or half-full fuel tank, changing tyres sooner or later, soft or hard tyres: It's not just the drivers who influence the outcome. It's only when nimble minds in the team directors box react correctly not just to routine, but also unexpected situations, that they can make the right decisions. Formula One racing is high speed chess with 800 horsepower under the hood.

The departure points for this strategic game are decided on the Friday of every Grand Prix weekend. In the open training sessions teams and drivers alike look for just the right undercarriage, gearbox and aerodynamic settings to give them the optimum performance during Sunday's race. During Saturday's training session it's all about qualifying, earning the best possible placement in the starting grid. To this end the cars are extensively modified: the gear ratio is set out on a flying start lap. The radiator levels and the air entry chambers are dramatically reduced: The less air resistance, the higher the speeds the car can reach on the straightaways - only a minimum of engine cooling is required for a single lap. The top teams even install engines designed solely for qualifying: Powerful 10 cylinder motors with that little bit of extra horsepower, which wouldn't, in this form at least, make it through an entire race. Even the undercarriages are set more aggressively: For a single lap tyre wear is not a factor.

The Question on Everybody´s mind: What's the Competition Doing?

The qualifying result is a basis of discussion for the ensuing briefing in which the driver, engineers and technical directors come up with their strategy for the upcoming race. To outsiders, it's no doubt an incomprehensible range of variables which influence these decisions. Of course one question is inevitable: What can be done to throw off the opposition? The first priority though is the team's own car. Prior to qualifying the drivers and the teams have already decided which tyres to use in the race. Now the question is whether these tyres will stand up to the wear and tear on

Schumacher Follows Brawn′s Orders

race day. Although the softer compound may have helped the driver achieve a better starting position in qualifying, because it's not as durable, it might force an additional change of tyres during the race. This depends upon the undercarriage of the car itself and the driving style and skill of each particular driver. Anyone who´s overheated his car's tyres by jamming on the brakes or spinning the tyres from a standing start will know how unforgiving tyres can be. The temperature on the day of the race, and in particular the temperature of the asphalt are important factors too, but that of course can't be determined until Sunday.

Similar factors come into play regarding fuel. While your average driver measures fuel in terms of litres, Formula One teams measure it in terms of weight. Full fuel tanks are accordingly heavier and cost time - on an average track as much as 0.2 seconds per lap for every extra 10 kilograms of fuel. Cars which begin the race with less fuel are faster, but they're also forced to refuel sooner - and if the team is employing a one pit stop strategy, it will also have to spend longer in the pits. Those which start the race with full tanks are lighter and faster by the time those who started with less than full tanks are turning off into the pits to refuel. The first option is useful for drivers starting from the front row of the grid: They're not bound to be held up by slower competitors. The second option is better for drivers starting from further back in the pack, because this will allow them to make up time towards the half-way point of the race - that is of course, provided the competitors follow the other strategy...

Spectacular Breakdowns Make Things Even More Interesting

Most important are the pit stops. It's not just how long the actual refuelling process takes, it's how long it takes to enter and exit the pits. If the entrance and exit is narrow an tricky as it is at Monaco, getting in and out of the pits will take much longer than it will at the Hungaroring for example, where the entry and exit routes are much shorter and can be driven at higher speeds. The pit stops prove more than anything else that Formula One really is a team sport. With the exception of the starts of races, pit stops are where more things can go wrong than anywhere else in a Grand Prix race. So it's no wonder that the teams practice pit stop procedures ad nauseam. They go through it a good 150 times prior to the start of the season, 20 times every Thursday before a race, and still another 20 times on the Sunday morning of the race. Despite all this hard work things still often go wrong, and if you happen to notice a car circling the track on 3 wheels, then it's probably a Ferrari. But more about that later....

Often the unexpected happens during the course of a race and this demands quick, but complex decision-making. For example, during a safety-car phase it's usually advantageous to make an early pit stop. While the actual time it will take for the pit stop will be about the same as it otherwise would be, the rest of the field can't travel as fast and as far in same time frame.

The start of another training session: Before the race the teams and driver look to find the right car settings and tyres for race day.

Strategists of the Racetrack: McLaren boss Ron Dennis (above left) and Mercedes Motor Sports Director Norbert Haug (below) set the tone at McLaren-Mercedes. At Jordan it's the team's owner. At the French Grand Prix at Magny Cours Eddie Jordan (above) sent a crew member a couple of kilometres towards the approaching rain and knew almost to the minute when the rain would begin.

Watching the competition: Benetton driver Alexander Wurz studying the quali-fying times monitor - it shows who's fast where.

If shortly before a planned pit stop a driver is being held up by slower cars there's no point in wasting time on trying to overtake them, because following the pit stop the driver would be stuck behind the same slow pokes all over again. In this case too it makes sense to head to the pits at the next opportunity.

On the other hand sometimes it makes sense not to stop until later - or if possible - not at all: for example, when the driver ahead has just turned into the pits. Now, with almost empty fuel tanks the driver remaining on the track has the opportunity to drive three or four fast laps and move ahead of his competitor without actually having to overtake him. Heinz-Harald Frentzen went one step better at Magny Cours this year: because of his Jordan's exceptionally large fuel capacity and his fuel-efficient style of driving he didn't even make a second fuelling stop - and won. That wasn't Jordan's only strategic coup of the day. Team boss Eddie Jordan had one of the crew drive four kilometres towards where the weather pattern was coming from. Using a mobile phone the crew member helped predict when the rain would start at the track almost to the exact minute...

Then Ross Brawn Played his Joker...

However the best tactician of them all on the Formula One circuit is Britain's Ross Brawn, the former nuclear physicist turned Ferrari's Technical Director. Working with Michael Schumacher Brawn has elevated pit strategy to a higher level. The main advantage this British-German combination have over other teams is that whatever Brawn tells Schumacher to do, he does, with unfailing precision.

Take the 1998 Hungarian Grand Prix for example, a boring race until the first pit stops. Mika Hakkinen and David Coulthard were in the lead, and looked to be on their way to a one-two finish. Ferrari's number one was still stranded back in third. On the 25th of 77 laps the German became the first driver to head into the pits, with both silver arrows doing the same shortly afterwards. It looked as if all three were employing a two stop strategy. Wrong! Michael Schumacher took off on a series of fast laps gaining ground on the two McLarens. On lap 43 Brawn played his joker: The German headed for his second pit stop earlier than expected, but only got half the usual volume of fuel, and the pit stop was three seconds faster than usual. Then on his way was clear, because after the two McLarens had completed their second pit stops Schumacher was in the lead. "Ross told me I had 19 laps to open up a 25 second lead". Schumacher did as he was told: "It was just like driving qualifying laps..." The rest as they say is history.

**7th Race of the World Championship 1999,
Circuit de Nevers, Magny-Cours (F), 27th June 1999**

He who laughs

....laughs best. Few would have predicted that Heinz-Harald Frentzen would come out on top in the French Grand Prix. But just two weeks after his serious accident in Canada, the Jordan driver made it to the top step of the podium.

Rain lover: Wet weather specialist Heinz-Harald Frentzen delivers the goods.

An odd mix on the podium: Mika Hakkinen, Heinz-Harald Frentzen and Rubens Barrichello (from left).

ast....

The first Stewart: Three times Rubens Barrichello held the lead, but it wasn't good enough for his first victory.

F ollowing an exciting Canadian Grand Prix, all the Formula One world feared this race would be the exact opposite. The "Circuit de Nevers" in the middle of nowhere about 200 kilometres south of Paris has the reputation of being an unimaginative and sterile track which hardly lends itself to exciting motor sport. That's the theory at least. In 1999 though reality turned out to be quite another matter. The French Grand Prix turned out to be not just the most fascinating of the Formula One season so far, but would also go down as one of the most exciting in motor racing history.

The scene for this unforgettable thriller was set in qualifying. While on Friday Magny Cours baked in a hot summer sun, Saturday saw clouds move in and just before the final training session a light rain began to spray the 4.25 kilome-tre course. McLaren-Mercedes and Ferrari, the two great rivals of the current season elected to wait for the weather to improve. Rubens Bar-richello, Jean Alesi and Olivier Panis though had other ideas. All three took their chances and

The starting grid was akin to a parody.

began their qualifying sessions irrespective of the wet track. It turned out to be a wise gamble - the rain just got heavier during the course of the day. By the time the rest of the teams had seen the error of their ways, it was already too late. Bar-richello secured just the second pole position of his career. His only other came at Spa-Francor-champs in 1994, when the Brazilian took advan-tage of a drying track to record the best qualify-ing result.

The rest of the starting grid was curious to say the least: points leader Mika Hakkinen could do no better than 14th, Ralf Schumacher started from the eighth row, and Eddie Irvine qualified in 17th. The only favourite to live up to expec-tations was David Coulthard. The Scot did well enough on the water-logged track to qualify for the second row - ahead of Heinz-Harald Frentzen and Michael Schumacher. All the ingredients for a spine-tingling race were present.

On Sunday the race itself began on a dry track, but the weather forecasters all agreed: rain would soon return. Rubens Barrichello got off to the best start ahead of Jean Alesi, but his joy was short-lived. By the second lap David

Costly error: Eddie Irvine waited too long and only qualified in 17th.

Fastest lap: David Coulthard was knocked out by a faulty alternator.

Coulthard, who was clearly the fastest man off the mark had passed Jean Alesi and was fast closing the gap between himself and the leading Stewart-Ford. On lap six the inevitable happened - Coulthard gunned his silver arrow out into the lead and put his toe down. Just three laps later the Scotsman had opened up a seven second lead on Barrichello.

But Coulthard's joy was also short-lived. On lap nine the electronics in his rather unreliable Mercedes put an end to his hopes of crossing the finish line ahead of the rest. "The engine just died", he lamented after the race. "It's a shame because things were going very well."

"Now even the safety car's going to fly off the track."

That made way for Rubens Barrichello to take the lead for the second time in this Grand Prix. But when peering into his rear-view mirror he likely couldn't have believed his eyes. It must have seemed like deja-vu - yet again a silver arrow was bearing down on him. Over the first few laps Mika Hakkinen had made good eight places, and by the time his team-mate had been forced to retire he was into the top five. Shortly after that the Finn overtook Michael Schumacher's Ferrari in the "Adelaide" hairpin turn." Later the defending champion remarked "I hadn't even got off to all that good a start. I was quite surprised at how easy it was to overtake. My car was balanced perfectly and that allowed me to drive aggressively." On lap 15 Frentzen and Jean Alesi watched the Finn whiz by, putting Hakkinen in second. On lap 20 it was Barrichello's turn.

But then the rain began. It was so heavy that despite the fact that all of the teams had quickly switched to wet weather tyres, the cars began to aqua-plane. "I was screaming at my team over the radio, to get the safety car sent out", recounted Frentzen after the race. The Jordan driver was still

in considerable pain following his crash in Montreal. The heavy rain had even built up into large puddles on various parts of the track. One of them claimed Jean Alesi. When he hit it, the gifted wet weather driver's car looked as if it had temporarily transformed itself into a speed boat, before it skidded off the track. Stranded at the side of the road, the Frenchman broke into one of his trademark maniacal fits of rage.

Up until this point Englishman Damon Hill was looking good. But alas it turned out to be another weekend to forget for this veteran, who has never been convinced of the virtues of the new grooved version of Formula One tyres. After a collision with Pedro de la Rosa in pit lane, he returned to the track in last place - that was before he suffered an electrical failure. Following the race, the former world champion announced his retirement. However he failed to specify precisely when he would call it a career.

For a full 11 laps the safety car set the pace, but its amber warning lights did nothing to prevent Jacques Villeneuve, Alexander Wurz, Marc Gené, and Alex Zanardi from skidding out of the race. Eddie Irvine went into a spin and dropped back to last place. Out in front, Rubens Barrichello was again a happy man. Thanks to a particularly quick pit stop he had taken the lead for a third time, this time ahead of Mika Hakkinen. "The conditions were so bad, at one point I thought even the safety car would fly off the track", recalled the Brazilian later.

On lap 35 Oliver Gavin steered his Mercedes Coupe into the pits, and the race was on again. Just three laps later Hakkinen made a bid to re-take the lead from Barrichello, but was unsuccessful. The McLaren driver went into a spin, and fell back to seventh place. "It was still very wet there, especially along the ideal driving line", is how the Finn explained his driving mistake, which may have cost him victory.

Now it was Michael Schumacher's turn. The two-time world champion whose Ferrari had been carefully adapted for wet conditions began his attack on the Stewart-Ford driver ahead of him. On lap 42 it happened: in "Adelaide" Schumacher sneaked alongside Barrichello, but the

Sibling rivalry: Ralf catches up to big brother Michael.

Eleven laps to go and still in first - Mika Hakkinen.

The third Mercedes: The safety car.

From the starting row to a fit of maniacal rage: Jean Alesi fell victim to aquaplaning before the safety car was sent out.

Nothing but agro - Michael Schumacher never got past fifth.

French GP

Not a happy camper: In France Damon Hill considered calling it a career.

A man with a bright future: Rubens Barrichello performed well at Magny-Cours.

Brazilian was able to meet the challenge until they hit the start of the curve. Two laps later though he couldn't. "Schumi" went out into the lead - it was the fifth time the lead had changed hands on a Grand prix track which is normally known for producing routine, boring contests.

But the race was long from over. Although the Ferrari man was able to build his lead up to a considerable nine seconds over the next seven laps, he too met an unkind fate. "Suddenly I had trouble shifting gears, only the first two were available", he later explained. In an early pit stop he received not just fuel and new tyres, but also a new electronic steering wheel. The German returned to the race in sixth.

Rubens Barrichello must have wondered

what was going on. Yet again he was back in first. But sure enough, yet again there was a silver arrow bearing down on him - Mika Hakkinen, who passed him on the 60th of 72 laps. But it wasn't to be the defending champion's day either. Just like Barrichello, Hakkinen had to make another pit stop to refuel. This wasn't the case for Heinz-Harald Frentzen. The German profited not just from his fuel-efficient driving style, but also from his Jordan-Mugen-Honda's 110 litre fuel tank, which holds a full 20 litres more than the rest. "When I drove into the pits for a change of tyres, the length of time it took for refuelling made me a little nervous. It wasn't until later that I realised that it was a good move." At first Frentzen was even a little annoyed. "With the

tank filled the car was quite heavy and difficult to keep on the track."

For the last seven laps the lead never changed, and a delighted Heinz-Harald Frentzen, two injured knees and all, crossed the finish line in first for his second career Formula One victory. But behind him there was still a heated battle for fourth place. Michael Schumacher's gearbox problem had been solved, but now he had a problem with tyre pressure. "The car was handling terribly, I couldn't steer properly at all." Brother Ralf and team-mate Eddie Irvine though had no such problems. While "Schumi Two" made short work of overtaking his sibling, for "Crazy Eddie" this was taboo. It was forbidden under the terms of his contract - for now.

Fighting through the pain: Despite a cracked kneecap Heinz-Harald Frentzen won the French Grand Prix and his boss, Eddie Jordan celebrated along with him

Statistics

Course length:	4,25 km
Distance of race:	72 (= 306 km)
Start time:	13.00 UTC
Weather on day of race:	cloudy, than rain, short dry periods in middle of race
Attendance:	107 000
1998 Results:	1. Michael Schumacher (D, Ferrari F300), 1 h 34'35"026
	2. Eddie Irvine (GB, Ferrari F300), +19"575 s
	3. Mika Hakkinen (FIN, McLaren-Mercedes MP4/13), +19"747 s
Pole position 1998:	Mika Hakkinen (McLaren-Mercedes MP4/13), 1'14"929 m
Fastest Lap 1998:	David Coulthard (GB, McLaren-Mercedes MP4/13), 1'17"523 m
Fastest pit stop 1998:	Alexander Wurz (A, Benetton-Playlife B198), 24"101 s

Monotonous, but with a lot of opportunities to overtake

"The Magny-Cours track is relatively monotonous for the driver and isn´t one of my favourites. The Circuit de Nevers only really has one challenging curve, the right-left combination after the starting/finish line. Apart from that you can take various lines into the Adelaide hairpin and block out your opponents."

Heinz-Harald Frentzen

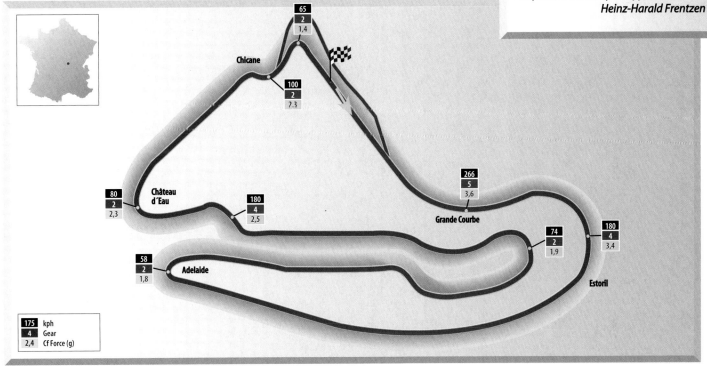

Results

	Driver	Team	Pit stops	Laps	Time (hours)	Average speed	Behind 1st	prev. driver
1.	Heinz-Harald Frentzen	Jordan-Mugen-Honda	1	72	1 h 58'24"343	154,965	–	–
2.	Mika Hakkinen	McLaren-Mercedes	2	72	1 h 58'35"435	154,724	11"092 s	
3.	Rubens Barrichello	Stewart-Ford	2	72	1 h 59'07"775	154,024	43"432 s	32"340 s
4.	Ralf Schumacher	Williams-Supertec	2	72	1 h 59'09"818	153,980	45"475 s	2"043 s
5.	Michael Schumacher	Ferrari	2	72	1 h 59'12"224	153,928	47"881 s	2"406 s
6.	Eddie Irvine	Ferrari	2	72	1 h 59'13"244	153,906	48"901 s	1"020 s
7.	Jarno Trulli	Prost-Peugeot	2	72	1 h 59'22"114	153,715	57"771 s	8"870 s
8.	Olivier Panis	Prost-Peugeot	2	72	1 h 59'22"874	153,699	58"531 s	0"760 s
9.	Ricardo Zonta	BAR-Supertec	2	72	1 h 59'53"107	153,053	1'28"764 m	30"233 s
10.	Luca Badoer	Minardi-Ford	2	71	1 h 59'05"221	151,937	1 lap	1 lap
11.	Pedro de la Rosa	TWR-Arrows	2	71	1 h 59'48"956	151,013	1 lap	43"735 s

Driver	Team	Pit stops	in lap	Reason f. retiring	Position before retiring
Giancarlo Fisichella	Benetton-Playlife	1	43	spun out	9
Damon Hill	Jordan-Mugen-Honda	2	32	spark failure	14
Alessandro Zanardi	Williams-Supertec	1	27	spun out	11
Jacques Villeneuve	BAR-Supertec	2	26	spun out	9
Alexander Wurz	Benetton-Playlife	1	26	spun out	12
Marc Gené	Minardi-Ford	1	26	spun out	15
Jean Alesi	Sauber-Petronas	1	25	spun out	3
David Coulthard	McLaren-Mercedes	0	10	spun out	1
Pedro Diniz	Sauber-Petronas	0	7	electrical trouble	11
Johnny Herbert	Stewart-Ford	0	5	power transmission	22
Toranosuke Takagi	TWR-Arrows [1]	2		disqualified	11

1.) Takagi finished 11th, but was disqualified due to a rule infraction.

French GP

**7th Race of the World Championship 1999,
Circuit de Nevers, Magny-Cours (F), 27th June 1999**

Starting Grid

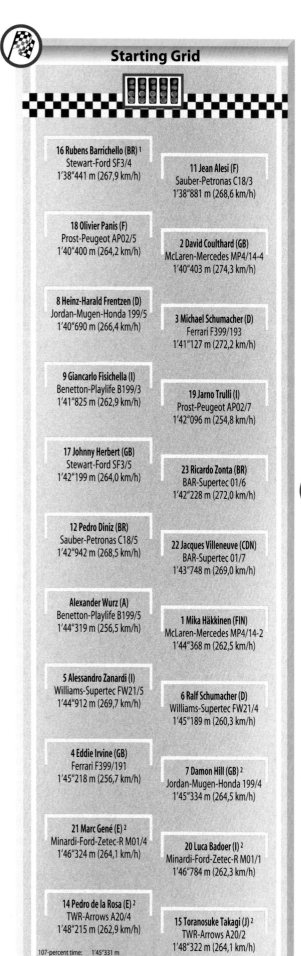

16 Rubens Barrichello (BR) [1]
Stewart-Ford SF3/4
1'38"441 m (267,9 km/h)

11 Jean Alesi (F)
Sauber-Petronas C18/3
1'38"881 m (268,6 km/h)

18 Olivier Panis (F)
Prost-Peugeot AP02/5
1'40"400 m (264,2 km/h)

2 David Coulthard (GB)
McLaren-Mercedes MP4/14-4
1'40"403 m (274,3 km/h)

8 Heinz-Harald Frentzen (D)
Jordan-Mugen-Honda 199/5
1'40"690 m (266,4 km/h)

3 Michael Schumacher (D)
Ferrari F399/193
1'41"127 m (272,2 km/h)

9 Giancarlo Fisichella (I)
Benetton-Playlife B199/3
1'41"825 m (262,9 km/h)

19 Jarno Trulli (I)
Prost-Peugeot AP02/7
1'42"096 m (254,8 km/h)

17 Johnny Herbert (GB)
Stewart-Ford SF3/5
1'42"199 m (264,0 km/h)

23 Ricardo Zonta (BR)
BAR-Supertec 01/6
1'42"228 m (272,0 km/h)

12 Pedro Diniz (BR)
Sauber-Petronas C18/5
1'42"942 m (268,5 km/h)

22 Jacques Villeneuve (CDN)
BAR-Supertec 01/7
1'43"748 m (269,0 km/h)

Alexander Wurz (A)
Benetton-Playlife B199/5
1'44"319 m (256,5 km/h)

1 Mika Häkkinen (FIN)
McLaren-Mercedes MP4/14-2
1'44"368 m (262,5 km/h)

5 Alessandro Zanardi (I)
Williams-Supertec FW21/5
1'44"912 m (269,7 km/h)

6 Ralf Schumacher (D)
Williams-Supertec FW21/4
1'45"189 m (260,3 km/h)

4 Eddie Irvine (GB)
Ferrari F399/191
1'45"218 m (256,7 km/h)

7 Damon Hill (GB) [2]
Jordan-Mugen-Honda 199/4
1'45"334 m (264,5 km/h)

21 Marc Gené (E) [2]
Minardi-Ford-Zetec-R M01/4
1'46"324 m (264,1 km/h)

20 Luca Badoer (I) [2]
Minardi-Ford-Zetec-R M01/1
1'46"784 m (262,3 km/h)

14 Pedro de la Rosa (E) [2]
TWR-Arrows A20/4
1'48"215 m (262,9 km/h)

15 Toranosuke Takagi (J) [2]
TWR-Arrows A20/2
1'48"322 m (264,1 km/h)

107-percent time: 1'45"331 m

Best Laps

In Training on Friday (m)

1.	M. Schumacher	1'17"912	12.	Hill	1'19"591
2.	Irvine	1'18"199	13.	Fisichella	1'19"651
3.	Häkkinen	1'18"251	14.	Villeneuve	1'20"002
4.	Coulthard	1'18"468	15.	Trulli	1'20"121
5.	Zanardi	1'18"746	16.	Panis	1'20"285
6.	Frentzen	1'18"779	17.	Diniz	1'20"528
7.	Alesi	1'18"908	18.	de la Rosa	1'20"655
8.	Barrichello	1'18"950	19.	Zonta	1'20"681
9.	R. Schumacher	1'19"069	20.	Takagi	1'21"418
10.	Herbert	1'19"266	21.	Badoer	1'21"506
11.	Wurz	1'19"491	22.	Gené	1'21"928

In the Race on Sunday (m)

1.	Coulthard	1'19"227	12.	Wurz	1'21"409
2.	Häkkinen	1'19"758	13.	Fisichella	1'21"423
3.	R. Schumacher	1'20"313	14.	Villeneuve	1'21"461
4.	Irvine	1'20"328	15.	Zanardi	1'21"983
5.	Alesi	1'20"848	16.	Hill	1'22"021
6.	Barrichello	1'20"878	17.	de la Rosa	1'22"535
7.	Zonta	1'20"881	18.	Diniz	1'22"629
8.	Frentzen	1'20"994	19.	Takagi	1'22"664
9.	M. Schumacher	1'21"014	20.	Gené	1'22"844
10.	Trulli	1'21"330	21.	Badoer	1'22"900
11.	Panis	1'21"403	22.	Herbert	1'25"608

Total Pit Stop Times

Lap	Time (s)	Lap	Time (s)	Lap	Time (s)
21 Panis	27"102	22 Alesi	30"292	50 Irvine	25"461
21 Irvine	63"796	22 Frentzen	32"800	52 R. Schumacher	25"953
21 Fisichella	33"768	22 M. Schumacher	27"946	54 M. Schumacher	31"627
21 Wurz	55"787	22 R. Schumacher	32"593	57 Panis	24"974
21 Villeneuve	31"957	22 Trulli	27"465	59 Trulli	24"315
21 Hill	46"939	22 Zonta	32"892	60 de la Rosa	32"798
21 de la Rosa	32"181	22 Zanardi	34"142	61 Zonta	30"411
21 Takagi	60"845	22 Badoer	30"794	65 Häkkinen	25"480
21 Gené	31"260	22 Hill	49"740	64 Barrichello	25"993
22 Barrichello	31"067	25 Villeneuve	28"289	67 Badoer	23"462
22 Häkkinen	28"769	28 Takagi	36"014		

The Race Lap by Lap

Start: Barrichello and Alesi maintain their positions, Coulthard slips into third. **Lap 1:** Hakkinen has already made good five places. **Lap 2:** Coulthard overtakes Alesi. Frentzen follows in fourth, then it´s M. Schumacher. **Lap 6:** Coulthard takes the lead. Hakkinen is sixth. **Lap 9:** The Finn challenges M. Schumacher ahead of the hairpin turn. Schumacher counters the first attempt, but one lap later Hakkinen moves into fifth. **Lap 10:** Coulthard rolls out of the running with gearbox trouble. **Lap 15:** Hakkinen struggles past Frentzen. Barrichello leads ahead of Alesi. **Lap 19:** Alesi makes a braking error, Hakkinen takes his opportunity to more into second. As predicted, a half hour into the race it begins to rain heavily. **Lap 21:** Almost the entire field switches to wet weather tyres. Frentzen has a long pit-stop as his fuel tank is filled to the brim. **Lap 25:** Alesi spins and is out. **Lap 26:** The safety-car makes an appearance - too late for Alesi, who shakes his fist from the sidelines. There´s so much water on the track that even behind the safety-car Zonta, Villeneuve, Wurz and Zanardi spin out. **Lap 36:** The race is on again. **Lap 38:** Hakkinen challenges Barrichello, spins out and continues in seventh. **Lap 39:** M. Schumacher overtakes Frentzen and is second. **Lap 44:** Following two failed attempts Schumacher overtakes Barrichello and is in the lead. **Lap 54:** M. Schumacher has his steering wheel replaced and is back to sixth, with persistent electronics problems. **Lap 57:** Hakkinen seizes second from Frentzen. **Lap 60:** Barrichello loses the lead to Hakkinen. **Lap 65:** Barrichello and Hakkinen have to refuel, Frentzen moves into first. **Lap 70:** R. Schumacher pinches fourth place from his brother, Irvine remains behind. **Lap 72:** Frentzen wins.

Standings

Driver/Points

1.	Mika Häkkinen	40
2.	Michael Schumacher	32
3.	Eddie Irvine	26
4.	Heinz-Harald Frentzen	23
5.	Ralf Schumacher	15
6.	Giancarlo Fisichella	13
7.	David Coulthard	12
8.	Rubens Barrichello	10
9.	Damon Hill	3
10.	Johnny Herbert	2
11.	de la Rosa	1
	Panis	1
	Alesi	1
	Wurz	1
	Trulli	1
	Diniz	1

Team

1.	Ferrari	58
2.	McLaren-Mercedes	52
3.	Jordan-Mugen-Honda	26
4.	Williams-Supertec	15
5.	Benetton-Playlife	14
6.	Stewart-Ford	12
7.	Prost-Peugeot	2
	Sauber-Petronas	2
9.	TWR-Arrows	1

1) Lap time (top speed in qualifying); 2) Allowed to start despite not achieving 107 per cent qualifying time.

Suddenly the focus of attention: Heinz-Harald Frentzen.

Happy Harry: Frentzen obviously feels comfortable at Jordan-Mugen-Honda

The Other German

For years Heinz-Harald Frentzen has been overshadowed by his more famous Formula One compatriot, Michael Schumacher.

But over the past season this non-conformist has managed to find a place in the hearts of the German fans, while at the

same time moving well up in the drivers standings.

But whether he's managed to drive his way into Damon Hill's heart is another matter. The German outperformed the former world champion at Williams in 1997 to the point that Hill was ousted as number one driver, and eventually moved over to Jordan. Then it happened again - Frentzen wound up following Hill to Jordan and made the Englishman look so average, that Damon Hill chose to end his driving career.

Thinking back but a couple of years, it's a development few would have laid money on. Heinz-Harald Frentzen had all but been written off as a top Formula One driver. The knock on him was that he was too nice (rare for a German), too soft, too comfortable and perhaps worst of all, had an apparently terminal case of bad luck. To be fair the Fleet Street tabloids never gave the man from Moenchen-Gladbach, once home of one of Europe's top football sides, much of a chance. They didn't shed a tear over the fact that the German never managed to get his feet under the table in his two years at Williams, and they overlooked the point that he missed winning his first ever race with the English team due to a technical defect...making good on that shortly afterwards at Imola... and that on race day it was Frank Williams and Patrick Head who sent the fastest man in training onto a rainy Monaco track outfitted with slicks. The fact that despite all this, the German driver came second in the world championship to Jacques Villeneuve didn't seem to be worth mentioning, possibly because it wasn't

in keeping with their view of Frentzen as a failure.

Today though things have changed. After a year in Eddie Jordan's stable, not only has Frentzen re-established himself in the elite class of Formula One drivers, but he's also rediscovered his sense of humour. He obviously feels comfortable and appreciated at Jordan. That couldn't have been said about his time at Williams. "Some people think I've changed", the 32 year-old diplomatically puts it. "I'm simply happy to be at Jordan. Maybe that's a big change in itself..."

In fact Frentzen, who's a more complicated character than many of his counterparts, rose like a phoenix from the ashes to deliver a near flawless season on the track. He won the rain-soaked French Grand Prix at Magny Cours, as well as the Italian Grand Prix at Monza. Only a technical failure prevented him from a win at the Nurburgring which, had he crossed the finish line in first, would have brought him to within a point of Mika Hakkinen at the top of the table. The great question mark about his future, which existed going into the season has been erased. The people left

Influence: When Heinz-Harald speaks, the Jordan team listens. The German clearly appreciates the fact that his suggestions are put into the development of the car's design.

asking questions about Frentzen are in Grove. Williams are left wondering how they could have misread Frentzen´s vast potential.

While they may have been a tough two years for him at Williams, they're two years the son of a German undertaker wouldn't change for the world. "Sometimes adversity can be one of the best motivators", comments Frentzen. "The people who've been working with me this season worked with a different Heinz-Harald Frentzen three or five years ago. That made it easier to become acclimatised to the team and the car." It's well apparent that the chemistry between the Monaco resident and the Jordan team is just right. "He has a terribly dry and black sense of humour", smiles chief design engineer Mike Gascoyne. "He likes to pull people's legs, but he's done a great job and everyone's loves him. His mechanics would travel through hell for him."

But what is the reason behind what for the motor racing public, has been an astounding comeback? There are a number of factors which have had a positive effect on Frentzen´s performance. First, he feels that the people at Jordan understand him, and take him seriously. For example when he requests a change to the car the technical staff build it into the car's development, without calling their driver's request into question. "Heinz is pleased with the way his suggestions are put into practice", says Mike Gascoyne. "Perhaps he lost his confidence at Williams because they didn't pay as much attention to what he was saying."

Ford Reportedly Offered £10 Million....

As well some of the rule changes have worked in the Jordan driver's favour: The fourth groove in the front tyres demands a very sensitive touch - Frentzen has the reputation among his competitors for being the driver with the most sensitive foot on the accelerator in the entire field. "You have to struggle more with the current Formula One cars", says the three time Grand Prix winner. The tyres don't stick to the road as well, so it's easier to go into a skid. This calls for the driver to exert more control on the car, and for a driver who likes to push the car to its limit at all times.

Another advantage has been that at Jordan Frentzen was teamed up again with Mike Gascoyne, the team's chief designer. He's the man who designed the ´93 and ´94 Sauber team cars, the ones in which Heinz-Harald first came to Formula One prominence. Not just that but in the Mugen-Honda Jordan has one of the best ten cylinders on the circuit, and the Japanese concern, which will officially return to Grand Prix racing next year is working hard on technical development. So things can only get better in the 2000 season.

But Jordan isn't the only team sold on Frentzen´s qualities as a driver. Ford is said to have offered him £10 million to move to the

Even without Michael Schumacher sometimes the Germans dominate the winners podium: Heinz-Harald Frentzen and Ralf Schumacher at the Italian Grand Prix.

Determined concentration: At the Nurburgring HHF earned his second pole position.

Strong performance: Frentzen led the pack in the race too until a mysterious technical defect forced him to retire.

Jaguar team for the 2001 season. Frentzen, who will race for Jordan next year as well doesn't waste a lot of time thinking about such rumours. "Everything's going well, but I work very hard at what I do", he explains. "When that begins paying off more victories, things will get easier."

Nevertheless 1999 was a very good season for Heinz-Harald Frentzen, even if his short-lived hopes of a shot at the drivers championship were dashed at the Nurburgring and in Malaysia. The German, who's about to become a father - his fiancée Tanja Nigge is expecting - takes a pragmatic view. "I don´t view it as having lost the drivers championship. In my view what we did was we secured third place in the constructors championship ahead of Williams and Stewart, and in so doing, achieved more than we had hoped to." Mike Gascoyne adds: "The drivers championship aside, as far as I'm concerned Heinz is this year's superstar".

Love of his life: Frentzen´s long-time fiancée Tanja Nigge is about to make Heinz-Harald a father for the first time.

Back to the Rhythm: Formula One team boss and amateur drummer Eddie Jordan set the beat for getting Heinz-Harald Frentzen´s Grand Prix career back on track.

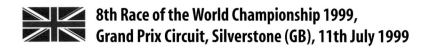
A crucial techr

The Formula One world held its collective

breath as title hopeful Michael

Schumacher crashed out and in so doing

change the complexion of the battle for

the world championship.

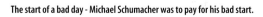

The start of a bad day - Michael Schumacher was to pay for his bad start.

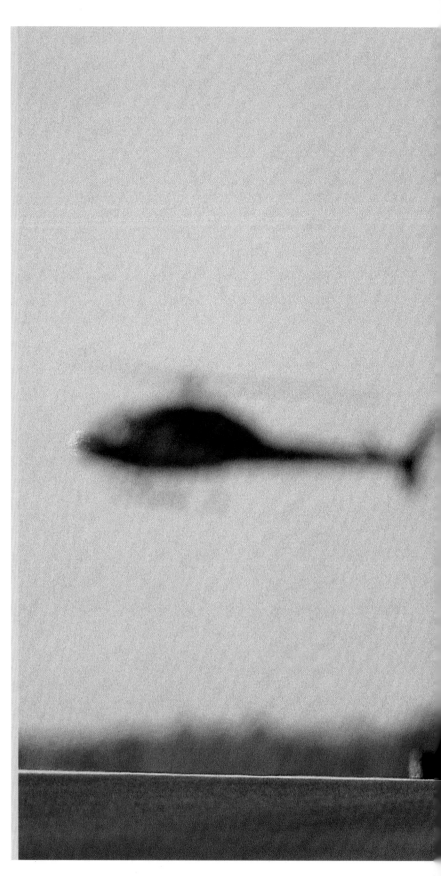

cal failure

Right: His title aspirations were to end early - Michael Schumacher.
Below: The Flying Scot - David Coulthard on the way to his first win of the season.

Part of the reason for Schumi´s crash: Villeneuve and Zanardi can't get it into gear for the green light.

Bad patch over? David Coulthard celebrated his first win of the season.

Michael Schumacher´s aspirations for this year´s drivers championship ended before the British Grand Prix was even a lap old. The German was trying to make up for a bad start, and attempting to overtake teammate Eddie Irvine on the hangar straight, when Schumacher´s Ferrari shot across the front of Ferrari's number two, through a gravel trap and into a triple tyre wall in front of the barriers. He hit the tyres at a speed of about 200 kph, in an incident which took one's thoughts back to Imola on the first of May 1994. Whereas the similarly shocking accident 5 years earlier claimed Ayrton Senna´s life, this time, to everyone´s relief it was soon clear that Schumacher had survived. Fans at Silverstone and fans tuning in all over the world looked on with amazement as just seconds later, Schumacher attempted to free himself from the cockpit - to no avail.

The twice world champion had sustained a double break of the lower right leg and bruising to the chest. Considering the speed at which he'd hit the wall, Schumacher could consider himself lucky, even if it did damage his aura of near perfection, and the myth of that top Formula One drivers are virtually indestructible. Senna´s fatal

accident had a similar effect. When lesser drivers are involved in such crashes, one of the stock explanations is simply that they're not as good as the very best of their era.

Hakkinen confirmed that he was at the top of his game.

Still another parallel between the Schumacher and Senna accidents is that in both cases technical failure rendered them powerless to do anything but await their fate, unable to take evasive action. As the Italian courts were continuing to deal with the question of what really was the cause of Senna´s fatal crash, the Ferrari team swiftly announced what they believed caused Schumacher´s car to bolt off course. Their explanation: a deficiency in the braking system. But video footage from the on-board camera, which in the meantime appears to have disappeared tells a very different story. It shows that Schumacher was desperately trying to steer the wheel

to keep the car on the track, but the front wheels obviously weren't responding. Incidentally one of the possibilities the courts dealing with the Senna crash are looking into is a possible failure in the steering system.

The race continued without Schumacher. Defending champion Mika Hakkinen had already proved that he was at the top of his game in qual-

Good result: Pedro Diniz secured his second championship point.

Herr Consistency - in England Heinz-Harald Frentzen collected still more championship points.

Battle of Britain: After the first refuelling pit stop Irvine was behind Co

Early joy: Irvine is still in second ahead of Coulthard.

Oranjes: The Royal Automobile Club grid girls would have fit in well at a Dutch national team match.

The right tactics: Ralf Schumacher on the way to his second pit stop.

ifying. It only took him one attempt to record a time nobody else was to approach - a lap of 1.24.943 minutes. It was the flying Finn's sixth pole position in just the eighth race of the season - an incredible record. Michael Schumacher, who like team-mate Eddie Irvine was faced with the problem of the front tyres on his Ferrari wearing too quickly, didn't have much of a chance to

better Hakkinen. But to his credit the talented German did make it into the first row, along side his arch-rival. Behind them were: David Coulthard and Eddie Irvine followed by the two Jordan-Mugen-Honda drivers in row three, Heinz-Harald Frentzen and Damon Hill. William's number one Ralf Schumacher and Stewart-Ford's Rubens Barrichello lined up at number seven and eight in the grid respectively.

But the first start went completely wrong. Schumacher crawled off the mark, allowing Coulthard and Irvine to roar past. Jacques Villeneuve and Alessandro Zanardi didn't even budge. The Canadian had gearbox trouble while the Italian had managed to stall his Williams

car's engine. The race officials swiftly decided to suspend the race, and while the McLaren drivers learned of the decision via their radios, Michael Schumacher didn't receive the message - with tragic result.

As the rest of the drivers were getting prepared to line up for a second start, none of them was more nervous than Michael's brother Ralf. "It wasn't a very good feeling getting back into the cockpit after the crash", the 24 year-old later admitted. "But I'm a professional and I have a job to do. I knew that Michael had been injured, but I also knew that it wasn't life-threatening. That helped. As well my pit crew constantly kept me up to date on Michael's condition".

A Finnish tragedy in two acts: First Mika had a bad pit stop, then the world champion lost a wheel.

British GP

The re-start was almost a carbon copy of the first. Hakkinen catapulted himself off the mark and moved into the lead. Behind him Irvine slipped past Coulthard and for the first half of the race had little trouble maintaining his position between the two silver arrows. "At this point Eddie was accelerating out of the curves much faster than I was", the handsome Scot told reporters later. But Hakkinen was still the fastest man on the track, consistently driving marginally faster laps than any of his closest pursuers be they Irvine, Coulthard, Frentzen, Ralf Schumacher or Damon Hill. Everything was going very much the blonde's way - that is until his first pit stop. That's when everything started to change.

Mika limped to the pits on three wheels.

Although the leading McLaren´s 9.2 second fuelling stop wasn't particularly fast, it wasn't an immediate cause for concern. But it soon became apparent that he did have a serious problem. He'd hardly got back onto the track when he let his team-mate overtake him, and steered back into the pits. This time he spent 27 seconds there, as mechanics worked feverishly to correct a problem with his rear left wheel. By the time he returned to the track this time he'd dropped all the way back to 11th, but undaunted he recorded the fastest lap of the race so far. It was all for nought. Suddenly his rear left wheel flew off, fortunately without injuring any other drivers or spectators.

This time Hakkinen and his Mercedes limped into the pits on just three wheels. The mechanics installed a new tyre and he was off again. But it wasn't long before team boss Ron Dennis called him back in. Because the mechanics had not been able to identify the problem, he chose to pull Hakkinen out of the race, rather than risk an injury to his number one driver.

In the meantime Hakkinen´s deputy was leading the field. Paradoxically David Coulthard had inherited the lead due to his team-mate's bad luck: as the mechanics were working on Hakkinen´s car, Irvine's route to his own pit crew was obstructed, causing him to overshoot the mark. The result: his pit stop took a full 12 instead of seven seconds. "That cost me the race", lamented the Northern Irishman afterwards.

Up until the second round of pit stops began on lap 40, Coulthard´s lead on the 5.14 kilometre course was less than a second. These second fuel stops would be what would decide the race for good. The McLaren team got Coulthard in and out of there in just 6.3 seconds. The Ferraris took 7.1 seconds for the same procedure on Eddie Irvine's car. "DC" left the pits ahead of Irvine by the skin of his teeth, on the way to his fifth Formula One victory. "It was my biggest win so far", smiled Mclaren´s number two. "It had always been a dream of mine to win the British Grand Prix."

The excitement continued in the battle for third place. The Jordan mechanics were so quick in getting fourth placed Heinz-Harald Frentzen´s car refuelled, that he returned to the track within striking distance of his compatriot, Ralf Schu-

True love isn't just skin deep - a British Jordan fan.

Victory at home: Briton David Coulthard.

macher. But the younger German kept his wits about him, and earned the last spot on the podium. "I can thank Williams for that", he said diplomatically. "The new aerodynamics package made it possible to keep up with at least Jordan, if not McLaren and Ferrari."

Frentzen wasn't quite so pleased. "Damon and I earned five points for the constructors standings, defending third place", commented Heinz-Harald. "But I know I could have done better today, and naturally that bothers me a bit."

Champagne spray: David Coulthard enjoys a shower of the bubbly on the winners podium.

Statistics

Course length:	5,14 km
Distance of race:	60 (= 308,296 km)
Start time:	13.00 UTC
Weather on day of race:	clear and mild
Attendance:	90 000
1998 Results:	1. Michael Schumacher (D, Ferrari F300) , 1 h 47'02"450
	2. Mika Hakkinen (FIN, McLaren-Mercedes MP4/13), +22"465 s
	3. Eddie Irvine (GB, Ferrari F300), +29"199 m
Pole position 1998:	Mika Hakkinen (McLaren-Mercedes MP4/13), 1'23"271 m
Fastest Lap 1998:	Michael Schumacher (Ferrari F300), 1'35"704 m
Fastest pit stop 1998:	Eddie Irvine (Ferrari F300), 26"509 s

Good aerodynamics are a must for the high-speed curves

"Silverstone provides drivers with many challenges. You know right away when you've driven a fast lap. That's extremely satisfying. Good aerodynamics are a must on this former airport course, particularly in the Copse or Becketts curves. The exits from the narrow turns on the other hand require good traction."

David Coulthard

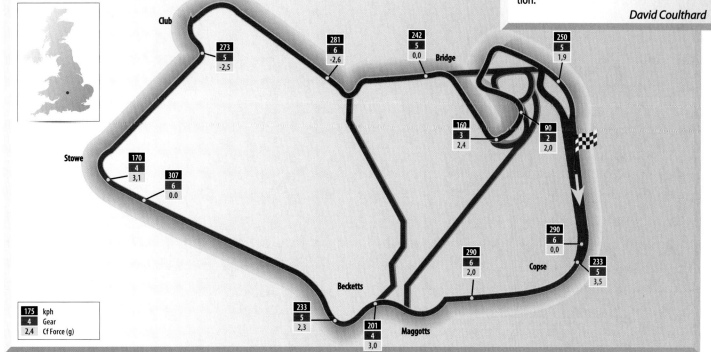

Results

Driver	Team	Pit stops	Laps	Time (hours)	Average speed	Behind 1st	prev. driver
1. David Coulthard	McLaren-Mercedes	2	60	1 h 32'30"144	199,970	–	–
2. Eddie Irvine	Ferrari	2	60	1 h 32'31"973	199,904	1"829 s	–
3. Ralf Schumacher	Williams-Supertec	2	60	1 h 32'57"555	198,987	27"411 s	25"582 s
4. Heinz-Harald Frentzen	Jordan-Mugen-Honda	2	60	1 h 32'57"933	198,974	27"789 s	0"378 s
5. Damon Hill	Jordan-Mugen-Honda	2	60	1 h 33'08"750	198,589	38"606 s	10"817 s
6. Pedro Diniz	Sauber-Petronas	2	60	1 h 33'23"787	198,056	53"643 s	15"037 s
7. Giancarlo Fisichella	Benetton-Playlife	2	60	1 h 33'24"758	198,022	54"614 s	0"971 s
8. Rubens Barrichello	Stewart-Ford	3	60	1 h 33'38"734	197,529	1'08"590 m	13"976 s
9. Jarno Trulli	Prost-Peugeot	2	60	1 h 33'42"189	197,408	1'12"045 m	3"455 s
10. Alexander Wurz	Benetton-Playlife	2	60	1 h 33'42"267	197,405	1'12"123 m	0"078 s
11. Alessandro Zanardi	Williams-Supertec	2	60	1 h 33'47"268	197,229	1'17"124 m	5"001 s
12. Johnny Herbert	Stewart-Ford	3	60	1 h 33'47"853	197,209	1'17"709 m	0"585 s
13. Olivier Panis	Prost-Peugeot	2	60	1 h 33'50"636	197,111	1'20"492 m	2"783 s
14. Jean Alesi	Sauber-Petronas	3	59	1 h 33'12"794	195,137	1 lap	1 laps
15. Marc Gené	Minardi-Ford	2	58	1 h 33'41"812	192,897	2 laps	1 laps
16. Toranosuke Takagi	TWR-Arrows	2	58	1 h 33'15"047	191,751	2 laps	33"235 s

Driver	Team	Pit stops	in lap	Reason f. retiring	Position before retiring
Ricardo Zonta	BAR-Supertec	2	42	suspension	14
Mika Hakkinen	McLaren-Mercedes	3	36	suspension	16
Jacques Villeneuve	BAR-Supertec	1	30	power transmission	10
Luca Badoer	Minardi-Ford	1	7	gearbox	20
Pedro de la Rosa	TWR-Arrows	0	1	gearbox	19
Michael Schumacher	Ferrari	0	0	didn´t restart	–

British GP

8th Race in the World Championship 1999,
Silverstone Grand Prix Circuit (GB), 11th July 1999

Starting Grid

1 Mika Häkkinen (FIN) [1]
McLaren-Mercedes MP4/14-2
1'24"804 m (308,4 km/h)

3 Michael Schumacher (D)
Ferrari F399/193
1'25"223 m (305,6 km/h)

2 David Coulthard (GB)
McLaren-Mercedes MP4/14-4
1'25"594 m (309,2 km/h)

4 Eddie Irvine (GB)
Ferrari F399/191
1'25"677 m (306,8 km/h)

8 Heinz-Harald Frentzen (D)
Jordan-Mugen-Honda 199/5
1'25"991 m (309,0 km/h)

7 Damon Hill (GB)
Jordan-Mugen-Honda 199/4
1'26"099 m (305,6 km/h)

16 Rubens Barrichello (BR)
Stewart-Ford SF3/4
1'26"194 m (305,8 km/h)

6 Ralf Schumacher (D)
Williams-Supertec FW21/4
1'26"438 m (304,7 km/h)

22 Jacques Villeneuve (CDN)
BAR-Supertec 01/7
1'26"719 m (301,9 km/h)

11 Jean Alesi (F)
Sauber-Petronas C18/6
1'26"761 m (302,6 km/h)

17 Johnny Herbert (GB)
Stewart-Ford SF3/5
1'26"873 m (305,5 km/h)

12 Pedro Diniz (BR)
Sauber-Petronas C18/5
1'27"196 m (303,2 km/h)

5 Alessandro Zanardi (I)
Williams-Supertec FW21/5
1'27"223 m (305,8 km/h)

19 Jarno Trulli (I)
Prost-Peugeot AP02/7
1'27"227 m (301,1 km/h)

18 Olivier Panis (F)
Prost-Peugeot AP02/5
1'27"543 m (302,3 km/h)

23 Ricardo Zonta (BR)
BAR-Supertec 01/6
1'27"669 m (304,3 km/h)

9 Giancarlo Fisichella (I)
Benetton-Playlife B199/7
1'27"857 m (305,9 km/h)

10 Alexander Wurz (A)
Benetton-Playlife B199/5
1'28"010 m (303,7 km/h)

15 Toranosuke Takagi (J)
TWR-Arrows A20/2
1'28"037 m (304,8 km/h)

14 Pedro de la Rosa (E)
TWR-Arrows A20/4
1'28"148 m (301,1 km/h)

20 Luca Badoer (I)
Minardi-Ford-Zetec-R M01/1
1'28"695 m (301,5 km/h)

21 Marc Gené (E)
Minardi-Ford-Zetec-R M01/4
1'28"772 m (301,6km/h)

107-percent time: 1'30"740 m

Best Laps

In Training on Friday (m)			
1. Häkkinen	1'26"981	12. Alesi	1'28"472
2. R. Schumacher	1'27"004	13. Fisichella	1'28"546
3. Irvine	1'27"061	14. Frentzen	1'28"595
4. **Coulthard**	1'27"155	15. Wurz	1'28"740
5. Barrichello	1'27"158	16. Trulli	1'28"883
6. M. Schumacher	1'27"327	17. Badoer	1'29"130
7. Hill	1'27"381	18. Herbert	1'29"201
8. Diniz	1'27"931	19. Gené	1'29"416
9. Villeneuve	1'27"981	20. de la Rosa	1'29"439
10. Zanardi	1'28"162	21. Takagi	1'29"630
11. Zonta	1'28"238	22. Panis	1'30"372

In the Race on Sunday (m)			
1. Häkkinen	1'28"309	12. Zanardi	1'30"522
2. Irvine	1'28"782	13. Zonta	1'30"611
3. **Coulthard**	1'28"846	14. Wurz	1'30"625
4. Hill	1'29"252	15. Panis	1'30"793
5. Frentzen	1'29"330	16. Trulli	1'30"964
6. R. Schumacher	1'29"414	17. Villeneuve	1'31"342
7. Barrichello	1'29"493	18. Gené	1'31"612
8. Diniz	1'29"819	19. Badoer	1'32"409
9. Herbert	1'30"103	20. Takagi	1'32"442
10. Fisichella	1'30"296		
11. Alesi	1'30"334		

Total Pit Stop Times

Lap	Time (s)	Lap	Time (s)	Lap	Time (s)	Lap	Time (s)
6 Badoer	76"216	24 R. Schumacher	26"294	31 Trulli	27"606	41 Wurz	27"017
19 Gené	27"733	24 Diniz	27"098	31 Zonta	29"855	41 Zonta	28"716
20 Fisichella	26"888	24 Trulli	26"098	33 Alesi	32"397	41 Takagi	31"186
20 Takagi	27"446	25 Häkkinen	28"118	34 Alesi	43"003	42 **Coulthard**	25"275
21 Alesi	27"134	25 Barrichello	28"178	38 Panis	27"253	42 Barrichello	27"399
21 Wurz	27"306	25 Zonta	26"603	39 Zanardi	28"324	42 Fisichella	27"202
22 Zanardi	26"277	26 Irvine	30"644	40 R. Schumacher	28"977	45 Frentzen	25"333
23 Hill	27"912	26 Häkkinen	47"874	40 Herbert	27"271	46 Hill	25"162
23 Herbert	25"790	26 Panis	26"391	40 Gené	26"854	47 Barrichello	28"595
24 **Coulthard**	26"351	29 Villeneuve	30"877	41 Irvine	26"084	49 Herbert	31"021
24 Frentzen	28"993	29 Häkkinen	58"018	41 Diniz	28"095		

The Race Lap by Lap

Start: Hakkinen gets off to the best start, Coulthard accelerates past M. Schumacher, Irvine too passes the German. Villeneuve and Zanardi stay put at the starting line, which causes the abandonment of the start. While the McLaren drivers are notified of this by two-way radio and there for let up on the gas, the Ferrari drivers continue on. While overtaking Irvine on the Stowe Corner, M. Schumacher races into a stack of tyres. Restart after a 40 minute break: Hakkinen goes out into the lead followed by Irvine, Coulthard, Frentzen, and R. Schumacher. This time de la Rosa can't get it into gear and the safety-car heads out onto the track. **Lap11:** The leading trio of Hakkinen, Irvine and Coulthard are 15 seconds ahead of Frentzen. **Lap 24:** Pit stops for Coulthard and Frentzen. The Scotsman remains in third, Heinz-Harald continually falls further behind R. Schumacher who had a quicker pit stop. **Lap 25:** Hakkinen stops for the first time. Irvine leads until his pit stop one lap later. **Lap 26:** Hakkinen loses speed, Coulthard goes into the lead. Irvine returns from the pits in second. Hakkinen goes to the pits to have his wheels checked. **Lap 28:** Hakkinen records the fastest lap of the day. **Lap 29:** The Finn loses his right rear wheel, but is able to limp into the pits. The safety-car comes out because the wheel is lying on the track. **Lap 31:** The race is on again. **Lap 35:** Hakkinen parks his car in the pits due to safety concerns. Coulthard and Irvine battle it out for the lead, followed by R. Schumacher, Frentzen, Barrichello and Hill. **Lap 41:** Irvine's second pit stop. **Lap 42:** Coulthard's stop is shorter, he builds on his lead. **Lap 47:** Barrichello has his front tyres replaced and falls back out of the points. **Lap 49:** Frentzen and R. Schumacher battle for third. **Lap 60:** David Coulthard completes his first win of the season.

Standings

Driver/Points			
1. Mika Häkkinen	40	13. de la Rosa	1
2. Michael Schumacher	32	Panis	1
4. Eddie Irvine	32	Alesi	1
5. Heinz-Harald Frentzen	26	Wurz	1
6. David Coulthard	22	Trulli	1
7. Ralf Schumacher	19		
8. Giancarlo Fisichella	13		
9. Rubens Barrichello	10		
10. Damon Hill	5		
11. Johnny Herbert	2		
Pedro Diniz	2		

Team	Points
1. Ferrari	64
2. McLaren-Mercedes	62
3. Jordan-Mugen-Honda	31
4. Williams-Supertec	19
5. Benetton-Playlife	14
6. Stewart-Ford	12
7. Sauber-Petronas	3
8. Prost-Peugeot	2
9. TWR-Arrows	1

1.) Lap time (top speed in qualifying).

A parting jam session? Damon Hill played a few chords on the electric guitar to mark his last British Grand Prix.

Safety Fast

This season saw the fifth anniversary of Formula One's "black weekend". In 1994 Brazilian superstar Ayrton Senna and Austrian driver Roland Ratzenberger died at the San Marino Grand Prix at Imola. This tragedy woke up FIA to the fact that something urgently had to be done. Since then much has been done to improve safety for both Formula One drivers and the fans in the stands as well.

Uninjured: The giant rubber bands in front of the stacks of tyres helped prevent injury to Mika Hakkinen after his tyre blew at over 300 kph at Hockenheim.

The newest generation of noses on Formula One cars are designed to collapse in order to lessen the impact for the driver.

Tragic: Ayrton Senna – he demanded improved safety provisions at the very stretch of track where Roland Ratzenberger fatally crashed.

What do Michael Schumacher, Jacques Villeneuve, Pedro Diniz, Heinz-Harald Frentzen and Ricardo Zonta have in common? All five have FIA, the world motor racing body to thank for the fact that they survived serious crashes with relatively minor injuries. Ten years ago the crashes that each of these drivers was involved in would have likely ended their careers - at best. But since the tragic deaths of Ayrton Senna and Roland Ratzenberger at Imola in 1994, FIA President Max Mosley has made the safety of the drivers one of the world motor racing body's top priorities. Some of the resulting rule changes have had a major impact on the track and some of them may have even saved the lives of: Michael Schumacher (at Silverstone), Zonta (in his native Brazil), Frentzen (in Canada), Villeneuve (at Spa), and Diniz (at the Nurburgring).

One of the most important innovations is that today, before a Formula One chassis is approved for use in a race, it must withstand a series of frontal, side and rear-end crash tests. But it's not enough to ensure that the carbon fibre monocoque can stand up to such impacts without the cockpit being damaged. There's another problem to be dealt with. At the speeds at which a Formula One driver can crash, even if the cockpit is undamaged, he's subject to such force within the cockpit at impact, that serious internal injuries are highly probable. For this reason more and more effort is going into developing ways of absorbing the shock. FIA is developing ways of ensuring that the car breaks down as much of the impact as possible. For example the carbon fibre nose of a current Formula One car disintegrates, practically into dust, while slowing the card down significantly during just a few milliseconds. The impact the driver is exposed to is significantly reduced.

The interiors of the cockpits have also been improved to reduce possible injury to the drivers. The walls of the cockpit are now lined with an energy-absorbing foam. Among other things this helps protect drivers from serious neck or spinal injuries during a side impact. This innovation proved vital when Heinz Harald Frentzen experienced a high speed side impact at this season's Canadian Grand Prix. Apart from injuries to his knees, he came out of it relatively unscathed.

FIA's newest development which was introduced for the 1999 season has also proved its worth. It's a specially-designed driver's seat which can be removed from a damaged car with an injured driver still sitting in it. It's particularly useful in rescuing a driver who's lost consciousness, or who's suspected to have suffered a spinal injury. They can remove the driver strapped into the seat, transport him as such to hospital, and even, if need be, x-ray him, still strapped into the seat. This drastically reduces

The countdown: A Formula One driver is required to be able to exit his cockpit within five seconds. Michael Schumacher passed the test in Malaysia.

New safety seat: It allows rescuers to remove the entire seat with the driver strapped in. It became mandatory in 1999.

Useless: Steel cables are designed to prevent the wheels from flying away during an accident and endangering other drivers and spectators.

the risk of the driver suffering further, possibly serious injury while being rescued and transported to hospital. Unfortunately it wasn't long before the seat, which was developed by one of the Stewart team's corporate partners, had to be tested in practice. It helped stabilise Pedro Diniz when he rolled his car at the Nurburgring, and helped in the removal of Michael Schumacher from his smashed Ferrari at Silverstone.

Not all FIA innovations work.

Some of the worst dangers can be little things one might not immediately think of. Ayrton Senna might have survived the horrendous crash of his Williams-Renault into the concrete wall at the Parabolica curve. But what killed him was a splintered piece of metal from the front suspension system. Since 1997 FIA has regulations in place which specify that such parts must be constructed to collapse in the event of a crash in a manner which is unlikely to threaten the safety of the driver. The world motor racing body has also introduced an innovation which hasn't worked so well. Following the mass crash at the 1998 Belgian Grand Prix FIA made it mandatory for wheels to be tied to the chassis by a steel/carbon fibre chord in order to prevent wheels that are knocked off on impact from rocketing around the stands like giant Frisbees. But it became clear when Mika Hakkinen

Lucky break: Even though the roll bar on Pedro Diniz´ Sauber broke at the Nurburgring, the Brazilian emerged unscathed.

Thanks to the new, higher cockpit walls (yellow area), which protect a driver´s head and spinal chord, he escaped serious injury.

A special thanks to Karl Wendlinger: At Monaco Alexander Wurz benefitted from the new safety measures.

Ayrton Senna´s 1994 death at Imola caused FIA to begin looking at ways of increasing the level of safety at Grand Prix races.

lost a wheel at Silverstone that this simply isn't enough.

It's not just the Formula One cars themselves which are being made safer. Track officials are being forced to undertake increasingly expensive measures to improve the safety of the individual courses themselves, even if the measures taken so far are not nearly enough. Michael Schumacher´s crash at Silverstone wouldn't have been as serious had Silverstone been outfitted with huge rubber safety bands. As it was, the German sped at almost full speed into first a pile of tyres, then a concrete wall. Hockenheim though does have such rubber safety bands - as Mika Hakkinen thankfully noted after a spectacular incident in which one of his tyres blew while he was travelling at high speed.

Tyre stacks are a less than ideal but cost-effective compromise.

Even if FIA´s comprehensive testing has determined that the used tyre barriers are the best compromise between function and cost, they certainly aren't the ideal solution. When the racers crash into these piles of tyres, sometimes they can become tangled up in the old rubber, causing the cars to come to an even more abrupt halt than might otherwise have been the case. Olivier Panis learned this painful experience the hard way during the 1997 Canadian Grand Prix. Had the Frenchman hit a concrete wall the same way, it would have bounced off and spun to a gradual halt. But as it was, the

The Safety Evolution

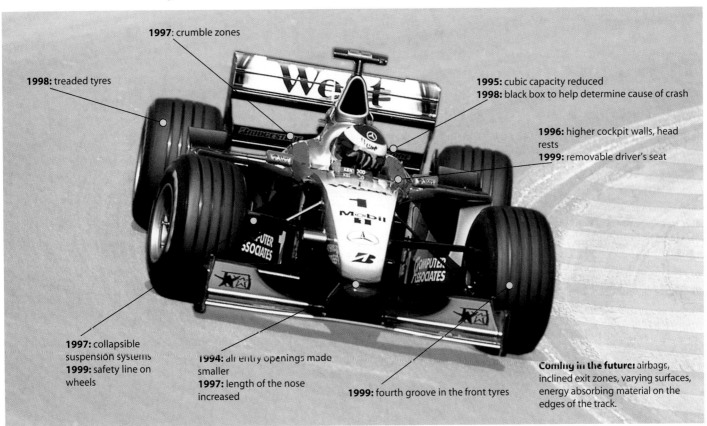

1997: crumble zones

1998: treaded tyres

1995: cubic capacity reduced
1998: black box to help determine cause of crash

1996: higher cockpit walls, head rests
1999: removable driver's seat

1997: collapsible suspension systems
1999: safety line on wheels

1994: air entry openings made smaller
1997: length of the nose increased

1999: fourth groove in the front tyres

Coming in the future: airbags, inclined exit zones, varying surfaces, energy absorbing material on the edges of the track.

Monaco Grand Prix winner wound up breaking both of his legs. The organisers of the Monaco Grand Prix are so far the only ones to opt for a modern and extremely expensive solution. In 1995 they had collapsible water tanks installed. They're also considering installing so-called "air-fences". But the water tanks weren't introduced until a serious accident there brought pressure to bear as well. One year earlier Austrian Sauber driver Karl Wendlinger crashed sideways into a rigid barrier. He sustained life-threatening injuries which prematurely ended his Formula One career.

Gravel or asphalt - which is better?

Schumacher's crash at Silverstone has served to re-ignite discussion over which is the better surface alongside the track, asphalt or gravel. There are advantages and disadvantages to each. Tar for example is the best surface to slow down a car in a spin. But if the car has first lost a wheel or two, things are completely dif-

ferent: only a gravel surface can be relied upon to slow it down - but only if the car isn't travelling at too high a speed. In that case the car can skid on unimpeded like a hovercraft crossing the channel.

Much less spectacular, but a detail which nevertheless could have prevented the German's fateful crash at Silverstone: light diodes in the cockpit to inform drivers of yellow or red flags, danger areas or even the abandonment of a race. This has already been extensively tested.

Still in the testing phase: Illuminated signals on the track and in the cockpit designed to warn drivers better than flag signals.

Involuntary crash test: Crumble zones in the rear of the car also help to reduce impact.

Out of Mic

He showed the critics: Eddie Irvine felt at home in his new role.

Even "Crazy Eddie" isn't foolish enough to squander the chance of a lifetime. Eddie Irvine had always claimed he was capable of being a number one driver on the Formula One circuit, and in Austria he silenced any remaining critics, celebrating his greatest Grand Prix success.

The worst possible scenario: Seconds into the race David Coulthard collides with team-mate Mika Hakkinen.

nael's Shadow

Austrian GP

Putting one over on Bernie: Only a few fans manage to watch Formula One without buying a ticket.

But the man who was most talked about in the week leading up to the race wasn't even there. The possible cause of Michael Schumacher's spectacular crash at Silverstone was so much on the mind of the collective Formula One world it had almost become an obsession. And perhaps more important was the question as to how long it would be before the talented German would again grace Formula One fans with his unique skill. Theory after theory gained credence among the pundits, none of which, in this charged atmosphere seemed ridiculous enough not to be taken seriously. Investigative motor sport journalists rushed to prove or disprove Heinz-Harald Frentzen's theory that a hand-operated accelerator such as those found on motorcycles could allow his compatriot to return to the starting grid as soon as the German Grand Prix one week later.

Only one thing was certain going into the Austrian Grand Prix at Spielberg: Michael Schumacher's spectacular crash at Silverstone had blown the battle for the 1999 Formula One world championship wide open. Schumacher's longtime understudy, Northern Ireland's Eddie Irvine had already been pushing for changes in his contract following his victory at Melbourne in the first race of the season. Now, ahead of the Austrian Grand Prix his wish had come true. With Schumacher out indefinitely, Ferrari named him

their new number one driver while the German was in rehab, throwing their entire technical support behind him, as their only serious contender for the world championship. Now though the man from Ulster would be subject to a new pressure which had hitherto always been placed firmly on Schumacher's broad shoulders - the pressure to win.

With Irvine effectively having replaced Schumacher, Ferrari had to find someone to replace

Right: Completely committed: Eddie Irvine didn't let damage to his Ferrari slow him down. **Below:** A dream come true - Mika Salo's first race for Ferrari.

Determination of a champion: Mika Hakkinen fought back to finish third.

Happy Heinz-Harald: Frentzen drove another flawless race.

A lot of smoke over nothing. Olivier Panis practised starts - without success.

Irvine as number two. They turned to a driver well-known in Formula One circles, the "other Mika" - Mika Salo. The 32 year old Finn brought with him the experience of 71 Grand Prix races, three of those having come earlier in the current season when he helped BAR out of a jam by filling in for the injured Riccardo Zonta. Not only that, but with his seventh and eighth place finishes, he turned in the new team's best performances of the season. At about the same time Michael Schumacher was slamming into a row of tyres at Silverstone, Salo was at Heathrow boarding a plane to Helsinki. He'd hardly arrived home when the phone rang with his manager Mike Greasley on the other end. Greasley, a close friend of Jean Todt from their rally world championship days, informed Salo that a ticket to Bologna was waiting for him at the airport, and the flight was leaving in an hour. A long-time dream was about to become reality.

What very few people know is that this was to be his second trip to Maranello. The first time Salo was there not as Ferrari's new Formula One driver, but as a customer. He was there to take delivery of his new Spyder 355. This time though the Finnish talent was in for more than just the standard tour of the plant.

Salo returned to Helsinki to get married.

"I felt welcome from the very first second", beamed Ferrari's first Scandinavian driver since the more or less unsuccessful Swede Stefan Johannsson (1985 -1986, 32 races, no wins) "Ross Brawn is a nice chap and we had a very long and detailed discussion." One day later Salo was out on Ferrari's Fiorano test track on his first laps in

the F399. "It was really something special", smiled the second-fastest Finn. But just three days later Salo had to temporarily put his work at Fiorano on hold to return to Helsinki where he was to marry his girlfriend of many years, Noriko Endo.

There was no dispute over where the happy couple should spend their honeymoon, the unanimous choice - Spielberg, Austria. Salo's debut as a Ferrari driver went better than expected: with a lap time of 1.12.414 minutes, the Finn qualified in a respectable seventh, just a half second behind the driver ahead of him. The first couple of rows in the starting grid though were filled with familiar faces: Mika Hakkinen, followed by David Coulthard, then Irvine, Jordan's Heinz-Harald Frentzen, and Rubens Barrichello.

Many Formula One "experts" believed Mika Hakkinen's road to a second consecutive world championship would begin in the small alpine republic. Who could stop him? If the experts were infallible there would be no reason to run the races, you could feed the information into a computer, and know the winner in a matter of seconds. The Austrian Grand Prix proved why that isn't the case.

The experts were right about at least one thing: Mika Hakkinen took off from his pole position and established himself right away at the front of the pack. The 22 cars made it through the "Castrol" curve without incident. That couldn't be said about the next one though, the "Remus" curve. David

Left: Although Jean Alesi passed the Benetton driven by Alexander Wurz (right), later he overheard an instruction to refuel. Below: A matter of interpretation, Tora Takagis' idea of the ideal driving line.

Exception: In Austria Ralf Schumacher committed a rare error.

Austrian GP

Coulthard made a braking error approaching the curve at the end of a straightaway on which the cars can hit a top speed of 290 kph. He hit Hakkinen ahead of him resulting in no major damage to either car, but with huge consequences for his team-mate. Hakkinen was thrown into a spin, and by the time he was able to re-enter the race, the entire rest of the field had cruised by. Not just that, but in the resulting fray the front wing of Mika Salo´s Ferrari was demolished in a dispute with the rear spoiler of Johnny Herbert's Ford.

Ross Brawn opened up his bag of tricks.

"A nightmare", moaned Coulthard later. "The worst thing that could have happened to me, knocking my own team-mate out of the race before the end of the lap." However the accident did nothing to hinder Coulthard´s progress. Having ended the race for his team-mate, Coulthard found himself in the lead, followed by Rubens Barrichello, who had slipped past Irvine in the "Remus" curve. The three of them then promptly began to take off from the rest, including Frentzen, Villeneuve (!), Ralf Schumacher, and a surprising Pedro Diniz, who had had a great start out of 16th in the grid, and has already climbed into ninth. By the time of his pit stop he'd even made it up to fifth.

Meanwhile, something exciting was developing way at the back of the pack. Sauber driver Jean Alesi, who'd started from 17th after a disastrous qualifying, and Mika Hakkinen both began quests to overtake as many competitors as possible. Twenty laps later the two of them had made their ways all the way up to places six and seven. By lap 30 the McLaren driver had climbed into fifth, and was continuing to complete faster laps than anyone else.

On lap 39 Coulthard, held up by slow pokes who didn't feel like letting him past, stopped in the pits to refuel. In 10.5 seconds he was back on the track. Barrichello, who had paid his mechanics a visit moments earlier, had taken 12.5 seconds. Hakkinen´s pit stop on lap 40 though took just 9.6 seconds. Eddie Irvine was out of sight.

Ferrari's master tactician Ross Brawn had brought his bag of tricks with him to Austria too, this time the former nuclear physicist's inspired strategic manoeuvres were for the benefit of Eddie Irvine. For his part the Northern Irishman was driving flawlessly, and had opened up a lead of 22.6 seconds on the Scotsman by the time he steered into the pits on lap 44. After a masterful pit stop by the Ferrari mechanics, Irvine returned to the race still well in the lead, and it was clear that the silver arrows had been beaten. Irvine had proved his critics wrong - once again.

While Irvine was well away, there were still a few interesting developments behind him. Rubens Barrichello had already surrendered third

Eddie Irvine didn't give David Coulthard a chance.

Sporting directors: Haug (Mercedes, left), Berger (BMW).

place to Hakkinen when the Brazilian was forced to retire on lap 55 due to engine failure. That was a lucky break for Heinz-Harald Frentzen. The German inherited fourth from "Rubinho", followed by Austria´s Alexander Wurz and Pedro Diniz. The underrated Sauber driver thus secured his third world championship point.

Michael Schumacher though had the last word. "I'm pleased that Ferrari won", he told reporters through his press spokesman. "We obviously had the right strategy." As if his former understudy had nothing to do with it...

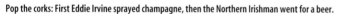

Pop the corks: First Eddie Irvine sprayed champagne, then the Northern Irishman went for a beer.

Statistics

Course length:	4,319 km
Distance of race:	71 (= 306,649 km)
Start time:	13.00 UTC
Weather on day of race:	overcast, cool
Attendance:	55 000
1998 Results:	1. Mika Hakkinen (FIN, McLaren-Mercedes MP4/13), 1 h 30'44"086
	2. David Coulthard (GB, McLaren-Mercedes MP4/13), +5"289 s
	3. Michael Schumacher (D, Ferrari F300), +39"093 s
Pole position 1998:	Giancarlo Fisichella (I, Benetton-Playlife B198), 1'29"598 m
Fastest Lap 1998:	David Coulthard (McLaren-Mercedes MP4/13), 1'12"878 m
Fastest pit stop 1998:	Esteban Tuero (RA, Minardi-Ford M198), 15"285 s

A Fast Course With Some Good Opportunities to Overtake

"The A-1 is an interesting track with its up and downhill stretches and fast average lap times. The mixture of fast and slow curves provide variety, but the first two are too sharp and there aren't any real high speed curves. On the other hand this alpine course offers some good opportunities for overtaking."

Eddie Irvine

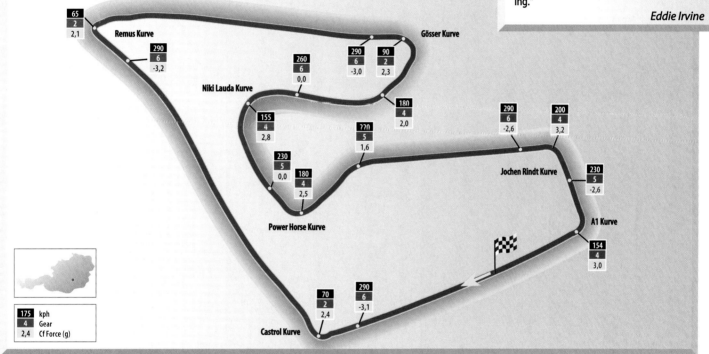

Results

Driver	Team	Pit stops	Laps	Time (hours)	Average speed	Behind 1st	prev. driver
1. Eddie Irvine	Ferrari	1	71	1 h 28'12"438	208,587	–	–
2. David Coulthard	McLaren-Mercedes	1	71	1 h 28'12"751	208,575	0"313 s	–
3. Mika Hakkinen	McLaren-Mercedes	1	71	1 h 28'34"720	207,712	22"282 s	21"969 s
4. Heinz-Harald Frentzen	Jordan-Mugen-Honda	1	71	1 h 29'05"241	206,526	52"803 s	30"521 s
5. Alexander Wurz	Benetton-Playlife	1	71	1 h 29'18"796	206,004	1'06"358 m	13"555 s
6. Pedro Diniz	Sauber-Petronas	2	71	1 h 29'23"371	205,828	1'10"933 m	4"575 s
7. Jarno Trulli	Prost-Peugeot	1	70	1 h 28'28"541	205,025	1 lap	1 lap
8. Damon Hill	Jordan-Mugen-Honda	1	70	1 h 28'29"690	204,981	1 lap	1"149 s
9. Mika Salo	Ferrari	2	70	1 h 28'35"747	204,747	1 lap	6"057 s
10. Olivier Panis	Prost-Peugeot	1	70	1 h 28'40"035	204,582	1 lap	4"288 s
11. Marc Gené	Minardi-Ford	1	70	1 h 29'25"126	202,863	1 lap	45"091 s
12. Giancarlo Fisichella [1]	Benetton-Playlife	1	68	1 h 25'51"478	205,240	retirement	retirement
13. Luca Badoer	Minardi-Ford	3	68	1 h 28'58"188	198,061	3 laps	3'06"710 m
14. Johnny Herbert	Stewart-Ford	2	67	1 h 29'20"589	194,333	4 laps	1 lap
15. Ricardo Zonta [1]	BAR-Supertec	1	63	1 h 19'59"481	204,094	retirement	retirement

Driver	Team	Pit stops	in lap	Reason f. retiring	Position before retiring
Rubens Barrichello	Stewart-Ford	1	56	engine	4
Jean Alesi	Sauber-Petronas	1	50	fuel shortage	6
Pedro de la Rosa	TWR-Arrows	1	39	spun out	16
Alessandro Zanardi	Williams-Supertec	0	36	fuel shortage	13
Jacques Villeneuve	BAR-Supertec	0	35	power transmission	12
Toranosuke Takagi	TWR-Arrows	0	26	engine	15
Ralf Schumacher	Williams-Supertec	0	9	spun out	6

1) Didn´t complete race but counted due to distance driven.

Austrian GP

Starting Grid

1 Mika Häkkinen (FIN) [1]
McLaren-Mercedes MP4/14-5
1'10"954 m (294,7 km/h)

2 David Coulthard (GB)
McLaren-Mercedes MP4/14-7
1'11"153 m (298,3 km/h)

4 Eddie Irvine (GB)
Ferrari F399/191
1'11"973 m (293,1 km/h)

8 Heinz-Harald Frentzen (D)
Jordan-Mugen-Honda 199/5
1'12"266 m (299,7 km/h)

16 Rubens Barrichello (BR)
Stewart-Ford SF3/4
1'12"342 m (297,8 km/h)

17 Johnny Herbert (GB)
Stewart-Ford SF3/5
1'12"488 m (297,2 km/h)

3 Mika Salo (FIN)
Ferrari F399/195
1'12"514 m (292,3 km/h)

6 Ralf Schumacher (D)
Williams-Supertec FW21/6
1'12"515 m (292,6 km/h)

22 Jacques Villeneuve (CDN)
BAR-Supertec 01/7
1'12"833 m (292,2 km/h)

10 Alexander Wurz (A)
Benetton-Playlife B199/4
1'12"850 m (305,5 km/h)

7 Damon Hill (GB)
Jordan-Mugen-Honda 199/4
1'12"901 m (293,0 km/h)

9 Giancarlo Fisichella (I)
Benetton-Playlife B199/7
1'12"924 m (302,9 km/h)

19 Jarno Trulli (I)
Prost-Peugeot AP02/7
1'12"999 m (289,5 km/h)

5 Alessandro Zanardi (I)
Williams-Supertec FW21/5
1'13"101 m (294,4 km/h)

23 Ricardo Zonta (BR)
BAR-Supertec 01/5
1'13"172 m (290,4 km/h)

12 Pedro Diniz (BR)
Sauber-Petronas C18/5
1'13"223 m (291,8m km/h)

11 Jean Alesi (F)
Sauber-Petronas C18/6
1'13"226 m (291,3 km/h)

18 Olivier Panis (F)
Prost-Peugeot AP02/5
1'13"457 m (297,6 km/h)

20 Luca Badoer (I)
Minardi-Ford-Zetec-R M01/1
1'13"606 m (290,4 km/h)

15 Toranosuke Takagi (J)
TWR-Arrows A20/2
1'13"641 m (294,2 km/h)

14 Pedro de la Rosa (E)
TWR-Arrows A20/4
1'14"139 m (290,4 km/h)

21 Marc Gené (E)
Minardi-Ford-Zetec-R M01/4
1'14"363 m (292,2 km/h)

107-percent time: 1'15"921 m

1.) Lap time (top speed in qualifying).

Best Laps

In Training on Friday (m)			
1. Hill	1'13"303	12. Zanardi	!'14"049
2. Häkkinen	1'13"325	13. Badoer	!'14"203
3. Coulthard	1'13"376	14. Gené	1'14"333
4. Zonta	1'13"685	15. Frentzen	1'14"558
5. Alesi	1'13"696	16. Salo	1'14"608
6. R. Schumacher	1'13"711	17. Trulli	1'14"724
7. Diniz	1'13"740	18. Fisichella	1'14"785
8. Villeneuve	1'13"840	19. Panis	1'15"028
9. Irvine	1'13"883	20. Wurz	!'15"107
10. Barrichello	1'13"923	21. de la Rosa	1'15"651
11. Herbert	!'14"008	22. Takagi	1'16"067

In the Race on Sunday (m)			
1. Häkkinen	1'12"107	12. Wurz	1'13"654
2. Herbert	1'12"641	13. Hill	1'13"960
3. Irvine	1'12"787	14. Villeneuve	1'13"977
4. Coulthard	1'12"855	15. Zonta	1'14"063
5. Diniz	1'13"093	16. Trulli	1'14"112
6. Frentzen	1'13"176	17. Zanardi	1'14"381
7. Alesi	1'13"228	18. Gené	1'14"517
8. Barrichello	1'13"278	19. Badoer	1'14"622
9. Panis	1'13"465	20. de la Rosa	1'14"914
10. Salo	1'13"481	21 Takagi	1'15"361
11. Fisichella	1'13"579	22. R. Schumacher	1'16"173

Total Pit Stop Times

Lap		Time (s)	Lap		Time (s)	Lap		Time (s)
1	Herbert	308"686	39	Coulthard	28"174	52	Diniz	24"802
2	Badoer	41"011	39	Herbert	28"512			
3	Salo	37"716	40	Häkkinen	27"429			
20	Badoer	28"890	41	Salo	26"754			
24	Diniz	27"706	43	Fisichella	28"413			
25	Alesi	26"127	44	Irvine	26"545			
30	de la Rosa	31"683	44	Frentzen	26"611			
35	Gené	30"547	44	Wurz	27"225			
36	Badoer	34"606	45	Trulli	26"150			
38	Barrichello	30"620	45	Hill	27"389			
38	Zonta	29"764	46	Panis	25"921			

The Race Lap by Lap

Start: The two McLaren drivers get off to the best start. Ahead of the Remus curve Coulthard tries to sneak past Hakkinen but throws his team-mate into a spin. The reigning world champion continues the race in last place. Salo rear-ends Herbert, who has to head to the pits for a new rear wing. Coulthard leads ahead of Barrichello, Irvine and Frentzen. Diniz moves up to ninth from 16th in the starting grid. **Lap 4:** After three laps with a broken front wing Salo has the nose of his Ferrari replaced in the pits. **Lap 8:** Hakkinen overtakes Hill and is already in 13th. The leading order remains the same. **Lap 9:** R. Schumacher spins off the track in a duel with Diniz. **Lap 11:** Hakkinen passes Trulli and is 11th. Coulthard is already 10 seconds ahead of Barrichello, Irvine is just behind in third. **Lap 19:** In the last four laps Alesi and Hakkinen have passed Wurz, Zonta, Fisichella and Villeneuve. **Lap 34:** The world champion hasn't given up: He seizes fourth from Frentzen. **Lap 36:** Zanardi is out after running out of fuel. **Lap 37:** Before the leaders begin heading to the pits the order is: Coulthard, Barrichello, Irvine, Hakkinen, Frentzen. **Lap 39:** The leading Scot heads to the pits, Irvine remains on the track and drives record laps on an almost empty fuel tank. **Lap 45:** When the Northern Irishman returns to the track following his pit stop, he's in the lead. **Lap 50:** Hakkinen moves into third ahead of Barrichello. **Lap 51:** Alesi forgets to refuel and his engine dies. **Lap 56:** Barrichello is forced out due to engine problems. Frentzen takes fourth place. Out in front Irvine is keeping Coulthard at bay. **Lap 71:** Irvine crosses the finish line first ahead of Coulthard in hot pursuit and gives Ferrari renewed hopes for a world championship. Hakkinen finishes third, Frentzen is in the points yet again.

Standings

Driver/Points					
1. Mika Häkkinen	44		12. Johnny Herbert	2	
2. Eddie Irvine	42		13. Jean Alesi	1	
3. Michael Schumacher	32		Pedro de la Rosa	1	
4. Heinz-Harald Frentzen	29		Olivier Panis	1	
5. David Coulthard	28		Jarno Trulli	1	
6. Ralf Schumacher	19				
7. Giancarlo Fisichella	13				
8. Rubens Barrichello	10				
9. Damon Hill	5				
10. Alexander Wurz	3				
Pedro Diniz	3				

Team	Points
1. Ferrari	74
2. McLaren-Mercedes	72
3. Jordan-Mugen-Honda	34
4. Williams-Supertec	19
5. Benetton-Playlife	16
6. Stewart-Ford	12
7. Sauber-Petronas	4
8. Prost-Peugeot	2
9. TWR-Arrows	1

Alone in the forest: Benetton´s Giancarlo Fisichella had a rough time on the A-1.

Buying into the image

The face of Formula One motor racing is about to change - radically. Where one once found an abundance of independent teams like McLaren or Williams pursuing their passion for motor racing, soon it will be multinational car making firms starting from the first row. These global players don't measure success simply in trophies and laurel wreaths, but in turnover, profits and shareholder value.

Back in the 1950's Mercedes, Ferrari, Maserati, or Alfa Romeo were the storied names of Formula One motor racing. But then the technically superior teams like Lotus, Brabham an Cooper began their rise, spelling the downfall of the big names. Today a new generation of big names are emerging on the Formula One scene. For a long time many of them were simply involved in the sport as the companies providing the engines, but now increasingly, they're stepping into roles as fully fledged team partners. As we enter a new century, the car makers are getting back into the game in such a big way, that it's just a matter of time before they establish themselves as actual teams in their own right once again. For example Mercedes has taken over a large part of McLaren, and half-way through the season Ford bought Stewart. The Ford bosses are dreaming of building up a top Formula One squad under the name Jaguar, just like Fiat did with Ferrari following their purchase of the Italian team in the 1960's. It's not just the big corporations' technical resources and their reputations that Formula One bosses appreciate, but their financial power is also welcome, too. It may be possible to temporarily delay the impact of the loss of adver-

tising revenue from tobacco companies, but by 2006 at the latest, this will hit the sport hard, when a European Union ban on tobacco companies advertising sporting events comes into effect.

The involvement of the car makers is different from their involvement all those years ago in two respects: first, back then it was companies which were already well known as motor sporting brands which got involved in Formula One in order to highlight their technical capabilities. Today big corporations get involved in an effort to spruce up their images, hoping the consumer will associate some of that sporting image with some of their less than exciting consumer products, even if that product bears not the slightest resemblance to a Formula One car.

If this works it will be a case of back to the future for some companies. Take BMW for example. If Williams' new partner, who get on board in the 2000 season begin celebrating victories on the podium as they hope they will, this will allow them to market these victories as being victories for BMW, not the victories of some plant in central England which is vaguely connected to the German car maker. BMW is joining Williams as an equal partner. The fact that the

team will be known as BMW-Williams is a clear indication that there is no question of a return to conditions as they were back in the 1980's when BMW was supplying the world championship turbo engines for Brabham, but had to fight tooth and nail just to get tiny stickers with its logo on the sides of the cars. However the Bavarian Motor Works have repeatedly stated that it is not interested in actually buying into the team.

In this way the Munich company differs from its arch rivals on the German autobahn: Mercedes has significantly expanded its activities on the Formula One circuit beyond this role and these days only does business with partners, who, as Sporting Director Norbert Haug puts it, "fit into the Mercedes-Benz system". These are stable long-term partnerships which are based on buying into those major partners. Large shares of both engine development company Ilmor (25 per cent), and of TAG McLaren (40 per cent), mean Daimler Chrysler has a significant say in their activities. It's not just on the Grand Prix track that Mercedes is involved in these partnerships either. One non-Formula One project has resulted with the development of the Mercedes SLR sports car.

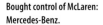

Bought control of McLaren: Mercedes-Benz.

Has financial control of Ferrari: Fiat

Renault: The trendsetters of the '80's may be back in 2001.

Honda: Supplier to both Jordan and BAR in the 2000 season.

Leaving: Peugeot hasn't been satisfied with its returns.

Ford's leaving, Jaguar's on its way: The American concern has renamed its Stewart Team for the 2000 season.

Preparing his biggest deal so far: Formula One supremo Bernie Ecclestone, replacing tobacco sponsors with car makers and now planning to go onto the stock market.

Formula One has never been so popular...

Even if Formula One supremo Bernie Ecclestone does need the involvement of these big motoring concerns, so far they've been overplaying any traditional links. The best example is they way they welcomed Jaguar "back to Formula One". While Jaguar does have a proud tradition in motor racing in general, the brand has never ever been represented on the Formula One circuit. However Jaguar's parent company Ford, which willingly agreed to leave the circuit to make way for the new team, still holds the record as the engine maker with the most all-time Grand Prix victories (175).

The move is really all about the marketing of the Ford corporation's consumer products. "We bought the Stewart team and engine producer Cosworth in order to allow us to pursue our long-term strategy directly and unfiltered", explains Ford boss Jac Nasser. Project leader Neil Ressler adds: "Motor sport must support our brands." For Ford's subsidiary Jaguar, entering the Formula One circuit projects a young, sporty image, which they hope will allow them to successfully compete with Mercedes and Ferrari in the consumer market as well. And as Jaguar boss Wolfgang Reitzle hastens to point out, there's no hiding the fact that BMW, just like Jaguar won't just be measuring their Formula One success in terms of Grand Prix wins, but in associated increases in consumer sales as well.

Seen in this light, Honda bucked the trend with its decision to get involved as an engine producer for British American Racing. The Japanese concern dropped the idea of building a chassis for their prized engine, and put their British Formula One subsidiary up for sale. This means BAR and Jordan will profit from their engine development even more intensively next season.

Another Japanese car maker will be watching with particular interest to see how Honda does next season. One of it's main competitors, Toyota has already taken the decision to enter Formula One racing. However, they're far from decided on whether to enter a car of their own, or simply deliver the engine. In the final analysis which road Toyota choose to take will depend on the Grand Prix and public relations results of their main rival.

The last of the independent engine producers is Supertec, and this company is widely believed to simply be keeping the seat warm for Renault, which is expected to re-enter the sport in 2001. The trend setters of the late 1970's, when they revolutionised the Formula One world with their turbo engine and their own chassis, are expected to enter a partnership with Alain Prost. The four time world champion driver, who was disappointed by his association with Peugeot, and who recently moved his headquarters nearer to Renault's research centre the "Technocentre" would likely be willing to allow Renault to buy a significant share of his team.

But the fact that marketing seems to be the main factor in deciding whether car companies do or don't get involved in Formula One racing brings with it hidden dangers. While teams themselves often remain in the sport for decades, the engine producers tend to come and go, depending upon their current marketing strategy. Because there are only three places available on the podium, a car maker that doesn't enjoy success very quickly, can just as quickly become discouraged, because when it comes to marketing through sporting events, nobody likes a loser.

Despite the risk of failure though, a lot of multi-national car makers obviously think Formula One is a good deal. With the sport more popular than ever the value of the publicity of the international television exposure that goes with it may be incalculable.

Partner and Sponsor: BMW doesn't want to buy Williams.

Ford is out: The most successful Grand Prix car maker is leaving...

...to make way for its Jaguar subsidiary.

About to enter the Formula One, but in what capacity?

"Mika 2" lets Irv

ne through

Three races, three certain victories thrown away: At Hockenheim Mika Hakkinen didn't make any progress towards defending his title either. Surprisingly the victorious Eddie Irvine wasn't in any mood for a celebration.

Left: Mika Hakkinen in hot pursuit of a win at Hockenheim - in vain. Below: Super-sub - Ferrari Team Boss Jean Todt congratulates Mika Salo.

Always giving it his all: Jacques Villeneuve flew off the track in the very first curve.

If any further proof was needed, the German Grand Prix proved once and for all that the battle between McLaren-Mercedes driver Mika Hakkinen and Ferrari's Eddie Irvine was quite similar to the old story of the turtle and the hare, but with one exception: no matter how quickly the McLaren driver took off ahead of his Northern Irish challenger, the only one of them who would cross the finish line would be the Ferrari. If it wasn't one thing getting in the way of victory for the flying Finn it was another: a defective wheel fastening at Silverstone, being hit by his own team-mate and the lack of a team order at the A-1 Ring and a refuelling disaster and blown tyre at Hockenheim. Put it all together and despite the fact that Michael Schumacher, the man expected to be his main challenger was out for the better part of

The parade didn't last long - Barrichello was knocked out early.

Strong effort Heinz-Harald Frentzen had the second fastest lap in qualifying.

the season, it's almost a wonder Hakkinen didn't chose to put himself out of his own misery by committing suicide in southern Germany. In his first three Grand Prix races without the German former champion, the McLaren driver had earned all of four points. Instead of marching confi-

Made it onto the podium at Hockenheim: Heinz-Harald Frentzen.

"A once in a lifetime feeling", smiled Heinz-Harald.

dently towards the world championship McLaren-Mercedes were threatening to challenge BAR for the title of biggest Formula One laughing stock. After the German Grand Prix Eddie Irvine helped rub salt into their wounds when he observed, "McLaren shot themselves in the foot".

But first things first. The long Hockenheim course, with its particular characteristics is known for separating the good from the bad in terms of Formula One cars. This is because the straight-aways through the woods demand that the wings be set absolutely parallel to the track to ensure that the aerodynamics are absolutely perfect, to allow the driver to push the car to it´s very limit. Naturally the car engine's performance is a key factor. Then the drivers are forced to drive around the narrow "Motodrom" with practically no assistance from the spoilers. This separates the wheat from the chaff: the only cars that do well on this stage are cars with sufficient mechanical grip, cars with chassis which hold the road well even without the help of the downward force of air produced by the spoilers.

The top speed measurements ahead of the Jim Clark chicane told the story: the strongest in the field were the Ferraris and the Mercedes which were reaching speeds of up to 355.7 kph.

But so were another team's cars - the Sauber-Petronas are also outfitted with Ferrari's V10 engine. In the Motodrom, the stadium area, the best performers were Mercedes, Heinz-Harald Frentzen´s Jordan-Mugen-Honda and Ralf Schumacher´s Williams - which was most remarkable considering the fact that Schumacher got such a good performance out of the inferior Supertec engine. The Ferrari drivers on the other hand were losing tenths of seconds negotiating the winding curves in the stadium area - time they had gained on the straightaways.

The biggest surprise in Saturday's qualifying was Heinz-Harald Frentzen, even if Mika Hakkinen did edge him out for the pole position at the very last minute due to a lap which was five one hundredths of a second faster. The hundreds of thousands of spectators got quite a show. While Germany's biggest star was out due to injury, the man usually in his shadow seemed to be step-

The master of qualifying: In Germany too Mika Hakkinen took pole position.

Poor performance: In the final training session Eddie Irvine found himself behind his team-mate.

Phantom of the track: Michael Schumacher via satellite.

Walk much? Ricardo Zonta failed to finish again.

Get well wishers - Michael Schumacher fans.

When Finns celebrate: Mika fans in Hockenheim - they didn't specify which Mika.

ping into his footsteps. "It´s a once in a lifetime feeling", smiled the son of a German undertaker, understandably proud of his performance.

The Monaco resident though couldn't have been proud of his start to the race itself. He developed too much wheel spin and in relative terms crawled away from the starting line. Before the first curve David Coulthard and Ferrari's reserve man Mika Salo sped past. Eddie Irvine´s start wasn't much better. He allowed Rubens Barrichello in the lighter Stewart-Ford to trap him behind Frentzen. The fifth best in qualifying effectively wound up beginning his assault on the lead from sixth. "I noticed that the oil temperature warning light was coming on", explained the Northern Irishman later, "so I tried to avoid the slipstreams of the car in front of me".

The man in front of him was soon Heinz-Harald Frentzen: the Rhinelander´s Jordan was relatively heavy, with his team having opted for just one pit stop, just as had most of the rest of the teams. Rubins Barrichello though was planning two pit stops and, with less fuel in the tank, was

able to go on the attack. He quickly made use of his weight advantage, overtaking the German with little trouble on the third lap. But the Brazilian wasn't smiling for long - on the sixth lap his car's hydraulics system failed. "I couldn't accelerate and I couldn't shift gears", complained the frustrated South American. "It's about time we

Fisichella got no help from team-mate Alex Wurz.

stopped giving away points so unnecessarily."

Similar thoughts must have been going through the head of BAR´s number one driver Jacques Villeneuve: in the 10th race of the season the French-Canadian failed yet again to make it to the finish line. This time however Villeneuve couldn't blame it on his mechanically troubled racer. He made a mistake braking going into the

first curve. He spun out, taking Sauber driver Pedro Diniz with him. Giancarlo Fisichella though was possibly even more annoyed for again finishing out of the points. He'd got off to a good start, but team-mate Alexander Wurz got off to a fantastic start, moving up five positions. Later though the Austrian wound up obstructing the Italian. "I was faster than him and I wanted to overtake him so as not to fall out of reach of the leaders", explained an embittered "Fisico" later. The long-legged Austrian though wasn't co-operating: at the entrance to the Motodrom the two blue and white cars made contact, with Fisichella winding up in the gravel and demolishing both the front wing and the front suspension system of his Benetton. It was more damage than his car could handle, and on lap seven his German Grand Prix was over.

At the front of the pack Mika Hakkinen was defending his lead, but only just - the rest of the leaders were hardly two seconds behind him. In second place was "Mika 2", the Mika of the Salo variety. The second fastest Finn found himself

Much ado about nothing: Minardi driver Luca Badoer finished out of the points yet again.

Didn't let things get him down: Ralf Schumacher was fourth despite having a slower car.

under intense pressure from David Coulthard. The Scotsman was swerving impatiently from side to side in the rear-view mirror of Salo´s Ferrari. On lap 10 "DC" launched his attack: in the "Ostkurve" chicane he manoeuvred his McLaren-Mercedes up alongside the Finn. But the apparent attempt to overtake "the other Mika" ended in failure. "I wasn't trying to overtake him", the handsome Scotsman with the square jaw told reporters later. "Salo had hit the brakes surprisingly early, I was just trying to avoid him." In addition to the unplanned trip to the pits, Coulthard was later assessed a stop-and-go penalty. On this day anything better than fifth was simply beyond the McLaren-Mercedes driver's reach.

For team-mate Mika Hakkinen though things couldn't have looked better - until his pit stop that is. It was the refuelling system that would transform what should have been a routine pit stop into a McLaren-Mercedes disaster. By the time the mechanics had finally gone for the fuelling system reserved for Coulthard, a pit stop eternity had passed. Instead of being in and out of there in the usual seven seconds, it took all of 24.3 seconds. Hakkinen returned to the race having dropped from first all the way back to fourth. It was an angry but determined Finnish driver who returned to the track. He caught up with Frentzen in the woods and was hoping to return to the Motodrom in third place when it happened: at well over 300 kph one of his rear tyres blew up, sending the defending world champion into a wild spin off the track, just missing the barrier, crossing the asphalt, skidding over the gravel, before coming to a jarring stop in a stack

Great show: Not only did Michael Schumacher´s replacement turn in a good performance, he could have won the German Grand Prix.

A scary moment for Mika Hakkinen and all Formula One fans: As he enters the Motodrom one of the tyres on his McLaren-Mercedes explodes. He misses the barrier by a margin of millimetres (above), before skidding across the gravel (left) and into a stack of tyres. Unlike in Australia in 1994, this time he is not injured.

Couldn't convert a fabulous start into points: Alexander Wurz.

A Genius and his driver: Ross Brawn (right) and Eddie Irvine.

of tyres. "Suddenly Mika's car swung out, parts were flying all over the place, and my vision was clouded by tyre debris", reported Frentzen later, who was only a few metres behind and

"I gave the trophy to Mika Salo - it was his victory."

therefore had a front row view of the mishap. "I had to hit the brakes quite hard, because I didn't known where Mika's car was at that moment. After his crash I was really worried about Mika, but then I saw him getting out of his car uninjured on a large video screen."

After that the results of the German Grand Prix were already as good as cast in stone. Mika Salo, who found himself leading a Grand Prix race for the first time in his Formula one career let Irvine pass him to allow the Northern Irishman to take over the lead. Then it was Salo who was faced with the constant pressure of Heinz-Harald Frentzen. "I even passed a message along to Eddie via the pit crew, asking him to drive faster," Salo told reporters later. What he didn't know at the time was that Irvine was again battling against abnormally high oil pressure.

Apart from that Ralf Schumacher drove a perfect race once again. Despite being saddled with an inferior car, by the sixth lap the Williams driver had fought his way from 11th in the starting grid to a place in the points, and improved even upon that, crossing the finish line in fourth.

Just married, and now her man makes an appearance on the podium in his first race for Ferrari: Noriko Salo (left) had good news to send home to Japan.

A shortened work day: Pedro Diniz was torpedoed at the start by Villeneuve.

"He drove every lap with total commitment", said Team Boss Frank Williams, who's known to pay compliments as willingly as handing out pay rises. Ralf's team-mate Alessandro Zanardi on the other hand fell victim to a failed differential on the rear axle. Just about everything that could go wrong, seemed to go wrong for the man who left the Champ Car Series to return to Formula One. Eddie Irvine had a lot to celebrate, but wasn't in a celebratory mood. "I gave the winner's trophy to Salo - today's win was his."

Statistics

10th Race in the World Championship 1999, Hockenheimring (D), 1st August 1999

Course length:	6,823 km
Distance of race:	45 (= 307,035 km)
Start time:	13.00 UTC
Weather on day of race:	clear and hot
Attendance:	100 000
1998 Results:	1. Mika Hakkinen (FIN, McLaren-Mercedes MP4/13), 1 h 20'47"984
	2. David Coulthard (GB, McLaren-Mercedes MP4/13), +0"427 s
	3. Jacques Villeneuve (CDN, Williams-Mecachrome FW20), +2"578 s
Pole position 1998:	Mika Hakkinen (McLaren-Mercedes MP4/13), 1'41"838 m
Fastest Lap 1998:	Mika Hakkinen (McLaren-Mercedes MP4/13), 1'44"946 m
Fastest pit stop 1998:	Ralf Schumacher (D, Jordan-Mugen-Honda 198), 27"554 s

In terms of set up it's difficult to find the optimal compromise

"The combination of long straightaways through the woods, where we reached the highest speeds all season, and the winding curves of the Motodrom is unique on the Grand Prix calendar. You need find the right compromise between low air resistance on the straightaways and the most possible grip in the curves."

Eddie Irvine

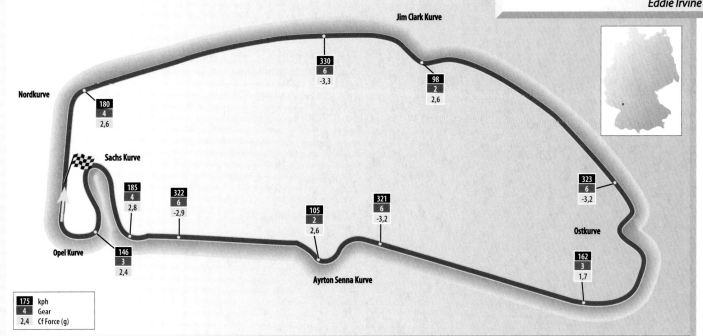

Results

Driver	Team	Pit stops	Laps	Time (hours)	Average speed	Behind 1st	prev. driver
1. Eddie Irvine	Ferrari	1	45	1 h 21'58"594	224,723	–	–
2. Mika Salo	Ferrari	1	45	1 h 21'59"601	224,677	1"007 s	–
3. Heinz-Harald Frentzen	Jordan-Mugen-Honda	1	45	1 h 22'03"789	224,468	5"195 s	25"582 s
4. Ralf Schumacher	Williams-Supertec	1	45	1 h 22'11"403	224,140	12"809 s	0"378 s
5. David Coulthard	McLaren-Mercedes	3	45	1 h 22'15"417	223,957	16"823 s	10"817 s
6. Olivier Panis	Prost-Peugeot	2	45	1 h 22'28"473	223,367	29"879 s	15"037 s
7. Alexander Wurz	Benetton-Playlife	1	45	1 h 22'31"927	223,211	33"333 s	0"971 s
8. Jean Alesi	Sauber-Petronas	3	45	1 h 23'09"885	221,513	1'11"291 s	13"976 s
9. Marc Gené	Minardi-Ford	1	45	1 h 23'46"912	219,881	1'48"318 m	3"455 s
10. Luca Badoer	Minardi-Ford	1	44	1 h 22'14"172	219,036	1 lap	0"078 s
11. Johnny Herbert [1]	Stewart-Ford	1	41	1 h 13'24"080	223,091	retirement	retirement

Driver	Team	Pit stops	in lap	Reason f. retiring	Position before retiring
Pedro de la Rosa	TWR-Arrows	1	38	crash	11
Mika Hakkinen	McLaren-Mercedes	1	26	crash	1
Alessandro Zanardi	Williams-Supertec	0	22	differential	13
Ricardo Zonta	BAR-Supertec	1	21	engine	16
Toranosuke Takagi	TWR-Arrows	0	16	engine	16
Damon Hill	Jordan-Mugen-Honda	0	14	retired	11
Jarno Trulli	Prost-Peugeot	0	11	engine	11
Giancarlo Fisichella	Benetton-Playlife	1	8	suspension	19
Rubens Barrichello	Stewart-Ford	0	7	hydraulics	19
Jacques Villeneuve	BAR-Supertec	0	1	collission	12
Pedro Diniz	Sauber-Petronas	0	1	collission	16

1) Counted due to distance driven.

German GP

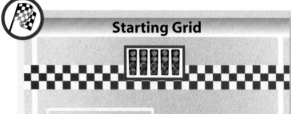

10th Race in the World Championship 1999, Hockenheimring (D), 1st August 1999

Starting Grid

1 Mika Häkkinen (FIN) [1]
McLaren-Mercedes MP4/14-2
1'42"950 m (352,0 km/h)

8 Heinz-Harald Frentzen (D)
Jordan-Mugen-Honda 199/5
1'43"000 m (349,7 km/h)

2 David Coulthard (GB)
McLaren-Mercedes MP4/14-4
1'43"288 m (351,6 km/h)

3 Mika Salo (FIN)
Ferrari F399/193
1'43"577 m (353,8 km/h)

4 Eddie Irvine (GB)
Ferrari F399/191
1'43"769 m (355,7 km/h)

16 Rubens Barrichello (BR)
Stewart-Ford SF3/4
1'43"938 m (343,4 km/h)

18 Olivier Panis (F)
Prost-Peugeot AP02/5
1'43"979 m (349,7 km/h)

7 Damon Hill (GB)
Jordan-Mugen-Honda 199/4
1'44"001 m (347,6 km/h)

19 Jarno Trulli (I)
Prost-Peugeot AP02/7
1'44"209 m (344,4 km/h)

9 Giancarlo Fisichella (I)
Benetton-Playlife B199/7
1'44"338 m (349,4 km/h)

6 Ralf Schumacher (D)
Williams-Supertec FW21/4
1'44"468 m (341,6 km/h)

22 Jacques Villeneuve (CDN)
BAR-Supertec 01/7
1'44"508 m (344,7 km/h)

10 Alexander Wurz (A)
Benetton-Playlife B199/4
1'44"522 m (348,8 km/h)

5 Alessandro Zanardi (I)
Williams-Supertec FW21/5
1'45"034 m (346,3 km/h)

21 Marc Gené (E)
Minardi-Ford-Zetec-R M01/4
1'45"331 m (342,5 km/h)

12 Pedro Diniz (BR)
Sauber-Petronas C18/5
1'45"335 m (349,2 km/h)

17 Johnny Herbert (GB)
Stewart-Ford SF3/5
1'45"454 m (350,1 km/h)

23 Ricardo Zonta (BR)
BAR-Supertec 01/5
1'45"460 m (346,5 km/h)

20 Luca Badoer (I)
Minardi-Ford-Zetec-R M01/1
1'45"917 m (344,8 km/h)

14 Pedro de la Rosa (E)
TWR-Arrows A20/4
1'45"935 m (339,6 km/h)

11 Jean Alesi (F)
Sauber-Petronas C18/6
1'45"962 m (352,4 km/h)

15 Toranosuke Takagi (J)
TWR-Arrows A20/2
1'46"209 m (340,1 km/h)

107-percent time: 1'50"156 m

1) Lap time (top speed in qualifying); 2) Ten second stop and go penalty.

Best Laps

In Training on Friday (m)

1.	Trulli	1'45"677	12.	Zanardi	1'47"043
2.	Irvine	1'46"225	13.	R. Schumacher	1'47"334
3.	Fisichella	1'46"243	14.	Diniz	1'47"513
4.	Coulthard	1'46"411	15.	Villeneuve	1'47"513
5.	Barrichello	1'46"418	16.	Alesi	1'47"551
6.	Panis	1'46"516	17.	Frentzen	1'47"802
7.	Salo	1'46"542	18.	Herbert	1'47"985
8.	Hill	1'46"851	19.	Badoer	1'48"953
9.	Wurz	1'46"859	20.	Zonta	1'48"978
10.	Häkkinen	1'46"866	21.	Takagi	1'49"059
11.	Gené	1'46"913	22.	de la Rosa	1'49"207

In the Race on Sunday (m)

1.	Coulthard	1'45"270	12.	Wurz	1'48"455
2.	Panis	1'46"823	13.	Hill	1'48"925
3.	Häkkinen	1'47"433	14.	Zonta	1'49"179
4.	Frentzen	1'47"619	15.	Trulli	1'49"285
5.	Irvine	1'47"687	16.	Zanardi	1'49"835
6.	Fisichella	1'47"785	17.	Gené	1'49"894
7.	Barrichello	1'47"788	18.	Badoer	1'49"942
8.	Salo	1'47"945	19.	Takagi	1'50"286
9.	R. Schumacher	1'48"083	20.	de la Rosa	1'50"534
10.	Alesi	1'48"334			
11.	Herbert	1'48"408			

Total Pit Stop Times

Lap		Time (s)	Lap		Time (s)	Lap	Time (s)
1	Alesi	29"324	23	Salo	28"013		
3	Fisichella	36"599	23	Herbert	29"557		
10	Coulthard	32"399	23	Wurz	27"123		
15	Zonta	41"028	24	Häkkinen	42"414		
16	Alesi	25"796	24	R. Schumacher	27"704		
18	Panis	26"089	26	Coulthard [2]	28"022		
20	Gené	30"279	28	Alesi	26"636		
21	Frentzen	28"919	30	Panis	26"567		
21	de la Rosa	31"350	39	Coulthard	25"168		
22	Irvine	27"362					
22	Badoer	29"538					

The Race Lap by Lap

Start: Salo gets off to a great start and is second behind Hakkinen heading into the Nordkurve. Coulthard out accelerates Frentzen, Barrichello slips past Irvine. At the approach to the first curve Gené bumps Villeneuve, who crashes out, taking Diniz with him. **Lap 3:** Barrichello seizes fourth place from Frentzen. Coulthard is on Salo´s tail, but can't get past. **Lap 6:** Hill is thrown from the track for the first time in a duel with Wurz. **Lap 10:** The hotly pursuing Coulthard makes contact with Salo´s rear tyre, the Scot's front wing breaks. After a planned pit stop he's in tenth. **Lap 13:** Hill makes a mistake braking in the Ostkurve. Shortly after leaving the track for the second time he retires due to brake trouble. **Lap 16:** Coulthard overtakes eighth-placed Panis on the edge of the track in the Ostkurve chicane and is assessed a stop and go penalty. **Lap 19:** Barrichello´s strong performance ends with an hydraulics failure. **Lap 22:** Irvine makes a pit stop. The Northern Irishman returns to the track ahead of Frentzen and has thus taken over third. Hakkinen leads ahead of Salo. **Lap 23:** Salo stops for fuel, but remains in second. **Lap 24:** When Hakkinen stops for fuel the crew has trouble with the fuelling system. By the time his car is refuelled from Coulthard´s pumps, Salo, Irvine, and Frentzen have all overtaken him. **Lap 26:** Hakkinen overtakes Frentzen but the left-rear tyre blows on the world champion's car as his Mercedes is travelling at more than 300 kph. The Finnish driver is sent into a spin and eventually hits a stack of tyres at a significantly reduced speed. Salo allows Irvine to take over the lead. **Lap 40:** Coulthard comes in for a regular pit stop and outfitted with fresh tyres, overtakes Panis. **Lap 41:** Herbert, in fifth place is forced to retire due to a defective gear box. **Lap 45:** Frentzen can't catch the two leaders. Irvine wins ahead of Salo, R. Schumacher ends a lonely race in fourth.

Standings

Driver/Points

1.	Eddie Irvine	52
2.	Mika Häkkinen	44
3.	Heinz-Harald Frentzen	33
4.	Michael Schumacher	32
5.	David Coulthard	30
6.	Ralf Schumacher	22
7.	Giancarlo Fisichella	13
8.	Rubens Barrichello	10
9.	Mika Salo	6
10.	Damon Hill	5
11.	Alexander Wurz	3
11.	Pedro Diniz	3
13.	Johnny Herbert	2
	Olivier Panis	2
15.	Pedro de la Rosa	1
	Jean Alesi	1
	Jarno Trulli	1

Team

1.	Ferrari	90
2.	McLaren-Mercedes	74
3.	Jordan-Mugen-Honda	38
4.	Williams-Supertec	22
5.	Benetton-Playlife	16
6.	Stewart-Ford	12
7.	Sauber-Petronas	4
8.	Prost-Peugeot	3
9.	TWR-Arrows	1

Huge crowds despite the absence of Michael Schumacher - Hockenheim 1999.

Lowlander in a Slump

Full blooded racer or pretender ? That's the question the Formula One world was asking about David Coulthard in 1999. Over the course of the season his performances provided evidence to support both theories. Although he stayed in the running for the championship for most of the season, he simply lacked consistency.

He's the kind of man every mother would like to have her daughter marry, and a lot of daughters would have no objections. Always dressed like a model for men's fashions and without a single hair out of place, David Coulthard stands out from the regular crowd of Formula One drivers. His wife is no less striking either - American model Heidi Wichlinski. Not just that but "DC" earns millions of pounds a year as a Grand Prix driver for the most successful team in Formula One history. It all seems like the perfect life, but there's one thing still missing: a Formula One drivers championship.

It's certainly possible to become a Formula One legend as a perennial runner-up too, as England's Stirling Moss proved. But while Moss' legend revolves around the fact that he was always faced with impossible odds, among other things being up against the superior Fangio, Coulthard has no such arguments. He's faced with the criticism of so far not having been able to take advantage of his glowing opportunities.

The past season was the most difficult of his career. He entered 1999 as one of the favourites for the world championship, but managed only a couple of Grand Prix wins, while suffering one set back after another. Sometimes it was his fault, but on the other hand he was also denied what should have been a dozen championship points by a series of technical failures. Despite his problems, until the last two races of the season Coulthard was in the running for what would have been his first Formula One championship. What bothered the proud Scotsman even more than these missed opportunities though was the criticism he faced in the media. It seemed to shake his self-confidence: "I'm more afraid of beating myself, than being beaten by others."

This doesn't sound much like the man who gave the silver arrows their first win. It came in the first race of the 1997 season: in Melbourne Coulthard sent a signal that McLaren-Mercedes was competitive once again. "A very important moment and a great relief for the entire team", is how the 28 year-old describes the win today. One year later he could have won again, but he waved team-mate Mika Hakkinen past him, since Hakkinen had been mistakenly ordered into the pits by his crew. It was an extremely sporting gesture, appreciated particularly in Britain, where, unlike in some other countries, sportsmanship and fair play remain virtues. However others saw in Coulthard's sporting gesture a serious flaw. His critics argued that this proved that he didn't have the hard-nosed win at all costs attitude that it takes to be a champion. But Coulthard has no illusions about the tough world of Formula One racing: "I know nobody's going to return the favour. I want to defeat all of my opponents, but I want to do it cleanly."

That wasn't to be an experience the Scottish driver would enjoy often in 1999. Following his performance at Imola where he was widely criticised for lacking the killer instinct, he went over the top over and over again. There was his senseless challenge of his team-mate in Austria, an overly hasty challenge on Mika Salo, and his misguided attempt to overtake Panis on the edge of the track at Hockenheim. As if that wasn't bad enough, he also lost his unofficial title of "top Brit" to Ferrari driver Eddie Irvine. Last but not least Johnny Herbert left him behind and drove to victory at the Nurburgring, a Grand Prix in which Coulthard squandered what had appeared to be an unassailable lead.

David Coulthard had a couple of problems to contend with this past season. For one thing team-mate Mika Hakkinen entered the season with fresh self-confidence, built up by his 1998 drivers championship win. While David had often been the faster of the two drivers in their first two seasons at McLaren, in 1999 Coulthard was seldom able to compensate for Mika's superior mental toughness. What didn't help matters either was the fact that it seemed the 1999 edition of their Mercedes wasn't nearly as easy to handle as it had been in previous years.

"I'm concentrating on the future."

Perhaps the key to the whole puzzle is to be found in Coulthard's personality. He's straightforward, honest, fair, and down to earth. His background has a lot to do with that, coming as he does from the village of Twynholm in the Scottish lowlands, a place he describes as "a beautiful and peaceful area, and a good place to return to, to help get life back into perspective". This is hardly necessary: his father taught him all about running the family business, a shipping

The model at David's side: American Heidi Wichlinski.

company. But David wasn't to take over the shipping company because Duncan Coulthard had once bought his young son a go-cart. "But I was always realistic. It was only when I began winning in Formula Ford that I started to think about making a career of motor racing", Coulthard says, who in the next breath adds that he would have also been happy as the manager of his dad's shipping company.

This Scotsman is loyal not only to his family, but also to his employer. Whether it's the many public appearances he's required to make, or standing up for the team following technical failures, David can always be depended upon. Occasionally though he does question his actions. "Perhaps I've been too honest by admitting my own errors." But giving his all for the team doesn't include fouling drivers from other teams. "I was very hurt when Michael claimed that I had deliberately knocked him out of the race at Spa-Francorchamps in 1998." Following a week of accusations against Coulthard, even the German eventually admitted that it hadn't been the Scotsman's intention.

But it's not as if Coulthard doesn't enjoy a laugh, even if it comes at the expense of his usually flawlessly styled hair. In 1997 he celebrated his first McLaren victory, by having his hair coloured silver, paying off a bet with Mercedes Sporting Director Norbert Haug. Now he's looking towards the future, and it would suit him just fine if he had the opportunity to colour his hair again in the 2000 season, to celebrate his first Formula One championship.

Hoping for a turn for the better:
McLaren-Mercedes driver David
Coulthard (28).

Light at the end o

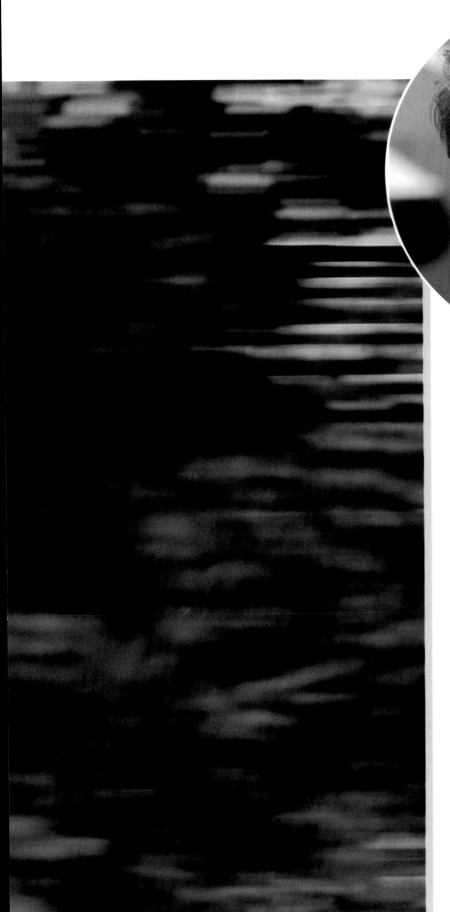

Is Mika Hakkinen no longer capable of winning? Following the setbacks of the past few Grand Prix races the McLaren-Mercedes driver was looking for an answer to this question - and got one.

For a while Mika Hakkinen appeared to be drifting aimlessly through the woods - in Hungary the defending champion returned to past form.

the tunnel

Completed McLaren´s double-victory at the Hungaroring: David Coulthard finished second despite a nightmare of a start.

F or a lot of fans the Hungarian Grand Prix got underway under a cloud of disappointment: No, Michael Schumacher would not make his comeback in Budapest, despite rumours to the contrary being spread through some of the media. But Ferrari fans did have something to be optimistic about: The narrow Puszta course with its wealth of curves is just the sort of track on which the reds from Maranello have the edge on their rivals - on paper at least. There are no particularly sharp curves or high curbs which have a tendency to play havoc with the aerodynamics of the F399 when the driver needs a little leeway. Most of the pundits figured that in Hungary Eddie Irvine was set to make it three wins in a row, but as we've seen before this season, the pundits are far from infallible.

Coulthard´s start was a nightmare.

Beginning in qualifying Irvine's hottest pursuer set out to prove that predictions are sometimes not worth the paper they're printed upon. The Finnish driver coolly drove his way to his ninth pole position of the current Grand Prix season and the 19th pole position of his career. What made this best qualifying time even more special was that Hakkinen did it in his very first qualifying lap. Try as he might not one of Irvine's four attempts was up to the standard of his McLaren rival. In the modern Formula One world 107 thousandths of a second can be a very

long time indeed.

Hakkinen´s team-mate, David Coulthard, didn't have an answer to his arch-rival's qualifying time either. The Scot's best time was all of 0.228 seconds off Mika´s standard-setting mark. For the tenth time this season Coulthard would have to line up in the grid behind the reigning world champion, on the losing end of a duel between team-mates upon which enormous importance is placed. These figures seemed to indicate that David Coulthard, despite the fact that his team operates without a team order was rapidly slipping back into the shadow of his consistently faster Finnish team-mate.

To make matters worse "DC"´s start went up in the smoke and dust kicked up by his rear tyres. In fact his start was so bad, that by the end of the lap he'd slipped back to fifth from his third position in the starting grid - all this on a track on which Thierry Boutsen once managed to keep Ayrton Senna at bay for the entire 77 lap race. "That was bad", groaned Coulthard later. "And at first I thought I´d started well." Giancarlo Fisichella and Heinz-Harald Frentzen put him in the picture, even if their advantage had to do partly with the fact that they had selected the softer Bridgestone tyres, which gave them the edge in terms of traction.

At the front of the pack it was a familiar sight with silver followed by red. Hakkinen wasted no time and stormed out of his pole position and made it to the first curve in first, followed closely, for a short time at least by Eddie Irvine. But the McLaren driver didn't let up, opening up his lead tenth of a second by tenth of a second, with the image of Irvine in his rear

Didn't have the answer: Salo qualified in 18th.

Didn't stand up to the pressure: Irvine had to let Coulthard past.

And then came Mika: Hakkinen lapped Salo on the 22nd lap, with nothing left to get in the way of victory.

Finished fourth despite the wrong fuelling strategy: Heinz-Harald Frentzen profited from Fisichella's misfortune.

Strong performance, but no cigar: Ralf Schumacher fought his way up from 16th to ninth.

view mirror becoming ever smaller. No wonder: Irvine was struggling with a technical difficulty. "After two or three laps I started having trouble with my tyres", quipped Ferrari's erstwhile number one.

But that was a poor excuse since the standings leader had had three open training sessions and Sunday morning's warm up to determine the best settings to get the optimal performance out of his Bridgestones. It's nothing new that the Hungaroring is particularly hard on tyres. It has a wealth of medium to fast and particularly long curves which means the tyres are constantly being put under pressure. So a driver who selects settings which are overly aggressive is bound to quickly overtax his tyres. "The car was shaking at the front and the back", complained "Fast Eddie". "Even if we sometimes struggle in qualifying, it's unusual for us not to be fast enough in the race..."

For Alex Zanardi things were even worse. Throughout the season he too had been stuck on the losing end of a qualifying duel with a faster team-mate, in this case Ralf Schumacher. On the Hungaroring the driver who'd returned to Formula One from America was better than his German team-mate, and this narrowed the margin in the Williams qualifying derby to 7-4. But qualifying positions 15 and 16 meant the two Williams drivers weren't likely to enjoy a banner weekend. For Zanardi came a new incident to chalk up to his season to forget. In the warm up his car died due to a defective crankshaft sensor. In the race itself the Italian too enjoyed the distinguishment of being the one to lead the way in terms of mechanical failures. Just as had been the case at Interlagos, Barcelona and Hockenheim, the electronic differential crippled his Williams. The light at the end of the tunnel had turned out to be that of an oncoming train.

On the subject of not completing races, Jacques Villeneuve remained a model of consistency. For the eleventh time in eleven races, the French-Canadian didn't make it over the finish line. This time it was the clutch on his BAR Supertec which let him down on the 60th of 77 laps. Not bad considering this was the longest he'd managed to stay on the track all season, but still not much consolation for a former world champion. Team-mate Ricardo Zonta did manage to finish the race, admittedly though he was 13th, and two laps behind...

During the first round of pit stops nothing changed at the front of the pack. In Hungary Mika Hakkinen enjoyed the luxury of trouble-

The Finnish Grand Prix: Hungary was full of Mika fans.

BAR's Villeneuve went farther than ever before.

Not pretty but effective: Jordan's ugly middle wing.

Famous visitors to the pits: Sylvester Stallone is still dreaming of shooting a Formula One movie.

A lot smoke about nothing: Ferrari didn't have a chance against McLaren - more than just a dip in form?

free pits stops. In 7.4 seconds the flying Finn was back on his way. While Fisichella and Frentzen, in third and fourth respectively had their tyres changed on laps 28 and 30, Coulthard, who until then had been close behind them, remained out on the track. As a result of a couple of extremely fast laps and a 7.3 second pit stop, the Scotsman took over third. Now it was open season on Eddie Irvine.

Heinz-Harald Frentzen was disappointed by his refuelling stop. "I went to the pits too early" he said. "Then I lost a lot of time stuck behind Giancarlo. Our strategy could have been better." But the German was in luck. An impressive performance by the Italian in his Benetton-Supertec was brought to an abrupt end when his car lost fuel pressure. This also allowed Rubens Barrichello, who was using a one stop strategy and had until then driven a flawless race, to move up into fifth. Frentzen´s team-mate Damon

An Englishman in Magyarorszag: Damon Hill felt at home in Budapest.

From figures on paper to paper tiger.

Hill suddenly found himself on track to finish in the points, having moved into sixth.

But the race was still far from over. While Mika Hakkinen was on his own out in front, David Coulthard was giving the number two man, Eddie Irvine, a hard time in the battle for the silver medal. The two drivers both headed to the pits on lap 58, almost as if driving in formation. Although the Ferrari took half a second longer, he was able to hang on to second place. In the lap ahead of the pit stop Irvine had put an

additional seven tenths of a second between himself and his pursuer. "David was driving faster than me", the Northern Irishman later recounted. "But it would have been difficult for him to overtake me, so I concentrated on avoiding error on the refuelling stop."

Although the pit stop went off without a hitch, Irvine was continuing to battle technical problems. "I had more trouble with the tyres and was having trouble controlling the car. The Ferrari was being dragged out of the curves, the perfect invitation for David Coulthard to overtake. "I don't think I could have caught him otherwise", the Scot admitted. "So my only chance was to force him into a mistake. It worked."

That suited Mika Hakkinen just fine. At the Hungaroring he proved he was back and that Grand Prix races are decided on the track, not on paper.

A new hair tonic: David Coulthard plays hair care specialist for team-mate Mika Hakkinen.

Beautiful scenery: Hungary is worth a visit.

Roadrunner not front-runner: Even the popular cartoon figure couldn't help Williams.

Statistics

11th Race in the World Championship 1999, Hungaroring, Budapest (H), 15th August 1999

Course length:	3,972 km
Distance of race:	77 (= 305,844 km)
Start time:	13.00 UTC
Weather on day of race:	cloudy, warm
Attendance:	110 000
1998 Results:	1. Michael Schumacher (D, Ferrari F300), 1 h 45'25"550
	2. David Coulthard (GB, McLaren-Mercedes MP4/13), +9"433 s
	3. Jacques Villeneuve (CDN, Williams-Mecachrome FW20), +44"444 s
Pole position 1998:	Mika Hakkinen (FIN, McLaren-Mercedes MP4/13), 1'16"973 m
Fastest Lap 1998:	David Coulthard (McLaren-Mercedes MP4/13), 1'19"989 m
Fastest pit stop 1998:	Jean Alesi (F, Sauber-Petronas C17) 28"993 s

Few opportunities to pass, but an interesting track

"At the Hungaroring the race tends to be decided to a large extent in qualifying because it's practically impossible to overtake here. It's not easy to find the right settings for this course which is hell for tyres. What you need most is sufficient down force. The course itself is fun, and what's even better is that so many Finnish fans always make the trip."

Mika Hakkinen

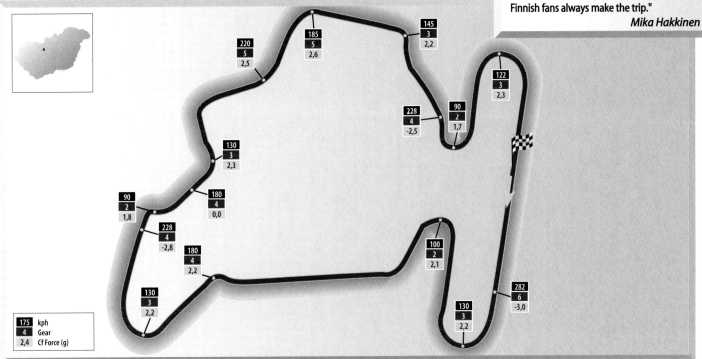

175	kph
4	Gear
2,4	Cf Force (g)

Results

	Driver	Team	Pit stops	Laps	Time (hours)	Average speed	Behind 1st	prev. driver
1.	Mika Hakkinen	McLaren-Mercedes	2	77	1 h 46'23"536	172,524	–	–
2.	David Coulthard	McLaren-Mercedes	2	77	1 h 46'33"242	172,262	9"706 s	9"706 s
3.	Eddie Irvine	Ferrari	2	77	1 h 46'50"764	171,791	27"228 s	17"522 s
4.	Heinz-Harald Frentzen	Jordan-Mugen-Honda	2	77	1 h 46'55"351	171,668	31"815 s	4"587 s
5.	Rubens Barrichello	Stewart-Ford	1	77	1 h 47'07"344	171,031	43"808 s	11"993 s
6.	Damon Hill	Jordan-Mugen-Honda	2	77	1 h 47'19"626	171,310	55"726 s	11"918 s
7.	Alexander Wurz	Benetton-Playlife	2	77	1 h 47'24"548	170,891	1'01"012 m	5"286 s
8.	Jarno Trulli	Prost-Peugeot	2	76	1 h 46'44"214	169,733	1 lap	1 lap
9.	Ralf Schumacher	Williams-Supertec	2	76	1 h 46'53"291	169,493	1 lap	9"077 s
10.	Olivier Panis	Prost-Peugeot	1	76	1 h 47'06"627	169,142	1 lap	13"336 s
11.	Johnny Herbert	Stewart-Ford	1	76	1 h 47'29"749	168,535	1 lap	23"122 s
12.	Mika Salo	Ferrari	1	75	1 h 46'28"748	167,906	2 laps	1 lap
13.	Ricardo Zonta	BAR-Supertec	3	75	1 h 46'29"795	167,878	2 laps	1"067 s
14.	Luca Badoer	Minardi-Ford	2	75	1 h 46'50"082	167,347	2 laps	20"287 s
15.	Pedro de la Rosa	TWR-Arrows	2	75	1 h 46'58"088	167,138	2 laps	8"006 s
16.	Jean Alesi [1]	Sauber-Petronas	3	74	1 h 43'41"491	170,121	retirement	retirement
17.	Marc Gené	Minardi-Ford	1	74	1 h 46'56"006	164,515	3 laps	3'14"515 m

Driver	Team	Pit stops	in lap	Reason f. retiring	Position before retiring
Jacques Villeneuve	BAR-Supertec	2	61	clutch	14
Giancarlo Fisichella	Benetton-Playlife	1	53	fuel pressure	5
Toranosuke Takagi	TWR-Arrows	1	27	drive shaft	20
Pedro Diniz	Sauber-Petronas	0	20	spun out	9
Alessandro Zanardi	Williams-Supertec	0	11	differential	22

1) Didn't complete race, but counted due to distance driven.

Hungarian GP

Starting Grid

1 Mika Häkkinen (FIN)
McLaren-Mercedes MP4/14-4
1'18"156 m (286,7 km/h) [1]

4 Eddie Irvine (GB)
Ferrari F399/191
1'18"263 m (278,9 km/h)

2 David Coulthard (GB)
McLaren-Mercedes MP4/14-6
1'18"384 m (285,7 km/h)

9 Giancarlo Fisichella (I)
Benetton-Playlife B199/7
1'18"515 m (279,6 km/h)

8 Heinz-Harald Frentzen (D)
Jordan-Mugen-Honda 199/5
1'18"664 m (279,4 km/h)

7 Damon Hill (GB)
Jordan-Mugen-Honda 199/4
1'18"667 m (279,3 km/h)

10 Alexander Wurz (A)
Benetton-Playlife B199/4
1'18"733 m (279,5 km/h)

16 Rubens Barrichello (BR)
Stewart-Ford SF3/4
1'19"095 m (278,2 km/h)

22 Jacques Villeneuve (CDN)
BAR-Supertec 01/8
1'19"127 m (280,7 km/h)

17 Johnny Herbert (GB)
Stewart-Ford SF3/5
1'19"389 m (279,3 km/h)

11 Jean Alesi (F)
Sauber-Petronas C18/6
1'19"390 m (279,5 km/h)

12 Pedro Diniz (BR)
Sauber-Petronas C18/7
1'19"782 m (278,4 km/h)

19 Jarno Trulli (I)
Prost-Peugeot AP02/7
1'19"788 m (279,9 km/h)

18 Olivier Panis (F)
Prost-Peugeot AP02/5
1'19"841 m (278,9 km/h)

5 Alessandro Zanardi (I)
Williams-Supertec FW21/5
1'19"924 m (283,4 km/h)

6 Ralf Schumacher (D)
Williams-Supertec FW21/6
1'19"945 m (282,0 km/h)

23 Ricardo Zonta (BR)
BAR-Supertec 01/5
1'20"060 m (278,9 km/h)

3 Mika Salo (FIN)
Ferrari F399/195
1'20"369 m (278,2 km/h)

20 Luca Badoer (I)
Minardi-Ford-Zetec-R M01/1
1'20"961 m (274,6 km/h)

14 Pedro de la Rosa (E)
TWR-Arrows A20/4
1'21"328 m (273,0 km/h)

15 Toranosuke Takagi (J)
TWR-Arrows A20/2
1'21"675 m (271,3 km/h)

21 Marc Gené (E)
Minardi-Ford-Zetec-R M01/4
1'21"867 m (271,8 km/h)

107-percent time: 1'23"627 m

1) Lap time (top speed in qualifying).

Best Laps

In Training on Friday (m)			
1. Irvine	1'19"476	12. Panis	1'21"525
2. Häkkinen	1'19"722	13. Badoer	1'21"635
3. Coulthard	1'20"117	14. Fisichella	1'21"673
4. Barrichello	1'20"547	15. Alesi	1'22"009
5. Salo	1'20"989	16. Hill	1'22"182
6. Frentzen	1'21"185	17. Zonta	1'22"290
7. Zanardi	1'21"251	18. Trulli	1'22"360
8. Wurz	1'21"456	19. Gené	1'22"380
9. R. Schumacher	1'21"481	20. Diniz	1'23"096
10. Herbert	1'21"486	21. Takagi	1'23"216
11. Villeneuve	1'21"504	22. de la Rosa	1'24"064

In the Race on Sunday (m)			
1. Coulthard	1'20"699	12. Trulli	1'21"936
2. Häkkinen	1'20"710	13. Villeneuve	1'21"975
3. Alesi	1'20"830	14. Diniz	1'22"452
4. Frentzen	1'20"991	15. Herbert	1'22"455
5. Irvine	1'21"010	16. Panis	1'22"587
6. Hill	1'21"180	17. Salo	1'22"681
7. Zonta	1'21"343	18. Badoer	1'23"456
8. Fisichella	1'21"469	19. de la Rosa	1'23"520
9. Wurz	1'21"539	20. Zanardi	1'24"297
10. Barrichello	1'21"707	21. Gené	1'24"807
11. R. Schumacher	1'21"745	22. Takagi	1'25"483

Total Pit Stop Times

Lap		Time (s)	Lap		Time (s)	Lap		Time (s)	Lap		Time (s)
23	Villeneuve	31"005	30	Frentzen	29"146	50	Frentzen	30"123	60	Zonta	31"554
25	Takagi	30"757	31	Häkkinen	30"002	50	Trulli	29"957	69	Alesi	33"622
28	Fisichella	30"796	32	Alesi	29"850	50	Villeneuve	32"393			
28	R. Schumacher	32"494	33	Coulthard	29"284	51	Wurz	30"613			
28	de la Rosa	31"412	33	Zonta	31"816	51	R. Schumacher	29"889			
29	Irvine	30"786	33	Gené	35"960	51	Badoer	30"681			
29	Hill	33"109	38	Herbert	34"625	52	de la Rosa	31"660			
29	Wurz	30"132	38	Panis	32"556	54	Alesi	46"069			
29	Trulli	29"468	40	Barrichello	33"654	55	Häkkinen	30"692			
29	Zonta	32"999	44	Salo	31"394	58	Irvine	28"868			
29	Badoer	30"310	48	Hill	31"063	58	Coulthard	28"593			

The Race Lap by Lap

Start: Hakkinen reaches the first curve ahead of Irvine, Coulthard is behind Fisichella and Frentzen. Following them are Hill, Barrichello and Wurz. **Lap 4:** Hakkinen is almost a second faster per lap than Irvine, whose team-mate Salo is in 20th. **Lap 9:** R. Schumacher overtakes team-mate Zanardi - 15th position. **Lap 16:** Hakkinen remains ahead of Irvine and begins lapping competitors. **Lap 20:** The Sauber pits tell Diniz to allow the faster Alesi to pass. The Brazilian does as he's told and spins off the track. **Lap 28:** Within a few laps the first six head to the pits. **Lap 33:** Coulthard, the last of the front-runners to head to the pits profits from the tactic and returns to the track in third. **Lap 40:** Barrichello refuels and drops back to eighth. **Lap 42:** Hakkinen continues to lead ahead of Irvine. Coulthard pursues the Northern Irishman. The rest of the pack: Fisichella, Frentzen, Hill, Alesi. **Lap 52:** During his second pit stop Fisichella's motor dies and he's out.

Frentzen moves into fourth, Hill is sixth because after just one pit stop he's moved ahead of the Englishman. **Lap 55:** Hakkinen enters the box with such a big lead that he returns in the lead as well. **Lap 58:** A race in the pits - Irvine and Coulthard make their second stop and leave the pits in the same order. **Lap 63:** Under pressure from Coulthard, Irvine makes an error which costs him second place, Coulthard slips past. **Lap73:** Frentzen attacks Irvine but can't overtake him. **Lap 77:** Hakkinen wins the Hungarian Grand Prix unchallenged, Coulthard is second ahead of third placed Irvine, then Frentzen, Barrichello and Hill.

Standings

Driver/Points			
1. Eddie Irvine	56	Pedro Diniz	3
2. Mika Häkkinen	54	13. Johnny Herbert	2
3. David Coulthard	36	Olivier Panis	2
Heinz-Harald Frentzen	36	15. Pedro de la Rosa	1
5. Michael Schumacher	32	Jean Alesi,	1
6. Ralf Schumacher	22	Jarno Trulli	1
7. Giancarlo Fisichella	13		
8. Rubens Barrichello	12		
9. Mika Salo	6		
Damon Hill	6		
11. Alexander Wurz	3		

Team	Points
1. Ferrari	94
2. McLaren-Mercedes	90
3. Jordan-Mugen-Honda	42
4. Williams-Supertec	22
5. Benetton-Playlife	16
6. Stewart-Ford	14
7. Sauber-Petronas	4
8. Prost-Peugeot	3
9. TWR-Arrows	1

Mini-Comeback: In Hungary Mika Hakkinen drove to his fourth win of the season.

Certainly not Wu

Big talk, disappointing results: Craig Pollock´s team no-where near lived up to his hype.

Disappointed: Former Champion Jacques Villeneuve did-n't have a lot to smile about at BAR.

nder-BAR

They proved to be the biggest flop of the 1999 season: never before had a Formula One team splashed out so much cash for so little return on the track. British American Racing and Team Boss Craig Pollock all talked a good game until their performances in their debut season threatened to turn them into the laughing stocks of the Grand Prix circuit.

The goals they set for themselves were high and ambitious: Team Manager Craig Pollock and Chief Designer Adrian Reynard even spoke optimistically of the chances of British American Racing (BAR) winning their very first Formula One race. But following 15 of the 16 Grand Prix races their record was a sobering one to say the least: instead of challenging for honours, BAR found themselves still chasing their first Grand Prix point. Contrary to their hopes of a world championship in their first season, they found themselves dead last in the constructors standings. Number one driver Jacques Villeneuve, world champion in 1997, needed a full 12 races before managing to cross the finish line with BAR for the first time. Seldom has the gap between wishful thinking and reality been so wide.

Needless to say it's not been a good year for former physical education teacher Craig Pollock. For one thing the Scotsman certainly can't be pleased that despite the team's £70 million budget, in its first season the team has been notable only for its series of technical cock ups, behind the scene controversies, and delusions of grandeur. To make matters worse the team has run up a deficit of about $30 million. Craig Pollock first had the idea to set up his own Formula One team when Jacques Villeneuve won his first race in the American Champ Car Series in Elkhart Lake in 1994. Two years later the fearless French-Canadian known for his daring manoeuvres moved to the reigning Formula One champions and at the wheel of his Williams-Renault won the world championship in only his second season. The "crash-kid" with the constantly changing hair colour had arrived as a motor racing superstar.

$500 Million for Five Years

At the same time Jacques´ manager Craig Pollock, who at the time was still teaching at a Swiss private school was working hard on turning the dream of founding his own Formula One team into reality. He already had experience in starting up a motor racing team from scratch. With the American cigarette maker "Players" behind him, he'd started up the Forsythe-Green team in the Champ Car Series. Players belongs to the British American Tobacco Company (BAT) and the firm's chief of marketing, Tom Moser turned out to be just the contact and ally that Pollock had so long been searching for. Moser was willing to put a lot of cash on the table to ensure that two of BAT´s most successful products "Lucky Strike" and "555", got high profile exposure on an international level. He signed a five year deal with BAR worth half a billion dollars. "In terms of finances", boasted Craig Pollock, "we're already among the top four on the Formula One circuit".

The team was barely on its feet on the financial side of life when the 41 year-old went out and started shopping. Basically all he needed to

Background: The BAR Disaster

Supposedly didn't do enough for BAR: Adrian Reynard.

No chance to show off his talent: Ricardo Zonta

Luxurious: BAR´s huge Motor home in the drivers´ area is notable for its decadence.

Wasted and frustrated at BAR: Jacques Villeneuve.

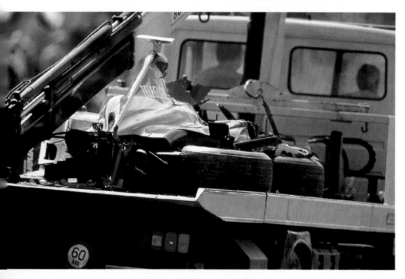

A lot of twisted metal: Ricardo Zonta and Jacques Villeneuve spent a lot of the season making short work of BAR´s troubled cars. In Spa-Francorchamps alone they wrote off two of them.

Sensitive: The technical side was a problem throughout the season. At least 90 per cent of their parts came from outside producers.

complete his new Formula One team was one thing - everything. He needed a competent pit crew and engineers, a competitive engine, and drivers capable of winning. The first piece of the puzzle was Ken Tyrell´s entire team, whom he tried to sign on for almost £1.4. But the Tyrell team wasn't amused by this sudden change in management, and almost all of them opted to move to Honda to help the Japanese concern develop its own Formula One car.

The majority of his current staff of 250 came from the pit crews of various Formula One teams. Head Designer Andy Green came from Jordan, Aerodynamics Specialist Willem Toet was lured away from Ferrari, Development Engineer John Dickenson came from McLaren, Race Engineer Jock Clear handed in his notice at Williams, and Team Manager Greg Field left behind him the "United Colors of Benetton". Head Constructor Malcolm Oastler came from Reynard. It's no wonder that Pollock had quickly made himself unpopular with the opposing managers.

As if that wasn't enough, the ambitious Scott certainly did nothing to befriend the sport's governing body, FIA or "Mr Formula One", Bernie Ecclestone. His plans to send his Formula One cars into battle with varying paint jobs according to sponsor met with far more opposition than he had bargained for. "In football the eleven players

BAR raced into crisis at high speed.

on the team don't take to the pitch in varying jerseys", the Formula One godfather argued, apparently forgetting the fact that goalkeepers aren't even allowed to wear the same jersey as the rest of the squad. "I have a duty to act in the best interests of BAT", answered the insolent Pollock. In the end though the comparatively snotty nosed kid was forced to bow to the grey establishment, and sent his cars out in identical "uniforms", just like a good little boy. But not satisfied with his backing down on the issue, the FIA World Council summoned him to a meeting to discuss his would-be transgression.

In the meantime his new team was beginning to take shape. At Brackley, in Formula One's answer to Silicon Valley, the 41,000 square metre BAR-acks, which even for the Grand Prix world was to be of mammoth proportions was well on its way to being completed. The design and construction of BAR´s first racer was moving along well, too. The engine came from Supertec who were continuing to produce the Renault ten cylinder RS09, after the French car maker had pulled out of the Formula One. In early October 1998, one week ahead of schedule, the first of these models, the "BAR 01" was supposed to be tested at Silverstone. It never happened - Bridgestone had failed to deliver the tyres in time. Test driver Jean-Christophe Boullion flew home and valu-

able time and money vanished into thin air. It was time that BAR could have used, since the new car turned out to be extremely prone to problems.

In terms of drivers though, Pollock signed on a couple of top names. The now veteran Jacques Villeneuve and the reigning GT world champion Ricardo Zonta. Pollock reckoned he had all the ingredients for an effortless march to victory in the Formula One. However, as we all know, it simply wasn't to be. While Villeneuve repeatedly failed to finish races due to a wide range of technical problems, Zonta suffered serious injury at his home race in Brazil. British American Racing was finally moving at high speed - into crisis. BAR drivers managed to cross the finishing line only nine times in their first 30 races. That was good enough for a grand total of zero points - or as the American side of the British-American collaboration would put it "one big goose egg".

Pollock´s Problems

It wasn't long before Pollock found himself juggling more problems than he could shake a stick at. "Adrian Reynard has let us down", complained Jacques Villeneuve, whining about what he considered the lack of commitment from the constructor. "Reynard isn't BAR", argued Adrian. "There are a lot of people competing for my valuable time: my wife, my five children, and firms

like BAR, not to mention Jacques Villeneuve, and this is the order in which I choose to set my priorities..."

Following the Monaco Grand Prix Craig Pollock lost his patience too. replacing Team Manager Greg Field with the man who until then had been running the testing team, Robert Synge. It wasn't long before the first restructuring took place. Financial Manager Rick Gorne took over as Director of Operations and Malcolm Oastler was promoted to the position of Technical Director, which until then had been Reynard´s job. What was most surprising though was the fact that Tom Moser, who until then had been BAT´s marketing director, moved to BAR. He was put in charge of finding more cash for the troubled Formula One team.

British American Racing doesn't have a lot to show for its first year on the Grand Prix circuit. What's worse is that for finishing well below the top ten, BAR has failed to finish high enough to earn a significant financial goody from Mr Ecclestone, because only the best ten teams are entitled to a rebate on their travelling costs. According to Craig Pollock, that would be almost £6 million, which BAR could certainly put to good use. Not just that, but the deal Pollock thought he had sealed with Honda was left in serious peril.

Only One Can Win

Ferrari was in trouble: At Spa-Francorchamps McLaren driver David Coulthard got back into the race for the world championship, even if team-mate Mika Hakkinen could really have used the ten points in aid of his title defence. Unlike Ferrari, McLaren doesn't have a team order.

Scotland´s pride on the Formula One circuit: David Coulthard took advantage of the fact that McLaren doesn´t have a team order and passed team-mate Mika Hakkinen on the first curve, driving to victory.

Heinz-Harald´s Biggest Fan: Team Boss Eddie Jordan.

Kept his championship hopes alive: David Coulthard.

Needed Salo to watch his back: Eddie Irvine of Ferrari.

Hanging over the Belgian Grand Prix was one big question on a lot of people's minds: Would McLaren-Mercedes carelessly throw away the drivers world championship by allowing Mika Hakkinen and David Coulthard to take points away from each other?

The real source of debate was an incident that annoyed not only the Finnish defending champion, but also a lot of observers. It happened in the very first lap at the sharp "La Source" turn. Coulthard who went into the race on 36 points in the drivers championship, 18 behind his teammate, got off to a much better start than Hakkinen and swung out wide on the curve and past the Finn. Hakkinen naturally wasn't prepared to give way, and separated by a matter of millimetres the two silver arrows catapulted themselves out of the curve - at which point they even made slight contact. "If that had gone wrong we would have looked like idiots", complained the disgruntled world champion.

What was annoying him even more was that during the race McLaren does not work the basis of a team order as does Ferrari. This meant Coulthard had no reason not to go after his second Grand Prix win of the season. "Both drivers have the same raw material to work with, and it's

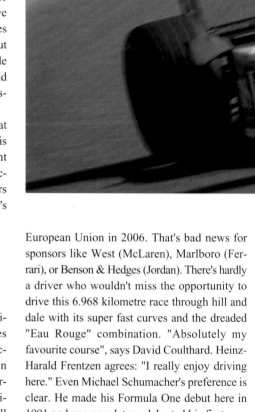

Jacques Villeneuve loves crashes.

up to each of them to win races or the championship for themselves", explained Mercedes Sporting Director Norbert Haug. "We're a racing team, and as much as we can we will refrain from influencing the race from outside. It's normal that drivers overtake one another." Hakkinen's more concise but telling comment: "They'll never learn..."

Spa-Francorchamps, the track known as the "Ardennes roller coaster" is located on the Belgian side of the border with Germany. The 1999 race could turn out to be the last time the Formula One will come to this last of the true "drivers courses". That's because Belgium has already put into place a ban on tobacco advertising at sporting events, a ban which is to take effect across the

European Union in 2006. That's bad news for sponsors like West (McLaren), Marlboro (Ferrari), or Benson & Hedges (Jordan). There's hardly a driver who wouldn't miss the opportunity to drive this 6.968 kilometre race through hill and dale with its super fast curves and the dreaded "Eau Rouge" combination. "Absolutely my favourite course", says David Coulthard. Heinz-Harald Frentzen agrees: "I really enjoy driving here." Even Michael Schumacher's preference is clear. He made his Formula One debut here in 1991 and one year later celebrated his first ever Grand Prix win here, and had several other spectacular races at Spa-Francorchamps.

Jacques Villeneuve has a very special relationship with "Eau Rouge" in particular. It's almost become a tradition for the fearless French-Canadian to do something spectacular on the 280 kph downhill stretch, which would make the hair of even the most seasoned Formula One fan stand on end.

Alessandro Zanardi may well have wished he had never returned from America.

Ricardo Zonta can only look on with envy: Frentzen reached the podium for the fifth time.

Go, Johnny, go: Things didn´t go well for Herbert in Belgium either.

Last year´s winner salvaged a single point: Damon Hill.

Hoping for a non-existent team order? Mika Hakkinen.

Could have finished fourth: Ralf Schumacher fell victim to a cynical Ferrari strategy.

"My best accident in Formula One so far", declared the 1997 world champion after last year's crash here. But he quickly added: "I've had better ones on the oval tracks in the States".

This year the son of the late Ferrari star Gilles Villeneuve, who was no less daring was apparently out to outdo himself. During qualifying the BAR driver took the "Eau Rouge" with the pedal to the metal, not letting off by as much as a millimetre. This experiment ended with a predictable result which couldn't have been any clearer: His BAR, which is troubled at the best of times swung out in the most famous curve on the Formula One circuit, shot straight off the track and

slammed into the stack of tyres. Villeneuve's immediate reaction to this terrible crash was to call his pit team on the radio to inquire as to whether the reserve car was ready to go.

The French-Canadian made himself comfortable in the cockpit of the so-called "T-car" in time to watch on the monitor as his team-mate Ricardo Zonta took on the same stretch of track. Under his helmet the Quebecois driver must have been turning green with envy as he watched Zonta complete an even more spectacular crash than he had managed to pull off - destroying his BAR too. Now Villeneuve had a challenge to live up to. He took the stretch at precisely the same speed as

the first time and to BAR´s relief but possibly to his own disappointment, made the curve.

Heinz-Harald Frentzen observed the BAR show with mixed feelings. While the crashes were amusing in a way, at one point he was forced to break off a qualifying lap as a result. "That's definitely not the best way to find out what the settings on the car should be", he said slightly annoyed. "The main thing is that nobody was injured." Despite the inconvenience the German had a good outing at qualifying - good enough to place him third in the starting grid, even if he did lag behind the pole sitter by almost a full second. Once again it was Mika Hakkinen who

Better luck next year Jarno: Trulli is on his way to Jordan.

A bus stop for photographers - the "Bus Stop" chicane at Spa-Francorchamps.

Too many questions - not enough answers: Mika Hakkinen struggles to explain why he couldn´t catch team-mate David Coulthard.

turned in the best time, while David Coulthard lined up alongside him in the first row.

What improved the Finn's mood even more was that his main rival Eddie Irvine was forced to line up in sixth place all the way behind Damon Hill and Ralf Schumacher. Ferrari's current number two, Mika Salo qualified in ninth. The Ferraris, who following Michael Schumacher's crash at Silverstone were on a high with two consecutive wins, had clearly slipped into the doldrums.

Mika Salo closed the door on Fast Eddie.

Gradually even Formula One people who dislike Michael Schumacher began admitting that the German's work in the continuing development of the F399 was being sorely missed.

Unlike in past years the entire field managed to negotiate the narrow "La Source" without the usual crack ups. While David Coulthard, as mentioned, sneaked by Mika Hakkinen, Irvine won his duel with Ralf Schumacher, moving up one position. Damon Hill though got off to a bad start. He allowed himself to fall from fourth all the way back to seventh before the race was a lap old. The rest of the race was also atypical for Spa-Francorchamps - it proceeded without a lot of drama. Coulthard worked on increasing his lead, moving 6.4 seconds ahead of Hakkinen within the first ten laps. Had the Finn's car sustained damage while it was being overtaken by the Scottish McLaren? "No, nothing like that", said Mika. "There was no point in staying close to

David. The engine doesn't run as cool in a slipstream and in terms of aerodynamics it also means added risk."

An excuse? Maybe there was another explanation, perhaps Hakkinen was expecting his team to order Coulthard to let him take over the lead. Or perhaps the slight collision had so annoyed him that it had distracted his concentration. What the real reason was, we may never know. Shortly afterwards though it was Mika who got an instruction from the pits "PUSH". "We were concerned about our drivers because they were on a one stop strategy", explained McLaren boss Ron Dennis.

The best of the rest on the day was Heinz-Harald Frentzen who also spent most of his time all alone on the track and unchallenged in third.

Ralf Schumacher also came up with a good performance. In his inferior Williams-Supertec he established himself in fifth off the start and at due to his one stop strategy was at one point even threatening Irvine in fourth. Then the Ferrari team pulled a trick that was frowned upon not just by the younger Schumacher and his Williams team. While Irvine was in the pits on lap 32 having his tyres changed for the second time, Ferrari ordered Ralf´s older brother's replacement, Mika Salo, to get in Schumacher's way and hold him back until Irvine was back in the race. "It really surprised me to see Salo follow that sort of order from the pits", exclaimed a visibly upset Patrick Head, Technical Director and co-owner of Williams. "Ferrari has employed cynical tactics such as this more than once this season. I prefer the sporting attitude of McLaren-Mercedes. They've earned the championship, and I hope that they get it!"

Proud of Ralf: Frank Williams.

Heinz-Harald Frentzen got another chance to pop the cork.

Statistics

Course length:	6,968 km
Distance of race:	44 (= 306,592 km)
Start time:	13.00 UTC
Weather on day of race:	cloudy, warm
Attendance:	90 000
1998 Results:	1. Damon Hill (GB, Jordan-Mugen-Honda 198) 1 h 43'47"407
	2. Ralf Schumacher (D, Jordan-Mugen-Honda 198), +0"932 s
	3. Jean Alesi (F, Sauber-Petronas C17), +7"240 s
Pole position 1998:	Mika Hakkinen (FIN, McLaren-Mercedes MP4/13), 1'48"682 m
Fastest Lap 1998:	Michael Schumacher (D, Ferrari F300), 2'03"766 m
Fastest pit stop 1998:	Damon Hill (Jordan-Mugen-Honda 198) 30"663 s

The Ardennes roller coaster is every driver's dream.

"Spa is a true driver's course. This fantastic track offers the perfect combination of long straightaways, fast curves, and a difficult hairpin turn. Driving a well set up car to its limit in qualifying is an incomparable feeling. Putting your toe down through the Eau Rouge really gets the adrenaline flowing."

David Coulthard

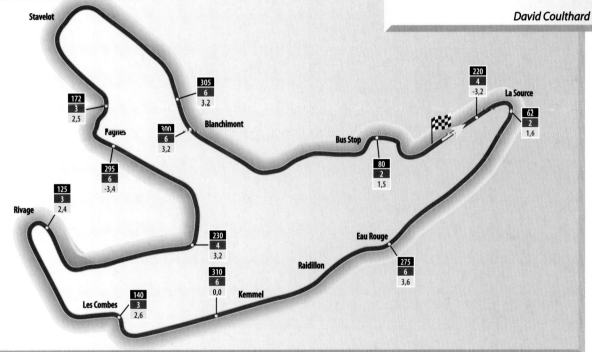

175 / 4 / 2,4	kph / Gear / Cf Force (g)

Results

Driver	Team	Pit stops	Laps	Time (hours)	Average speed	Behind 1st	prev. driver
1. David Coulthard	McLaren-Mercedes	2	44	1 h 25'43"057	214,595	–	–
2. Mika Hakkinen	McLaren-Mercedes	2	44	1 h 25'53"526	214,159	10"469 s	–
3. Heinz-Harald Frentzen	Jordan-Mugen-Honda	2	44	1 h 26'16"490	213,209	33"433 s	22"964 s
4. Eddie Irvine	Ferrari	2	44	1 h 26'28"005	212,736	44"948 s	11"515 s
5. Ralf Schumacher	Williams-Supertec	1	44	1 h 26'31"124	212,608	48"067 s	3"119 s
6. Damon Hill	Jordan-Mugen-Honda	2	44	1 h 26'37"973	212,328	54"916 s	6"849 s
7. Mika Salo	Ferrari	2	44	1 h 26'39"306	212,273	56"249 s	1"333 s
8. Alessandro Zanardi	Williams-Supertec	2	44	1 h 26'50"079	211,835	1'07"022 m	10"773 s
9. Jean Alesi	Sauber-Petronas	2	44	1 h 26'56"905	211,557	1'13"848 m	6"826 s
10. Rubens Barrichello	Stewart-Ford	2	44	1 h 27'03"799	211,278	1'20"742 m	6"894 s
11. Giancarlo Fisichella	Benetton-Playlife	1	44	1 h 27'15"252	210,816	1'32"195 m	11"453 s
12. Jarno Trulli	Prost-Peugeot	2	44	1 h 27'19"211	210,657	1'36"154 m	13"959 s
13. Olivier Panis	Prost-Peugeot	2	44	1 h 27'24"600	210,440	1'41"543 m	5"389 s
14. Alexander Wurz	Benetton-Playlife	1	44	1 h 27'40"802	209,792	1'57"745 m	16"202 s
15. Jacques Villeneuve	BAR-Supertec	1	43	1 h 25'49"704	209,447	1 lap	1 lap
16. Marc Gené	Minardi-Ford	2	43	1 h 26'19"557	208,240	1 lap	29"853 s

Driver	Team	Pit stops	in lap	Reason f. retiring	Position before retiring
Pedro de la Rosa	TWR-Arrows	2	36	power transmission	17
Luca Badoer	Minardi-Ford	2	34	suspension	16
Ricardo Zonta	BAR-Supertec	1	34	gearbox	19
Johnny Herbert	Stewart-Ford	1	28	spun out	14
Pedro Diniz	Sauber-Petronas	1	20	crash	18
Toranosuke Takagi	TWR-Arrows	0	1	clutch	19

Belgian GP

12th Race in the World Championship 1999, Circuit de Spa-Franchorchamps (B), 29th August 1999

Starting Grid

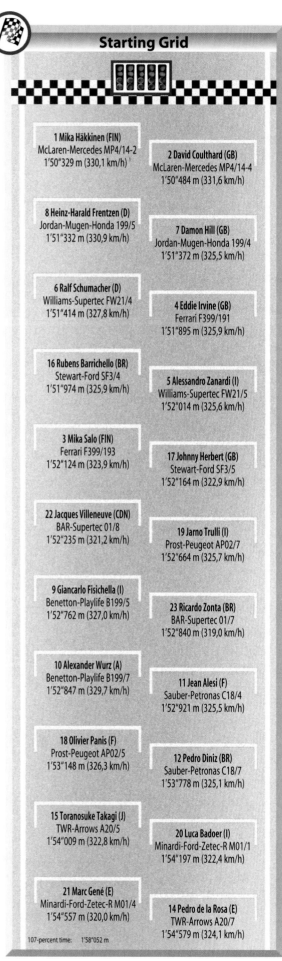

1 Mika Häkkinen (FIN)
McLaren-Mercedes MP4/14-2
1'50"329 m (330,1 km/h) [1]

2 David Coulthard (GB)
McLaren-Mercedes MP4/14-4
1'50"484 m (331,6 km/h)

8 Heinz-Harald Frentzen (D)
Jordan-Mugen-Honda 199/5
1'51"332 m (330,9 km/h)

7 Damon Hill (GB)
Jordan-Mugen-Honda 199/4
1'51"372 m (325,5 km/h)

6 Ralf Schumacher (D)
Williams-Supertec FW21/4
1'51"414 m (327,8 km/h)

4 Eddie Irvine (GB)
Ferrari F399/191
1'51"895 m (325,9 km/h)

16 Rubens Barrichello (BR)
Stewart-Ford SF3/4
1'51"974 m (325,9 km/h)

5 Alessandro Zanardi (I)
Williams-Supertec FW21/5
1'52"014 m (325,6 km/h)

3 Mika Salo (FIN)
Ferrari F399/193
1'52"124 m (323,9 km/h)

17 Johnny Herbert (GB)
Stewart-Ford SF3/5
1'52"164 m (322,9 km/h)

22 Jacques Villeneuve (CDN)
BAR-Supertec 01/8
1'52"235 m (321,2 km/h)

19 Jarno Trulli (I)
Prost-Peugeot AP02/7
1'52"664 m (325,7 km/h)

9 Giancarlo Fisichella (I)
Benetton-Playlife B199/5
1'52"762 m (327,0 km/h)

23 Ricardo Zonta (BR)
BAR-Supertec 01/7
1'52"840 m (319,0 km/h)

10 Alexander Wurz (A)
Benetton-Playlife B199/7
1'52"847 m (329,7 km/h)

11 Jean Alesi (F)
Sauber-Petronas C18/4
1'52"921 m (325,5 km/h)

18 Olivier Panis (F)
Prost-Peugeot AP02/5
1'53"148 m (326,3 km/h)

12 Pedro Diniz (BR)
Sauber-Petronas C18/7
1'53"778 m (325,1 km/h)

15 Toranosuke Takagi (J)
TWR-Arrows A20/5
1'54"009 m (322,8 km/h)

20 Luca Badoer (I)
Minardi-Ford-Zetec-R M01/1
1'54"197 m (322,4 km/h)

21 Marc Gené (E)
Minardi-Ford-Zetec-R M01/4
1'54"557 m (320,0 km/h)

14 Pedro de la Rosa (E)
TWR-Arrows A20/7
1'54"579 m (324,1 km/h)

107-percent time: 1'58"052 m

1) Lap time (top speed in qualifying).

Best Laps

In Training on Friday (m)			
1. Coulthard	1'53"577	12. Wurz	1'55"486
2. Häkkinen	1'54"021	13. Panis	1'55"541
3. Fisichella	1'54"066	14. Zanardi	1'55"743
4. Frentzen	1'54"678	15. Badoer	1'56"090
5. Hill	1'54"982	16. Takagi	1'56"263
6. R. Schumacher	1'54"889	17. Diniz	1'56"310
7. Herbert	1'54"975	18. Villeneuve	1'56"429
8. Salo	1'55"032	19. de la Rosa	1'56"749
9. Irvine	1'55"242	20. Trulli	1'56"765
10. Alesi	1'55"271	21. Gené	1'56"885
11. Barrichello	1'55"484	22. Zonta	1'57"717

In the Race on Sunday (m)			
1. Häkkinen	1'53"955	12. Panis	1'56"681
2. Coulthard	1'54"088	13. Gené	1'56"789
3. Hill	1'54"954	14. Fisichella	1'57"037
4. Salo	1'55"299	15. Herbert	1'57"094
5. Frentzen	1'55"412	16. Wurz	1'57"526
6. Irvine	1'55"582	17. Villeneuve	1'57"619
7. Zanardi	1'55"786	18. Badoer	1'57"929
8. R. Schumacher	1'55"964	19. Diniz	1'58"179
9. Alesi	1'56"016	20. de la Rosa	1'58"480
10. Barrichello	1'56"131	21. Zonta	1'58"918
11. Trulli	1'56"367		

Total Pit Stop Times

Lap	Time (s)	Lap	Time (s)	Lap	Time (s)	Lap	Time (s)
12 Panis	30"260	17 Barrichello	33"038	27 Panis	29"909	32 Barrichello	29"874
13 Badoer	32"123	18 Häkkinen	29"917	28 Hill	29"480	34 Salo	28"379
14 Alesi	32"343	18 Irvine	28"824	29 Alesi	29"849		
14 Trulli	29"281	19 Coulthard	29"025	29 Gené	31"109		
14 Gené	30"399	21 Zanardi	30"818	29 de la Rosa	31"700		
14 de la Rosa	30"309	21 Fisichella	35"960	30 Trulli	28"683		
15 Herbert	32"282	21 Zonta	33"351	31 Häkkinen	31"749		
15 Diniz	31"008	22 R. Schumacher	32"824	31 Zanardi	28"711		
16 Hill	28"743	22 Wurz	32"561	32 Coulthard	28"784		
17 Frentzen	29"533	26 Villeneuve	31"944	32 Frentzen	28"275		
17 Salo	29"990	26 Badoer	31"758	32 Irvine	29"522		

The Race Lap by Lap

Start: Hakkinen is in motion too early, he hits the brakes to avoid a penalty. At the same moment the red lights go out. Coulthard gets off the mark better than his team-mate. In the "La Source" hairpin turn Hakkinen tries to slip past the Scot, the cars make contact. The Finn gives way. Frentzen tries to take advantage of the situation, but can't match the McLaren´s acceleration and remains in third. Irvine, R. Schumacher, Zanardi, Wurz and Hill give chase. **Lap 12:** Coulthard increases his lead on Hakkinen, R. Schumacher moves away from team-mate Zanardi, who's in a battle with Hill and Salo over sixth. **Lap 16:** Hill is the first of the leaders to head to the pits. **Lap 17:** Frentzen and Salo steer in for servicing. **Lap 18:** Hakkinen refuels ahead of Coulthard, who remains in first following the pit stop. R. Schumacher, using a one stop strategy takes over second from the world champion. **Lap 20:** Hakkinen passes the German at the end of a straightaway.

Lap 21: Diniz spins out in Eau Rouge but doesn't hit anything. Coulthard leads by ten seconds ahead of Hakkinen, followed by Frentzen, Irvine and Hill. **Lap 22:** R. Schumacher´s only refuelling stop. He returns to the track ahead of Salo who then overtakes him. **Lap 30:** R. Schumacher is faster the fifth-placed Salo who holds him up until he stops for fuel. The point of the exercise: to ensure that Ferrari colleague Eddie Irvine has enough of a lead on Schumacher to take his second pit stop. **Lap 32:** The Northern Irishman returns to the track ahead of the German and remains in fourth. **Lap 36:** Coulthard still leads, 15 seconds ahead of Hakkinen. The strategic move that the defending champion is probably expecting never happens. **Lap 44:** The Scotsman wins ahead of his team-mate, followed by Frentzen, Irvine, R. Schumacher, and Hill.

Standings

Driver/Points			
1. Mika Häkkinen	60	11. Pedro Diniz	3
2. Eddie Irvine	59	13. Johnny Herbert	2
3. David Coulthard	46	Olivier Panis	2
4. Heinz-Harald Frentzen	40	14. Pedro de la Rosa	1
5. Michael Schumacher	32	Jean Alesi	1
6. Ralf Schumacher	24	Jarno Trulli	1
7. Giancarlo Fisichella	13		
8. Rubens Barrichello	12		
9. Damon Hill	7		
10. Mika Salo	6		
11. Alexander Wurz	3		

Team	Points
1. McLaren-Mercedes	106
2. Ferrari	97
3. Jordan-Mugen-Honda	47
4. Williams-Supertec	24
5. Benetton-Playlife	16
6. Stewart-Ford	14
7. Sauber-Petronas	4
8. Prost-Peugeot	3
9. TWR-Arrows	1

A nice view in the pits at the Belgian Grand Prix.

An Understudy with Ambition

No Formula One driver is more controversial: Despite his status as a Ferrari man, World Championship favourite Eddie Irvine is the most down to earth driver in the starting grid. The Northern Irishman has more of a connection to his surroundings than many others.

From number two to number one: The 1999 season took an almost unbelievable turn for Eddie Irvine.

Eddie Irvine loves life. Typical conformist, dull Formula One driver? Not this self-willed Northern Irishman. That sort of criticism bothers him about as much as it would his driving colleagues Heinz-Harald Frentzen or Jean Alesi. He couldn't care less about public opinion. When he grants interviews he doesn't speak in the slick manner of a marketing puppet. Eddie says what's on his mind, uncensored and in an English with a bit of a rough edge. It's not vulgar, but it is the slang used on the streets of his homeland, fresh and sometimes funny. Not just that but he speaks in sound bytes. He's a journalist's dream - a seemly inexhaustible source of good one-liners and cheeky comments.

For example there was the time when he won his first Formula One race - the 82nd Grand Prix race of his career. After the race he ran into his former boss Eddie Jordan who, since one of his drivers had finished second, was being interviewed by a British TV reporter who had worked as Jordan's spokesperson in the days when Irvine was still there. This is what happened in front of a rolling camera:

Jordan (to Irvine): "Hey you - I made you!"

Irvine "Oh, the first among the losers..."

Jordan (whose team won its first Grand Prix at Spa in 1998): "Ya, it's a long way to victory, but we made it there first...."

Irvine (with reference to the transfer fee that Jordan got when he sold Irvine to Ferrari): "I may not have got you a lot of points but I made you a rich man."

Jordan: "That's right, Ferrari was our biggest sponsor back then..."

No question: Irvine loves to clown around like no other driver since Gerhard Berger, who even managed to get the humourless superstar Ayrton Senna into the act once in a while. But nonetheless this Northern Irish Jewel of 82 Grand Prix race had suddenly drawn more than a little attention. The reason is simple: Eddie Irvine had long relegated himself to the role of number two man at Ferrari behind Michael Schumacher. Despite his

position, "I - WANT - TO - WIN - RACES", the Northern Irishman stresses repeatedly, before turning serious: "Money isn't the top priority, although as a professional I wouldn't drive for peanuts. What's really important is to be sitting in a competitive car. It's about investing in my career. Villeneuve would never accept number two status. If he didn't have his famous last name he'd accept the same conditions as I."

This too is typical Eddie Irvine: In an almost complete absence of envy, he recognises that Michael Schumacher is in a position of far more power than he has. Almost every other Formula One driver seems to believe that he is just about the best driver of all time. The system seems to force them to think this way. Not Eddie: "I understand why I have to get out of the way in certain situations", he explains. "I have no problem with my image as the number two man. I know where I stand in the team. What's important is the overriding conclusion that for me the Ferrari deal makes a whole lot of sense."

The Paparazzi Stayed Hot On Irvine's Heels.

In 1997 in Argentina Irvine voluntarily held back and didn't challenge Jacques Villeneuve, settling for second place. In Suzuka - in the same year - he could have won, but obeyed the two-way radio instructions from his team, and allowed Schumacher to pass. It was only at the first race of this season when both McLaren-Mercedes and his team-mate were knocked out early, that Eddie finally got his just desserts: after appearing on the lower steps of the podium some 16 times, finally he got to the top step, and this despite the fact that during winter testing he'd only had a mere day and a half to get to know the new F399. Naturally this was the perfect opportunity for his cheeky side to come to the surface: "Michael took a lot of preparation work off my hands to ensure that the car was reliable", he chuckled. "My hat goes off to him, he did a great job. Last year I did all the tyre testing and he collected all the wins. Maybe

it's time for us to exchange roles..."

Melbourne 1999 - Eddie Irvine's great breakthrough? "Now they're even taking me seriously as a driver back in Italy", laughed Irvine. "Public opinion has made a 180 degree turn. I've never had to give so many interviews in my life. Even the paparazzi are hot on my heels." So had the cocky extrovert finally reached his ultimate goal? Eddie surprised a lot of people with a completely different view of the situation. "No - this win was of particular importance for my mechanics and my race engineer Luca Baldisserri. I'm paid for not winning under certain circumstances. But these guys, they work day and night to get my car ready. They work their backsides off, often with little reward." Eddie Irvine - a man with a social conscience?

He's always good for a different assessment of a situation. Sure, he enjoys his fame, his income, and all of the other trappings that go with his privileged position - a Falcon jet for business trips, a helicopter for travelling around Ireland, stately residences at home and in Italy, a fleet of Ferraris for street use - Eddie Irvine definitely has it okay. As a practising single, who likes to land his helicopter in the parking lot of his favourite local, he also knows how to use such things to his advantage.

Is this all fulfilment for a superficial person? No. Irvine is rough around the edges but also careful in his own way. He is for example the father of a young girl, even if he isn't with the daughter's mother any longer. He's a caring father who looks after the needs of his small family from more than just a financial point of view.

Driving as the number two things were a lot

simpler than they have been as one of the new favourites for the drivers championship, a role he was thrust into soon after Michael Schumacher's crash as Silverstone which knocked the German out of action for most of the rest of the season. Soon the Northern Irishman was to experience the pressure to win that his German team-mate had always shouldered up until then, and it was an experience that wasn't all together to the Irishman's liking. Irvine didn't appear to be completely comfortable steeping into Schumacher's role as test driver either. But despite such difficulties the man from Conlig in County Down feels he's ready to be number one. The party animal is leaving Ferrari to become the number one driver at the Jaguar team beginning in 2000. There's no telling just how Eddie Irvine will fare at Jaguar next season, or in fact how the team which in 1999 competed as Stewart-Ford, will fare with Ford's subsidiary at the helm. But here's no need to worry about how Eddie Irvine the man. He'll remain the same fun-loving character he's always been. Just as well.

They'd go through hell for him: Eddie is admired by his mechanics.

Practising single: Eddie loves to chat-up the girls.

Rough around the edges but with a heart of gold: Below his arrogant exterior Eddy has a strong character.

Italian GP

A New

GRAN PREMIO CAMPARI D'ITALIA 1999

The first German one-two result when Michael Schumacher isn't one
of them. The victorious Heinz-Harald Frentzen (middle) at the post-
race press conference with second placed Ralf Schumacher (left) and
Mika Salo (right).

None of the front-runners in the battle for the Formula One championship
was able to make much progress at
the 1999 Italian Grand Prix - not the
McLaren-Mercedes drivers Mika
Hakkinen or David Coulthard, and not
Eddie Irvine of Ferrari either. The man
who profited from their woes was
Jordan driver Heinz-Harald Frentzen.

Contender

His second win of the season: Heinz-Harald Frentzen took advantage of his opportunity.

Made his team-mate look bad: Mika Salo on the podium.

There's an old saying in motor racing. It goes: "To finish first, you first have to finish..." It doesn't take a rocket scientist to figure out why. But it's an old saying that Mika Hakkinen will want to take to heart following the 1999 Italian Grand Prix. The Finnish driver experienced one of the darkest days of his Formula One career at Monza in 1999, after it had all got off to such a good start. In fact before it all went wrong, it appeared that there was nothing that could have prevented the two McLaren-Mercedes drivers from finishing one-two...

In qualifying it was business as usual: Mika Hakkinen outdid himself yet again. The fastest man in Finland - not taking into consideration the performances of rally stars Juha Kankkunen and Tommi Mälinen for the time being, realised every racing car driver's dream: driving the perfect lap. The Finn took the pole position yet again, this time with a lap time of 1.22.432 minutes - a new track record.

So it was only logical that Hakkinen, under such favourable circumstances, not to mention that his main competitors had more or less met their qualifying Waterloos, was looking forward to Sunday with a good deal of optimism. Eddie Irvine could qualify no better than eighth in the land of Ferrari. That amounted to a minor disaster. What was even more embarrassing was the fact that he qualified behind his temporary Ferrari team-mate, Mika Salo. David Coulthard had his problems as well. He couldn't get the car settings right and had to make do with third in the starting grid.

But while a couple of the traditional leaders were having their problems, others were finding Monza to their liking. Williams driver Alex Zanardi earned a place in the second row with team-mate Ralf Schumacher right behind him in fifth. Rubens Barrichello qualified ahead of Eddie Irvine, too, well positioned to make a good showing in the race. But up in the front row someone who would later be the toast of the town was already extremely satisfied. Heinz-Harald Frentzen surprised everybody with the second best training time. "I even thought I had a shot at the pole position", said the straightforward German. "We were already very fast in the testing laps here, and my team had prepared the car very well."

"The first few laps were interesting."

It was a beautiful sunny day at the Monza track, but the forest was rocking. One hundred and forty thousand fans jammed the park to see the action along the 5.77 kilometre long course. The "Tifosi" weren't to be disappointed, the race on what is currently the fastest Formula One track was not to be a yawner.

As expected Mika Hakkinen got off the mark quickest and moved out into the lead. Frentzen didn't get away nearly as well. The Jordan driver was forced to cut in behind Alex Zanardi in the first chicane, which is known for frequent crashes off the start. Zanardi had already left David Coulthard in his dust. Although the Italian driver appeared to have left his slump behind him, the Williams driver didn't have much of a chance against the sheer power from the Honda engine under the Jordan car's hood. Frentzen re-established himself in second place just a few metres later.

Behind the first three there was a lot more action: Ralf Schumacher was under intense pressure from both Coulthard and Mika Salo. "The first few laps were really quite interesting", smiled Ralf Schumacher after the race. "I tried make my car wide the best I could..." "Wide isn't the word for it", complained Salo. "I was coming at him from one side, and David was pursuing him from the other. Even though we were both faster on the straightaways, we didn't get past him." The German, whose Williams-Supertec has a good 50 horsepower less than either the Mercedes or the Ferrari, kept his nerve and his eyes on both rear-view mirrors. It wasn't long until the pressure let up.

Red sea: The grid girls in Ferrari colours.

Poor performance: David Coulthard finished fifth.

Looked good: Rubens Barrichello fought his way up to fourth.

Technical difficulty: Jean Alesl looked great in open training until the Ferrari engine in his Sauber let him down.

A lot of smoke about nothing: Eddie Irvine was disappointing.

Que bella cantina: Ferrari's cook at work.

Thanks for coming out! Villeneuve was still after his first point.

Their hearts beat in ten-cylinder time: Ferrari fans at Monza.

An angry Mika Hakkinen tossed his steering wheel away.

At the front of the pack Hakkinen was driving a textbook race, increasing his lead on Frentzen every lap. In the meantime Rubens Barrichello was causing a stir. The Brazilian cheekily out-manoeuvred McLaren´s David Coulthard and slipped past him to move into sixth on the slow curve at the end of the starting straightaway. Eight laps later Salo too fell victim to the ambitious Stewart-Ford driver. Eddie Irvine was still lingering back in eighth place.

The battle between the two Williams drivers for third was anti-climatic. After having given the underside of his car a massage on the rough edge of the track, on lap 17 Champ Car champion Alex Zanardi let his team-mate pass without a fight. "Something seemed to be dragging on the ground", shrugged the Italian. "It seems that something had become lose on the underside of the car..." Not long after that he lost fourth place, too, this time to Rubens Barrichello.

For a while after that the Italian Grand Prix was threatening to degenerate into a bore. That changed though on lap 30, when the race took a completely unexpected turn. The spectators on hand as well as millions of television viewers held their collect breath. Thoroughly unchallenged, Mika Hakkinen went off the track. In an outburst of frustration he ripped out the steered wheel and tossed it away, before throwing his driver's gloves to the ground. He then proceeded behind a hedge, hoping to find some privacy,

Nothing to show for the pole position: Mika Hakkinen.

and wept openly. What he likely didn't know at the time was that a television camera filming from a helicopter was beaming live pictures of him around the world as he battled to fight back the tears.

It took a while before the Finn finally regained his composure. "The whole weekend I've been taking the first curve in second gear", the reigning world champion explained. "This time though I accidentally put it into first gear. The rear wheels partially locked up and I spun off with a stalled engine." What contributed to his accident, was the fact that he'd manipulated the gearshift on the steering wheel so slowly, that an electronic safety that could have prevented the mistake, wasn't activated. "A gear shifting error that normally wouldn't happen to me in ten thousand test kilometres. But I will make sure that this is the last error I make this year." The fact that Hakkinen broke down in tears had won him

Reason to smile: Frentzen.

A setback for a contender: Eddie Irvine.

Discontent: Some fans doubted the need for Michael Schumacher to be out for so long.

much more sympathy than disdain. Perhaps Formula One fans were pleased to see that a normally so cool, well trained professional is also only human. But at the same time it revealed the intense pressure the Finnish driver was feeling. After the race, the world champion apologised to each and every mechanic on the team.

Heinz-Harald Frentzen was just as surprised as the millions of others when he saw what had happened. He was suddenly in the lead. "I hadn't been able to catch Mika so I was just trying to drive as fast as I could while at the same time not putting any more strain than necessary on my tyres. After Mika was out I just concentrated on maintaining my lead on Ralf and in bringing the baby home." That was said in typical Heinz-Harald Frentzen style. Few people knew at the time that there was a hidden meaning to what he had just said. Frentzen and Tanja Nigge, his long-time companion were expecting a child...

But the race still wasn't over, even though Frentzen was not to be seriously challenged

again. The German only temporarily surrendered the lead to Mika Salo while he was in the pits. Ferrari´s number two had been held up by Zanardi during the first half of the race, but through an extremely fast pit stop he managed to climb past Barrichello, and, driving extremely

Ralf met the challenge with poise.

fast laps launched an challenge on Schumacher. Ralf though responded with the poise of his older brother, by driving his fastest laps of the day as well. Despite Salo´s gallant effort, it was soon over. Frentzen won ahead of Ralf, Salo and Barrichello. Behind them the surprisingly lacklustre David Coulthard, who was battling and under steering problem, and Eddie Irvine carved up the final three world championship points. "We knew that Monza wouldn't be suited to us", said

the Northern Irishman in an effort to fend off criticism. The main problem for Ferrari was that to be successful at Monza the drivers have to use the high edges of the track to their advantage, and this is pure poison for the sensitive aerodynamics of the F399, which seems to demand a consistent and even driving surface.

While Monza had turned out to be bad news for McLaren-Mercedes and Ferrari in 1999, it was good news for the drivers championship. With just three races left in the season the competition was wide open with four drivers in with a realistic shot at the title. Hakkinen and Irvine were in the lead level on points with 60, Frentzen was in third with 50, and Coulthard was just two behind him with 48. "We've taken every opportunity to earn points, and here we took advantage of a fantastic opportunity", grinned an elated Heinz-Harald Frentzen. "If McLaren continue to make so little of their potential, Eddie and I will have the best shots at winning the world championship..."

An early end: Giancarlo Fisichella collided with Pedro Diniz on the second lap and rolled into the wall.

Statistics

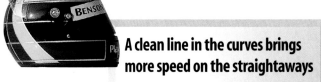

Course length: 5,77 km

Distance of race: 53 (= 305,81 km)

Start time: 13.00 UTC

Weather on day of race: sunny and warm

Attendance: 140 000

1998 Results:
1. Michael Schumacher (D, Ferrari F300) 1 h 17'09"672
2. Eddie Irvine (GB, Ferrari F300) – 37"977 s
3. Ralf Schumacher (D, Jordan-Mugen-Honda 198) – 41"152 s

Pole position 1998: Michael Schumacher (Ferrari F300), 1'25"289 m

Fastest Lap 1998: Eddie Irvine (Ferrari F300), 1'24"987 m

Fastest pit stop 1998: Damon Hill (GB, Jordan-Mugen-Honda 198) 19"154 s

A clean line in the curves brings more speed on the straightaways

"The atmosphere at Monza is great. You need a sensitive touch on this high speed course because we drive it with very small wings, so the cars are especially touchy. The key spot is the Curva Parabolica - any mistake will be punished on the following straightaway."

Heinz-Harald Frentzen

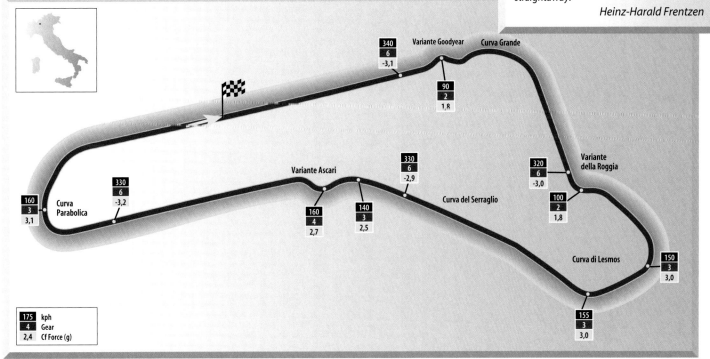

175	kph
4	Gear
2,4	Cf Force (g)

Results

Driver	Team	Pit stops	Laps	Time (hours)	Average speed	Behind 1st	prev. driver
1. Heinz-Harald Frentzen	Jordan-Mugen-Honda	1	53	1 h 17'02"923	237,938	–	–
2. Ralf Schumacher	Williams-Supertec	1	53	1 h 17'06"195	237,770	3"272 s	–
3. Mika Salo	Ferrari	1	53	1 h 17'14"855	237,328	11"932 s	8"660 s
4. Rubens Barrichello	Stewart-Ford	1	53	1 h 17'20"533	237,034	17"630 s	5"698 s
5. David Coulthard	McLaren-Mercedes	1	53	1 h 17'21"065	237,008	18"142 s	0"512 s
6. Eddie Irvine	Ferrari	1	53	1 h 17'30"325	236,536	27"402 s	9"260 s
7. Alessandro Zanardi	Williams-Supertec	1	53	1 h 17'30"970	236,503	28"047 s	0"645 s
8. Jacques Villeneuve	BAR-Supertec	1	53	1 h 17'44"720	235,806	41"797 s	13"750 s
9. Jean Alesi	Sauber-Petronas	1	53	1 h 17'45"121	235,788	42"198 s	0"401 s
10. Damon Hill	Jordan-Mugen-Honda	1	53	1 h 17'59"182	235,078	56"259 s	14"061 s
11. Olivier Panis [2]	Prost-Peugeot	2	52	1 h 16'30"578	235,090	retirement	retirement

Driver	Team	Pit stops	in lap	Reason f. retiring	Position before retiring		
Johnny Herbert	Stewart-Ford	1	41	clutch	11		
Toranosuke Takagi	TWR-Arrows	1	36	spun out	7		
Pedro de la Rosa	TWR-Arrows	1	36	suspension	14		
Mika Häkkinen	McLaren-Mercedes	1	30	spun out	1		
Jarno Trulli	Prost-Peugeot	1	30	engine overheated	14		
Ricardo Zonta	BAR-Supertec	1	26	defective breaks	15		
Luca Badoer	Minardi-Ford	0	24	collision	16		
Alexander Wurz	Benetton-Playlife	0	12	gearbox	18		
Pedro Diniz	Sauber-Petronas	0	2	collision	12		
Giancarlo Fisichella	Benetton-Playlife	0	2	collision	15		
Marc Gené	Minardi-Ford	0	1	collision	20		

1) Didn't complete race but counted due to distance driven.

Italian GP

**13th Race in the World Championship 1999,
Autodromo di Monza, 12th September 1999**

Starting Grid

1 Mika Häkkinen (FIN)
McLaren-Mercedes MP4/14-5
1'22"432 m (355,3 km/h) [1]

8 Heinz-Harald Frentzen (D)
Jordan-Mugen-Honda 199/5
1'22"926 m (348,7 km/h)

2 David Coulthard (GB)
McLaren-Mercedes MP4/14-7
1'23"177 m (352,9 km/h)

5 Alessandro Zanardi (I)
Williams-Supertec FW21/5
1'23"432 m (340,1 km/h)

6 Ralf Schumacher (D)
Williams-Supertec FW21/6
1'23"636 m (342,3 km/h)

3 Mika Salo (FIN)
Ferrari F399/195
1'23"657 m (348,4 km/h)

16 Rubens Barrichello (BR)
Stewart-Ford SF3/4
1'23"739 m (351,4 km/h)

4 Eddie Irvine (GB)
Ferrari F399/191
1'23"765 m (347,4 km/h)

7 Damon Hill (GB)
Jordan-Mugen-Honda 199/4
1'23"979 m (348,7 km/h)

18 Olivier Panis (F)
Prost-Peugeot AP02/5
1'24"016 m (348,4 km/h)

22 Jacques Villeneuve (CDN)
BAR-Supertec 01/6
1'24"188 m (342,5 km/h)

19 Jarno Trulli (I)
Prost-Peugeot AP02/2
1'24"293 m (347,3 km/h)

11 Jean Alesi (F)
Sauber-Petronas C18/4
1'24"591 m (349,4 km/h)

10 Alexander Wurz (A)
Benetton-Playlife B199/4
1'24"593 m (353,5 km/h)

17 Johnny Herbert (GB)
Stewart-Ford SF3/5
1'24"594 m (348,6 km/h)

12 Pedro Diniz (BR)
Sauber-Petronas C18/7
1'24"596 m (347,0 km/h)

9 Giancarlo Fisichella (I)
Benetton-Playlife B199/7
1'24"682 m (349,0 km/h)

23 Ricardo Zonta (BR)
BAR-Supertec 01/7
1'25"114 m (344,6 km/h)

20 Luca Badoer (I)
Minardi-Ford-Zetec-R M01/1
1'25"348 m (345,8 km/h)

21 Marc Gené (E)
Minardi-Ford-Zetec-R M01/4
1'25"695 m (344,6 km/h)

14 Pedro de la Rosa (E)
TWR-Arrows A20/7
1'26"383 m (341,8 km/h)

15 Toranosuke Takagi (J)
TWR-Arrows A20/5
1'26"509 m (342,7 km/h)

107-percent time   1'28"202 m

Best Laps

In Training on Friday (m)			
1. R. Schumacher	1'24"507	12. Herbert	1'25"551
2. Trulli	1'24"692	13. Frentzen	1'25"577
3. Zanardi	1'24"823	14. Fisichella	1'25"701
4. Panis	1'25"007	15. Wurz	1'25"742
5. Alesi	1'25"030	16. Irvine	1'25"897
6. Häkkinen	1'25"102	17. Salo	1'25"931
7. Villeneuve	1'25"307	18. Gené	1'26"069
8. Coulthard	1'25"347	19. Zonta	1'26"181
9. Diniz	1'25"388	20. Badoer	1'26"633
10. Hill	1'25"397	21. de la Rosa	1'27"542
11. Barrichello	1'25"499	22. Takagi	1'27"931

In the Race on Sunday (m)			
1. R. Schumacher	1'25"579	12. Hill	1'26"342
2. Salo	1'25"630	13. Irvine	1'26"387
3. Barrichello	1'25"825	14. Trulli	1'26"493
4. Coulthard	1'25"832	15. Zonta	1'26"945
5. Alesi	1'25"911	16. Wurz	1'28"338
6. Frentzen	1'25"917	17. de la Rosa	1'28"516
7. Panis	1'25"953	18. Badoer	1'28"914
8. Zanardi	1'26"047	19. Takagi	1'29"216
9. Häkkinen	1'26"060		
10. Herbert	1'26"253		
11. Villeneuve	1'26"338		

Total Pit Stop Times

Lap	Time (s)	Lap	Time (s)	Lap	Time (s)
1 de la Rosa	168,645	33 Alesi	20"781		
16 Panis	19"569	34 Hill	22"442		
17 Trulli	19"446	35 Frentzen	19"299		
24 Takagi	38"995	35 Irvine	18"961		
25 Zonta	29"057	35 Villeneuve	20"931		
27 Herbert	25"630	36 Salo	19"301		
29 Barrichello	23"128	36 Coulthard	20"137		
31 de la Rosa	21"741				
31 Zanardi	21"573				
32 Panis	20"722				
33 R. Schumacher	21"102				

The Race Lap by Lap

Start: Hakkinen and Zanardi get off to the best starts. While Frentzen is spinning his wheels the Italian moves into second. The big loser is Coulthard who moves into fifth place behind R. Schumacher and Salo. **Lap 1:** Frentzen overtakes Zanardi. Further back de la Rosa and Gené make contact, the Spaniard is forced to retire. **Lap 2:** Fisichella´s attempt to overtake Diniz fails, with both ending their races in a cloud of dust. **Lap 10:** Hakkinen is 4.5 seconds ahead of Frentzen. R. Schumacher is applying pressure behind third placed Zanardi, they're followed by Salo, Coulthard and Barrichello. **Lap 11:** The Brazilian blocks the Scot out and is in sixth. **Lap 17:** Zanardi lets his team-mate Schumacher past. Hakkinen is well in the lead. Title contender Irvine is in eighth. **Lap 24:** The second Minardi driver is also eliminated by an Arrows driver: Takagi hits Badoer from behind, but can continue. The Italian is out. **Lap 25:** Barrichello overtakes the trou-

ble-plagued Zanardi and is in fourth. **Lap 27:** The Italian is passed again: Salo takes over fifth. **Lap 30:** The McLaren team gives Hakkinen the signal "push". On the same lap the Finn chooses the wrong gear and slides off the track ahead of the first chicane. Frentzen takes over the lead ahead of R. Schumacher, Salo, Coulthard and Irvine. Barrichello steers into the pits to refuel. **Lap 33:** Within the next three laps the leaders all make pit stops. The order of the first three remains the same, but Coulthard and Irvine are now behind Barrichello. **Lap 42:** Coulthard embarks on a number of failed attempts to oust Barrichello from third place and on lap 50 goes off the track. **Lap 53:** Frentzen celebrates his second win of the season. R. Schumacher is a surprising second, Ferrari driver Salo reaches the last step on the podium.

Standings

Driver	Points
1. Mika Häkkinen	60
Eddie Irvine	60
3. Heinz-Harald Frentzen	50
4. David Coulthard	48
5. Michael Schumacher	32
6. Ralf Schumacher	30
7. Rubens Barrichello	15
8. Giancarlo Fisichella	13
9. Mika Salo	10
10. Damon Hill	7
11. Alexander Wurz	3
Pedro Diniz	3
13. Johnny Herbert	2
Olivier Panis	2
15. Pedro de la Rosa	1
Jean Alesi	1
Jarno Trulli	1

Team	Points
1. McLaren-Mercedes	108
2. Ferrari	102
3. Jordan-Mugen-Honda	57
4. Williams-Supertec	30
5. Stewart-Ford	17
6. Benetton-Playlife	16
7. Sauber-Petronas	4
8. Prost-Peugeot	3
9. TWR-Arrows	1

1). Lap time (top speed in qualifying).

For the Love of Money

Should winners be determined at the boardroom table? It wasn't the first time that the Formula One's adjudicators had to rule on an issue of a few millimetres or the odd kilogram, but seldom have FIA officials been so charitable as they were when they overturned Ferrari's double disqualification at the Malaysian Grand Prix.

Length, width, height - the measurements of Formula One cars are required to meet some very strict regulations. According to the rule book any infringement of these regulations shall result in automatic disqualification. Seen in this light, it's no surprise that the sporting commissioners in Malaysia were so strict with Ferrari. The reversal of their decision by the judges in Paris charged with hearing Ferrari's appeal shouldn't come as a surprise either. That decision came in the spirit of one of the Formula One's guiding principles - keeping the competition interesting, and the fan's tuned in. There's an old saying sometimes quoted by those who would doubt earthly justice: "On the high seas and in the courtroom you're at the mercy of all mighty God." The all mighty when it comes to handing out justice in the Formula One world is a man by the name of Ecclestone. More often than not, decisions regarding questions of a sporting nature just happen to coincide with what the Formula One supremo feels is best. That's because Charles Bernard Ecclestone, better known as Bernie, isn't one to allow some minor technicality like a breach of the rules spoil his lucrative show. Too much depends on an exciting race for the championship, which, if at all possible, should be decided in the last race of the season.

That's why it wasn't just Ferrari and their fans who were gnashing their teeth three and a half hours after the chequered flag was dropped in Sepang. When the sports commissioners, on the basis of a report by technical delegate Joachim Bauer, decided to disqualify both Ferrari cars, the Formula One godfather must have seen hundreds of thousands of pound notes drifting away from him. The more interesting the battle for the drivers championship is, the more television viewers tune in all over the world, and

the more viewers you have, the more you can charge for television advertising time.

That meant it was time for action. Statements about the details of the rule breaches were quickly destroyed, and concerns were publicly raised about the championship being diminished, if it were decided anywhere but on the track. It all added up to the desired result: the gentlemen from Maranello were found not guilty, with the championship to be decided in the very last race of the season.

Schumacher's First Brush with the Rules came in 1994.

It's all possible due to the vague wording of FIA's technical regulations. These grey zones provide plenty of scope, for example, to reign

in a team that might be running away with things. The best example of this came at the start of the 1998 season. After the two McLaren-Mercedes drivers had run away with the Australian Grand prix, FIA turned around and banned their braking system, which had clearly been legal.

Michael Schumacher has also made almost regular appearances in front of FIA judges. While no-one pretends that the German is a model of fair play and sportsmanship, in fact, the main reason he so often winds up in FIA's bad books is because he's too successful, having been a contender for the drivers championship five out of the last six years.

Schumacher's record with the FIA "justice department" stretches back to 1994. Following the death of Ayrton Senna, Schumacher was

Despite a sensational performance at the Belgian Grand Prix, Michael Schumacher left empty handed....

Team Manager Ken Tyrell took the term „leaded fuel" too literally: In 1984 Tyrell's drivers were stripped of all of their championship points.

threatening to run away with the title. His big mistake came at Silverstone, the home race of his only remaining challenger for the title, Damon Hill. During a warm-up lap he illegally overtook Hill, who had taken the pole position. The British officials handed the championship points leader a ten second penalty. On the orders of his team, Schumacher though remained on the course while Benetton's strategists looked for a way to get around the decision. The German was then shown the black flag, the signal that he'd been disqualified. But he ignored the signal lap after lap, not turning into the pits to serve his penalty until late in the race.

The result: FIA withdrew his six points for finishing second and barred him for the following two races. While Benetton was still appealing that decision, the English/Italian team stepped on the next landmine: The newly introduced device to measure the clearance between he bottom of the car and the road showed that Benetton's car was in violation of the regulation - by a mere millimetre. That cost Michael Schumacher a magnificently-driven victory at Spa-Francorchamps. This time though the team had really been a victim of bad timing. Shortly afterwards FIA amended the regulations, but too late for Benetton. Schumacher's disqualification naturally stood, and his lead in the points table continued to melt away.

In 1995 FIA Left the Drivers Alone.

One year later the powers that be seemed to have a change of heart, or was it that they weren't taking their jobs as seriously? Fuel samples taken from both David Coulthard's Williams and Michael Schumacher's Benetton at the Brazilian Grand Prix, didn't correspond to the ones the teams had provided prior to the season. This

... the favourite for the championship was disqualified because the wooden device designed to measure the clearance between car and track found it was a millimetre outside of the rules.

The biggest rivalry of the ´80´s ended in 1989 with a bang: McLaren drivers Ayrton Senna and Alain Prost collided.

Poisonous atmosphere: Not long after this picture was taken Alain Prost (left) and Ayrton Senna were hardly on friendly terms.

blue cars driven by Stefan Bellof and Martin Brundle had been underweight the whole season, but the cars only had to be weighed after the race. To ensure that the cars were heavy enough to make the cut, Tyrell created a special "blend" of fuel. When the cars stopped in the pits for their final fuelling stops of the day, what would flow into the tanks would be not just fuel, but lots of small lead balls as well. Although they were eventually caught out, and Tyrell were stripped of all

of their championship points, nobody could really stay mad at "Uncle Ken" for long. After all they were the only ones competing using cars outfitted with conventional engines against an entire field of turbo-charged cars.

The sports officials really got into the act in 1989. Superstar Ayrton Senna, locked in a close fight for the championship with team-mate Alain Prost, had to win the second last race of the season - the Japanese Grand Prix at Suzuka, if he

Lenient decision: After the 1995 Belgian Grand Prix, Williams and Benetton Renault were in front of the judges again. David Coulthard (below) and...

time FIA was lenient, since it was determined that the illegal fuel didn't give either driver an unfair advantage. Michael Schumacher and David Coulthard kept their points for finishing first and second respectively. The teams though paid for their indiscretions by losing their points in the constructors championship.

"Uncle Ken" Used Leaded Fuel...

While not all infractions result from carelessness, it's rare that teams break the rules deliberately. One of the best examples of this sort of thing was provided by the Tyrell team, who "earned" their 15 points in 1984 with the help of a crafty but illegal trick. Team Manager Ken Tyrell took the term "leaded fuel" too literally. The

was to keep his hopes of winning the title alive. That was a point that wasn't lost on the Frenchman, who prevented Senna from overtaking him by sharply turning his steering wheel, and sending both of them off of the track. While the little Frenchman was cheerfully getting out of his car, Senna, was busy trying to get back onto the track, with some help from a couple of friendly and strong men pushing his car to get it started. He went on to win the race, but his joy was short-lived. The regulation regarding "the use of outside help" allowed FIA to disqualify the Brazilian, and hand the world championship to Alain Prost, the preferred contender all along.

In 1997, too, decisions handed down by the racing commissioners ensured that the season was an interesting one. Williams driver and championship points leader Jacques Villeneuve was penalised for ignoring a yellow flag, and as a repeat offender he was barred from driving in the Japanese Grand Prix. Since the decision was not yet final, the French-Canadian drove in Suzuka anyway, with the clear intention of trying to make life difficult for Michael Schumacher, and with no guarantee any points he earned in the race would be counted. FIA upheld the decision and withdrew the two additional points he did claim in Japan.

McLaren Wins the Title, FIA Takes it Away.

It didn't really matter much. Just 14 days later, at the drivers championship showdown at Jerez in Spain, Michael Schumacher lost his temper and committed his most infamous act so far, ramming Quebec's "enfant terrible". Villeneuve got past him though and won the Formula One championship. Then not only did the unsportsmanlike German have to face the scorn of the media, even at home, but he was forced to appear before the FIA judges once again. They promptly stripped him of every one of his championship points.

That case casts the FIA judges in the light of highly principled guardians of justice. But the exact opposite can also be said of Ferrari's successful appeal which came just in time for the 1999 season finale in Suzuka. The judges' bizarre decision to overturn the decision of the Malaysian sporting commissioners, who had ruled the turning vanes on both Ferraris illegal was as slap in the face not only to the Malaysian FIA delegates, but to every other Formula One team. McLaren-Mercedes, whose driver, Mika Hakkinen had been awarded the win when Eddie Irvine and Michael Schumacher were disqualified, were dismayed by the turn of events. The German car maker reacted to the decision in a written statement: "Once the last race of the season is over, it will be time to clarify the question of whether the highest class of motor racing is being administered according to clear rules which are supported by all of the participants without reservation." To put it more simply, Ferrari shouldn't be given preferential treatment, and there should be no fiddling of the rules to ensure that the competition is kept artificially exciting for the lucrative television market.

...Michael Schumacher held onto their championship points despite the use of illegal fuel.
Both teams were stripped of their points towards the constructors championship.

European GP

**14th Race in the World Championship 1999,
Nurburgring (D), 26th September 1999**

Below: A scene from a lucky landing - Pedro Diniz rolled several times,
Alex Zanardi (above) had great difficulty avoiding him.

Big picture and above: The next impact crushed the rear end and the roll bar, a rear
wheel almost wedges itself between the driver's helmet and the ground.

Johnny was good

The European Grand Prix had something for everyone: drama, mayhem, and rain - tears, joy, and jubilation. The Nurburgring provided it all, in no small part due to the bizarre weather patterns over this border region of western Germany. While the traditional leaders on the Grand Prix circuit had a horrendous day, others, like Johnny Herbert, Jarno Trulli, Jackie Stewart and Pedro Diniz had a rare opportunity to celebrate.

In the end the car comes to a stop upside down. The Formula One world holds its collective breath...

...but the rescue crew soon signals that all is well: incredibly Pedro Diniz escapes with nothing but a few bruises.

European GP

The 1999 European Grand Prix would not be looked back on fondly by most of Formula One's top drivers. A whole slew of them were made into losers here. But where there are losers, as famous as they might be, there are always winners. The luckiest man on the day was Pedro Diniz. Just a few metres after the start this son of a Brazilian millionaire spectacularly rolled his Sauber-Petrona. Despite the fact that the racer's roll bar was destroyed in the process, astonishingly, Diniz emerged unscathed.

The region near Germany's western border, where the Nurburgring is located, is known for its changeable and unpredictable weather. The weekend of the 1999 European Grand Prix was to be no exception. It all began promptly in qualifying. The heavens opened up at eleven o'clock in the morning, with the rain stopping just before the final training session. Naturally the track didn't dry out right away.

Heinz-Harald Frentzen, coming off his win at Monza, was at the centre of the media circus, and

until then he'd had a terrible weekend. He missed his first open training due to gearbox trouble. Then on Saturday there was more hard luck - his car's engine had to be replaced due to an hydraulics problem. But soon the Jordan mechanics discovered that there was a problem with the replacement engine too, so it had to be hauled out and replaced with yet another engine - all of this in the space of an hour and ten minutes. Frentzen wasn't able to complete an entire laps, but his section times put him up in the same class

First victory at Monza, then a surprising pole position in Germany's Eifel region: Everything seemed to be going Heinz-Harald Frentzen´s way.

Right: A weekend to forget - at the Nurburgring Eddie Irvine's Ferrari team became the laughing stocks of the motor sport media. Far right: More than a little unhappy - Giancarlo Fisichella threw away what would have been his first Grand Prix win.

Right: Strong performance - Ralf Schumacher might have won too, had one of the tyres on his Williams not blown. Far right: Would have liked to have given Stewart their first victory - Rubens Barrichello.

with Mika Hakkinen.

It was no wonder then that nerves in the Jordan pits were getting steadily frayed as qualifying continued, mainly without Frentzen. "I'm going to have to apologise to the lads in the pits", the German later smiled. "We had a difference of opinion about when I should head out onto the track, we even got into a yelling match." The reason for the dispute was that as had been the case

"Let there not be fire!", prayed Diniz

at the French Grand Prix, it appeared likely that the rain could start again at any moment, so the team's owner, Eddie Jordan and Frentzen´s race engineer Trevor Foster wanted to send their number one driver out sooner rather than later. "Wait a few minutes for it to dry out", countered the man behind the wheel, and he was right. Ten minutes prior to the end of qualifying Frentzen rolled out of the pits with enough fuel not just for one quick lap, but for several. The 32 year old´s plan was to spend the first lap or so getting acclimatised to the difficult road conditions before really going for it. It worked. With his first real lap he catapulted himself to the top of the list of best times. The expressions in the Jordan camp brightened up in tandem with the sky above the Nurburgring.

Shortly afterwards however, other drivers were recording faster lap times. Then Frentzen beat them all. He headed to the pits in just the same way he would normally do during a race and had new tyres installed, before burning up the asphalt on an almost perfect lap, bettering the times of both of the McLarens, David Coulthard and Mika Hakkinen plus Ralf Schumacher. Both Ferrari drivers had nightmares with Irvine and Salo qualifying in ninth and twelfth respectively.

It was still more evidence that in terms of speed, Jordan had passed Ferrari, and were now second only to McLaren-Mercedes.

The German also got off the mark faster than all the rest, ahead of the two Mercedes. He was the first into the Castrol-S curve and moved out into the lead. It was a vastly different story for his team-mate Damon Hill, who had his engine stall midway through the curve, resulting in a serious crash. Alexander Wurz was caught off guard by the slowing Jordan, and in his effort to avoid Hill, he hit Pedro Diniz. The Sauber car was thrown up into the air, rolling several times before it finally came to rest upside down on the grass. A shocked Formula One world held its collective breath. But when the first track attendants arrived at the scene and rolled the destroyed racer back onto it's wheels, the Brazilian stretched out his arm and gave the thumbs up. "Tell everyone I'm okay." While waiting for his rescuers, Diniz had reason to fear the worst. "I was getting wet. First it was a warm liquid, so I knew that was coolant. Then it was a cold liquid, possibly petrol. All that was going through my head was: just don't let there be a fire..."

That was of course the cue for the safety-car to swing into action. Soon after it returned to the pits, Frentzen began increasing his lead ahead of Mika Hakkinen, David Coulthard, Ralf Schumacher and Giancarlo Fisichella. While Eddie Irvine had overcome a bad start on the restart, and had used his superior speed on the straightaways to catch Prost-Peugeot's Olivier Panis, Giancarlo turned out to be a tougher nut to crack. The Italian was cheekily zipping around the track ahead of the Northern Irishman, with Irvine unable to find an opening. It wasn't until the Benetton driver in his Veedol-Z made an error, that Fast Eddie was able to take advantage. The top four meanwhile were well on their way, having left the rest behind.

Those who know the Nurburgring know what

Neither here nor there: Ralf Schumacher was fourth in qualifying.

On the way to his most satisfying victory: Johnny Herbert.

Improvisation is a virtue: Marc Gené earned his first point.

Rain or shine: The Nurburgring always attracts the fans.

Dark clouds on the horizon: Frequent changes of weather are as much a part of the "ring" as the Nurburg castle in the background.

Inconsolable: Badoer missed his last chance for a point.

The drama of the first curve: Hill (far right) loses speed, Wurz (across the track) tries to avoid him and hits Diniz (yellow mirror).

was bound to happen next: it was almost certain to start raining, and it did. But in a fashion typical for the bizarre weather patterns of this region, it didn't start raining all over the track, the weather-god reserved this exclusive honour for the Dunlop turn at the most westerly point of the course. That left everyone with a dilemma on their hands: what to do? Regular treaded or wet weather tyres? Rain specialist Heinz-Harald Frentzen who's known for having the most sensitive foot on the accelerator on the circuit cruised through the puddles with no worries, confident

Ten points cast to the wind: David Coulthard.

Jam-packed: The Nurburgring was sold out.

Frentzen didn't see any of the involuntary comedy.

that the weather would soon improve. Ralf Schumacher, who was somehow getting sufficient performance out of his inferior Williams-Supertec to put considerable pressure on David Coulthard, seemed to like the varying track conditions, too. On lap 19 the junior German saw his opportunity in the few metres between the last curve and the entry to the finish line straightaway and moved past the doubtless disgruntled Scot - a very nice manoeuvre.

That was the sort of move that on this day, several contenders for the drivers championship could only dream of. In fact both McLaren and Ferrari were plagued by misadventures that one had to see to believe. Mika Hakkinen, who doesn't like driving on a wet track steered into the pits on lap 19 to get wet weather tyres installed. That turned out to be a mistake. That was nothing compared to what was about to develop in the Ferrari camp. The Reds' pit performance on this day approached the drama of a tragic comedy. Instead of Eddie Irvine who had opted to blindly follow Mika Hakkinen by opting for wet weather tyres, it was Mika Salo who arrived first in the pits on lap 20. The Finn had just finished demolishing his front wing. Irvine, who was running critically low on fuel followed Salo in to the pits, one lap after he was supposed to. That's a recipe for confusion to begin with. Not just that, but for good measure Ferrari's tactician Ross Brawn decided to change strategy, and ordered regular tyres installed. The crew was thrown into complete

chaos with crew members running about like mad desperately trying to rescue a rapidly deteriorating situation. Predictably, something went wrong - a tyre was missing. Nobody among the professionally trained and experienced Ferrari crew could find the elusive chunk of rubber. It took an Italian television crew member to solve the mystery of Ferrari's missing tyre. It was a full 28 seconds before Irvine was able to speed off, back into the fray.

While Hakkinen had by then dropped back to tenth, Irvine returned to the track two places behind his Finnish rival. On lap 23 the champion though returned to the pits to get regular tyres again, which forced him all the way back into what for him is a very uncustomary 14th position. What made matters worse was that because he'd made his second refuelling stop too early, he couldn´t be certain of having enough fuel to last for the balance of the race. The usually swift McLaren driver just dropped further and further back, with even the lesser lights at the back overtaking him.

Out in front, Frentzen had missed this show of black comedy. He had problems of his own. On the now dry track, Ralf Schumacher was getting too close for comfort. There was only a short let up in pressure when Schumacher made his first trip to the pits, for David Coulthard soon picked up where the German had left off. Frentzen and Coulthard both headed to the pits on lap 32. This duel wasn't decided in the pits, but just seconds later. Frentzen´s Jordan-Mugen-Honda rolled into the Castrol-S and out of the race with an electronics problem. "Everything was going perfectly in the first half of the race," moaned the visibly disappointed Frentzen. "I left the pits ahead of David, and then suddenly everything was dead. But these things happen in motor sport."

The happiest man in the world: Jackie Stewart.

Romantic scenes in the Eifel region. The chaotic weather casts the European Grand Prix in an artistic light.

"Bedtime for a sleepy cameraman.

That meant David Coulthard was in the lead, with the opportunity to pick up some very valuable points which could have immensely enhanced his chances of winning his first drivers championship. It wasn't to be: on lap 38 the Scotsman made a critical error. "It's the first time this season that I've flown off the course", he grimaced. "I hit a white track edge marker as I was braking - that's all it took." One man's misfortune is another man's opportunity: Ralf Schumacher moved into the lead. The German fans could hardly believe their eyes, particularly after his nearest challenger, Giancarlo Fisichella skidded off the track on lap 42, losing nine seconds on the leader.

Two laps later Ralf headed to the pits to get outfitted with dry weather tyres, and returned to the track in third behind Johnny Herbert. When the Englishman went for his tyre change, Schumacher moved up into second. But there was another surprise in store: "Fisico" flew off the track for a second time, thus ending his hopes of earning his first Grand Prix victory. "My mistake", balled the crestfallen, teary-eyed Italian, "the chance of a lifetime! But my headrest had

come undone, and it distracted me for a moment..."

Now the Nurburgring was rocking, with local lad Ralf Schumacher out in the lead and victory apparently within his grasp. But one lap later the right rear tyre of his Williams blew, just a second after he had passed the entrance to the pits and noticed the strange vibrations. "Unfortunately the tyre just exploded", the 24 year-old told reporters. It couldn't have happened at a more inopportune time for the young German. He manoeuvred his crippled racer around the track for another full lap, before guiding it into the pits. Despite the mishap, his boss, Frank Williams was pleased. "Ralf drove another brilliant race. He didn't make even the slightest error." Shortly after the race the wheel-chair general put his money where his mouth was, giving Schumacher a pay rise, and signing him to a contract extension which runs until 2003.

So who was leading now? The Formula One world could hardly believe it - it was Stewart driver Johnny Herbert. On this day the Englishman

"Honestly, I was fighting for my life..."

had done everything right, always heading to the pits at precisely the right time, and always choosing the right tyres. "Just as I was about to head to the pits on lap 35, it started to rain. I saw this big dark cloud overhead so I opted for wet weather tyres. It was a good move."

Johnny´s team-mate Rubens Barrichello thought otherwise. "I originally wanted wet weather tyres, too, but then I noticed a patch of blue sky. I figured the track would dry out quickly so I opted for grooved slicks. Since we'd also chosen the harder blend, in the laps that followed it became very difficult to keep the car on the track. To be honest, I was fighting for my life."

There was still no end to the drama. While Herbert was unchallenged out in the lead, Barrichello was challenging Jarno Trulli in second place. But despite intense pressure from the

"Let it rain now": Phil Collins in the Stewart Box.

Still not a single point: Jacques Villeneuve.

Mysterious: An electrical defect stopped Frentzen.

The man of the hour: Herbert (left) got his third Grand Prix victory.

A classic duel: Mika Hakkinen against Eddie Irvine - but this time the two championship contenders were only battling for sixth position.

Twenty-six years ago he stood on the very same winners podium: Team Manager Jackie Stewart enjoys a champagne shower.

The boss: Walter Kafitz is the head of Nurburgring Ltd.

Brazilian, the Prost driver didn't flinch. "A fair fight", said the Italian afterwards. "I know the Nurburgring well from the Formula 3." Minardi driver Luca Badoer meanwhile was thrilled to be in fourth - until the gearbox in his Minardi self-destructed that is. The Italian, who has never collected a single Formula One point, and for whom this was likely his last Grand Prix season, was inconsolable.

This not only moved Ralf Schumacher up a spot, Jacques Villeneuve inherited fifth - giving the former world champion his best shot so far at earning his first points of the season. He was to be denied yet again. Five laps before the finish the clutch on his BAR-Supertec gave up the ghost.

Among the others who were benefiting from all of this bad luck was Mika Hakkinen, who'd driven in a fuel efficient manner during the rain but on the dry track was one of the fastest once again. He was now challenging Eddie Irvine for the last championship point. On his third attempt on lap 61, the Finn badgered Irvine into making a mistake, which Hakkinen used to cruise past. Soon afterwards the reigning world champion overtook Marc Gené, who was delighted with the single point. It was the first point of the season for Minardi - something which in terms of television revenues is worth its weight in gold.

Nobody would have begrudged Johnny Herbert this win, except perhaps team-mate Rubens Barrichello, who had mixed feelings. "Deep down in my heart of course I'm happy for Johnny, up until today he'd had a really rough season. On the other hand I would have liked to have been the one to give Stewart their first win..."

For Jackie Stewart, who won his last race as a driver at the Nurburgring in 1973, it was the culmination of a dream. The win ensured that the three time world champion was able to see his name entered into the list of winners once again, a rare opportunity since the team is to be re-named Jaguar in 2000. "I'm incredibly proud of this team", the champagne-soaked Scot exclaimed. Naturally he had climbed up onto the podium, too.

Statistics

14th Race in the World Championship 1999, Nürburgring (D), 26th September 1999

Course length:	4,556 km
Distance of race:	66 (= 300,696 km)
Start time:	13.00 UTC
Weather on day of race:	partly cloudy with occasional showers
Attendance:	142 000
1998 Results:	1. Mika Hakkinen (FIN, McLaren-Mercedes MP4/13) 1 h 32'14"789
	2. Michael Schumacher (D, Ferrari F300), – 2"211 s
	3. David Coulthard (GB, McLaren-Mercedes MP 4/14), – 34"164 s
Pole position 1998:	Michael Schumacher (Ferrari F300), 1'18"561 m
Fastest Lap 1998:	Mika Häkkinen (McLaren-Mercedes MP4/13), 1'20"450 m
Fastest pit stop 1998:	Mika Häkkinen (McLaren-Mercedes MP4/13), 24"858 s

On a dry track you can take the Hatzenbach bend at 270 kph

"The Nurburgring is a good mixture of slow turns and curves that can be taken in third or fourth gear. The best feature is the Hatzenbach bend which we can take about 270 kph. The great unknown about this track is always the weather. As is the case in Spa, rain can start at any time, and sometimes only affects one area of the track."

Johnny Herbert

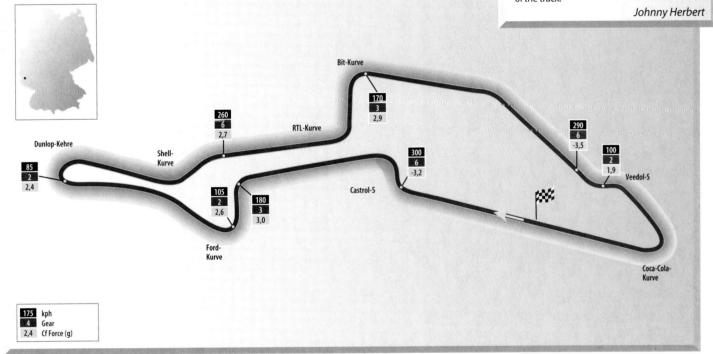

175	kph
4	Gear
2,4	Cf Force (g)

Results

Driver	Team	Pit stops	Laps	Time (hours)	Average speed	Behind 1st	prev. driver
1. Johnny Herbert	Stewart-Ford	2	66	1 h 41'54"314	177,034	–	–
2. Jarno Trulli	Prost-Peugeot	3	66	1 h 42'16"933	176,381	22"618 s	22"619 s
3. Rubens Barrichello	Stewart-Ford	1	66	1 h 42'17"180	176,374	22"865 s	0"247 s
4. Ralf Schumacher	Williams-Supertec	3	66	1 h 42'33"822	175,987	39"507 s	16"642 s
5. Mika Häkkinen	McLaren-Mercedes	2	66	1 h 42'57"264	175,230	1'02"950 m	23"449 s
6. Marc Gené	Minardi-Ford	1	66	1 h 42'59"468	175,167	1'05"154 m	2"204 s
7. Eddie Irvine	Ferrari	3	66	1 h 43'00"997	175,124	1'06"683 m	1"529 s
8. Ricardo Zonta	BAR-Supertec	3	65	1 h 42'08"914	173,936	1 lap	1 lap
9. Olivier Panis	Prost-Peugeot	2	65	1 h 42'18"099	173,676	1 lap	9"185 s
10. Jacques Villeneuve [1]	BAR-Supertec	1	62	1 h 35'55"300	173,828	retirement	retirement

Driver	Team	Pit stops	in lap	Reason f. retiring	Position before retiring
Luca Badoer	Minardi-Ford	1	54	gearbox	4
Pedro de la Rosa	TWR-Arrows	2	53	gearbox	12
Giancarlo Fisichella	Benetton-Playlife	1	49	spun out	1
Mika Salo	Ferrari	2	45	defective brakes	14
Toranosuke Takagi	TWR-Arrows	2	43	spun out	15
David Coulthard	McLaren-Mercedes	1	38	spun out	1
Jean Alesi	Sauber-Petronas	2	36	power transmission	10
Heinz-Harald Frentzen	Jordan-Mugen-Honda	1	33	electrical	1
Alessandro Zanardi	Williams-Supertec	0	11	spun out	17
Damon Hill	Jordan-Mugen-Honda	0	1	power transmission	12
Alexander Wurz	Benetton-Playlife	0	1	crash	14
Pedro Diniz	Sauber-Petronas	0	1	crash	13

1) Didn't complete race, but counted due to distance driven.

Starting Grid

8 Heinz-Harald Frentzen (D)
Jordan-Mugen-Honda 199/5
1'19"910 m (298,0 km/h) [1]

2 David Coulthard (GB)
McLaren-Mercedes MP4/14-7
1'20"176 m (302,6 km/h)

1 Mika Häkkinen (FIN)
McLaren-Mercedes MP4/14-5
1'20"376 m (300,4 km/h)

6 Ralf Schumacher (D)
Williams-Supertec FW21/6
1'20"444 m (293,0 km/h)

18 Olivier Panis (F)
Prost-Peugeot AP02/5
1'20"638 m (297,1 km/h)

9 Giancarlo Fisichella (I)
Benetton-Playlife B199/7
1'20"781 m (297,7 km/h)

7 Damon Hill (GB)
Jordan-Mugen-Honda 199/4
1'20"818 m (302,0 km/h)

22 Jacques Villeneuve (CDN)
BAR-Supertec 01/6
1'20"825 m (296,6 km/h)

4 Eddie Irvine (GB)
Ferrari F399/191
1'20"842 m (301,0 km/h)

19 Jarno Trulli (I)
Prost-Peugeot AP02/2
1'20"965 m (295,1 km/h)

10 Alexander Wurz (A)
Benetton-Playlife B199/4
1'21"144 m (296,7 km/h)

3 Mika Salo (FIN)
Ferrari F399/195
1'21"314 m (299,5 km/h)

12 Pedro Diniz (BR)
Sauber-Petronas C18/7
1'21"345 m (294,0 km/h)

17 Johnny Herbert (GB)
Stewart-Ford SF3/5
1'21"379 m (296,1 km/h)

16 Rubens Barrichello (BR)
Stewart-Ford SF3/4
1'21"490 m (299,8 km/h)

11 Jean Alesi (F)
Sauber-Petronas C18/4
1'21"634 m (298,4 km/h)

23 Ricardo Zonta (BR)
BAR-Supertec 01/7
1'22"267 m (294,6 km/h)

5 Alessandro Zanardi (I)
Williams-Supertec FW21/5
1'22"284 m (298,7 km/h)

20 Luca Badoer (I)
Minardi-Ford-Zetec-R M01/1
1'22"631 m (290,3 km/h)

21 Marc Gené (E)
Minardi-Ford-Zetec-R M01/4
1'22"760 m (291,1 km/h)

15 Toranosuke Takagi (J)
TWR-Arrows A20/5
1'23"401 m (288,9 km/h)

14 Pedro de la Rosa (E)
TWR-Arrows A20/7
1'23"698 m (288,0 km/h)

107-percent time   1'25"504 m

Best Laps

In Training on Friday (m)			
1. Häkkinen	1'20"578	12. Frentzen	1'21"933
2. Salo	1'20"920	13. Herbert	1'21"982
3. Panis	1'21"134	14. Hill	1'22"207
4. Irvine	1'21"338	15. Badoer	1'22"311
5. R. Schumacher	1'21"385	16. Zanardi	1'22"321
6. Coulthard	1'21"461	17. Wurz	1'22"427
7. Barrichello	1'21"505	18. Diniz	1'22"462
8. Fisichella	1'21"636	19. de la Rosa	1'22"853
9. Trulli	1'21"750	20. Gené	1'22"872
10. Villeneuve	1'21"850	21. Zonta	1'23"604
11. Alesi	1'21"884	22. Takagi	1'24"282

In the Race on Sunday (m)			
1. Häkkinen	1'21"282	12. Salo	1'23"404
2. Coulthard	1'21"835	13. Gené	1'23"657
3. Frentzen	1'22"082	14. Trulli	1'23"742
4. R. Schumacher	1'22"237	15. Badoer	1'23"745
5. Fisichella	1'22"244	16. Panis	1'23"905
6. Irvine	1'22"332	17. Zanardi	1'24"300
7. Villeneuve	1'22"564	18. Takagi	1'24"848
8. Barrichello	1'22"960	19. de la Rosa	1'24"857
9. Herbert	1'23"010		
10. Zonta	1'23"067		
11. Alesi	1'23"097		

Total Pit Stop Times

Lap	Time (s)	Lap	Time (s)	Lap	Time (s)
12 de la Rosa	30"908	24 Zonta	26"818	35 Badoer	57"181
19 Panis	28"712	27 R. Schumacher	26"564	35 Alesi	31"224
19 Zonta	28"855	28 Trulli	27"025	37 Barrichello	32"592
19 Takagi	28"478	28 Alesi	31"720	40 Irvine	28"754
20 Häkkinen	31"727	32 Frentzen	26"050	44 R. Schumacher	29"356
20 Salo	59"290	32 Coulthard	26"816	44 Zonta	29"241
21 Irvine	48"124	32 Fisichella	25"972	46 de la Rosa	1'09"242
22 Takagi	26"499	33 Villeneuve	32"375	47 Herbert	26"922
23 Panis	32"793	34 Gené	30"081	48 Trulli	26"646
23 Salo	27"553	35 Herbert	33"009	49 Irvine	25"726
24 Häkkinen	27"484	35 Trulli	27"726	50 R. Schumacher	33"687

The Race Lap by Lap

Start: Abandoned after Gené's motor dies. Restart: Frentzen hits the Castrol-S curve first, Hakkinen overtakes Coulthard. Hill's Jordan dies in the curve. Alesi swerves off into the grass, Wurz towards the middle of the track and hits Diniz. The Brazilian's Sauber rolls several times, coming to rest upside down. **Lap 2:** Safety car phase. Diniz is rescued. **Lap 6:** At the restart Frentzen remains ahead of Hakkinen, Coulthard, R. Schumacher, and Fisichella. Irvine overtakes Panis in sixth. **Lap 17:** Irvine overtakes Fisichella when he temporarily leaves the track. R. Schumacher pursues Coulthard. **Lap 18:** Rain begins on the northern portion of the track. Schumacher outfoxes Coulthard. **Lap 20:** Hakkinen changes to rain tyres, Frentzen loses him. When Irvine heads to the pits they only have three tyres ready - 20 seconds are lost. **Lap 23:** The rain ends, Hakkinen changes to dry weather tyres and is 14th. **Lap 32:** Frentzen and Coulthard drive to the pits at the same time, and return to the track in the same order, but moments later Frentzen is eliminated by an electrical failure. **Lap 35:** Herbert gets wet weather tyres. **Lap 38:** Coulthard skids off the track, R. Schumacher takes over the lead. **Lap 43:** The leader gets new dry road tyres in the pits. **Lap 49:** Fisichella - now the leader - spins out. **Lap 50:** Tyre blows on R. Schumacher's Williams, who is until then, back in the lead. Herbert moves into first. **Lap 55:** Badoer is in tears - he was in fourth when the gearbox on his Minardi breaks down. **Lap 57:** Second-placed Trulli is under pressure from Barrichello. **Lap 63:** The two favourites for the championship battle for seventh place. Hakkinen badgers Irvine into an error and overtakes him. No points for BAR yet again: Villeneuve is in fifth when his engine fails. **Lap 65:** Hakkinen catches Gené and moves into sixth. **Lap 66:** Herbert gives Stewart-Ford their first Formula One win.

Standings

Driver/Points			
1. Mika Häkkinen	62	Damon Hill	7
2. Eddie Irvine	60	13. Alexander Wurz	3
3. Heinz-Harald Frentzen	50	Pedro Diniz	3
4. David Coulthard	48	15. Oliver Panis	2
5. Ralf Schumacher	33	16. Pedro de la Rosa	1
6. Michael Schumacher	32	Jean Alesi	1
7. Rubens Barrichello	19	Marc Gené	1
8. Giancarlo Fisichella	13		
9. Johnny Herbert	12		
10. Mika Salo	10		
11. Jarno Trulli	7		

Team	Points
1. McLaren-Mercedes	110
2. Ferrari	102
3. Jordan-Mugen-Honda	57
4. Williams-Supertec	33
5. Stewart-Ford	31
6. Benetton-Playlife	16
7. Prost-Peugeot	9
8. Sauber-Petronas	4
9. TWR-Arrows	1
10. Minardi-Ford	1

1) Lap time (top speed in qualifying).

Eyewitness to a fiasco: Ferrari boss Luca di Montezemolo.

Can He Come Back?

His title hopes ended in a stack of tyres: When the brakes on Michael Schumacher's Ferrari failed, causing him to crash into the barrier, the primary concern was about how badly he'd been injured. But the doctor who examined him had barely completed his diagnosis when speculation began about how quickly the German would be able to return to the cockpit.

Above: Niki Lauda (right) made the most spectacular comeback in Formula One history. After his fiery crash at the old Nurburg-ring the Austrian received the last sacrament. Six weeks later he was back at the starting line and missed winning the drivers championship by a single point. Below: Missed eight races. Patrick Depailler broke both legs in a 1980 hang-gliding accident.

One thing that Formula One history has taught us, is that it's virtually impossible to predict how well any given driver will perform following a serious accident. There's no more truth to the old saying "every crash slows you down", than to the wildly optimistic predictions that filled the tabloids following Michael Schumacher's operation. The theories that he could return after just six weeks, with his car outfitted with a hand-operated accelerator and special padding for his legs turned out to be about as realistic as expecting to see a Minardi car starting from the pole position. Despite the fact that his superior physical fitness and his burning desire to win gave him a decided edge in the recovery process, his doctors came to the quick conclusion that he would have to sit out for a period of at least three months - about the same length of time it took Prost driver Olivier Panis to recover after his accident two years earlier.

A video address to his disciples at Hockenheim was listened to with intense interest throughout the Formula One world, and it revealed two new pieces of information: "I'm only human", was the overachiever's first admission. He also spoke for the first time about the heel injury which had torpedoed his hopes of making his comeback at Monza. The 14 weeks between his accident at Silverstone and the two-time world champion's comeback at the Malaysian Grand Prix were filled with speculation, cancellations, denials of rumours and even an audience with the Pope. When he did finally return to the cockpit, he looked so much like the Schumacher of old, that it seemed clear that he would be a force to be reckoned with in the battle for the 2000 drivers championship.

Quicker returns to the cockpit though have been plagued with problems. Richard Zonta, who had to sit out the start of the season due to leg injuries, felt fit enough to race at Imola. But the Formula One's head doctor, Sid Watkins wasn't about to take the racer's word for it. He made Zonta go through a simple test - he made him jump onto the floor from a chair. He failed the test, and Watkins didn't give the BAR driver the approval he needed to enter the race.

Olivier Panis wouldn't have any problem with that kind of test - in part due to two massive steel plates in his legs. But until those plates, which were implanted following his 1997 crash in Montreal, were removed, the former Formula 3000 champion performed, as Panis put it, "as if the hand brake was permanently on."

He made his comeback just 13 weeks later, but his full recovery didn't just come later, but too late. When he crashed in Montreal he was third in the drivers standings, but in 1998, the first complete season after his accident, he couldn't get used to the new treaded tyres, and failed to earn a single championship point.

Karl Wendlinger had the misfortune of crashing in 1994, before the introduction of the new higher cockpit walls. In Monaco the Austrian hit the wall sideways at high speed. He was in a coma for four weeks, but with the help of Austrian fitness guru Willi Dungl he got back onto his feet and returned to the track after an absence of 13 races. Team Boss Peter Sauber kept his word, given shortly after Wendlinger's crash: "Whenever Karli is fit again, we'll have a car for him." Despite this unusual support from his team, Karl never regained his confidence in the cockpit. After five Grand Prix races in 1995, his team gave up on him.

One driver found it easier to put his own crash behind him than that of one of his competitors. Rubens Barrichello literally lived under the cloud of Ayrton Senna's fatal crash in 1994.

The beginning of the end. Karl Wendlinger sustained severe head injuries in his 1994 crash at Monte Carlo. His comeback for Sauber only lasted a few races.

The Brazilian had little trouble dealing with his spectacular crash into the guard fence at Imola, but the death of Senna, his mentor, created a gap in his life which he was unable to fill. He lost the person he most looked up to, and at the same time, as Senna´s heir-apparent, he was lumbered with the pressure to replace his compatriot in the hearts of the Brazilian fans.

This year's winner at the Nürburgring almost had his career ended before it even began. Johnny Herbert was involved in an horrific crash on the Formula 3000 circuit which damaged his legs to such an extent that the doctors could only shake their heads over his ambition to continue his racing career. But the little Englishman beat the odds. In 1989, even before he was able to walk again, he was driving to a fourth place finish in his sensational debut for Benetton in Brazil. Unfortunately though it was a one off, since complications resulting from his original injuries prevented him from driving to his full potential.

Patrick Depailler was also competitive in the first race of his comeback. When the little Frenchman returned to the cockpit of his Alfa Romeo after missing eight races in 1980 he appeared to be even more self-confident than he had been before his accident, in which he suffered multiple breaks in both legs - in a hang-gliding accident.

"I was born to drive race cars..."

The most spectacular comeback of them all though had to be Nick Lauda´s return to the cockpit at Monza in 1976. Horrendously scarred by the burns he'd suffered in his crash at the Nurburgring, just six weeks later he was ready to race again, to keep alive his chances of winning the drivers championship. That didn't sit well with his boss, Enzo Ferrari. Convinced that Lauda wouldn't survive at all, or at best would never drive again, Ferrari had gone out and hired a replacement. Lauda earned points right away, but mentally he still wasn't quite back to his old self. In the race which decided the drivers championship, the rain-soaked Japanese Grand Prix at Fuji, he retired to the pits voluntarily. "Too dangerous", was his only comment, before he caught a plane back to Europe. It was only when he arrived in Vienna that he learned that England's

James Hunt had won the championship by a single point. By 1977 though he'd recovered his mental toughness winning the drivers championship. When a reporter asked him how he felt one year later, Lauda asked: "One year after what?"

What is it about Austrians and fire? Lauda´s compatriot Gerhard Berger survived a fiery crash at Imola in 1989. The completely full fuel tanks on his Ferrari exploded in flames when he crashed in the Tamburello high-speed curve. For weeks later his hair on the back of his neck stood on end every time he saw as much as the flame of a lighter. But that didn't stop the Austrian daredevil from climbing back into the pits after just 3 weeks on the mend. Not just that, but Berger won another Formula One race before the season was out.

As terrible as the burns to these two drivers were, they pale in comparison to what one driver experienced, who would later go on to become one of the all-time greats. In 1953 Juan Manuel Fangio spent six long months in a corset cast after sustaining several vertebral fractures when he crashed into a tree at the Parco di Monza. Fangio overcame his fears to climb into the cockpit of a new Alfa Romeo. Following a few careful laps he knew that "I´ve got to do it", and he returned to the Formula One circuit. The Argentinean went on to win four drivers championships and set records for Grand Prix wins as well as the number of races started.

Mika Hakkinen is familiar with a similar sequence of events - first a life-threatening crash, then the world championship. In the final training session at the 1995 Australian Grand Prix he blew a tyre and crashed into a wall at almost full speed. He was left in a coma, and it took him the whole winter to recover from this terrible accident. In 1998 he won the drivers championship.

All of the best drivers, like Michael Schumacher, are able to put any fears they may have out of their minds once the race starts. "Right after the accident I thought about retiring", Schumacher admitted in his first interview following his crash at Silverstone. The reason he came back was simple: "I was born to drive race cars. That's what I enjoy doing."

For weeks the sight of the flame from a lighter frightened him: Austrian Gerhard Berger crashed into a wall at Imola in 1989.

Needed an entire winter break to recover, following his terrible crash in Australia in 1995: Mika Hakkinen.

Drove as if the handbrake was stuck: Prost driver Olivier Panis.

Faster than ever on his comeback: Michael Schumacher.

15th Race in the World Championship 1999, Sepang
International Circuit (MAL), 17th October 1999

A Moral Victory?

Well done: David Coulthard (behind) takes advantage of an error by Michael Schumacher to slip past the German.

metres

The most controversial Grand Prix race of the entire season wasn't decided until five days after the drivers crossed the finish line. An appeal court declared the disqualifications of Eddie Irvine and Michael Schumacher null and void. The turn of events raised new questions about the integrity of the sport's governing body.

Team effort: Eddie Irvine (in front) thanks Schumacher for his rare assistance to a team-mate.

Powerless: Mika Hakkinen couldn't find a way to beat Ferrari's blocking tactics.

Great start: Mika Hakkinen used the opening provided to him by team-mate David Coulthard (in front).

wo hours after Ferrari's one-two victory at the Malaysian Grand Prix, their joy had turned to bitter disappointment and dismay. The technical delegation from FIA, motor sport´s world governing body, declared the two Ferrari F399´s illegal due to turning vanes installed on the sides of both racers. The turning vanes the FIA delegates had determined, were ten millimetres too wide. As a result the sports commissioners had no choice but to disqualify both the winner, Eddie Irvine, and runner-up Michael Schumacher. Third-placed Mika Hakkinen was declared the winner. That handed the Finnish driver the championship for the second year running, but only on an interim basis, since Ferrari immediately filed for an appeal. At the same time Ferrari launched an aggressive media campaign, telling any reporter who would listen that the turning vanes, although technically illegal, didn't enhance the performance of their cars one bit. What had so been far from an uneventful Formula One season, finally had a nice juicy scandal on its hands.

The tabloids ate it all up, of course. The whole week between Ferrari's disqualifications and their day in court in Paris, the daily rags were filled with speculation about what really was behind, what appeared to be an inexcusable mistake by Ferrari. While one report suggested a "typical" impropriety by German commissioner Joachim Bauer, another claimed to have uncovered a case of espionage and sabotage. McLaren it was alleged, had long known about Ferrari's illegal turning vanes, and had waited until just the right moment to inform the officials.

What was also interesting was the sort of coalitions that were suddenly springing up, trying to influence public opinion, and by extension presumably, the opinions of the judges. Frank Williams who is known not to be particularly friendly with the Ferrari people, surprised just about everybody by supporting Ferrari. No wonder: If the disqualification were to be overturned, Stewart, who Williams is battling against for fourth in the constructors standings, would be awarded not ten, but instead just 5 points. Bearing this in mind, it's not hard to imagine whose side Jackie Stewart was on. Alas, the Formula One is a championship in which only one's personal interests seem to count for much these days. In fact though the sport was caught between a rock and a hard place: It stood to lose no matter what the judges decided. Upholding the disqualification would mean that the last race of the season would be virtually meaningless. On the other hand, reversing the decision would call the integrity of the sport into question. It was the "International Court of Appeal" which was charged with making this, on the surface at least, difficult decision. The five judges, one each from Portugal, Austria, Belgium, Holland, and Greece who FIA stressed over and over were completely independent and impartial, came to an astonishing decision. They found that Ferrari's turning vanes weren't 10 millimetres too wide after all, but merely a paltry five millimetres outside of legality. They determined that not only had the tech-

Remorseful: Ralf Schumacher paid for his mistake.

Offending wings: Ferrari hid the mounted spoilers.

In the best rallying tradition: Toranosuke Takagi started from last.

History lesson: Mercedes hopeful Nick Heidfeld in the vintage W154.

Spying in the pits? Ferrari's disqualification shocked the Formula One world.

Delighted: Johnny Herbert was again Stewart's best.

nical delegates in Malaysia used the wrong procedure to measure the Ferrari parts, but they'd also failed to use the correct measuring device. It was a crafty decision, since it placed the blame squarely on a group that didn't have a strong lobby in the media - the technical commissioners. Ferrari, Irvine and Schumacher all had their points back, and the drivers championship was wide open once again.

Back to the race.

But it no was no wider open than a series of unanswered questions. Why for example had even Ferrari openly admitted following the disqualifications that the parts were indeed illegal? Why had they been covering up the offending parts as soon as the cars were off the track, ever since they were first introduced at the Nurburgring? Why had the technical delegates in Malaysia been forced to work with the wrong measuring devices? Whatever the answers, the court's decision left a decidedly unpleasant aftertaste.

That didn't bother Michael Schumacher one bit. You could even argue that Sepang was a moral victory for the German driver, who, following a lay off of 98 days, looked as if he hadn't missed a lap. He not only qualified in pole position, but made several of the other top drivers look slow in the process. With 15 minutes left in the last qualifying session he bettered his teammate's best time by 1.1 seconds. The McLaren drivers David Hakkinen and Mika Hakkinen were left even further behind. After qualifying the German couldn't resist rubbing it in Eddie Irvine's face: "This was a great success not just for me but for the entire team", he said with a broad smile. "They've been under a lot of media pressure over the past few seeks. Now we've shown what the Ferrari is really capable of. Nobody seems to want to believe me, but I've been saying all along, we've got a bigger edge on McLaren than ever before."

Things didn't go nearly as well for another Rhinelander at the beautiful Sepang International Circuit. In fact Heinz-Harald Frentzen had a nightmare in qualifying. In his first session part of the interior of his cockpit began to come apart. "Something suddenly hit me in the neck, and I was so startled that I went into a spin." As a result the Jordan driver wound up in the gravel. The determined German jumped into the untested reserve car - which, as it turned out, had a problem with the brakes on the front left-hand wheel. The first half hour of qualifying was lost as the Jordan mechanics feverishly worked to correct the problem. Frentzen though was still undeterred, he headed out to the track and drove like a desperado, but his best on the day, was simply substandard. He qualified in a disappointing 14th position. But during the race itself, Frentzen

Strange bedfellows: Surprisingly Team Boss Frank Williams supported Ferrari.

Relieved: Team Boss Jean Todt congratulates Michael Schumacher.

The pit stop crawl: Despite his one stop strategy, Heinz-Harald Frentzen could do no better than sixth.

Michael Schumacher felt fit despite the heat.

You're welcome: Ferrari gave thanks with a one-two win.

Exotic: Malaysian grid girl in traditional dress.

proved that he really is much better than his troubled performance in qualifying. While the rest of the field were driving best laps on an average of 0.6 seconds worse then their qualifying times, Frentzen went and recorded a best lap that, had he done so well in qualifying, would have guaranteed him a place in the first row of the starting grid.

Michael Schumacher built on his pole position with a strong performance during the race itself. He reached the first curve in the lead and promptly began increasing his lead on the rest by a second per lap. At first a lot of spectators and commentators alike assumed that it was a two stop strategy, and thus a lighter car that was allowing him to leave the rest of the field behind. To their amazement, they were later to find out that they'd assumed wrong.

On lap three the two-time world champion interrupted his impressive demonstration to get down to his real business on the day: He started giving team-mate Eddie Irvine the support that the team had demanded Schumacher provide the Northern Irishman who was now the team's only shot at the drivers championship. Schumacher let off the accelerator long enough to allow Irvine to overtake him. But the cocky German got more than he bargained for: The pride of Scotland, David Coulthard, whose McLaren was considerably lighter due to his two pit stop strategy, suddenly pulled up alongside the Ferrari driver, and left him in his dust. "That wasn't part of my plan", the surprised Rhinelander later admitted. "I didn't expect David to launch a challenge at that point. He caught me by surprise - perhaps that had something to do with my long layoff." But Schumacher didn't let David by without a fight - at one point the cars even made contact. "My front wing was damaged, that's why my car was understeering from

then on", complained the Formula One returnee.

While Hakkinen was stranded behind the third place Ferrari, Coulthard was completing considerably faster laps, trying to hunt down Eddie Irvine. It appeared simply to be a matter of time before the Scotsman would catch the Northern Irishman.

Unsportsmanlike

"Our plan appeared to be working perfectly", said McLaren boss Ron Dennis later. "Eddie had a lot more to lose than David had - meaning he could have been all the more bold in his attempt to overtake him." Coulthard though never got the opportunity, due to a technical failure. On lap 15 he rolled out of the race due to a loss of fuel pressure. After that Hakkinen's job didn't get any easier, as Schumacher spent the rest of the race cutting off the faster Finn. "It was completely frustrating. Michael wasn't taking the curves at a regular speed, sometimes he'd brake earlier, sometimes later, so I had to be careful at all times not to run into him", explained a totally exhausted Mika Hakkinen following the race. While still out on the track, his frustration got the best of him at times, as he was seen making angry gestures at his German tormentor. Later though he was more conciliatory. "I can't blame Ferrari, we probably would have done the same thing in that situation." Ron Dennis didn't share his Finnish driver's assessment. "No, we wouldn't even consider doing something like that. We're not going to lodge a protest, but what they did is certainly not in the spirit of sportsmanship."

Ferrari's questionable tactic though did have the desired effect. Eddie Irvine remained in the lead even after completing his first pit stop. Although Schumacher later complained of understeering and that his tyres were wearing too quickly, ahead of his one and only pit stop he did manage to complete the two fastest laps of the weekend, enough to keep him ahead of his Scandinavian rival when he returned to the track, despite the fact that he took longer in the pits, because his fuel tank had to be filled to the brim. Hakkinen was to have even more problems. When he completed his last refuelling stop nine laps before the end of the race, he found himself behind European Grand Prix winner Johnny Herbert. The slight Englishman, who for the first time on the day had managed to get team-mate Rubens Barrichello out of his hair, defended third place like a tiger. It wasn't until the third lap from the finish that he made a small but crucial error. "Johnny took the curve a little too wide", recounted Hakkinen. "That caused him to lose momentum, and I was past."

The win allowed Northern Ireland's Eddie Irvine to significantly improve his chances of claiming the drivers world championship, even if he had to wait for a panel of judges in Paris to hand down a bizarre and questionable decision five days later, to confirm that the win and the lead in the championship table were indeed his.

Statistics

Course length:	5,542 km
Distance of race:	56 (= 310,352 km)
Start time:	7.00 UTC
Weather on day of race:	very warm, cloudy, very humid
Attendance:	80 000
1998 Results:	1999 was the first year the track was in use
Pole position 1998:	–
Fastest Lap 1998:	–
Fastest pit stop 1998:	–

It's difficult to achieve the right balance on the curves

"I really like this track. This course is extremely demanding, but that's precisely what makes it so much fun. It has a mixture of narrow, blind curves and longer, fast curves. Because of this variety it's difficult to find the right balance on the curves, despite the fact that you get a lot of grip. Enduring the heat during the race isn't a big problem."

Eddie Irvine

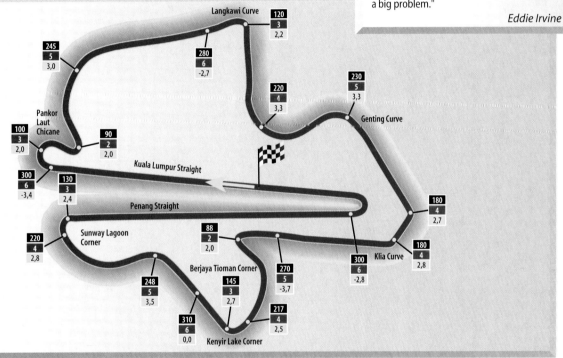

175	kph
4	Gear
2,4	Cf Force (g)

Results

Driver	Team	Pit stops	Laps	Time (hours)	Average speed	Behind 1st	prev. driver
1. Eddie Irvine	Ferrari	2	56	1 h 36'38"494	192,697	–	–
2. Michael Schumacher	Ferrari	1	56	1 h 36'39"534	192,655	1"040 s	–
3. Mika Häkkinen	McLaren-Mercedes	2	56	1 h 36'48"237	192,359	12"743 s	8"703 s
4. Johnny Herbert	Stewart-Ford	1	56	1 h 36'56"032	192,101	17"538 s	7"795 s
5. Rubens Barrichello	Stewart-Ford	2	56	1 h 37'10"790	191,615	32"296 s	14"758 s
6. Heinz-Harald Frentzen	Jordan-Mugen-Honda	1	56	1 h 37'13"378	191,530	34"884 s	2"588 s
7. Jean Alesi	Sauber-Petronas	2	56	1 h 37'32"902	190,891	54"408 s	19"524 s
8. Alexander Wurz	Benetton-Playlife	2	56	1 h 37'39"428	190,678	1'00"934 m	6"526 s
9. Marc Gené	Minardi-Ford	1	55	1 h 37'10"056	188,217	1 lap	1 lap
10. Alessandro Zanardi	Williams-Supertec	3	55	1 h 37'36"473	188,368	1 lap	26"417 s
11. Giancarlo Fisichella	Benetton-Playlife	3	52	1 h 38'14"562	176,003	4 laps	3 laps

Driver	Team	Pit stops	in lap	Reason f. retiring	Position before retiring
Jacques Villeneuve	BAR-Supertec	2	49	hydraulics	9
Pedro Diniz	Sauber-Petronas	2	45	spun out	9
Pedro de la Rosa	TWR-Arrows	1	31	engine	12
Luca Badoer	Minardi-Ford	1	16	engine	14
David Coulthard	McLaren-Mercedes	0	15	fuel pressure	2
Ralf Schumacher	Williams-Supertec	0	8	spun out	9
Toranosuke Takagi	TWR-Arrows	0	8	throttle	13
Ricardo Zonta	BAR-Supertec	0	7	spun out	15
Olivier Panis	Prost-Peugeot	0	6	engine	15
Damon Hill	Jordan-Mugen-Honda	0	1	collision	9
Jarno Trulli	Prost-Peugeot	0	0	engine	18

GP Malaysia

15th Race in the World Championship 1999, Sepang International Circuit (MAL), 17th Oktober 1999

Starting Grid

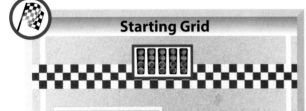

3 Michael Schumacher (D)
Ferrari F399/195
1'39"688 m (297,6 km/h) [1]

4 Eddie Irvine (GB)
Ferrari F399/196
1'40"635 m (298,8 km/h)

2 David Coulthard (GB)
McLaren-Mercedes MP4/14-6
1'40"806 m (299,7 km/h)

1 Mika Häkkinen (FIN)
McLaren-Mercedes MP4/14-4
1'40"866 m (299,1 km/h)

17 Johnny Herbert (GB)
Stewart-Ford SF3/3
1'40"937 m (296,1 km/h)

16 Rubens Barrichello (BR)
Stewart-Ford SF3/4
1'41"351 m (297,5 km/h)

10 Alexander Wurz (A)
Benetton-Playlife B199/4
1'41"444 m (292,5 km/h)

6 Ralf Schumacher (D)
Williams-Supertec FW21/6
1'41"558 m (284,4 km/h)

7 Damon Hill (GB)
Jordan-Mugen-Honda 199/4
1'42"050 m (295,7 km/h)

22 Jacques Villeneuve (CDN)
BAR-Supertec 01/6
1'42"087 m (295,2 km/h)

9 Giancarlo Fisichella (I)
Benetton-Playlife B199/7
1'42"110 m (296,3 km/h)

18 Olivier Panis (F)
Prost-Peugeot AP02/5
1'42"208 m (295,2 km/h)

23 Ricardo Zonta (BR)
BAR-Supertec 01/7
1'42"310 m (297,4 km/h)

8 Heinz-Harald Frentzen (D)
Jordan-Mugen-Honda 199/5
1'42"380 m (294,0 km/h)

11 Jean Alesi (F)
Sauber-Petronas C18/4
1'42"522 m (290,4 km/h)

5 Alessandro Zanardi (I)
Williams-Supertec FW21/3
1'42"885 m (295,0 km/h)

12 Pedro Diniz (BR)
Sauber-Petronas C18/5
1'42"933 m (290,0 km/h)

19 Jarno Trulli (I)
Prost-Peugeot AP02/7
1'42"948 m (297,2 km/h)

21 Marc Gené (E)
Minardi-Ford-Zetec-R M01/4
1'43"563 m (291,2 km/h)

14 Pedro de la Rosa (E)
TWR-Arrows A20/7
1'43"579 m (291,1 km/h)

20 Luca Badoer (I)
Minardi-Ford-Zetec-R M01/1
1'44"321 m (290,3 km/h)

15 Toranosuke Takagi (J)
TWR-Arrows A20/5
1'44"637 m (292,3 km/h)

107-percent time: 1'46"666 m

1) Lap time (top speed in qualifying).

Best Laps

In Training on Friday (m)

1.	Villeneuve	1'42"407	12.	Hill	1'43"417
2.	Coulthard	1'42"519	13.	Panis	1'43"500
3.	Alesi	1'42"701	14.	Frentzen	1'43"677
4.	Irvine	1'42"725	15.	Trulli	1'43"793
5.	M. Schumacher	1'42"875	16.	Badoer	1'44"818
6.	Diniz	1'43"006	17.	Zonta	1'44"968
7.	Barrichello	1'43"042	18.	R. Schumacher	1'45"164
8.	Häkkinen	1'43"153	19.	de la Rosa	1'45"397
9.	Wurz	1'43"311	20.	Zanardi	1'45"833
10.	Herbert	1'43"349	21.	Takagi	1'46"690
11.	Fisichella	1'43"403	22.	Gené	1'49"451

In the Race on Sunday (m)

1.	M. Schumacher	1'40"267	12.	Zanardi	1'42"056
2.	Frentzen	1'40"631	13.	Gené	1'42"490
3.	Barrichello	1'40"810	14.	Coulthard	1'42"940
4.	Fisichella	1'40"960	15.	de la Rosa	1'43"885
5.	Häkkinen	1'41"103	16.	Badoer	1'46"367
6.	Irvine	1'41"254	17.	R. Schumacher	1'46"418
7.	Alesi	1'41"328	18.	Takagi	1'46"441
8.	Herbert	1'41"383	19.	Zonta	1'46"444
9.	Diniz	1'41"639	20.	Panis	1'46"874
10.	Villeneuve	1'41"769			
11.	Wurz	1'41"950			

Total Pit Stop Times

Lap		Time (s)	Lap		Time (s)	Lap		Time (s)	Lap	Time (s)
1	Fisichella	410"649	27	Häkkinen	29"149	41	Irvine	28"224		
3	Zanardi	29"094	27	Gené	32"624	41	Alesi	29"338		
12	Badoer	35"453	28	M. Schumacher	32"523	47	Häkkinen	28"388		
19	Barrichello	30"266	28	Herbert	35"081	48	Zanardi	27"435		
20	Wurz	30"530	28	Zanardi	32"546					
20	Fisichella	29"839	30	Frentzen	30"607					
21	Alesi	30"425	37	Fisichella	29"249					
22	Villeneuve	30"515	38	Wurz	28"755					
22	Diniz	29"695	38	Villeneuve	30"817					
24	de la Rosa	32"443	39	Barrichello	29"983					
25	Irvine	28"899	39	Diniz	28"975					

The Race Lap by Lap

Start: Trulli´s engine gives up in the warm-up lap. Schumacher and Irvine get off the mark in front ahead of Coulthard and Häkkinen. **Lap 1:** Fisichella pushes Hill out, the Italian is forced into the pits. **Lap 4:** Schumacher, who is at first in front, slows down and allows Irvine to overtake him. **Lap 5:** Coulthard challenges Schumacher, the two cars make brief contact, Coulthard overtakes the German and is in second. **Lap 9:** Coulthard is chasing Irvine, Schumacher begins blocking Häkkinen. **Lap 15:** Coulthard is forced to retire due to a lack of fuel pressure. Irvine leads, four seconds ahead of Schumacher and Häkkinen. Behind them follow Barrichello, Herbert, Wurz, and Alesi. **Lap 18:** Barrichello catches up to Häkkinen, who's still being blocked by Schumacher. **Lap 19:** The Brazilian goes to the pits and returns in eighth. **Lap 22:** Irvine's lead is up to 10 seconds thanks to Schumacher´s blocking of Häkkinen. Villeneuve is in fifth behind Barrichello. **Lap 25:** Irvine's

first pit stop, he returns in fourth. **Lap 27:** Häkkinen refuels. Without the Finn behind him, Schumacher completes the fastest two laps of the weekend. **Lap 28:** The German makes his only pit stop, which takes 11 seconds to complete. He returns to the race behind Irvine but ahead of Häkkinen. **Lap 30:** Irvine leads, five seconds ahead of Schumacher, who still has Häkkinen under control. **Lap 39:** Barrichello´s second pit stop leaves him behind team-mate Johnny Herbert. **Lap 47:** To Ferrari's relief, Häkkinen too heads to the pits for a second refuelling stop. Schumacher leads ahead of Irvine, the Finn returns in fourth place behind Herbert. **Lap 53:** Schumacher lets Irvine overtake him for the second time. **Lap 54:** Häkkinen overtakes Herbert, and moves into third. **Lap 56:** Irvine wins ahead of Schumacher, Häkkinen, Herbert, and Barrichello.

Standings

Driver/Points		Team	Points
1. Eddie Irvine	70	1. Ferrari	118
2. Mika Häkkinen	66	2. McLaren-Mercedes	114
3. Heinz-Harald Frentzen	51	3. Jordan-Mugen-Honda	58
4. David Coulthard	48	4. Stewart-Ford	36
5. Michael Schumacher	38	5. Williams-Supertec	33
6. Ralf Schumacher	33	6. Benetton-Playlife	16
7. Rubens Barrichello	21	7. Prost-Peugeot	9
8. Johnny Herbert	15	8. Sauber-Petronas	4
9. Giancarlo Fisichella	13	9. TWR-Arrows	1
10. Mika Salo	10	10. Minardi-Ford	1
11. Jarno Trulli	7		

Driver/Points	
Damon Hill	7
13. Alexander Wurz	3
Pedro Diniz	3
14. Olivier Panis	2
15. Pedro de la Rosa	1
Jean Alesi	1
Marc Gené	1

Looked good: Michael Schumacher finished second despite a layoff of 98 days.

More Variety

Eastward expansion: Formula One motor sport added another stop in the Asia-Pacific region in 1999, taking its travelling circus to Malaysia for the first time. The successful debut of the Malaysian Grand Prix, which was widely praised throughout the world of motor sport, has served to place the bar very high indeed for other countries hoping to attract the Formula One.

Let nature be your guide: The leaves of the native hibiscus tree inspired the design of the roof over the stands at Sepang.

Michael Schumacher praised the brand new Sepang International Circuit as being both demanding and fun to drive. Perhaps it's no wonder that the German was so enthused with the track, since it was designed by his compatriot, Hermann Tilke, a renowned course designer who incidentally comes from the same region of Germany as the two-time Formula One champion.

"It's the spectators who count the most, because they're the paying customers", is Tilke´s philosophy, who in his free time is a passionate amateur race car driver. "We wanted to place them in the middle of the action, so they can not only see the race, but smell and feel it as well." The stands between the two straightaways have a capacity of 30,000 and are 1,400 metres long, making them the longest stands in the world. What makes the stands particularly special for the fans is the indoor shopping precinct with fan shops, fast food outlets, and conference rooms. Given that Malaysia is a Moslem country, there are also sufficient prayer rooms so that even god-fearing Muslims can enjoy the Formula One experience.

The roof over the stands is also aesthetically delightful. It's made up of several parts which spread out over the spectators like oversized leaves. This festival of light and glass finds its crescendo at the "roof of leaves" at the end of the stands. The structure in front of the hairpin turn ahead of the finishing straightaway has already established itself as Sepang´s international trademark.

The layout of the track is also exemplary for its individuality, and has already established itself as one of the best in the world. Michael Schumacher, who acted as a consultant, particularly with regards to the security of the new track, rates Sepang as his fourth-favourite course, behind such classics as Spa, Monte Carlo, and Suzuka. There are 15 curves, ranging from tight to medium fast to fast, and two long straightaways on this 5.542 kilometre-long course. Herman Tilke designed the course with a particular stress on making it challenging for the drivers.

"One important factor was making sure there would be opportunities for the drivers to overtake one another", he says. "We looked at a lot of tracks and analysed where and how drivers overtake each other." Slow curves before and after straight-

Future Formula One Sites

Indianapolis (USA) will return to the Formula One circuit in 2000. One curve and one straightaway from the legendary brickyard will be part of the new track inside the oval. Brands Hatch (GB) was once the site of the British Grand Prix and will return to the circuit in 2002, when it will replace Silverstone. This hilly course in southern England is another track being renovated by Tilke´s team. Zhuhai is a free trade zone in China and has already hosted a GT race. It's entry into the Formula One club is being held up by China's painfully slow bureaucratic jungle as well as the lack of sufficient infrastructure. In Germany work on the Lausitzring, located about 60 miles south of Berlin is to be completed in 2000. It's unlikely to get a Grand Prix race anytime soon, though. It will host Indy Racing League and other events. It's not expected that the Formula One circuit will add a date at the Kyalami course in South Africa anytime soon either.

aways tend to give drivers the best opportunities for overtaking. "But there's much more to it than that", says the 44 year-old designer. "The curves which lead into the straightaways have to be difficult enough that the drivers will be occasionally be forced into errors, which then gives opponents opportunities to accelerate past them."

Tilke´s first lap time was "one hour and 31 minutes - with an off-road vehicle". But based on data from several Formula One teams, Tilke and his team were able to accurately estimate speeds and average lap times while the bulldozers and lorries were still moving the earth. In return Tilke´s office in western Germany provided each of the teams with sufficient information well ahead of the race, so that even weeks before they headed to Malaysia, they were able to make preliminary settings on their cars. While the drivers are naturally most interested in the track itself, Formula One officials are just as interested in the infrastructure around the site. Sepang´s infrastructure could hardly be better, with its modern media centre, and located as it is right beside Kuala Lumpur's international airport and surrounded by five star hotels.

This second step into Asia is part of a long

term strategy. The idea started as a means of fleeing Europe and its ban on advertising by tobacco companies, but it's developed into a strategy of gaining a presence in all of the world's major markets. While it remains centred in Europe, the Formula One now has races on four different continents. When it adds races in China, South Africa, and the United States, the Formula One circuit will become a world championship in the truest sense of the word. For a wide range of reasons prospective Grand Prix hosts are cueing up for their chance to join this exclusive club. Hosting an event helps increase a city's tourism, its international reputation as a high tech centre, and as if that weren't enough, there's also the $80 million in extra spending which according to a FIA study is pumped into any given region which hosts a Formula One race.

Malaysia did everything right in its bid to become the first Asian country outside of Japan to host a Formula One event. Perhaps its most important move was winning the support of the Sauber and Stewart teams, which in turn gave them direct contact to the Formula One's decision maker, Bernie Ecclestone. Even Malaysia's Prime Minister got behind the project. China on the other hand, which already has a less impressive, but adequate track at Zhuhai, had to wait. "The Chinese simply don't have the right people to organise such a big event", is how Ecclestone explained his decision to make the world's most populous nation wait a little longer. But China is expected to get its own Grand Prix race in a few years. Hermann Tilke has been hired to bring Zhuhai up to Formula One standards: "When the Formula One comes to China, everything will be ready."

A day at the races: Local fans in the natural stands.

Shopping under palm leaves: The shopping precinct.

The designer: German race track architect Herman Tilke.

Big in Japan

Rivals of the track: Mika Hakkinen (left) snatched the drivers championship out of Eddie Irvine´s hands.

Classic: Mika Hakkinen had the best start (left) and went on to win the race – and a second consecutive drivers title.

The scene for the last race of the 1999 season couldn't have been set any better had it been scripted by a writer for the stages of London's west end: It all came down to one race with defending champion Mika Hakkinen facing Eddie Irvine, McLaren facing Ferrari. While the race itself didn't live to its billing, when all was over the controversy of the previous two weeks was forgotten and it seemed like the perfect ending.

The death of the dream of a 12th pole position: Jean Alesi (in background) forced Mika Hakkinen to leave the track during qualifying.

Seldom had a season finale been so hotly anticipated as the last race of the 1999 season in Suzuka. An international panel of judges, who FIA repeatedly insisted were impartial, had overturned the disqualification of Ferrari drivers Eddie Irvine and Michael Schumacher, meaning the championship would be decided on the track in Japan. When the race was over either Ferrari's Eddie Irvine or McLaren's Mika Hakkinen would be crowned champion.

Irvine prepared for the most important race of his Formula One career in his own way. He didn't seek out the wisdom of a Tibetan monk, he didn't work on his fitness in the Maldives, he didn't drive test laps at Silverstone either. The Northern Irishman chose to prepare for the big day by visiting his daughter and playing golf in Macau. He made a

quick trip to Paris to testify in Ferrari's appeal, but didn't learn about the judges' decision until he was already back in Tokyo. When he did hear the news he celebrated all night long. Sure, his days were taken up with public relations appearances, but there was still lots of time at night for parties and sushi bars. To Irvine this obviously seemed like the best possible preparation for a shot at the Formula One title.

His opponent in the battle for the drivers championship wasn't exactly the vision of a relaxed and fit defending champion either. In Japan, Mika Hakkinen's nerves seemed to be even more frayed and he appeared more exhausted than he did on the podium in Malaysia, when he looked so fatigued that he found it impossible to stand up straight. The enormous pressure on the Finnish driver's

shoulders appeared to be taking its toll. Irvine's outward cool confidence and Michael Schumacher's impressive return to the track at Sepang seemed to be eating away at Mika.

The McLaren-Mercedes driver's luck in qualifying did nothing to improve his mood either. After his exciting battle with Michael Schumacher it was Jean Alesi who got in Hakkinen's way. The Italian-French driver made a braking error behind the silver arrow driver on the last curve, rumbled over the grass, shot back out onto the track in front of Finn, and completed a pirouette. Mika was forced to take to the gravel to avoid hitting the Sauber car. Eleven times this season he'd captured pole position, but ahead of this most crucial race of the season, the honour went to Michael Schumacher.

In fact the German's impressive return to the track in Malaysia following a 98 day layoff had caught the entire Formula One world by surprise. In Japan he was only getting better. Even McLaren boss Ron Dennis, who's usually sparing with his comments on rival drivers and teams, expressed his awe. "To shave a second off his time so quickly is an impressive step. All you can do is scratch your head and trying to imagine any possible thing he could have done to manage this..." Insiders speculated that Ferrari had come up with a way of increasing traction, but it couldn't have been any aerodynamic aids just millimetres beyond legality. Was this the reason that Mika Hakkinen had been observed examining the red F399 anytime he got a chance to get up close to it?

While the cars were lined up for the start the technical commissioners in Japan came up with a surprise of their own. They proceeded to disconnect the electrical supplies in a number of selected Formula One racers for precisely three seconds. The

Hectic moments before the start: Michael Schumacher returned to the pits to get adjustments made to his car.

idea behind this unconventional measure was to make sure that any so called "volatile programmes" would be erased from the memories of the cars´ electronics systems, and therefore would no longer be accessible. One can only speculate on how such software provides drivers with an extra edge.

By the time the five red lights in front of the starting grid had gone out, Michael Schumacher had already had a busy race against time. Numerous times ahead of the inspection lap the German had returned to the pits to have a variety of settings on his car adjusted, including things like the angle of its front wings for example. "The car wasn't balanced as well as it had been in warm-up", he later told reporters. He passed the traffic light at the end of the pit lane just seconds before it turned red 15 minutes before the end of the start countdown. But he had yet another problem: "Even in the pre-start I noticed that the engine wasn't set properly, so I already feared that I wouldn't get off to the best start."

Schumacher´s fear turned out to be justified. His rear tyres spun too quickly off the start, while at the same time Mika Hakkinen catapulted himself into the first curve and was out in the lead. The Finn, whose nerves had earlier appeared so

Coulthard´s race was more interesting.

frayed, had obviously rediscovered his mental toughness, and at just the right time. While his German competitor was forced to fall into line behind him, Olivier Panis provided the big surprised of the first few seconds of the race. The Frenchman, who in Japan was likely competing in his last Grand Prix race, took advantage of the confusion amongst Eddie Irvine, Heinz-Harald Frentzen, and David Coulthard, and cheekily slipped his Prost-Peugeot past them and into third place. "I had a fantastic start", the winner of the 1996 Monaco Grand Prix revealed. My car was

No luck in Japan either: Williams driver Alessandro Zanardi didn´t earn a single point all season.

running so well that I was easily able to defend third for the next 18 laps. Then my alternator failed."

While this was going on, Hakkinen was unhindered out in front working on building up his lead by about half a second per lap. Following Panis were Irvine, Coulthard, Frentzen and Ralf Schumacher in his Williams-Supertec. Apart from the fact that a drivers champion would be decided on the day, the 1999 Japanese Grand Prix was looking about as exciting as watching grass grow. There was one interesting factor to keep one's eyes on, and that was the question of whether Schumacher were using the same pit stop strategy, or whether the McLaren driver would be making an extra trip to the pits. The answer came in the 19th and 22 laps when first Hakkinen and then Schumacher headed off to refuel. While the Finn was out for a full 8.8 seconds, the Ferrari was off and running again in just 6.3 seconds. It appeared as if Schumacher had only had his tank partially filled to keep his car light so he could do some sprinting. But on the day even this Ferrari strategy wasn't enough to give the German the edge he craved. Mika Hakkinen was in complete control all the way through.

Understand? The drivers championship standings in Japanese.

Their man triumphed in the end: Mercedes Sporting Director Norbert Haug (left) and McLaren´s Ron Dennis.

David Coulthard´s race was significantly more interesting. He'd managed to squeeze by Eddie Irvine during their first pit stops. Beginning on lap 30, the handsome Scot got up to Ferrari's old tricks they'd used against McLaren in Malaysia. He began blocking Eddie Irvine, so much so in fact that Heinz-Harald Frentzen and Ralf Schumacher were able to catch up. Ferrari though countered by pulling their title hopeful into the pits early on lap 32. In the following laps "DC" proved how fast he could really drive, reducing his lap times by as much as 3 seconds. Then the McLaren driver made an error: As he was preparing to enter the Spoon Turn his rear left tyre touched the grass. He lost control of his McLaren and at a good 280 kph he

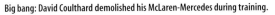
Big bang: David Coulthard demolished his McLaren-Mercedes during training.

Left the rest behind: Mika Hakkinen led for almost the entire race and won his second championship.

The season's most pleasant surprises: Ralf Schumacher (foreground) impressed in his Williams, Jordan's Frentzen even challenged for the drivers championship.

Teamwork I: Hakkinen and McLaren's designer Adrian Newey.

Teamwork II: Ferrari's tactician Ross Brawn and Eddie Irvine.

crashed into the barrier on the inside of the curve, giving his Mercedes a broken nose. It was a spectacular crash but Coulthard was extremely lucky: he escaped completely unscathed, used the momentum of the car coming out of the crash to get it back onto the track, and casually made his way to the pits to get his Mercedes a nose job. He then returned to the race in eighth place.

That didn't please Michael Schumacher one bit, and he claimed that Coulthard had unnecessarily held him up as he was trying to lap the Scot. "That was an unfair foul", the German cried, as if there could be any other kind of foul. "It would have been easy for him to let me past, but through his dirty tactics he made life difficult for me." When asked about Schumacher's comments,

Coulthard just chuckled. "You know Michael", he said. "He thinks there should be one set of rules for him, and another set of rules for everybody else." Schumacher's reaction to reporters' questions about parallels between Coulthard's behaviour in Japan, and his own blocking tactics in Malaysia gives credence to the Scotsman's theory. "It's not at all the same. Mika and I were battling over second place.

"One of us had to lose - it was me..."

This was a completely different set of circumstances."

Be that as it may, this duel had no influence on the drivers standings - and championship. It did though have a bearing on the constructors championship. Coulthard was forced to retire from the race due to gearbox trouble - apparently a result of his earlier crash. This was to cost McLaren the constructors title, and millions of pounds worth of prize money and television revenue. Ron Dennis couldn't have been pleased.

The only other excitement was provided by Heinz-Harald Frentzen and Ralf Schumacher. The two western Germans were locked in a heated battle for fourth place, which for Frentzen would mean a surprising third place in the drivers standings. Heinz-Harald prevailed, despite having to grapple with a crippled gearbox. "First gear was shot quite early in the race, then second went too", explained Frentzen. Ralf Schumacher's comment: "Although I was faster than Heinz, unfortunately I couldn't overtake him."

The last few metres of the race gave Mika Hakkinen a rare treat in sport: the opportunity to savour vic-

tory before the competition is actually over. He'd silenced his critics by leading the race from start to finish. He crawled around the track on his victory lap, and it wasn't hard to guess what sort of emotions he must have been experiencing. "1999 was a difficult year, because we unnecessarily gave away a lot of points. Having the drivers championship come down to the last race of the season is incredibly nerve-wracking. I hope I don't have to go through something like this again." Eddie Irvine was philosophical: "There's no point in moaning. One of us had to lose. As it turned out, it was me."

So it seemed the Formula One season had ended just like a relaxing paperback novel - with a happy ending. Everyone appeared to be satisfied. A relieved Mika Hakkinen celebrated his second drivers championship in a row. Ferrari got their first constructors championship since 1983, and Eddie Irvine could look back on his best season yet, even if it was all due to the injury to Schumacher at Silverstone. Despite having missed a large portion of the season, Schumacher could be content too, for following his layoff, he'd proved to everyone that he's just as fast as ever, and can be expected to take another run at Hakkinen's title next year. All's well, that ends well.

Gestures of reconciliation: Mika Hakkinen (right) and Eddie Irvine on the podium.

Statistics

Course length: 5,864 km

Distance of race: 53 (= 310,792 km)

Start time: 6.00 UTC

Weather on day of race: partly cloudy, warm

Attendance: 150 000

1998 Results:
1. Mika Hakkinen (FIN, McLaren-Mercedes MP4/13), 1 h 27'22"535
2. Eddie Irvine (GB, Ferrari F300), – 6"491 s
3. David Coulthard (GB, McLaren-Mercedes MP4/13), – 27"662 s

Pole position 1998: Michael Schumacher (D, Ferrari F300), 1'36"293 m

Fastest Lap 1998: Michael Schumacher (Ferrari F300), 1'40"190 m

Fastest pit stop 1998: Michael Schumacher (Ferrari F300), 29"396 s

The Drivers Enjoy the Challenge of this Course

"Suzuka is a great course. Most drivers love this track, even if there's hardly any opportunity to overtake. It demands the best from both the driver and the car. The series of curves at the start of the course determines whether you'll have a fast or slow lap. One of the best curves is the 130R - a very fast left turn, that you can take in sixth gear."

Mika Hakkinen

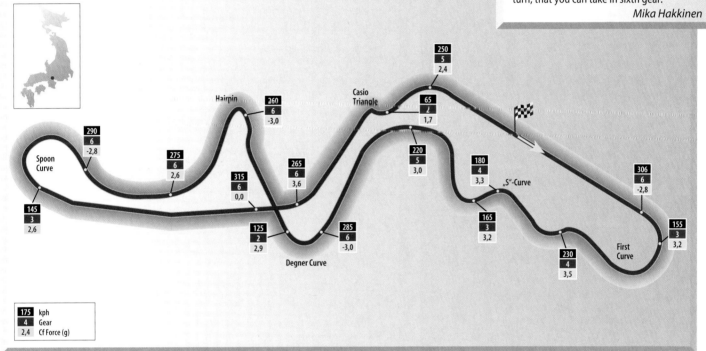

	kph
175	
4	Gear
2,4	Cf Force (g)

Results

Driver	Team	Pit stops	Laps	Time (hours)	Average speed	Behind 1st	prev. driver
1. Mika Häkkinen	McLaren-Mercedes	2	53	1 h 31'18"785	204,086	–	–
2. Michael Schumacher	Ferrari	2	53	1 h 31'23"800	203,899	5"015 s	–
3. Eddie Irvine	Ferrari	2	53	1 h 32'54"473	200,583	1'35"688 m	1'30"673 m
4. Heinz-Harald Frentzen	Jordan-Mugen-Honda	2	53	1 h 32'57"420	200,477	1'38"635 m	2"974 s
5. Ralf Schumacher	Williams-Supertec	2	53	1 h 32'58"279	200,446	1'39"494 m	0"859 s
6. Jean Alesi	Sauber-Petronas	2	52	1 h 31'31"101	199,784	1 lap	1 lap
7. Johnny Herbert	Stewart-Ford	2	52	1 h 31'33"352	199,702	1 lap	2"251 s
8. Rubens Barrichello	Stewart-Ford	2	52	1 h 31'34"255	199,669	1 lap	0"903 s
9. Jacques Villeneuve	BAR-Supertec	2	52	1 h 31'46"116	199,239	1 lap	11"861 s
10. Alexander Wurz	Benetton-Playlife	2	52	1 h 31'55"310	198,907	1 lap	9"164 s
11. Pedro Diniz	Sauber-Petronas	2	52	1 h 32'16"261	198,154	1 lap	20"951 s
12. Ricardo Zonta	BAR-Supertec	2	52	1 h 32'44"136	197,161	1 lap	27"875 s
13. Pedro de la Rosa	TWR-Arrows	2	51	1 h 31'39"478	195,641	2 laps	1 lap
14. Giancarlo Fisichella	Benetton-Playlife	2	47	1 h 23'50"733	197,085	retirement	retirement

Driver	Team	Pit stops	in lap	Reason f. retiring	Position before retiring
Toranosuke Takagi	TWR-Arrows	2	44	gearbox	15
Luca Badoer	Minardi-Ford	3	44	engine	16
David Coulthard	McLaren-Mercedes	2	40	gearbox	11
Marc Gené	Minardi-Ford	2	32	gearbox	14
Damon Hill	Jordan-Mugen-Honda	1	22	retired	17
Olivier Panis	Prost-Peugeot	1	20	electrical	14
Jarno Trulli	Prost-Peugeot	0	4	engine	9
Alessandro Zanardi	Williams-Supertec	0	1	electrical	16

1) Didn´t complete race, but counted due to distance driven.

Japanese GP

**16th Race in the World Championship 1999,
Suzuka Circuit (J), 31st October 1999**

Starting Grid

3 Michael Schumacher (D)
Ferrari F399/195
1'37"470 m (312,8 km/h) [1]

1 Mika Häkkinen (FIN)
McLaren-Mercedes MP4/14-4
1'37"820 m (311,9 km/h)

2 David Coulthard (GB)
McLaren-Mercedes MP4/14-6
1'38"239 m (315,5 km/h)

8 Heinz-Harald Frentzen (D)
Jordan-Mugen-Honda 199/5
1'38"696 m (309,2 km/h)

4 Eddie Irvine (GB)
Ferrari F399/196
1'38"975 m (308,7 km/h)

18 Olivier Panis (F)
Prost-Peugeot AP02/5
1'39"623 m (312,6 km/h)

19 Jarno Trulli (I)
Prost-Peugeot AP02/7
1'39"644 m (313,6 km/h)

17 Johnny Herbert (GB)
Stewart-Ford SF3/3
1'39"706 m (307,4 km/h)

6 Ralf Schumacher (D)
Williams-Supertec FW21/6
1'39"717 m (308,5 km/h)

11 Jean Alesi (F)
Sauber-Petronas C18/4
1'39"721 m (307,8 km/h)

22 Jacques Villeneuve (CDN)
BAR-Supertec 01/6
1'39"732 m (306,3 km/h)

7 Damon Hill (GB)
Jordan-Mugen-Honda 199/4
1'40"140 m (307,3 km/h)

16 Rubens Barrichello (BR)
Stewart-Ford SF3/4
1'40"140 m (306,9 km/h)

9 Giancarlo Fisichella (I)
Benetton-Playlife B199/7
1'40"261 m (304,7 km/h)

10 Alexander Wurz (A)
Benetton-Playlife B199/4
1'40"303 m (302,0 km/h)

5 Alessandro Zanardi (I)
Williams-Supertec FW21/3
1'40"403 m (310,4 km/h)

12 Pedro Diniz (BR)
Sauber-Petronas C18/5
1'40"740 m (305,9 km/h)

23 Ricardo Zonta (BR)
BAR-Supertec 01/7
1'40"861 m (304,5 km/h)

15 Toranosuke Takagi (J)
TWR-Arrows A20/5
1'41"067 m (307,7 km/h)

21 Marc Gené (E)
Minardi-Ford-Zetec-R M01/4
1'41"529 m (303,2 km/h)

14 Pedro de la Rosa (E)
TWR-Arrows A20/7
1'41"708 m (304,3 km/h)

20 Luca Badoer (I)
Minardi-Ford-Zetec-R M01/1
1'42"515 m (300,0 km/h)

107-percent time   1'44"293 m

Best Laps

In Training on Friday (m)

1.	Häkkinen	1'41"746	12. Wurz	1'43"430
2.	Coulthard	1'41"894	13. Alesi	1'43"485
3.	M. Schumacher	1'42"215	14. de la Rosa	1'43"599
4.	Barrichello	1'42"529	15. Gené	1'43"652
5.	Zanardi	1'42"718	16. Hill	1'43"720
6.	Panis	1'42"925	17. Zonta	1'43"776
7.	Fisichella	1'42"953	18. Takagi	1'43"804
8.	Villeneuve	1'43"047	19. Trulli	1'43"916
9.	Frentzen	1'43"235	20. Herbert	1'44"179
10.	Irvine	1'43"375	21. Diniz	1'44"423
11.	R. Schumacher	1'43"399	22. Badoer	1'45"543

In the Race on Sunday (m)

1.	M. Schumacher	1'41"319	12. Hill	1'43"939
2.	Häkkinen	1'41"577	13. Wurz	1'43"963
3.	Coulthard	1'42"106	14. Diniz	1'44"112
4.	R. Schumacher	1'42"567	15. Trulli	1'43"304
5.	Frentzen	1'42"972	16. Fisichella	1'44"379
6.	Panis	1'43"188	17. Zonta	1'44"869
7.	Irvine	1'43"297	18. Gené	1'45"359
8.	Barrichello	1'43"496	19. Badoer	1'45"377
9.	Alesi	1'43"668	20. de la Rosa	1'45"556
10.	Herbert	1'43"706	21. Takagi	1'46"150
11.	Villeneuve	1'43"898		

Total Pit Stop Times

Lap	Time (s)	Lap	Time (s)	Lap	Time (s)	Lap	Time (s)
15 Wurz	33"147	19 Alesi	33"320	32 Irvine	29"796	36 Herbert	36"468
15 Hill	39"703	19 Zonta	32"729	32 R. Schumacher	32"150	36 Alesi	32"166
16 Panis	31"053	19 Takagi	35"944	32 Badoer	37"510	37 M. Schumacher	30"717
16 Gené	31"469	20 R. Schumacher	31"046	33 Barrichello	32"731	37 Diniz	31"293
16 Fisichella	31"821	20 Barrichello	31"230	33 Wurz	33"148	38 Häkkinen	30"966
17 Herbert	33"574	20 Diniz	32"294	33 Zonta	32"300	41 Badoer	38"561
17 Villeneuve	32"563	22 M. Schumacher	29"771	33 Fisichella	32"136		
17 de la Rosa	39"950	22 Coulthard	31"042	34 Coulthard	42"726		
18 Badoer	32"320	23 Irvine	30"742	34 Villeneuve	32"514		
19 Häkkinen	32"520	31 Frentzen	30"362	34 de la Rosa	35"848		
19 Frentzen	30"741	31 Gené	39"882	35 Takagi	34"668		

The Race Lap by Lap

Start: Hakkinen gets off to the best start and is in front. Despite his quick reaction, M. Schumacher is slow off the mark due to spinning tyres. Behind the German, Panis claims third ahead of Irvine, Coulthard, and Frentzen. **Lap 1:** Zanardi rolls out with an electronics problem. That leaves him without a single point in his entire comeback season. **Lap 7:** Schumacher drops further behind Hakkinen, Panis is still ahead of Irvine. **Lap 15:** Hill skids out on the Spoon Corner. **Lap 19:** Pit stops for Hakkinen and Frentzen. Schumacher is in the lead, ten seconds ahead of the Finn. A defective alternator dashes Panis´ hopes of finishing in the points. **Lap 22:** M. Schumacher's pit stop leaves him behind Hakkinen once again. Coulthard also stops to refuel and returns in fourth, ahead of Frentzen. Hill gives up in the pits, and brings his Formula One career to a lacklustre end. **Lap 23:** Irvine returns to the track in fourth following a pit stop. Hakkinen leads ahead of M. Schumacher and Coulthard. **Lap 31:** M. Schumacher's fastest lap, which reduces Hakkinen´s lead. Coulthard holds back Irvine as well as Frentzen and R. Schumacher. Frentzen takes an early second pit stop. **Lap 32:** Irvine also heads to the pits early and is fifth. **Lap 34:** Without having to block Irvine anymore Coulthard is three seconds faster per lap than before - but only until he skids, hits the barrier, and tears the nose off of his Mercedes. **Lap 37:** After his second pit stop, M.Schumacher is blocked by Coulthard as the German is trying to lap the Scot. **Lap 38:** Hakkinen maintains the lead following his second pit stop and leads throughout the rest of the race. **Lap 53:** The Finn crosses the line first, successfully defending his drivers championship. M. Schumacher and Irvine finish second and third, Frentzen is fourth, and Ralf Schumacher is fifth. Alesi collects the final point of the season.

Standings

Driver/Points

1.	Mika Häkkinen	76	12.	Damon Hill	7
2.	Eddie Irvine	74	13.	Alexander Wurz	3
3.	Heinz-Harald Frentzen	54	14.	Pedro Diniz	3
4.	David Coulthard	48	15.	Olivier Panis	2
5.	Michael Schumacher	44	16.	Jean Alesi	2
6.	Ralf Schumacher	35	17.	Pedro de la Rosa	1
7.	Rubens Barrichello	21	18.	Marc Gené	1
8.	Johnny Herbert	15			
9.	Giancarlo Fisichella	13			
10.	Mika Salo	10			
11.	Jarno Trulli	7			

Team

1.	Ferrari	128
2.	McLaren-Mercedes	124
3.	Jordan-Mugen-Honda	61
4.	Stewart-Ford	36
5.	Williams-Supertec	35
6.	Benetton-Playlife	16
7.	Prost-Peugeot	9
8.	Sauber-Petronas	5
9.	TWR-Arrows	1
10.	Minardi-Ford	1

1). Lap time (top speed in qualifying).

115 Grand Prix races, 22 wins, 1996 Drivers Championship: Damon Hill´s record as he retired as a Formula One driver.

His title defence turned out to be the most difficult season of his Formula One career: Mika Hakkinen, world champion for the second year running.

In Defence of the
Championship

What many had expected to be a triumphant march to his second consecutive drivers championship turned out to be a difficult season for Mika Hakkinen, with the battle for the title coming down to the very last race. That was par for the course for the Finn, who's never really had it easy on the Formula One circuit.

The flying Finn has done it: Mika Hakkinen had made it into the elite group of Formula One drivers who have managed to win back to back drivers championships. Such great names as Jim Clark, Jackie Stewart, Emerson Fittipaldi, Niki Lauda and Nelson Piquet all failed to do so. Those who were successful include Alberto Ascari, Juan-Manuel Fangio, Jack Brabham, Alain Prost, Ayrton Senna, and Michael Schumacher.

Just two years after his first Formula One victory, which was simply handed to him, Mika Hakkinen has established himself among the truly great names of Grand Prix motor racing, and he's still only 31 years old with plenty of time to win further honours. Hakkinen grew up in a suburb of Helsinki and quickly made his way through the ranks of racing classes, mastering each before moving onto the next. He began early, and by the age of 18 had amassed five Kart championships. In 1987 he took the Swedish and Nordic Formula Ford series by storm, repeated his success in the GM Lotus Euro series and stepped up to the tough Formula Three competition in 1989. In 1990 he was champion, and felt he was ready to move on to Formula One.

But his first year in Grand Prix racing wasn't easy. He made his debut with the Lotus team at the US. Grand Prix in 1991, but despite the famous name of his new team, it was a team that was on its way out. However the quiet blonde did manage to make people sit up and take notice. In Phoenix he managed to qualify in 13th, despite having a clearly inferior car, and in his third race he finished in the points. At Imola he drove the sluggish Lotus from second last in the starting grid to a fifth place finish. It was the only time the Finn was to finish in the top six all season. In 1993 things went better for him as he finished in the points on a total of six occasions, including two fourth place finishes. Despite the improvement Hakkinen and

His favourite pose: Mika Hakkinen feels at home on the top step of the podium. In the past season the McLaren-Mercedes driver earned the privilege five times.

his manager, Keke Rosberg, concluded that there was no future for him at Lotus. That's when Hakkinen made a daring move: he signed on with McLaren, not as a Grand Prix driver, but as a test driver. "Although we knew that I wouldn't race for a whole year, Keke said the main thing was to get me working for McLaren", Hakkinen recalls today. "As usual, he was right."

But McLaren, which had won the constructors championship six times and the drivers championship seven times since 1984, was in a

free fall. Honda had pulled out at the team's engine building partner, forcing Ron Dennis and his team to go with a Ford engine for the 1993 season. Even Ayrton Senna was left without a chance against the Williams-Renault driven by arch-rival Alain Prost. Michael Andretti, the US. Cart champion and McLaren´s second driver was a complete disappointment. It all added up to good news for Hakkinen. "To my surprise Senna didn't like to test drive unless there was something new to try out. So I practically lived on the track at Silverstone, and probably spent

"I believed in McLaren-Mercedes every bit as much as I believed in my own talent."

more time behind the wheel than most of the other Formula One drivers."

After the Italian Grand Prix at Monza, Ron Dennis ran out of patience with Andretti. He sent the American back home to the United States. This was Mika´s big chance, and he made no mistake. Three days before his 25th birthday he qualified ahead of the great Ayrton Senna. Was this a reason for jubilation? "No, it all went according to plan", the newly-crowned champion reveals. "Third was nice. But my team-mate won the race..."

"I wanted to win the Formula One drivers championship in my very first season."

Senna moved to Williams the following season, and Hakkinen quickly became the unofficial number one. He was so much better than his new team-mate, Martin Brundle, that it appeared to simply be a matter of time before the Finn would take his first Grand Prix race. That turned out to be completely wrong. The new Peugeot engine wasn't good enough to help McLaren duplicate its successes of the previous years either. After just one year the French car maker was more or less forced to move to the Jordan team, because Ron Dennis had just caught a bigger fish: Mercedes Benz. But even for this new

Formula one dream team it was to be a long and sometimes painful road to their first Grand Prix victory.

This was a difficult time for the ambitious Finn: "Sure, I always wanted to be world champion", the Monaco resident recalls. "I wanted to win as a Kart driver, and I wanted to win even more as a Formula One driver. When I made my debut in 1991 I thought that's it, I'm going to be world champion, and I wanted to win the title in my very first season..." Did he ever think about giving up? "Had I been on my own I might have, but I had fabulous people around me who always encouraged me - Ron, the mechanics, Keke, my wife Erja and my family, a lot of good friends."

Just in case the frustration might become to great, his father had given him some good advice on how to deal with it. "Go out into the woods and chop down a couple of trees to help vent your anger", is what his father suggested he do as early as Mika´s Kart days. "Back then the problem wasn't that there were enough trees, the problem was there weren't enough forests", Hakkinen laughs today. "It's tough when you're unable to achieve what you want to. But I think I've been a very loyal driver. I believed in McLaren and Mercedes every bit as much as I believed in my own talent." With a smile he

adds: "We Finns are optimists - what other choice do you have in a country in which we hardly see the sun in the winter, even during the day?"

"You were really lucky."

The darkest hours, days and weeks of Mika´s career though didn't come in his native Finland, but down under in Australia. He blew a tyre in the last session of training ahead of the 1995 Australian Grand Prix in Adelaide. At more than 200 kph his McLaren flew into the air and crashed into a stack of tyres. "Blood was flowing from his mouth, his eyes were open, but lifeless", remembers Merome Cockings, one of the first doctors on the scene of the accident. When Hakkinen´s face began to turn blue due to a lack of oxygen, the doctors on the scene decided to perform an emergency tracheotomy. But shortly after he arrived at hospital, Hakkinen slipped into a coma. When he regained consciousness the next day, Sid Watkins was at his bed side. "You were really lucky", the Formula One's head doctor told the injured driver. "We didn't have to perform brain surgery..." Hakkinen´s reaction? "On the one hand I was relieved, but at the same time I was shocked, because then it became clear to me that I´d survived a very serious crash."

Information is power: Away from the track he's laid back, but on the track he's a model of concentration.

Champagne for everybody: Mika Hakkinen successfully defended his title.

Dialogue is the recipe for success: Mika´s title defence was made possible by good teamwork.

A calming influence: His wife Erja accompanies her husband to every Grand Prix race.

It took almost the entire winter break for him to recover. His girlfriend Erja, who's famous as a television presenter back in Finland, resigned from her job to be with Mika in Australia. Three months later Mika returned to the cockpit for the first time. Alain Prost, who was then still at McLaren remembers Hakkinen´s comeback well. "It was very moving. Mika was much faster right from the first lap than anyone had expected. And what was even more important was that he clearly still enjoyed being behind the wheel." In his next test laps at Estoril he turned in the fastest times of anyone. Later he scoffed at congratulations on his qualifying performance at the first race of the 1996 season, the Australian Grand Prix. "Fifth place, you call that good? That's no good at all! I came here to win!"

The first win remained elusive.

Still another year passed without McLaren-Mercedes recording its first win. The pressure was becoming enormous. "At that time I started to wonder if I was really good enough." Consumed with self-doubt, he began questioning his driving style. He switched from left foot braking, a system he'd introduced to Formula One racing, back to the conventional right foot braking system. "It had become clear to me that I had to optimise every aspect I possibly could."

It wasn't Hakkinen, but the surprising David Coulthard who gave the newly painted "silver arrows" their first Grand Prix win at the 1997 Australian Grand Prix. For Mika, who was giving it his all in pursuit of this goal, it seemed like his first win would never happen. What had appeared to be sure victories at Silverstone, the A-1 Ring in Austria or at the Nurburgring were all squandered due to technical failures. It wasn't until Coulthard handed him his first victory

in the last race of the season at Jerez, after McLaren had mistakenly called the Finn into the pits once too often, that Hakkinen´s luck finally turned. In 1998 Mika went on to win eight more Grand Prix races, he started from the pole position in nine races, recorded the fastest lap in seven races, and won the drivers championship.

Hakkinen´s Tears of Frustration Endeared Him to a lot of Fans

Following that strenuous season he embarked on a similarly stressful six week-long promotional tour, before taking a month's vacation in the Caribbean. Tanned and well-rested, Hakkinen returned to work, ready to defend his title. It was to turn out to be the most difficult season of his Formula One career - despite an impressive series of qualifying best times, and despite the absence for much of the season of arch-rival Michael Schumacher. The unreliability of his McLaren-Mercedes MP4/14 cost him just as many valuable championship points as did team-mate David Coulthard and his own unnecessary mistakes at Imola and at Monza. At one point the incredible pressure on Hakkinen´s shoulders made him break down in tears, in front of a live audience of millions.

But it was only his harshest critics who made fun of the usually so outwardly calm and collected champion. To the minds of most fans, Hakkinen´s emotional outburst added a human dimension to what is often seen as an unemotional, mechanical sport. If there was any doubt about his mental toughness, he came up with the right answer with his convincing win in the final race of the season in Japan. That's a big reason he has earned a place in the history books alongside names such as Ascari, Fangio, Brabham, Prost, Senna, and Schumacher.

All's Well, That Ends Well

At the end of a season full of dramatic events, unexpected turns, and surprising decision, it was the man who'd been the favourite all along, who wound up taking the drivers championship. Ferrari failed to secure the drivers title for a 20th time running, but could take consolation in their constructors championship, and the outlook for 2000 with a healthy Michael Schumacher.

Not a big help: Mikka Hakkinen (left) wasn't able to count on the support of team-mate David Coulthard.

One thing that jumps out at you when you look back at the 1999 season is that Mika Hakkinen's and McLaren-Mercedes' most dangerous opponents weren't Ferrari and Michael Schumacher or even Eddie Irvine - but McLaren-Mercedes themselves. The silver arrows in 1999 displayed an astounding knack for shooting themselves in the foot. While Ferrari's watchword this past season was reliabilitiy, with Eddie Irivine failing to cross the finish line only once, the British-German team repeatedly eliminated themselves, even though certainly in the first half of the season, and arguably throughout the entire 16 races, McLaren-Mercedes had the faster car.

In terms of reliability, the silver arrows had their biggest problems early in the campaign. In the first four races of the season, David Couthard failed to finish three times due to technical failure, Mika Hakkinen failed to reach the finish line once. Over a total of 32 starts, McLaren had their drivers knocked out by mechanical problems seven times, Ferrari just three times, including Michael Schumacher's spectacular crash at Silverstone.

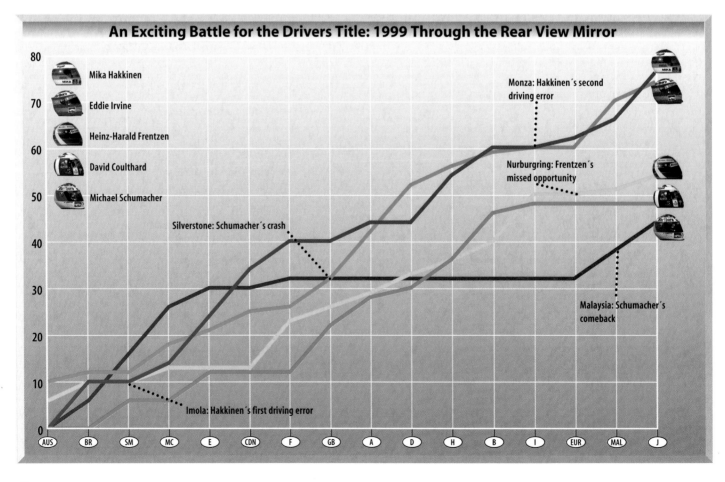

An Exciting Battle for the Drivers Title: 1999 Through the Rear View Mirror

- Mika Hakkinen
- Eddie Irvine
- Heinz-Harald Frentzen
- David Coulthard
- Michael Schumacher

Silverstone: Schumacher's crash

Imola: Hakkinen's first driving error

Monza: Hakkinen's second driving error

Nurburgring: Frentzen's missed opportunity

Malaysia: Schumacher's comeback

AUS BR SM MC E CDN F GB A D H B I EUR MAL J

Two happy drivers: the injury of Michael Schumacher at Silverstone allowed Eddie Irvine (left) to take a shot at the drivers title. It also allowed supersub Mika Salo to realise his dream of driving for Ferrari.

In terms of team orders, while Ferrari began the season with Michael Schumacher as their number one driver, with Irvine playing a supporting role until the German´s crash, Hakkinen and Coulthard were always in competition with each other. The Finn lost six points for example when the Scott ran into him from behind, knocked Hakkinen out of the race, and to add injury to insult, finished the race in second place. There was a similar case at the Belgian Grand Prix where McLaren allowed Coulthard to win, even though Hakkinen could really have used the extra points in the drivers championship. Had McLaren ordered Coulthard to let his Finnish team-mate past, Hakkinen would have gone into the final race two points ahead of, instead of four points behind Eddie Irvine.

Ferrari´s strategy was another matter entirely: Irvine had four points given to him by Mika Salo at Hockenheim, who had effectively won his first Grand Prix race, only to step on the brakes to let his Northern Irish team-mate overtake him. Michael Schumacher was ordered to do the same thing in Malaysia. It all added up to eight extra points for Irvine.

To make matters worse, the lack of a team order seemed to wear on Mika Hakkinen´s frayed nerves, as he helped place his own title defence in jeopardy by committing two avoidable errors and turning in a sub-standard performance during the changeable track conditions at the Nurburgring. While Eddie Irvine didn´t perform at the standard of a world champion in every race of the season, and while he did have a number of

poor qualifying outings, he didn´t display any glaring weaknesses. The future Jaguar driver didn´t make a single critical mistake.

The fact that McLaren-Mercedes was able to secure the drivers championship, after having been temporarily awarded the title, only to have it taken away by a panel of "independent" judges in Paris, and despite not having a team order like Ferrari, made this a particularly deserving win for Mika Hakkinen. All´s well that ends well, even if David Coulthard cost his team the constructors championship by finishing out of the points in each of the last three races, twice as a result of a driving error. That in turn cost the team tens of millions of pounds in lost prize money and television revenues.

Michael Schumacher has reason to be happy, too. After coming back after a layoff of almost 100 days he not only confirmed his reputation as one of the best drivers of all time, but in some people´s eyes improved his image, casting himself in the unusual light of team player. He did so while not being forced to watch Eddie Irvine become the first Ferrari drivers champion in 20 years. That´s an honour the German wants to claim for himself in 2000.

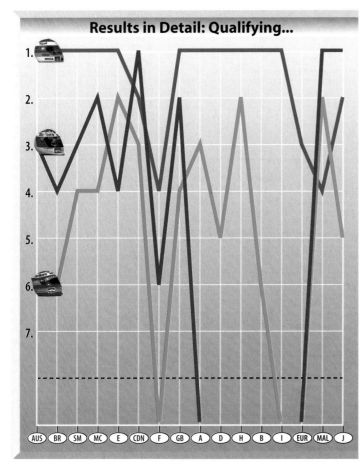

Results in Detail: Qualifying...

1.
2.
3.
4.
5.
6.
7.

AUS BR SM MC E CDN F GB A D H B I EUR MAL J

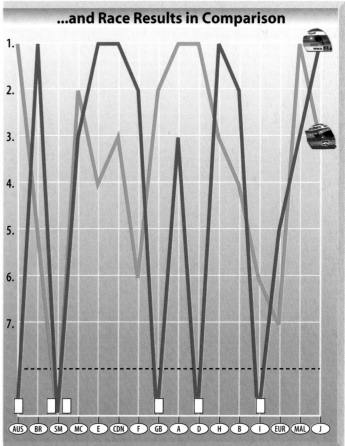

...and Race Results in Comparison

1.
2.
3.
4.
5.
6.
7.

AUS BR SM MC E CDN F GB A D H B I EUR MAL J

D = Race Not Completed Due to Technical Failure. F = Race Not Completed Due to Driving Error.

The Fourth German

He's so different, but so similar at the same time: Beginning in 2000 Nick Heidfeld will be the fourth German on the Formula One circuit. What sets him apart from his compatriots is his unassuming demeanour. But he shares with them a very important quality - he's fast. Before he'd appeared in a single Formula One race, he was the most sought- after driver on the "transfer market".

A frequent gesture: Nick Heidfeld was always one of the favourites on the tough Formula 3000 circuit.

A guiding hand: McLaren´s Ron Dennis helped the young German along the road to success.

he Germans are dominant: When Nick Heidfeld begins his Formula One career with Prost-Peugeot next season, Germans will make up almost a fifth of the starting grid, and German car makers will be supplying a similar percentage of the engines. You may not like it, but it's a fact. Not just that but they all come from the Rhine land in western Germany. Twenty-two year-old Nick is no exception.

Unlike the rest though, Heidfeld is actually quite shy. He's still trying to get adjusted to being in the spotlight, as he was at the press conference to announce his signing with Prost-Peugeot. Despite the tailor-made suits provided by one of the McLaren team's sponsors, he still feels more at home in a pair of racing overalls. Looking into his young face, it's easy to forget that at 22, Nick is the same age as Ralf Schumacher was when he made his Formula One debut. At the same time, nobody who's seen him drive doubts he has the talent and experience it takes to make it in racing´s highest league.

What makes this young man from Moenchen-Gladbach so endearing, is that he's so modest, particularly when it comes to how well he speaks English. "I took English at school", he reveals. "But I picked up most of it from the team. That could be why I use the odd naughty word." Chances are good that despite all the praise of late, he will remain just as down to earth in the crazy world of Grand Prix racing. "You can't let all the praise go to your head. The people around me provide me with a lot of stability. If all you're ever getting is pats on the back, you might be tempted to rest on your laurels." His girlfriend Patricia and Werner Heinz, his manager, don't likely have too difficult a time of keeping Heidfeld´s feet on the ground.

The Formula One newcomer's resume reads like a picture book: Kart, Formula Ford, Formula Three, Formula 3000, and now Formula One. Couple that experience with the support of one of the world's biggest car makers, and it all looks like a fairy tale career. But his road to the top wasn't as easy as it may appear at first glance, despite the fact that Mercedes first got behind him three years ago. Despite the Mercedes name, he didn't have much of an advantage over his competitors in the Formula Three or the Formula 3000. That's because just like at the Formula One level, there are very strict rules designed to ensure that all the cars have the same chance to win. The most important qualities for young drivers hoping to make it in the first class are a good mastery of the car, and the ability to overtake one's competitors, while avoiding unnecessary risks.

Heidfeld proved how good he is almost too early. In 1998, Nick's first year in a Formula 3000 cockpit, the young German beat Juan-Pablo Montoya, now the most talked about man in the American Champ Car series, several times. He just missed winning the drivers championship due to a mistake by his team. In retrospect, it turned out to be a stroke of luck. It gave him an extra year to improve and to prove that he is capable of dominating one of the highest classes in motor sport. "In the Formula 3000 we were working on a two-year plan. We'd never expected to get so close to the title in the first season", remembers Heidfeld today. Was it frustrating to get that close and then fail? "I entered my second season totally motivated. What made things a little difficult was that suddenly I was viewed as one of the favourites." With his four victories and the drivers championship though, he dealt with the added pressure like an old veteran. That was his ticket to the Formula One.

What's often forgotten is that Nick isn't as good as he is because he has a multi-national corporation and one of the best teams on the Formula One circuit behind him. He had to be good enough in the first place to attract the interest of Mercedes. The Stuttgart car make isn't in the habit of supporting losers. It was Mercedes after all who gave brothers Michael and Ralf Schumacher, as well as Heinz-Harald Frentzen the support early in their careers which helped them develop into the successful drivers they are today.

What three of these Germans have in common didn't start with the discovery of each of them by Mercedes. It began at the Schumacher family's go cart track outside of Cologne. It is of course where both Michael and Ralf first got behind the wheel. But several years ago the paths of the two-time world champion and the man tipped to follow in his footsteps crossed here too, as Michael explains. "I was training a few kids on the cart track, to pick up some pocket money. I´d teach them about finding the ideal driving line and a few other tricks I´d picked up. One of them was Nick, and I could tell right away that he had a lot of talent."

Heidfeld spent five years racing go carts, and from then on each season he would take another step up the ladder to success. The only exception was when he'd narrowly missed winning the championship in a particular class. Then he'd stick around another year to collect the title. In 1994, his first in a real racer, a Formula Ford 1600, he promptly won the championship. He did the same thing the following year in the 1800 class. That led him to the Formula Three circuit. Under the supervision of the experienced team manager Bertram Schaefer, Nick learned more about what it takes to win, and finished number three on the season.

About half-way through the 1997 season he was called up to the Mercedes junior team. For them he drove the Look silver arrow and crowned the season off with the title. In the same year he drove a fantastic race in the Formula Three race in Monaco, the renowned "little Grand Prix". He concluded his apprenticeship with the Formula 3000 championship this past season.

"Nick is mentally strong and is one of the rare drivers who can drive and think at the same time," says David Brown, who's responsible for Mercedes' youth programme and who was also Nick's manager for two years at West Competition in the Formula 3000. "It doesn't take everything he had for him to keep the car on the road, so he can analyse things as he's driving, such as whether something needs to be adjusted to improve the car's performance." As if that's not praise enough, Brown compares Heidfeld to some of the greatest drivers the world has ever seen: "Even if a car isn't performing at its best, he'll still go out there and drive a super lap, just like Nigel Mansell or Ayrton Senna always could."

When the rookie joins the team run by four time world champion Alain Prost next season, he'll be faced with working with an experienced but difficult character. While he is an extremely skilled driver, Jean Alesi is considered one of the most difficult team-mates you could imagine. But this doesn't seem to faze the young German: "I've managed to deal with everything I've come up against so far. Right now I want to learn a lot and become the best driver I can be. Heidfeld´s "best" just may turn out to be too much for the ageing Alesi. Other Formula One drivers would do well to take "Quick Nick" seriously as well.

The Heidfeld clan: Nick with his parents and girlfriend Patricia.

A Comeback Full of Peril

The man Williams was counting on to bring in some points and give them a shot at the constructors championship proved to be a bust.

Two time Champ Car champion Alex Zanardi was overshadowed in his Formula One comeback by the younger Ralf Schumacher.

T he record speaks for itself: in16 Grand Prix races Formula One returnee Alex Zanardi didn't earn a single championship point. To make matters worse, his younger team-mate Ralf Schumacher had earned a very respectable 35 points - every single Williams point of the season. In terms of qualifying times, the 24 year-old German also held the upper hand, bettering Zanardi´s time 11 out of 16 opportunities. Zanardi had be outclassed in every way.

Many had feared that the Italian was in for a nightmare season, but few had expected it to be so embarrassing. It must have been particularly demoralising, considering the fact that Zanardi had returned to the Formula One circuit as a much celebrated Champ Car champion and with the experience of 25 previous Grand Prix races under his belt between 1991 and 1994. Back in the Champ Car series he was a hero, having taken over from Jacques Villeneuve as the circuit's superstar, and having won the championship two years running. What's more, his daring, often cheeky braking and overtaking manoeuvres even heightened his profile on this side of the Atlantic. He gained a reputation for being the perfect tonic for a dull race. Frank Williams and Patrick Head made a quick decision. They let the unhappy Heinz-Harald Frentzen go to Jordan, got Zanardi back, and sent Williams test driver and Formula 3000 champions Juan Pablo Montoya to Chip Ganassi.

"I didn´t expect it to be this difficult."

But Zanardi was a failure on every account. "Even from watching on television, I knew that it would be difficult", admits the 33 year-old.

The smile has been wipe off of Alessandro Zanardi´s face: The Italian returned to the Formula One as a champions but quickly learned that he can't deal effectively with the current treaded tyres.

"But I didn't expect it to be this difficult. The current incarnation of Formula One cars aren't anything like what I consider to be a well-handling racer." The man from Bologna picked up where he left off as a Lotus driver in the 1994 Australian Grand Prix - following the pack in dead last. That season he earned but a single point, and 1999 has been even worse, with Zanardi failing to earn as much as a single point.

Has the once fearless Zanardi, who became a father at the end of last year, suddenly gone soft? "I hit the curves with a lot of speed, that's my problem", explains the Italian driver, who made his Formula One debut as a replacement for Michael Schumacher at Jordan. "The current tyres don't skid as easily into the curves but they build up a lot of power in the direction of the wheels. So you have to hit the brakes hard, firing the car into the curve, and then - bang! Hit the gas again. I prefer to drive more like Alain Prost: gentle, but always at the very limit. The way they are now, I hate these cars. With these cars I can't do all the things I'm used to doing."

Although the Williams bosses continue to make excuses for Zanardi´s poor showing, his place in the team next season is anything but secure. He's being challenged by some serious competition. If Montoya manages to win the Champ Car series in his debut season, he'd be seen as a worthy successor to Zanardi, even if Juan-Pablo has let it be known that he'd prefer to stay in America for another year. But he's not the only danger for Zanardi. Tom Kristensen is also being watched closely by Williams, particularly by Patrick Head, who seemingly never tires of singing his praises. The happy go lucky Dane, who made a big splash in the German Super Touring Cars Championship, has already tested Zanardi´s car.

"I'm not worried about my future", the Italian says relaxed. "I'm financially secure. If someday I find that I really can't adjust, my driving style to the demands of these cars, then it won't be any fun anymore. But until that happens I´ll keep trying."

A Question of Fitness

What the first Formula One season of a new millennium will bring with it is written in the stars. We looked into our crystal ball to bring you this look back at what the coming year has in store.

Australian Grand Prix

There's no doubt in the mind of BAR Team Manager Craig Pollock, BAR will win the first race of the season. Damon Hill has reconsidered and signs on for another season, this time with Minardi. In qualifying the McLaren-Mercedes dominate: five seconds faster than the competition. Michael Schumacher can't start since he's suffering from a cold. His Ferrari team-mate Rubens Barrichello wins his first Grand Prix race driving with slicks from 1997. McLaren´s protest is overturned by a Paris court one week later, because it was obviously an oversight, and Ferrari didn't derive any advantage. BAR drivers Villeneuve and Zonta are eliminated on the first lap after colliding with one another.

Brazilian Grand Prix

The race ends with a surprising win by Heinz-Harald Frentzen. Since Eddie Jordan adopted him as his son, Frentzen feels more at home than ever, and his performance behind the wheel approves accordingly. Barrichello had surrendered the lead during a pit stop - the Ferrari pits had run out of fuel. The team's boss, Jean Todt offers to resign. Michael Schumacher is still out of action, he's climbing Mount Everest to find out whether he's fit enough. Both BAR drivers fail to finish the race due to gearbox trouble.

San Marino Grand Prix

Damon Hill considers retirement: He didn't make it past the first curve. Mika Hakkinen is in the lead until his engine fails due to the computer game he's playing in the cockpit, and the Finn burst out in tears. Rubens Barrichello goes out into the lead way out in front of Hakkinen´s team-mate David Coulthard, but later the commissioners determine that Barrichello´s car has

an all-wheel drive system. The protest is rejected because Ferrari didn't not derive any advantage. Audi is suspected of sabotage. The BAR drivers can't start their engines at the start of the race.

British Grand Prix

Mika Hakkinen is in the lead until he loses a wheel. He burst out into tears again. Michael Schumacher is training with the German national football squad, but still doesn't feel fit enough for the Formula One. Since Eddie Jordan's mother has been cooking for Frentzen in the pits, the German feels even more at home and wins. Damon Hill says his personal good-byes to all the rest of the drivers, the mechanics, and even the spectators. The Englishman figures the time has come to retire.

European Grand Prix

Hill changes his mind and is in the starting grid at the Nurburgring. The weather plays havoc with the track, with a thunderstorm, snow, and sunshine all at the same time. McLaren plays it safe by outfitting Mika Hakkinen´s car with slicks on the front and winter tyres on the back. The Finn burst into tears over the fact that his mobile phone has been stolen, and skids off the track. Johnny Herbert wins because everybody ahead of him crashes out. Villeneuve and Zonta don't start because Craig Pollock lost the keys to the BAR garage.

Monaco Grand Prix

Surprise! The BAR drivers stumble over the qualifying hurdle. Michael Schumacher has a great comeback: Even though he's not completely fit he wins, crossing the finish line two laps ahead of his nearest competitor. Prince Rainier greets him: "Oh you again!"

Canadian Grand Prix

BAR is missing again. Most of the team has travelled on to France to make sure nothing goes wrong at the French Grand Prix. Without a car to drive in the race, Jacques Villeneuve addresses the spectators in an effort to win the undecided over to the "yes" side in Quebec's latest referendum on independence from Canada. Hakkinen wins after all of the rest of the field crash out on turn 15. The technical commissioners determine that the McLaren car is underweight. FIA disqualifies Hakkinen and declares a surprised Alessandro Zanardi the winner. McLaren´s appeal is rejected. "Rules are rules" argue the independent judges.

French Grand Prix

BAR doesn't show up. There are rumours the team has returned to Montreal to join the fight for Quebec independence. Schumacher still has a cold, and can't drive. Frentzen wins, motivated by an invitation from his boss to spend Christmas at the Jordan family home.

German Grand Prix

Schumacher can't start at Hockenheim either, but the German racing icon gives an address to the faithful broadcast all over the world on pay TV. His address gets better ratings than the Pope's Easter mass. On that news FIA calls off the race and declares Schumacher the winner, since Ferrari was deemed to be disadvantaged.

Hungarian Grand Prix

Damon Hill announces that the Hungarian Grand Prix will definitely be his last race. After the Englishman wins, to everyone´s complete surprise, he changes his mind.

Belgian Grand Prix

Schumacher is back: He leaves everyone in his wake in a rain-soaked race on his favourite track. Hakkinen can't start as he's being treated for a blocked tear duct. Both BAR cars crash in the "Eau Rouge". Eddie Jordan hires a psychologist, concerned that Frentzen might be suffering from loneliness.

Malaysian Grand Prix

Heinz-Harald Frentzen wins, after Eddie Jordan has plastic surgery which makes him look like Frentzen´s double. Both Bar drivers almost make it to the finish line, but give up just metres away. Villeneuve and Zonta collapse in their cockpits of exhaustion, no longer having the stamina to drive an entire race.

Ecclestone´s Successors

Bernie Ecclestone, 68, has effectively chosen his own successors to run the Formula One circuit. The German bank Deutsche Bank has bought half of the "Formula One Administration (FOA) for $1.3 billion. Following the deal, former Mercedes manager Helmut Werner plans to take Ecclestone´s company, which holds extensive television and commercial rights for the Formula One, onto the stock market. "The Formula One is a very profitable business", said the chairman of the board-designate. One can only guess at just how profitable it is. Turnover during the past year was just under $1 billion. The sale comes after several attempts by Ecclestone to sell off part of the business. Now the Formula One boss is speaking of retirement. Werner though stressed that: "Ecclestone is still the boss".

Deutsche Bank ⧄

Who's Driving for Whom in the Coming Year?
The Transfer Market

Their transfer one for one was the worst kept secret in the Formula One world. While Rubens Barrichello will be hoping to get his first Grand Prix win with Ferrari, Eddie Irvine is hoping to lead Jaguar (as the Stewart-Ford team will be known beginning next year), to the elite class of Formula One teams, while establishing himself as a number one driver. Alain Prost believes he has a good combination of experience and young blood in Jean Alesi and his new team-mate, Formula 3000 European champion Nick Heidfeld. Zanardi´s job at BMW-Williams could be on the line. Should Juan-Pablo Montoya win the Champ Car championship this season, there will be nothing left standing in the way of Williams moving their young Colombian talent over to their Formula One team.

Staying with Formula One: Mika Salo is moving to Sauber.

Drivers and Teams for the 2000 Season:

Ferrari	Michael Schumacher (D)/Rubens Barrichello (BR)
McLaren-Mercedes	Mika Häkkinen (FIN)/David Coulthard (GB)
Jordan-Honda	Heinz-Harald Frentzen (D)/Jarno Trulli (I)
Jaguar	Eddie Irvine (GB)/Johnny Herbert (GB)
BMW-Williams	Ralf Schumacher (D)/*Alessandro Zanardi (I)?*
Benetton-Playlife	Giancarlo Fisichella (I)/Alexander Wurz (A)
Prost-Peugeot	Jean Alesi (F)/Nick Heidfeld (D)
Sauber-Petronas	Mika Salo (FIN)/Pedro Diniz (BR)
TWR-Arrows/Supertec?	Pedro de la Rosa (E)/Toranosuke Takagi (J)?
Minardi-Supertec	Marc Gené (E)/*Pedro de la Rosa?*
BAR-Honda	Jacques Villeneuve (CDN)/Ricardo Zonta (BR)

The Return of BMW
The Bavarians are Back

BMW, the motoring partner of Williams as of the coming season have finally dared to make an appearance on a Formula One track, the A-1 in Austria. The first test laps of the German-made V 10 engine were driven under the watchful eyes of Williams Technical Director Patrick Head, who was favourably impressed. "Just two seconds slower as we've been with our current FW21. That's very good for a test car, with months to go before our first season with BMW."

In the testing stage: BMW returns to Formula One in 2000 as the motoring partner of Williams.

Rule Changes for the 2000 Season
Reality Rules

There will be a few small but significant changes to the Formula One rule book in 2000. If a race is abandoned and later restarted, the times of the drivers following the two starts will no longer be added up. The drivers will enter the starting grid in the order they were in when the race was abandoned. The timing computer will simply calculate how far drivers were behind the leader in terms of seconds. The idea is to make it easier for the spectators to keep track of the race. Which ever driver reaches the finish line first is the winner. Also, if the rear lights on a car fail to work during bad weather, the race officials can pull that car out of the race until it has had its rear lights repaired. Finally, drivers who have been forced to retire will now be allowed to cross the track under supervision, so they will no longer have to choose between being hit with a hefty fine and taking a very long detour on foot.

Toyota, Renault and Michelin Consider Entering Formula One

The Future Brings More Corporate Involvement

Corporate involvement in the Formula One is continuing to grow. Michelin, Toyota and Renault are all planning to return to Grand Prix motoring. The French tyre-making giant plans to return to given Japanese tyre-maker Bridgestone a run for its money in 2001. Toyota though doesn't plan to get involved until 2002 at the earliest. By that time Renault, a six time world champion and the most successful engine producer of the 1990´s will have a full season under its belt. The French concern is planning to make its comeback in 2001.

The 2000 Season Calendar

Spa Stays

Belgian Formula One fans have breathed a collective sigh of relief, while Grand Prix drivers have expressed their delight. The unique Spa-Francorchamps will remain on the Formula One calendar despite the restrictions of the fact that as of next season it will be illegal for tobacco companies to advertise at sporting events in Belgium. Bernie Ecclestone also bowed to pressure

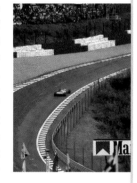

regarding the French Grand Prix. Although he owns an attractive alternative site in Le Castellet in the south of France, Ecclestone has confirmed that the French Grand Prix will remain at Magny-Cours through the 2004 season.

The 2000 Season:

12.03.	Australia (Melbourne)
26.03.	Brazil (Sao Paolo)
09.04.	San Marino (Imola, I)
23.04.	Great Britain (Silverstone)
07.05.	Spain (Barcelona)
21.05.	Europe (Nurburgring, D)
04.06.	Monaco (Monte Carlo)
18.06.	Canada (Montreal)
02.07.	France (Magny-Cours)
16.07.	Austria (A1-Ring)
30.07.	Germany (Hockenheim)
13.08.	Hungary (Hungaroring)
27.08.	Belgium (Spa-Francorchamps)
10.09.	Italy (Monza)
24.09.	USA (Indianapolis)
08.10.	Japan (Suzuka)
22.10.	Malaysia (Sepang)

News in Brief

Good News for Sauber

"Mr Red Bull", Dietrich Mateschitz, and Peter Sauber have agreed to buy up the portion of the Swiss Formula One team which until now had been held by business consultant Fritz Kaiser. Sauber, the team's founder, believes this will bring more stability to the management of the team. At the same time the Malaysian oil concern Petronas has renewed its sponsorship agreement with Sauber, which should help ensure that the C19 runs smoothly into the 2000 season.

A New Job Description

After Olivier Panis was unsuccessful in his search for a new Formula One team for the 2000 season, his manager, Keke Rosberg, found him an alternative. Next season Panis will compete driving a Mercedes CLK in the new German Touring Car Masters series and work part-time as a test driver for McLaren-Mercedes.

Telefonica to Buy Into Minardi?

The smaller Formula One teams too are looking to improve their chances in the coming season. Minardi team owner Giancarlo Minardi and his partner, Gabriele Rum are hoping to convince the Spanish communications giant Telefonica to buy into the lacklustre team. ...?

Prince Leaves Arrows

His association with the Formula One was short-lived: Public relations genius Prince Malik Ado Ibrahim, who was supposed to negotiate big sponsorship deals for the Arrows Team promised a lot but delivered little. That at least is how Arrows Team owner Tom Walkinshaw sees it, and he made no secret of his dissatisfaction, complaining bitterly about the Nigerian prince's lack of effectiveness. One thing that will have pleased Walkinshaw is that Malik is gone, but his money stays.

High Deposit Fee

Beginning next season new teams seeking entry into the Formula One circuit will be required to pay a $48 million entry deposit. The teams will get the money back in payments spread out over four years, provided they do actually get to the starting line. For every year they fail to do so they will forfeit $12 million. The new rule is designed to ensure that new teams are on solid financial ground following the failures in recent years of the Pacific, Simtec, Forti and Lola teams.

FIA Formula One Championship Drivers

1950	Giuseppe Farina (I)	Alfa Romeo 158/159
1951	Juan Manuel Fangio (RA)	Alfa Romeo 159
1952	Alberto Ascari (I)	Ferrari 500
1953	Alberto Ascari (I)	Ferrari 500
1954	Juan Manuel Fangio (RA)	Mercedes W196/Maserati 250 F
1955	Juan Manuel Fangio (RA)	Mercedes W196
1956	Juan Manuel Fangio (RA)	Lancia-Ferrari D50
1957	Juan Manuel Fangio (RA)	Maserati 250 F
1958	Mike Hawthorn (GB)	Ferrari Dino 246
1959	Jack Brabham (AUS)	Cooper-Climax T51
1960	Jack Brabham (AUS)	Cooper-Climax T53
1961	Phil Hill (USA)	Ferrari Dino 156
1962	Graham Hill (GB)	BRM P57
1963	Jim Clark (GB)	Lotus-Climax 25
1964	John Surtees (GB)	Ferrari 158
1965	Jim Clark (GB)	Lotus-Climax 33
1966	Jack Brabham (AUS)	Brabham-Repco BT19/BT20
1967	Denny Hulme (NZ)	Brabham-Repco BT20/BT24
1968	Graham Hill (GB)	Lotus-Ford 49/49B
1969	Jackie Stewart (GB)	Matra-Ford MS10/MS80
1970	Jochen Rindt (A)	Lotus-Ford 49C/72
1971	Jackie Stewart (GB)	Tyrrell-Ford 001/003
1972	Emerson Fittipaldi (BR)	Lotus-Ford 72
1973	Jackie Stewart (GB)	Tyrrell-Ford 005/006
1974	Emerson Fittipaldi (BR)	McLaren-Ford M23
1975	Niki Lauda (A)	Ferrari 312T
1976	James Hunt (GB)	McLaren-Ford M23
1977	Niki Lauda (A)	Ferrari 312T2
1978	Mario Andretti (USA)	Lotus-Ford 78/79
1979	Jody Scheckter (ZA)	Ferrari 312T3/312T4
1980	Alan Jones (AUS)	Williams-Ford FW07B
1981	Nelson Piquet (BR)	Brabham-Ford BT49C
1982	Keke Rosberg (SF)	Williams-Ford FW07C/FW08
1983	Nelson Piquet (BR)	Brabham-BMW BT52/BT52B
1984	Niki Lauda (A)	McLaren-TAG Porsche MP4/2
1985	Alain Prost (F)	McLaren-TAG Porsche MP4/2B
1986	Alain Prost (F)	McLaren-TAG Porsche MP4/2C
1987	Nelson Piquet (BR)	Williams-Honda FW11B
1988	Ayrton Senna (BR)	McLaren-Honda MP4/4
1989	Alain Prost (F)	McLaren-Honda MP4/5
1990	Ayrton Senna (BR)	McLaren-Honda MP4/5B
1991	Ayrton Senna (BR)	McLaren-Honda MP4/6
1992	Nigel Mansell (GB)	Williams-Renault FW14B
1993	Alain Prost (F)	Williams-Renault FW15C
1994	Michael Schumacher (D)	Benetton-Ford B194
1995	Michael Schumacher (D)	Benetton-Renault B195
1996	Damon Hill (GB)	Williams-Renault FW18
1997	Jacques Villeneuve (CDN)	Williams-Renault FW19
1998	Mika Häkkinen (FIN)	McLaren-Mercedes MP4/13
1999	Mika Häkkinen (FIN)	McLaren-Mercedes MP4/14

FIA Formula One Champions - Constructors

1958	Vanwall
1959	Cooper-Climax
1960	Cooper-Climax
1961	Ferrari
1962	BRM
1963	Lotus-Climax
1964	Ferrari
1965	Lotus-Climax
1966	Brabham-Repco
1967	Brabham-Repco
1968	Lotus-Ford
1969	Matra-Ford
1970	Lotus-Ford
1971	Tyrrell-Ford
1972	Lotus-Ford
1973	Lotus-Ford
1974	McLaren-Ford
1975	Ferrari
1976	Ferrari
1977	Ferrari
1978	Lotus-Ford
1979	Ferrari
1980	Williams-Ford
1981	Williams-Ford
1982	Ferrari
1983	Ferrari
1984	McLaren-TAG Porsche
1985	McLaren-TAG Porsche
1986	Williams-Honda
1987	Williams-Honda
1988	McLaren-Honda
1989	McLaren-Honda
1990	McLaren-Honda
1991	McLaren-Honda
1992	Williams-Renault
1993	Williams-Renault
1994	Williams-Renault
1995	Benetton-Renault
1996	Williams-Renault
1997	Williams-Renault
1998	McLaren-Mercedes
1999	Ferrari

Most Drivers Championships

5	Juan-Manuel Fangio (51/54/55/56/57)
4	Alain Prost (85/86/89/93)
3	Jack Brabham (59/60/66)
3	Jackie Stewart (69/71/73)
3	Niki Lauda (75/77/84)
3	Nelson Piquet (81/83/87)
3	Ayrton Senna (88/90/91)
2	Alberto Ascari (52/53)
2	Graham Hill (62/68)
2	Jim Clark (63/65)
2	Emerson Fittipaldi (72/74)
2	Michael Schumacher (94/95)
2	Mika Häkkinen (98/99)

Most Best Car Titles

9	Williams
8	Ferrari
8	McLaren
7	Lotus
2	Cooper
2	Brabham
1	Vanwall
1	BRM
1	Matra
1	Tyrrell
1	Benetton

Engine Manufactures with the Most Championships

10	Ford
9	Ferrari
6	Honda
6	Renault
4	Climax
2	Repco
2	Porsche

Most Grand Prix Victories

51	Alain Prost
41	Ayrton Senna
35	Michael Schumacher
31	Nigel Mansell
27	Jackie Stewart
25	Jim Clark
25	Niki Lauda
24	Juan Manuel Fangio
23	Nelson Piquet
22	Damon Hill
16	Stirling Moss
14	Jack Brabham
14	Emerson Fittipaldi
14	Graham Hill
14	Mika Häkkinen
13	Alberto Ascari
12	Mario Andretti
12	Alan Jones
12	Carlos Reutemann
11	Jacques Villeneuve
10	James Hunt
10	Ronnie Peterson
10	Jody Scheckter
10	Gerhard Berge
6	David Coulthard
4	Eddie Irvine
3	Johnny Herbert
3	Heinz-Harald Frentzen

Teams with the Most GP Victories

125	Ferrari	16	Cooper
123	McLaren	15	Renault
103	Williams	10	Alfa Romeo
79	Lotus	9	Maserati
35	Brabham	9	Matra
27	Benetton	9	Mercedes
23	Tyrrell	9	Vanwall
17	BRM	9	Ligier

Engine Manufacturers with the Most GP Victories

175	Ford	12	Alfa Romeo
125	Ferrari	11	Maserati
95	Renault	9	BMW
71	Honda	9	Vanwall
40	Climax	8	Repco
28	Mercedes	4	Mugen-Honda
26	Porsche	3	Matra
18	BRM	1	Weslake

Most Pole Positions

65	Ayrton Senna
33	Jim Clark
33	Alain Prost
32	Nigel Mansell
29	Juan Manuel Fangio
24	Niki Lauda
24	Nelson Piquet
23	Michael Schumacher
21	Mika Häkkinen
20	Damon Hill
18	Mario Andretti
18	René Arnoux
17	Jackie Stewart
16	Stirling Moss
14	Alberto Ascari
14	James Hunt
14	Ronnie Peterson
13	Jack Brabham
13	Graham Hill
13	Jacky Ickx
13	Jacques Villeneuve
12	Gerhard Berger

Drivers with the Most GP Starts

256	Riccardo Patrese
210	Gerhard Berger
208	Andrea de Cesaris
204	Nelson Piquet
199	Alain Prost
194	Michele Alboreto
187	Nigel Mansell
176	Graham Hill
176	Jacques Laffite
171	Niki Lauda
167	Jean Alesi
163	Thierry Boutsen
161	Ayrton Senna
158	Martin Brundle
152	John Watson
…	…
145	Johnny Herbert
128	Michael Schumacher
128	Mika Häkkinen
116	Damon Hill
113	Rubens Barrichello
97	Heinz-Harald Frentzen
96	Eddie Irvine
90	David Coulthard
83	Pedro Diniz
77	Mika Salo
65	Jacques Villeneuve

Statistics 1999

Teams with the Most GP Starts

635	Ferrari
508	McLaren
430	Tyrrell
420	Williams
391	Prost (Ligier)
353	Arrows
229	Benetton (Toleman)
253	Minardi
162	Jordan
129	Sauber
65	Stewart

Drivers with the Most GP Wins per Start (percentage)

47,1	Juan Manuel Fangio
41,9	Alberto Ascari
34,7	Jim Clark
27,3	Michael Schumacher
27,3	Jackie Stewart
25,6	Alain Prost
25,5	Ayrton Senna
24,2	Stirling Moss
19,0	Damon Hill
16,9	Jacques Villeneuve
16,6	Nigel Mansell
15,8	Tony Brooks

Drivers with the Most top 3-finishes

106	Alain Prost
80	Ayrton Senna
71	Michael Schumacher
60	Nelson Piquet
59	Nigel Mansell
54	Niki Lauda
47	Gerhard Berger
45	Carlos Reutemann
43	Jackie Stewart
42	Damon Hill
38	Mika Häkkinen
37	Riccardo Patrese

Driver Championship Standings 1999

1.	Mika Häkkinen (FIN)	76
2.	Eddie Irvine (IRL)	74
3.	Heinz-Harald Frentzen (D)	54
4.	David Coulthard (GB)	48
5.	Michael Schumacher (D)	44
6.	Ralf Schumacher (D)	35
7.	Rubens Barrichello (BR)	21
8.	Johnny Herbert (GB)	15
9.	Giancarlo Fisichella (I)	13
10.	Mika Salo (FIN)	10
11.	Jarno Trulli	7
12.	Damon Hill (GB)	7
13.	Alexander Wurz (A)	3
14.	Pedro Diniz (BR)	3
15.	Olivier Panis	2
16.	Jean Alesi (F)	2
17.	Pedro de la Rosa (E)	1
18.	Marc Géne	1

Constructors Championship 1999

1.	Ferrari	128
2.	McLaren-Mercedes	124
3.	Jordan-Mugen-Honda	61
4.	Stewart-Ford	36
5.	Williams-Mecachrome	35
6.	Benetton-Playlife	16
7.	Prost-Peugeot	9
8.	Sauber-Petronas	5
9.	Arrows	1
10.	Minardi	1

Drivers with the Most Victories 1999

5	Mika Häkkinen
4	Eddie Irvine
2	Michael Schumacher
2	Heinz-Harald Frentzen
2	David Coulthard
1	Johnny Herbert

Teams with the Most Victories 1999

7	McLaren-Mercedes
6	Ferrari
2	Jordan-Mugen-Honda
1	Stewart-Ford

Drivers with the Most Pole Positions 1999

11	Mika Häkkinen
3	Michael Schumacher
1	Rubens Barrichello
1	Heinz-Harald Frentzen

Teams with the Most Pole Positions 1999

11	McLaren-Mercedes
3	Ferrari
1	Stewart-Ford
1	Jordan-Mugen-Honda

Head to Head Training 1999

M. Schumacher – Irvine	9 : 1
Irvine – Salo	4 : 2
Villeneuve – Zonta	12 : 1
Villeneuve – Salo	3 : 0
Frentzen – Hill	14 : 2
Häkkinen – Coulthard	13 : 3
Barrichello – Herbert	13 : 3
Fisichella – Wurz	13 : 3
Alesi – Diniz	12 : 4
R. Schumacher – Zanardi	11 : 5
Badoer – Gené	10 : 5
Gené – Sarazin	1 : 0
Trulli – Panis	8 : 8
Takagi – De la Rosa	8 : 8

Drivers with the Most Fastest Laps per GP start

6	Mika Häkkinen
5	Michael Schumacher
3	David Coulthard
1	Eddie Irvine
1	Ralf Schumacher

Teams with the Most Fastest Laps per GP start

9	McLaren-Mercedes
6	Ferrari
1	Williams-Supertec

1950

Grand Prix, GB, Silverstone, 13.5.1950
70 x 4,649 km = 325,430 km.
1. Giuseppe Farina	Alfa Romeo 158	2:13.23,600 h
2. Luigi Fagioli	Alfa Romeo 158	2:13.26,200 h
3. Reg Parnell	Alfa Romeo 158	2:14.15,600 h

Grand Prix, MC, Monte Carlo, 21.5.1950
100 x 3,180 km = 318,000 km.
1. Juan Manuel Fangio	Alfa Romeo 158	3:13.18,700 h
2. Alberto Ascari	Ferrari 125	-1
3. Louis Chiron	Maserati 4CL/48	-2

Indianapolis 500, Indianapolis, 30.5.1950
138 x 4,023 km = 555,174 km.
1. Johnnie Parsons	Kurtis-Offenhauser	2:46.55,970 h
2. Bill Holland	Deidt-Offenhauser	-1
3. Mauri Rose	Deidt-Offenhauser	-2

Grand Prix, CH, Bremgarten, 4.6.1950
42 x 7,280 km = 305,760 km.
1. Giuseppe Farina	Alfa Romeo 158	2:02.53,700 h
2. Luigi Fagioli	Alfa Romeo 158	2:02.54,100 h
3. Louis Rosier	Lago-Talbot T26C-DA	-1

Grand Prix, B, Spa-Francorchamps, 18.6.1950
35 x 14,120 km = 494,200 km.
1. Juan Manuel Fangio	Alfa Romeo 158	2:47.26,000 h
2. Luigi Fagioli	Alfa Romeo 158	2:47.47,000 h
3. Louis Rosier	Lago-Talbot T26C-DA	2:49.45,000 h

Grand Prix, F, Reims-Gueux, 2.7.1950
64 x 7,816 km = 500,224 km.
1. Juan Manuel Fangio	Alfa Romeo 158	2:57.52,800 h
2. Luigi Fagioli	Alfa Romeo 158	2:58.18,500 h
3. Peter Whitehead	Ferrari 125	-3

Grand Prix, I, Monza, 3.9.1950
80 x 6,300 km = 504,000 km.
1. Giuseppe Farina	Alfa Romeo 159	2:51.17,400 h
2. D. Serafini / A. Ascari	Ferrari 375	2:52.36,000 h
3. Luigi Fagioli	Alfa Romeo 158	2:52.53,000 h

1950
1. Giuseppe Farina	40 P.
2. Juan Manuel Fangio	23 P.
3. Luigi Fagioli	12 P.

1951

Grand Prix, CH, Bremgarten, 27.5.1951
42 x 7,280 km = 305,760 km.
1. Juan Manuel Fangio	Alfa Romeo 159	2:07.53,640 h
2. Piero Taruffi	Ferrari 375	2:08.48,880 h
3. Giuseppe Farina	Alfa Romeo 159	2:09.12,950 h

Indianapolis 500, Indianapolis, 29.5.1951
200 x 4,023 km = 804,600 km.
1. Lee Wallard	Kurtis-Offenhauser	3:57.38,050 h
2. Mike Nazaruk	Kurtis-Offenhauser	3:59.25,310 h
3. J. McGrath/ M. Ayulo	Kurtis KK3000-Offenh.	4:00.29,420 h

Grand Prix, B, Spa-Francorchamps, 17.6.1951
36 x 14,120 km = 508,320 km.
1. Giuseppe Farina	Alfa Romeo 159	2:45.46,200 h
2. Alberto Ascari	Ferrari 375	2:48.37,200 h
3. Luigi Villoresi	Ferrari 375	2:50.08,100 h

Grand Prix, F, Reims-Gueux, 1.7.1951
77 x 7,816 km = 601,832 km.
1. L. Fagioli/J.M. Fangio	Alfa Romeo 159	3:22.11,000 h
2. J. F. Gonzales/A. Ascari	Ferrari 375	3:23.09,200 h
3. Luigi Villoresi	Ferrari 375	-3

Grand Prix, GB, Silverstone, 14.7.1951
90 x 4,649 km = 418,410 km.
1. Jose Froilan Gonzales	Ferrari 375	2:42.18,200 h
2. Juan Manuel Fangio	Alfa Romeo 159	2:43.09,200 h
3. Luigi Villoresi	Ferrari 375	-2

Grand Prix, D, Nürburgring, 29.7.1951
20 x 22,810 km = 456,200 km.
1. Alberto Ascari	Ferrari 375	3:23.03,300 h
2. Juan Manuel Fangio	Alfa Romeo 159	3:23.33,800 h
3. Jose Froilan Gonzales	Ferrari 375	3:27.42,300 h

Grand Prix, I, Monza, 16.9.1951
80 x 6,300 km = 504,000 km.
1. Alberto Ascari	Ferrari 375	2:42.39,300 h
2. Jose Froilan Gonzales	Ferrari 375	2:43.23,900 h
3. F. Bonetto/G. Farina	Alfa Romeo 159	-1

Grand Prix, E, Pedralbes, 28.10.1951
70 x 6,316 km = 442,120 km.
1. Juan Manuel Fangio	Alfa Romeo 159	2:46.54,100 h
2. Jose Froilan Gonzales	Ferrari 375	2:47.48,380 h
3. Giuseppe Farina	Alfa Romeo 159	2:48.39,640 h

1951
1. Juan Manuel Fangio	31 P.
2. Alberto Ascari	25 P.
3. Jose Froilan Gonzales	24 P.

1952

Grand Prix, CH, Bremgarten, 18.5.1952
62 x 7,280 = 451,360 km.
1. Piero Taruffi	Ferrari 500	3:01.46,100 h
2. Rudolf Fischer	Ferrari 500	3:04.23,300 h
3. Jean Behra	Gordini 16	-1

Indianapolis 500, Indianapolis, 30.5.1952
200 x 4,023 km = 804,600 km.
1. Troy Rottman	Kuzma-Offenhauser	3:52.41,880 h
2. Jim Rathman	Kurtis KK3000-Offenh.	3:56.44,240 h
3. Sam Hanks	Kurtis KK3000-Offenh.	3:58.53,480 h

Grand Prix, B, Spa-Francorchamps, 5.6.1952
36 x 14,120 km = 508,320 km.
1. Alberto Ascari	Ferrari 500	3:03.46,300 h
2. Giuseppe Farina	Ferrari 500	3:05.41,500 h
3. Robert Manzon	Gordini 16	3:08.14,700 h

Grand Prix, F, Rouen-les-Essarts, 6.7.1952
76 x 5,100 km = 386,600 km.
1. Alberto Ascari	Ferrari 500	3:00.00,000 h
2. Giuseppe Farina	Ferrari 500	-1
3. Piero Taruffi	Ferrari 500	-2

Grand Prix, GB, Silverstone, 19.7.1952
85 x 4,711 km = 400,435 km.
1. Alberto Ascari	Ferrari 500	2:44.11,000 h
2. Piero Taruffi	Ferrari 500	-1
3. Mike Hawthorn	Cooper T20-Bristol	-2

Grand Prix, D, Nürburgring, 3.8.1952
18 x 22,810 km = 410,580 km.
1. Alberto Ascari	Ferrari 500	3:06.13,300 h
2. Giuseppe Farina	Ferrari 500	3:06.27,400 h
3. Rudolf Fischer	Ferrari 500	3:09.22,400 h

Grand Prix, NL, Zandvoort, 17.8.1952
90 x 4,193 km = 377,370 km.
1. Alberto Ascari	Ferrari 500	2:53.28,500 h
2. Giuseppe Farina	Ferrari 500	2:54.08,600 h
3. Luigi Villoresi	Ferrari 500	2:55.02,900 h

Grand Prix, I, Monza, 7.9.1952
80 x 6,300 km = 504,000 km.
1. Alberto Ascari	Ferrari 500	2:50.45,600 h
2. Jose Froilan Gonzales	Maserati A6GCM	2:51.47,400 h
3. Luigi Villoresi	Ferrari 500	2:52.49,800 h

1952
1. Alberto Ascari	36 P.
2. Giuseppe Farina	24 P.
3. Piero Taruffi	22 P.

1953

Grand Prix, RA, Buenos Aires, 18.1.1953
97 x 3,912 km = 379,464 km.
1. Alberto Ascari	Ferrari 500	3:01.04,600 h
2. Luigi Villoresi	Ferrari 500	-1
3. Jose Froilan Gonzales	Maserati A6GCM	-1

Indianapolis 500, Indianapolis, 30.5.1953
200 x 4,023 km = 804,600 km.
1. Bill Vukovich	Kurtis KK500A-Offenh.	3:53.01,690 h
2. Art Kross	Kurtis KK4000-Offenh.	3:56.32,560 h
3. S. Hanks/D. Carter	Kurtis KK4000-Offenh.	3:57.13,240 h

Grand Prix, NL, Zandvoort, 7.6.1953
90 x 4,193 km = 377,370 km.
1. Alberto Ascari	Ferrari 500	2:53.35,800 h
2. Giuseppe Farina	Ferrari 500	2:53.46,200 h
3. F. Bonetto/J. Gonzales	Maserati A6SSG	-1

Grand Prix, B, Spa-Francorchamps, 21.6.1953
36 x 14,120 km = 508,320 km.
1. Alberto Ascari	Ferrari 500	2:48.30,300 h
2. Luigi Villoresi	Ferrari 500	2:51.18,500 h
3. Onofre Marimon	Maserati A6SSG	-1

Grand Prix, F, Reims, 5.7.1953
60 x 8,347 km = 500,820 km.
1. Mike Hawthorn	Ferrari 500	2:44.18,600 h
2. Juan Manuel Fangio	Maserati A6SSG	2:44.19,600 h
3. Jose Froilan Gonzales	Maserati A6SSG	2:44.20,000 h

Grand Prix, GB, Silverstone, 18.7.1953
90 x 4,711 km = 423,990 km.
1. Alberto Ascari	Ferrari 500	2:50.00,000 h
2. Juan Manuel Fangio	Maserati A6SSG	2:51.00,000 h
3. Giuseppe Farina	Ferrari 500	-2

Grand Prix, D, Nürburgring, 2.8.1953
18 x 22,810 km = 410,580 km.
1. Giuseppe Farina	Ferrari 500	3:02.25,000 h
2. Juan Manuel Fangio	Maserati A6SSG	3:03.29,000 h
3. Mike Hawthorn	Ferrari 500	3:04.08,600 h

Grand Prix, CH, Bremgarten, 23.8.1953
65 x 7,280 km = 473,200 km.
1. Alberto Ascari	Ferrari 500	3:01.34,400 h
2. Giuseppe Farina	Ferrari 500	3:02.47,330 h
3. Mike Hawthorn	Ferrari 500	3:03.10,360 h

Grand Prix, I, Monza, 13.9.1953
80 x 6,300 km = 504,000 km.
1. Juan Manuel Fangio	Maserati A6SSG	2:49.45,900 h
2. Giuseppe Farina	Ferrari 500	2:49.47,300 h
3. Luigi Villoresi	Ferrari 500	-1

1953
1. Alberto Ascari	34,5 P.
2. Juan Manuel Fangio	27,5 P.
3. Giuseppe Farina	26 P.

1954

Grand Prix, RA, Buenos Aires, 17.1.1954
87 x 3,912 km = 340,334 km.
1. Juan Manuel Fangio	Maserati 250F	3:00.55,800 h
2. Giuseppe Farina	Ferrari 625	3:02.14,800 h
3. Jose Froilan Gonzales	Ferrari 625	3:02.56,800 h

Indianapolis 500, Indianapolis, 31.5.1954
200 x 4,023 km = 804,600 km.
1. Bill Vukovich	Kurtis KK500A-Offenh.	3:49.17,270 h
2. Jimmy Bryan	Kuzma-Offenhauser	3:50.27,260 h
3. Jack McGrath	Kurtis KK500A-Offenh.	3:50.36,970 h

Grand Prix, B, Spa-Francorchamps, 20.6.1954
36 x 14,120 km = 508,320 km.
1. Juan Manuel Fangio	Maserati 250F	2:44.42,400 h
2. Maurice Trintignant	Ferrari 625	2:45.06,600 h
3. Stirling Moss	Maserati 250F	-1

Grand Prix, F, Reims, 4.7.1954
61 8,302 km = 506,442 km.
1. Juan Manuel Fangio	Mercedes-Benz W196	2:42.47,900 h
2. Karl Kling	Mercedes-Benz W196	2:42.48,000 h
3. Robert Manzon	Ferrari 625	-1

Grand Prix, GB, Silverstone, 17.7.1954
90 x 4,711 km = 423,949 km.
1. Jose Froilan Gonzales	Ferrari 625	2:56.14,000 h
2. Mike Hawthorn	Ferrari 625	2:57.24,000 h
3. Onofre Marimon	Maserati 250F	-1

Grand Prix, D, Nürburgring, 1.8.1954
22 x 22,810 km = 501,820 km.
1. Juan Manuel Fangio	Mercedes-Benz W196	3:45.45,800 h
2. Gonzales/Hawthorn	Ferrari 625	3:47.22,300 h
3. Maurice Tritingnant	Ferrari 625	3:50.54,400 h

Grand Prix, CH, Bremgarten, 22.8.1954
66 x 7,280 km = 480,480 km.
1. Juan Manuel Fangio	Mercedes-Benz W196	3:00.34,500 h
2. Jose Froilan Gonzales	Ferrari 625	3:01.323,00 h
3. Hans Herrmann	Mercedes-Benz W196	-1

Grand Prix, I, Monza, 5.9.1954
80 x 6,300 km = 504,000 km.
1. Juan Manuel Fangio	Mercedes-Benz W196	2:47.47,900 h
2. Mike Hawthorn	Ferrari 625	-1
3. U. Maglioli/Gonzales	Ferrari 625	-2

Grand Prix, E, Pedralbes, 24.10.1954
80 x 6,316 km = 505,280 km.
1. Mike Hawthorn	Ferrari 553 Squalo	3:13.52,100 h
2. Luigi Musso	Maserati 250F	3:15.05,300 h
3. Juan Manuel Fangio	Mercedes-Benz W196	-1

1954
1. Juan Manuel Fangio	42 P.
2. Jose Froilan Gonzales	25,14 P.
3. Mike Hawthorn	24,64 P.

1955

Grand Prix, RA, Buenos Aires, 16.1.1955
96 x 3,912 km = 375,552 km.
1. Juan Manuel Fangio	Mercedes-Benz W196	3:00.38,600 h
2. Gonz./Trintig./Farina	Ferrari 625	3:02.08,200 h
3. Far./Maglioli/Trintig.	Ferrari 625	-2

Grand Prix, MC, Monte Carlo, 22.5.1955
100 x 3,145 km = 314,500 km.
1. Maurice Trintignant	Ferrari 625	2:58.09,800 h
2. Eugenio Castellotti	Lancia D50	2:58.30,000 h
3. J. Behra/C. Perdisa	Maserati 250F	-1

Indianapolis 500, Indianapolis, 30.5.1955
200 x 4,023 km = 804,600 km.
1. Bob Sweikert	Kurtis KK500C-Offenh.	3:53.59,130 h
2. Bettenhausen/P. Russo	Kurtis KK500C-Offenh.	3:56.43,110 h
3. Jimmy Davies	Kurtis KK500B-Offenh.	3:57.31,890 h

GP 1955 – 1960

Grand Prix, B, Spa-Francorchamps, 5.6.1955
36 x 14,120 km = 508,320 km.
1. Juan Manuel Fangio	Mercedes-Benz W196	2:39.29,000 h
2. Stirling Moss	Mercedes-Benz W196	2:39.37,100 h
3. Giuseppe Farina	Ferrari 555	2:41.09,500 h

Grand Prix, NL, Zandvoort, 19.6.1955
100 x 4,193 km = 419,300 km.
1. Juan Manuel Fangio	Mercedes-Benz W196	2:54.23,800 h
2. Stirling Moss	Mercedes-Benz W196	2:54.24,100 h
3. Luigi Musso	Maserati 250F	2:55.20,900 h

Grand Prix, GB, Aintree, 16.7.1955
90 x 4,823 km = 434,523 km.
1. Stirling Moss	Mercedes-Benz W196	3:07.21,200 h
2. Juan Manuel Fangio	Mercedes-Benz W196	3:07.21,400 h
3. Karl Kling	Mercedes-Benz W196	3:08.33,000 h

Grand Prix, I, Monza, 11.9.1955
50 x 10,000 km = 500,000 km.
1. Juan Manuel Fangio	Mercedes-Benz W196	2:25.04,400 h
2. Piero Taruffi	Mercedes-Benz W196	2:25.05,100 h
3. Eugenio Castellotti	Ferrari 555	2:25.50,600 h

1955
1. Juan Manuel Fangio	40 P.
2. Stirling Moss	23 P.
3. Eugenio Castellotti	12 P.

1956

Grand Prix, RA, Buenos Aires, 22.1.1956
98 x 3,912 km = 383,376 km.
1. L. Musso/J. M. Fangio	Lancia-Ferrari D50	3:00.03,700 h
2. Jean Behra	Maserati 250F	3:00.28,100 h
3. Mike Hawthorn	Maserati 250F	-2

Grand Prix, MC, Monte Carlo, 13.5.1956
100 x 3,145 km = 314,500 km.
1. Sterling Moss	Maserati 250F	3:00.32,900 h
2. P. Collins/J. M. Fangio	Lancia-Ferrari D50	3:00.39,000 h
3. Juan Manuel Fangio	Maserati 250F	-1

Indianapolis 500, Indianapolis, 30.5.1956
200 x 4,023 km = 804,600 km.
1. Pat Flaherty	Watson-Offenhauser	3:53.28,840 h
2. Sam Hanks	Kurtis KK500C-Offenh.	3:53.49,300 h
3. Don Freeland	Phillips-Offenhauser	3:54.59,070 h

Grand Prix, B, Spa-Francorchamps, 3.6.1956
36 x 14,120 km = 508,320 km.
1. Peter Collins	Lancia-Ferrari D50	2:40.00,300 h
2. Paul Frère	Lancia-Ferrari D50	2:41.51,600 h
3. C. Perdisa/S. Moss	Maserati 250F	2:43.16,900 h

Grand Prix, F, Reims, 1.7.1956
61 x 8,302 km = 506,422 km.
1. Peter Collins	Lancia-Ferrari D50	2:34.23,400 h
2. Eugenio Castellotti	Lancia-Ferrari D50	2:34.23,700 h
3. Jean Behra	Maserati 250F	2:35.53,300 h

Grand Prix, GB, Silverstone, 14.7.1956
101 x 4,711 km = 475,766 km.
1. Juan Manuel Fangio	Lancia-Ferrari D50	2:59.47,000 h
2. de Portago/P. Collins	Lancia-Ferrari D50	-1
3. Jean Behra	Maserati 250F	-2

Grand Prix, D, Nürburgring, 5.8.1956
22 x 22,810 km = 501,820 km.
1. Juan Manuel Fangio	Lancia-Ferrari D50	3:38.43,700 h
2. Stirling Moss	Maserati 250F	3:39.30,100 h
3. Jean Behra	Maserati 250F	3:46.22,000 h

Grand Prix, I, Monza, 2.9.1956
50 x 10,000 km = 500,000 km.
1. Stirling Moss	Maserati 250F	2:23.41,300 h
2. P. Collins/J. M. Fangio	Lancia-Ferrari D50	2:23.47,000 h
3. Ron Flockhart	Connaught B-Alta	-1

1956
1. Juan Manuel Fangio	30 P.
2. Stirling Moss	27 P.
3. Peter Collins	25 P.

1957

Grand Prix, RA, Buenos Aires, 13.1.1957
100 x 3,912 km = 391,200 km.
1. Juan Manuel Fangio	Maserati 250F	3:00.55,900 h
2. Jean Behra	Maserati 250F	3:01.14,200 h
3. Carlos Menditeguy	Maserati 250F	-1

Grand Prix, MC, Monte Carlo, 19.5.1957
105 x 4,023 km = 422,415 km.
1. Juan Manuel Fangio	Maserati 250F	3:10.12,800 h
2. Tony Brooks	Vanwall VW7	3:10.38,000 h
3. Masten Gregory	Maserati 250F	-2

Indianapolis 500, Indianapolis, 30.5.1957
200 x 4,023 km = 804,600 km.
1. Sam Hanks	Epperly-Offenhauser	3:41.14,250 h
2. Jim Rathmann	Epperly-Offenhauser	3:41.35,750 h
3. Jimmy Brian	Kuzma-Offenhauser	3:43.28,250 h

Grand Prix, F, Rouen-les-Essarts, 7.7.1957
77 x 6,542 km = 503,734 km.
1. Juan Manuel Fangio	Maserati 250F	3:07.46,400 h
2. Luigi Musso	Lancia-Ferrari 801	3:08.37,200 h
3. Peter Collins	Lancia-Ferrari 801	3:09.52,400 h

Grand Prix, GB, Aintree, 20.7.1957
90 x 4,828 km = 434,523 km.
1. T. Brooks/S. Moss	Vanwall VW4	3:06.37,800 h
2. Luigi Musso	Lancia-Ferrari 801	3:07.03,400 h
3. Mike Hawthorn	Lancia-Ferrari 801	3:07.20,600 h

Grand Prix, D, Nürburgring, 4.8.1957
22 x 22,810 km = 501,820 km.
1. Juan Manuel Fangio	Maserati 250F	3:30.38,300 h
2. Mike Hawthorn	Lancia-Ferrari 801	3:30.41,900 h
3. Peter Collins	Lancia-Ferrari 801	3:31.13,900 h

Grand Prix, E, Pescara, 18.8.1957
18 x 25,579 km = 460,422 km.
1. Stirling Moss	Vanwall VW5	2:59.22,700 h
2. Juan Manuel Fangio	Maserati 250F	3:02.36,600 h
3. Harry Schell	Maserati 250F	3:06.09,500 h

Grand Prix, I, Monza, 8.9.1957
87 x 5,750 km = 500,250 km.
1. Stirling Moss	Vanwall VW5	2:35.03,900 h
2. Juan Manuel Fangio	Maserati 250F	2:35.45,100 h
3. Wolfgang of Trips	Lancia-Ferrari 801	-2

1957
1. Juan Manuel Fangio	40 P.
2. Stirling Moss	25 P.
3. Luigi Musso	16 P.

1958

Grand Prix, RA, Buenos Aires, 19.1.1958
80 x 3,912 km = 312,960 km.
1. Stirling Moss	Cooper T43-Climax	2:19.33,700 h
2. Luigi Musso	Ferrari Dino 246	2:19.36,400 h
3. Mike Hawthorn	Ferrari Dino 246	2:19.46,300 h

Grand Prix, MC, Monte Carlo, 18.5.1958
100 x 3,145 km = 314,500 km.
1. Maurice Trintignant	Cooper T45-Climax	2:52.27,900 h
2. Luigi Musso	Ferrari Dino 246	2:52.48,200 h
3. Peter Collins	Ferrari Dino 246	2:53.06,700 h

Grand Prix, NL, Zandvoort, 25.5.1958
36 x 16,023 km = 500,001 km.
1. Stirling Moss	Vanwall VW10	2:04.49,200 h
2. Harry Schell	BRM P25 (58)	2:05.37,100 h
3. Jean Behra	BRM P25 (58)	2:06.31,500 h

Indianapolis 500, Indianapolis, 30.5.1958
200 x 4,023 km = 804,600 km.
1. Jimmy Brian	Epperly-Offenhauser	3:44.13,800 h
2. George Amick	Epperly-Offenhauser	3:44.41,450 h
3. Johnny Boyd	Kurtis KK500G-Offenh.	3:45.45,750 h

Grand Prix, B, Spa-Francorchamps, 15.6.1958
24 x 14,100 km = 338,400 km.
1. Tony Brooks	Vanwall VW5	1:37.06,300 h
2. Mike Hawthorn	Ferrari Dino 246	1:37.27,000 h
3. Stuart Lewis-Evans	Vanwall VW4	1:40.07,200 h

Grand Prix, F, Reims 6.7.1958
50 x 8,302 km = 415,100 km.
1. Mike Hawthorn	Ferrari Dino 246	2:03.21,300 h
2. Stirling Moss	Vanwall VW10	2:03.45,900 h
3. Wolfgang of Trips	Ferrari Dino 246	2:04.21,000 h

Grand Prix, GB, Silverstone, 19.7.1958
75 x 4,711 km = 353,291 km.
1. Peter Collins	Ferrari Dino 246	2:09.04,200 h
2. Mike Hawthorn	Ferrari Dino 246	2:09.28,400 h
3. Roy Salvadori	Cooper T45-Climax	2:09.54,800 h

Grand Prix, D, Nürburgring, 3.8.1958
15 x 22,810 km = 342,150 km.
1. Tony Brooks	Vanwall VW4	2:21.15,000 h
2. Roy Salvadori	Cooper T45-Climax	2:24.44,700 h
3. Maurice Trintignant	Cooper T45-Climax	2:26.26,200 h

Grand Prix, P, Oporto, 24.8.1958
50 x 7,407 km = 370,350 km.
1. Stirling Moss	Vanwall VW10	2:11.27,800 h
2. Mike Hawthorn	Ferrari Dino 246	2:16.40,550 h
3. Stuart Lewis-Evans	Vanwall VW6	-1

Grand Prix, I, Monza, 7.9.1958
70 x 5,750 km = 402,500 km.
1. Tony Brooks	Vanwall VW5	2:03.47,800 h
2. Mike Hawthorn	Ferrari Dino 246	2:04.12,000 h
3. Phil Hill	Ferrari Dino 246	2:04.16,100 h

Grand Prix, MA, Ain Diab, 19.10.1958
53 x 7,618 km = 403,754 km.
1. Stirling Moss	Vanwall VW5	2:09.15,000 h
2. Mike Hawthorn	Ferrari Dino 246	2:10.39,800 h
3. Phil Hill	Ferrari Dino 246	2:10.40,600 h

1958
1. M. Hawthorn	42 P.	1. Vanwall	48 P.
2. S. Moss	41 P.	2. Ferrari	40 P.
3. T. Brooks	24 P.	3. Cooper-Climax	31 P.

1959

Grand Prix, MC, Monte Carlo, 10.5.1959
100 x 3,145 km = 314,500 km.
1. Jack Brabham	Cooper T51-Climax	2:55.51,300 h
2. Tony Brooks	Ferrari Dino 246	2:56.11,700 h
3. Maurice Trintignant	Cooper T51-Climax	-2

Indianapolis 500, Indianapolis, 30.5.1959
200 x 4,023 km = 804,600 km.
1. Rodger Ward	Watson-Offenhauser	3:40.49,200 h
2. Jim Rathmann	Watson-Offenhauser	3:41.12,470 h
3. Johnny Thomson	Lesovsky-Offenhauser	3:41.39,850 h

Grand Prix, NL, Zandvoort, 31.5.1959
75 x 4,193 km = 314,475 km.
1. Jo Bonnier	BRM P25 (59)	2:05.26,800 h
2. Jack Brabham	Cooper T51-Climax	2:05.41,000 h
3. Masten Gregory	Cooper T51-Climax	2:06.49,800 h

Grand Prix, F, Reims, 5.7.1959
36 x 16,023 km = 500,001 km.
1. Tony Brooks	Ferrari Dino 246	2:01.26,500 h
2. Phil Hill	Ferrari Dino 246	2:01.54,000 h
3. Jack Brabham	Cooper T51-Climax	2:03.04,200 h

Grand Prix, GB, Aintree, 18.7.1959
75 x 4,828 km = 362,102 km.
1. Jack Brabham	Cooper T51-Climax	2:30.11,600 h
2. Stirling Moss	BRM P25 (58)	2:30.33,800 h
3. Bruce McLaren	Cooper T54-Climax	2:30.34,000 h

Grand Prix, D, Avus, 2.8.1959
60 x 8,300 km = 498,000 km.
1. Tony Brooks	Ferrari Dino 246	2:09.31,600 h
2. Dan Gurney	Ferrari Dino 246	2:09.33,200 h
3. Phil Hill	Ferrari Dino 246	2:10.36,700 h

Grand Prix, P, Monsanto Park, 23.8.1959
62 x 5,440 km = 337,280 km.
1. Stirling Moss	Cooper T51-Climax	2:11.45,410 h
2. Masten Gregory	Cooper T51-Climax	-1
3. Dan Gurney	Ferrari Dino 246	-1

Grand Prix, I, Monza, 13.9.1959
72 x x 5,750 km = 414,000 km.
1. Stirling Moss	Cooper T51-Climax	2:04.05,400 h
2. Phil Hill	Ferrari Dino 246	2:04.52,100 h
3. Jack Brabham	Cooper T45-Climax	2:05.17,900 h

Grand Prix, USA, Sebring, 12.12.1959
42 x 8,369 km = 351,481 km.
1. Bruce McLaren	Cooper T54-Climax	2:12.35,700 h
2. Maurice Trintignant	Cooper T51-Climax	2:12.35,300 h
3. Tony Brooks	Ferrari Dino 246	2:15.36,600 h

1959
1. J. Brabham	31 P.	1. Cooper-Climax	40
2. T. Brooks	27 P.	2. Ferrari	32
3. S. Moss	25,5 P.	3. BRM	18

1960

Grand Prix, RA, Buenos Aires, 7.2.1960
80 x 3,912 km = 312,960 km.
1. Bruce McLaren	Cooper T45-Climax	2:17.49,500 h
2. Cliff Allison	Ferrari Dino 246	2:18.15,800 h
3. M. Trintignant/S. Moss	Cooper T45-Climax	2:18.26,400 h

Grand Prix, MC, Monte Carlo, 29.5.1960
100 x 3,145 km = 314,500 km.
1. Stirling Moss	Mercedes Benz W196	2:53.45,500 h
2. Bruce McLaren	Cooper T53-Climax	2:54.37,600 h
3. Phil Hill	Ferrari Dino 246	2:54.47,400 h

Indianapolis 500, Indianapolis, 30.5.1960
200 x 4,023 km = 804,600 km.
1. Jim Rathmann	Watson-Offenhauser	3:36.11,360 h
2. Rodger Ward	Watson-Offenhauser	3:36.24,030 h
3. Paul Goldsmith	Epperly-Offenhauser	3:39.18,580 h

Grand Prix, NL, Zandvoort, 6.6.1960
75 x 4,193 km = 314,475 km.
1. Jack Brabham	Cooper T53-Climax	2:01.47,200 h
2. Innes Ireland	Lotus 18-Climax	2:02.11,200 h
3. Graham Hill	BRM P48	2:02.43,800 h

Grand Prix, B, Spa-Francorchamps, 19.6.1960
36 x 14,100 km = 507,600 km.
1. Jack Brabham	Cooper T53-Climax	2:21.37,300 h
2. Bruce McLaren	Cooper T53-Climax	2:22.40,600 h
3. Olivier Gendebien	Cooper T51-Climax	-1

Grand Prix, F, Reims, 3.7.1960
50 x 8,302 km = 415,100 km.
1. Jack Brabham	Cooper T53-Climax	1:57.24,900 h
2. Olivier Gendebien	Cooper T51-Climax	1:57.13,200 h
3. Bruce McLaren	Cooper T53-Climax	1:58.16,800 h

Grand Prix, GB, Silverstone, 16.7.1960
77 x 4,711 km = 362,747 km.
1. Jack Brabham	Cooper T53-Climax	2:04.24,600 h
2. John Surtees	Lotus 18-Climax	2:05.14,200 h
3. Innes Ireland	Lotus 18-Climax	2:05.54,200 h

Grand Prix, P, Oporto, 14.8.1960
55 x 7,407 km = 407,385 km.
1. Jack Brabham	Cooper T53-Climax	2:19.00,030 h
2. Bruce McLaren	Cooper T53-Climax	2:29.58,000 h
3. Jim Clark	Lotus 18-Climax	2:20.53,260 h

Grand Prix, I, Monza, 4.9.1960
50 x 10,000 km = 500,000 km.
1. Phil Hill	Ferrari Dino 246	2:21.09,200 h
2. Richie Ginther	Ferrari Dino 246	2:23.36,800 h
3. Willy Mairesse	Ferrari Dino 246	-1

Grand Prix, USA, Riverside, 20.11.1960
75 x 5,271 km = 395,295 km.
1. Stirling Moss	Lotus 18-Climax	2:28.52,200 h
2. Innes Ireland	Lotus 18-Climax	2:29.30,200 h
3. Bruce McLaren	Cooper T53-Climax	2:30.14,200 h

1960
1. J. Brabham	43 P.	1.Cooper-Climax	48 P.
2. B. McLaren	34 P.	2. Lotus-Climax	34 P.
3. S. Moss	19 P.	3. Ferrari	26 P.

1961

Grand Prix, MC, Monte Carlo, 14.5.1961
100 x 3,145 km = 314,500 km.
1. Stirling Moss	Lotus 18-Climax	2:45.50,100 h
2. Richie Ginther	Ferrari 156	2:45.53,700 h
3. Phil Hill	Ferrari 156	2:46.31,400 h

Grand Prix, NL, Zandvoort, 5.6.1961
75 x 4,193 km = 314,475 km.
1. Wolfgang of Trips	Ferrari 156	2:01.52,100 h
2. Phil Hill	Ferrari 156	2:01.53,000 h
3. Jim Clark	Lotus 21-Climax	2:02.05,200 h

Grand Prix, B, Spa-Francorchamps, 18.6.1961
30 x 14,100 km = 423,000 km.
1. Phil Hill	Ferrari 156	2:03.03,800 h
2. Wolfgang of Trips	Ferrari 156	2:03.04,500 h
3. Richie Ginther	Ferrari 156	2:03.23,300 h

Grand Prix, F, Reims, 2.7.1961
52 x 8,302 km = 431,704 km.
1. Giancarlo Baghetti	Ferrari 156	2:14.17,500 h
2. Dan Gurney	Porsche 718	2:14.17,600 h
3. Jim Clark	Lotus 21-Climax	2:15.18,600 h

Grand Prix, GB, Aintree, 15.7.1961
75 x 4,828 km = 362,100 km.
1. Wolfgang of Trips	Ferrari 156	2:40.53,600 h
2. Phil Hill	Ferrari 156	2:41.39,600 h
3. Richie Ginther	Ferrari 156	2:41.40,400 h

Grand Prix, D, Nürburgring, 6.8.1961
15 x 22,810 km = 342,150 km.
1. Stirling Moss	Lotus 18/21-Climax	2:18.12,400 h
2. Wolfgang of Trips	Ferrari 156	2:18.33,800 h
3. Phil Hill	Ferrari 156	2:18.34,900 h

Grand Prix, I, Monza, 10.9.1961
43 x 10,000 km = 430,000 km.
1. Phil Hill	Ferrari 156	2:03.13,000 h
2. Dan Gurney	Porsche 718	2:03.44,200 h
3. Bruce McLaren	Cooper T55-Climax	2:05.41,400 h

Grand Prix, USA, Watkins Glen, 8.10.1961
100 x 3,701 km = 370,100 km.
1. Innes Ireland	Lotus 21-Climax	2:13.45,800 h
2. Dan Gurney	Porsche 718	2:13.50,100 h
3. Tony Brooks	BRM P48/57 Climax	2:14.34,800 h

1961
1. Phil Hill	34 P.	1. Ferrari	40 P.
2. W. of Trips	33 P.	2. Lotus-Climax	32 P.
3. Gurney/Moss	21 P.	3. Porsche	22 P.

1962

Grand Prix, NL, Zandvoort, 20.5.1962
80 x 4,193 km = 335,440 km.
1. Graham Hill	BRM P57	2:11.02,100 h
2. Trevor Taylor	Lotus 24-Climax	2:11.29,300 h
3. Phil Hill	Ferrari 156	2:12.23,200 h

Grand Prix, MC, Monte Carlo, 3.6.1962
100 x 3,145 km = 314,500 km.
1. Bruce McLaren	Cooper T60-Climax	2:46.29,700 h
2. Phil Hill	Ferrari 156	2:46.31,000 h
3. Lorenzo Bandini	Ferrari 156	2:47.53,800 h

Grand Prix, B, Spa-Francorchamps, 17.6.1962
32 x 14,100 km = 451,200 km.
1. Jim Clark	Lotus 25-Climax	2:07.32,300 h
2. Graham Hill	BRM P57	2:08.16,400 h
3. Phil Hill	Ferrari 156	2:09.38,800 h

Grand Prix, F, Rouen-les-Essarts, 8.7.1962
54 x 6,542 km = 353,268 km.
1. Dan Gurney	Porsche 804	2:07.35,500 h
2. Tony Maggs	Cooper T60-Climax	-1
3. Richie Ginther	BRM P57	-2

Grand Prix, GB, Aintree, 21.7.1962
75 x 4,823 km = 361,725 km.
1. Jim Clark	Lotus 25-Climax	2:26.20,800 h
2. John Surtees	Lola MK4-Climax	2:27.10,000 h
3. Bruce McLaren	Cooper T60-Climax	2:28.05,600 h

Grand Prix, D, Nürburgring, 5.8.1962
15 x 22,810 km = 342,150 km.
1. Jim Clark	Lotus 25-Climax	2:38.45,300 h
2. John Surtees	Lola MK4-Climax	2:38.47,800 h
3. Dan Gurney	Porsche 804	2:38.49,700 h

Grand Prix, I, Monza, 16.9.1962
86 x 5,750 km = 494,500 km.
1. Graham Hill	BRM P57	2:29.08,400 h
2. Richie Ginther	BRM P57	2:29.38,200 h
3. Bruce McLaren	Cooper T60-Climax	2:30.06,200 h

Grand Prix, USA, Watkins Glen, 7.10.1962
100 x 3,701 km = 370,100 km.
1. Jim Clark	Lotus 25-Climax	2:07.13,000 h
2. Graham Hill	BRM P57	2:07.22,200 h
3. Bruce McLaren	Cooper T60-Climax	-1

Grand Prix, ZA, EastLondon, 29.12.1962
82 x 3,920 km = 312,440 km.
1. Graham Hill	BRM P57	2:08.03,300 h
2. Bruce McLaren	Cooper T60-Climax	2:08.53,100 h
3. Tony Maggs	Cooper T60-Climax	2:08.53,600 h

1962
1. G. Hill	42 P.	1. BRM	42 P.
2. J. Clark	30 P.	2. Lotus-Climax	36 P.
3. B. McLaren	27 P.	3. Cooper-Climax	29 P.

1963

Grand Prix, MC, Monte Carlo, 26.5.1963
100 x 3,145 km = 314,500 km.
1. Graham Hill	BRM P57	2:41.49,700 h
2. Richie Ginther	BRM P57	2:41.54,300 h
3. Bruce McLaren	Cooper T66-Climax	2:42.02,500 h

Grand Prix, B, Spa-Francorchamps, 9.6.1963
32 x 14,100 km = 451,200 km.
1. Jim Clark	Lotus 25-Climax	2:27.47,600 h
2. Bruce McLaren	Cooper T66-Climax	2:32.41,600 h
3. Dan Gurney	Brabham BT7-Climax	-1

Grand Prix, NL, Zandvoort, 23.6.1963
80 x 4,193 km = 335,440 km.
1. Jim Clark	Lotus 25-Climax	2:08.13,070 h
2. Dan Gurney	Brabham BT7-Climax	-1
3. John Surtees	Ferrari 156	-1

Grand Prix, F, Reims, 30.6.1963
53 x 8,302 km = 440,006 km.
1. Jim Clark	Lotus 25-Climax	2:10.54,300 h
2. Tony Maggs	Cooper T66-Climax	2:11.59,200 h
3. Graham Hill	BRM P61	2:13.08,200 h

Grand Prix, GB, Silverstone, 20.7.1963
82 x 4,711 km = 386,302 km.
1. Jim Clark	Lotus 25-Climax	2:14.09,600 h
2. John Surtees	Ferrari 156	2:14.35,400 h
3. Graham Hill	BRM P57	2:14.47,200 h

Grand Prix, D, Nürburgring, 4.8.1963
15 x 22,810 km = 342,150 km.
1. John Surtees	Ferrari 156	2:13.06,800 h
2. Jim Clark	Lotus 25-Climax	2:14.24,300 h
3. Richie Ginther	BRM P57	2:15.51,700 h

Grand Prix, I, Monza, 8.9.1963
86 x 5,750 km = 494,500 km.
1. Jim Clark	Lotus 25-Climax	2:24.19,600 h
2. Richie Ginther	BRM P57	2:25.54,600 h
3. Bruce McLaren	Cooper T66-Climax	-1

Grand Prix, USA, Watkins Glen, 6.10.1963
110 x 3,701 km = 407,110 km.
1. Graham Hill	BRM P57	2:19.22,100 h
2. Richie Ginther	BRM P57	2:19.56,400 h
3. Jim Clark	Lotus 25-Climax	-1

Grand Prix, MEX, Mexico City, 27.10.1963
65 x 5,000 km = 325,000 km.
1. Jim Clark	Lotus 25-Climax	2:09.52,100 h
2. Jack Brabham	Brabham BT7-Climax	2:11.33,200 h
3. Richie Ginther	BRM P57	2:11.46,800 h

Grand Prix, ZA, East London, 28.12.1963
85 x 3,920 km = 333,200 km.
1. Jim Clark	Lotus 25-Climax	2:10.36,900 h
2. Dan Gurney	Brabham BT7-Climax	2:11.43,700 h
3. Graham Hill	BRM P57	-1

1963
1. J. Clark	54 P.	1. Lotus-Climax	54 P.
2. G. Hill/Ginther	29 P.	2. BRM	36 P.
4. J. Surtees	22 P.	3. Brabham-Climax	28 P.

1964

Grand Prix, MC, Monte Carlo, 10.5.1964
100 x 3,145 km = 314,500 km.
1. Graham Hill	BRM P261	2:41.19,500 h
2. Richie Ginther	BRM P261	-1
3. Peter Arundell	Lotus 25-Climax	-3

Grand Prix, NL, Zandvoort, 24.5.1964
80 x 4,193 km = 335,440 km.
1. Jim Clark	Lotus 25-Climax	2:07.35,400 h
2. John Surtees	Ferrari 158	2:08.29,000 h
3. Peter Arundell	Lotus 25-Climax	-1

Grand Prix, B, Spa-Francorchamps, 14.6.1964
32 x 14,100 km = 451,200 km.
1. Jim Clark	Lotus 25-Climax	2:06.40,500 h
2. Bruce McLaren	Cooper T73-Climax	2:06.43,900 h
3. Jack Brabham	Brabham BT7-Climax	2:07.28,600 h

Grand Prix, F, Rouen-les-Essarts, 24.6.1964
57 x 6,542 km = 372,894 km.
1. Dan Gurney	Brabham BT7-Climax	2:07.49,100 h
2. Graham Hill	BRM P261	2:07.13,200 h
3. Jack Brabham	Brabham BT7-Climax	2:08.14,000 h

Grand Prix, GB, Brands Hatch, 11.7.1964
80 x 4,265 km = 341,200 km.
1. Jim Clark	Lotus 25-Climax	2:15.07,000 h
2. Graham Hill	BRM P261	2:15.09,800 h
3. John Surtees	Ferrari 158	2:16.27,600 h

Grand Prix, D, Nürburgring, 2.8.1964
15 x 22,810 km = 342,150 km.
1. John Surtees	Ferrari 158	2:12.04,800 h
2. Graham Hill	BRM P261	2:13.20,400 h
3. Lorenzo Bandini	Ferrari 156	2:16.57,600 h

Grand Prix, A, Zeltweg, 23.8.1964
105 x 3,200 km = 336,000 km.
1. Lorenzo Bandini	Ferrari 156	2:06.18,230 h
2. Richie Ginther	BRM P261	2:06.24,410 h
3. Bob Anderson	Brabham BT11-Climax	-3

Grand Prix, I, Monza, 6.9.1964
78 x 5,750 km = 448,500 km.
1. John Surtees	Ferrari 158	2:10.51,800 h
2. Bruce McLaren	Cooper T73-Climax	2:11.57,800 h
3. Lorenzo Bandini	Ferrari 158	-1

Grand Prix, USA, Watkins Glen, 4.10.1964
110 x 3,701 km = 407,110 km.
1. Graham Hill	BRM P261	2:16.38,000 h
2. John Surtees	Ferrari 158	2:17.08,500 h
3. Jo Siffert	Brabham BT11-BRM	-1

Grand Prix, MEX, Mexico City, 24.10.1964
65 x 5,000 km = 325,000 km.
1. Dan Gurney	Brabham BT7-Climax	2:09.50,320 h
2. John Surtees	Ferrari 158	2:10.59,260 h
3. Lorenzo Bandini	Ferrari 1512	2:10.59,950 h

1964
1. J. Surtees	40 P.	1. Ferrari	45 P.
2. G. Hill	39 P.	2. BRM	42 P.
3. J. Clark	32 P.	3. Lotus-Climax	37 P.

GP 1965 – 1969

1965

Grand Prix, ZA, East London, 1.1.1965
85 x 3,920 km = 333,200 km.
1. Jim Clark	Lotus 33-Climax	2:06.46,000 h
2. John Surtees	Ferrari 158	2:07.15,000 h
3. Graham Hill	BRM P261	2:07.17,800 h

Grand Prix, MC, Monte Carlo, 30.5.1965
100 x 3,145 km = 314,500 km.
1. Graham Hill	BRM P261	2:37.39,600 h
2. Lorenzo Bandini	Ferrari 1512	2:38.43,600 h
3. Jackie Stewart	BRM P261	2:39.21,500 h

Grand Prix, B, Spa-Francorchamps, 13.6.1965
32 x 14,100 km = 451,200 km.
1. Jim Clark	Lotus 33-Climax	2:23.34,800 h
2. Jackie Stewart	BRM P261	2:24.19,600 h
3. Bruce McLaren	Cooper T77-Climax	-1

Grand Prix, F, Clermont-Ferrand, 27.6.1965
40 x 8,055 km = 322,200 km.
1. Jim Clark	Lotus 33-Climax	2:14.38,400 h
2. Jackie Stewart	BRM P261	2:15.04,700 h
3. John Surtees	Ferrari 158	2:17.11,900 h

Grand Prix, GB, Silverstone, 10.7.1965
80 x 4,711 km = 376,880 km.
1. Jim Clark	Lotus 33-Climax	2:05.25,400 h
2. Graham Hill	BRM P261	2:05.28,600 h
3. John Surtees	Ferrari 158	2:05.53,000 h

Grand Prix, NL, Zandvoort, 18.7.1965
80 x 4,193 km = 335,440 km.
1. Jim Clark	Lotus 33-Climax	2:03.59,100 h
2. Jackie Stewart	BRM P261	2:04.07,100 h
3. Dan Gurney	Brabham BT11-Climax	2:04.12,100 h

Grand Prix, D, Nürburgring, 1.8.1965
15 x 22,810 km = 342,150 km.
1. Jim Clark	Lotus 33-Climax	2:07.52,400 h
2. Graham Hill	BRM P261	2:08.08,300 h
3. Dan Gurney	Brabham BT11-Climax	2:08.13,800 h

Grand Prix, I, Monza, 12.9.1965
76 x 5,750 km = 437,000 km.
1. Jackie Stewart	BRM P261	2:04.52,800 h
2. Graham Hill	BRM P261	2:04.56,100 h
3. Dan Gurney	Brabham BT11-Climax	2:05.09,300 h

Grand Prix, USA, Watkins Glen, 3.10.1965
110 x 3,701 km = 407,110 km.
1. Graham Hill	BRM P261	2:20.36,100 h
2. Dan Gurney	Brabham BT11-Climax	2:20.48,600 h
3. Jack Brabham	Brabham BT11-Climax	2:21.33,600 h

Grand Prix, MEX, Mexico City, 5.6.1965
65 x 5,000 km = 325,000 km.
1. Richie Ginther	Honda RA272	2:08.32,100 h
2. Dan Gurney	Brabham BT11-Climax	2:08.34,900 h
3. Mike Spence	Lotus 33-Climax	2:09.32,200 h

1965

1. J. Clark	54 P.	1. Lotus-Climax	54 P.
2. G. Hill	40 P.	2. BRM	45 P.
3. J. Stewart	33 P.	3. Brabham-Climax	27 P.

1966

Grand Prix, MC, Monte Carlo, 22.5.1966
100 x 3,145 km = 314,500 km.
1. Jackie Stewart	BRM P261	2:33.10,600 h
2. Lorenzo Bandini	Ferrari 158/246	2:33.50,700 h
3. Graham Hill	BRM P261	-1

Grand Prix, B, Spa-Francorchamps, 12.6.1966
28 x 14,100 km = 394,800 km.
1. John Surtees	Ferrari 312	2:09.11,300 h
2. Jochen Rindt	Cooper T81-Maserati	2:09.53,400 h
3. Lorenzo Bandini	Ferrari 158/246	-1

Grand Prix, F, Reims, 3.7.1966
48 x 8,302 km = 398,496 km.
1. Jack Brabham	Brabham BT19-Repco	1:48.31,300 h
2. Micheal Parkes	Ferrari 312	1:48.40,800 h
3. Denny Hulme	Brabham BT20-Repco	-2

Grand Prix, GB, Brands Hatch, 16.7.1966
80 x 4,265 km = 341,200 km.
1. Jack Brabham	Brabham BT19-Repco	2:13.13,400 h
2. Denny Hulme	Brabham BT20-Repco	2:13.23,000 h
3. Graham Hill	BRM P261	-1

Grand Prix, NL, Zandvoort, 24.7.1966
90 x 4,193 km = 377,370 km.
1. Jack Brabham	Brabham BT19-Repco	2:39.29,000 h
2. Graham Hill	BRM P261	-1
3. Jim Clark	Lotus 33-Climax	-2

Grand Prix, D, Nürburgring, 7.8.1966
15 x 22,810 km = 342,150 km.
1. Jack Brabham	Brabham BT19-Repco	2:27.03,000 h
2. John Surtees	Cooper T81-Maserati	2:27.47,400 h
3. Jochen Rindt	Cooper T81-Maserati	2:29.35,600 h

Grand Prix, I, Monza, 4.9.1966
68 x 5,750 km = 391,000 km.
1. Ludovico Scarfiotti	Ferrari 312	1:47.14,800 h
2. Micheal Parkes	Ferrari 312	1:47.20,600 h
3. Denny Hulme	Brabham BT20-Repco	1:47.20,900 h

Grand Prix, USA, Watkins Glen, 2.10.1966
108 x 3,701 km = 399,708 km.
1. Jim Clark	Lotus 43-BRM	2:09.40,100 h
2. Jochen Rindt	Cooper T81-Maserati	-1
3. John Surtees	Cooper T81-Maserati	-1

Grand Prix, MEX, Mexico City, 23.10.1966
65 x 5,000 km = 325,000 km.
1. John Surtees	Cooper T81-Maserati	2:06.35,340 h
2. Jack Brabham	Brabham BT20-Repco	2:06.43,220 h
3. Denny Hulme	Brabham BT20-Repco	-1

1966

1. J. Brabham	42 P.	1. Brabham-Repco	42 P.
2. J. Surtees	28 P.	2. Ferrari	31 P.
3. J. Rindt	22 P.	3. Cooper-Maserati	30 P.

1967

Grand Prix, ZA, Kyalami, 2.1.1967
80 x 4,094 km = 327,520 km.
1 Pedro Rodriguez	Cooper T81-Maserati	2:05.45,900 h
2. John Love	Cooper T79-Climax	2:06.12,300 h
3. John Surtees	Honda RA273	-1

Grand Prix, MC, Monte Carlo, 7.5.1967
100 x 3,145 km = 314,500 km.
1. Denny Hulme	Brabham BT20-Repco	2:34.34,300 h
2. Graham Hill	Lotus 33-BRM	-1
3. Chris Amon	Ferrari 312	-2

Grand Prix, NL, Zandvoort, 4.6.1967
90 x 4,193 km = 377,370 km.
1. Jim Clark	Lotus 49-Ford	2:14.45,100 h
2. Jack Brabham	Brabham BT19-Repco	2:15.08,700 h
3. Denny Hulme	Brabham BT19-Repco	2:15.10,800 h

Grand Prix, B, Spa-Francorchamps, 18.6.1967
28 x 14,100 km = 394,800 km.
1. Dan Gurney	Eagle AAR104-Weslake	1:40.49,450 h
2. Jackie Stewart	BRM P83	1:41.52,400 h
3. Chris Amon	Ferrari 312	1:42.29,400 h

Grand Prix, F, Le Mans-Bugatti, 2.7.1967
80 x 4,422 km = 353,760 km.
1. Jack Brabham	Brabham BT24-Repco	2:13.21,300 h
2. Denny Hulme	Brabham BT19-Repco	2:14.10,800 h
3. Jackie Stewart	BRM P261	-1

Grand Prix, GB, Silverstone, 15.7.1967
80 x 4,711 km = 376,880 km.
1. Jim Clark	Lotus 49-Ford	1:59.25,600 h
2. Denny Hulme	Brabham BT24-Repco	1:59.38,400 h
3. Chris Amon	Ferrari 312	1:59.42,200 h

Grand Prix, D, Nürburgring, 6.8.1967
15 x 22,835 km = 342,525 km.
1. Denny Hulme	Brabham BT24-Repco	2:05.55,700 h
2. Jack Brabham	Brabham BT24-Repco	2:06.34,200 h
3. Chris Amon	Ferrari 312	2:06.34,700 h

Grand Prix, CDN, Mosport Park, 27.8.1967
90 x 3,957 km = 356,130 km.
1. Jack Brabham	Brabham BT24-Repco	2:40.40,000 h
2. Denny Hulme	Brabham BT24-Repco	2:41.41,900 h
3. Dan Gurney	Eagle AAR103-Weslake	-1

Grand Prix, I, Monza, 10.9.1967
68 x 5,750 km = 391,000 km.
1. John Surtees	Honda RA300	1:43.45,000 h
2. Jack Brabham	Brabham BT24-Repco	1:43.45,200 h
3. Jim Clark	Lotus 49-Ford	1:44.08,100 h

Grand Prix, USA, Watkins Glen, 1.10.1967
108 x 3,701 km = 399,708 km.
1. Jim Clark	Lotus 49-Ford	2:03.13,200 h
2. Graham Hill	Lotus 49-Ford	2:03.19,500 h
3. Denny Hulme	Brabham BT24-Repco	-1

Grand Prix, MEX, Mexico City, 22.10.1967
65 x 5,000 km = 325,000 km.
1. Jim Clark	Lotus 49-Ford	1:59.59,700 h
2. Jack Brabham	Brabham BT24-Repco	2:00.54,060 h
3. Denny Hulme	Brabham BT24-Repco	-1

1967

1. D. Hulme	51 P.	1. Brabham-Repco	63 P.
2. J. Brabham	46 P.	2. Lotus-Ford	44 P.
3. J. Clark	41 P.	3. Cooper-Maserati	28 P.

1968

Grand Prix, ZA, Kyalami, 1.1.1968
80 x 4,104 km = 328,320 km.
1. Jim Clark	Lotus 49-Ford	1:53.56,600 h
2. Graham Hill	Lotus 49-Ford	1:54.21,900 h
3. Jochen Rindt	Brabham BT24-Repco	1:54.27,000 h

Grand Prix, E, Jarama, 12.5.1968
90 x 3,404 km = 306,360 km.
1. Graham Hill	Lotus 49-Ford	2:15.20,100 h
2. Denny Hulme	McLaren M7A-Ford	2:15.36,000 h
3. Brian Redman	Cooper T86B-BRM	-1

Grand Prix, MC, Monte Carlo, 26.5.1968
80 x 3,145 km = 251,600 km.
1. Graham Hill	Lotus 49-Ford	2:00.32,300 h
2. Richard Attwood	BRM P126	2:00.34,500 h
3. Lucien Bianchi	Cooper T86B-BRM	-4

Grand Prix, B, Spa-Francorchamps, 9.6.1968
28 x 14,100 km = 394,800 km.
1. Bruce McLaren	McLaren M7A-Ford	1:40.02,100 h
2. Pedro Rodriguez	BRM P133	1:40.14,200 h
3. Jacky Ickx	Ferrari 312	1:40.41,700 h

Grand Prix, NL, Zandvoort, 23.6.1968
90 x 4,193 km = 377,370 km.
1. Jackie Stewart	Matra MS10-Ford	2:46.11,260 h
2. Jean-Pierre Beltoise	Matra MS11	2:47.45,190 h
3. Pedro Rodriguez	BRM P133	-1

Grand Prix, F, Rouen-les-Essarts 7.7.1968
60 x 6,542 km = 392,520 km.
1. Jacky Ickx	Ferrari 312	2:25.40,900 h
2. John Surtees	Honda RA301	2:27.39,500 h
3. Jackie Stewart	Matra MS10-Ford	-1

Grand Prix, GB, Brands Hatch, 20.7.1968
80 x 4,265 km = 341,200 km.
1. Juan Manuel Fangio	Lotus 49-Ford	2:01.20,300 h
2. Chris Amon	Ferrari 312	2:01.24,700 h
3. Jacky Ickx	Ferrari 312	-1

Grand Prix, D, Nürburgring, 4.8.1968
14 x 22,835 km = 319,690 km.
1. Jackie Stewart	Matra MS10-Ford	2:19.03,200 h
2. Graham Hill	Lotus 49-Ford	2:23.06,400 h
3. Jochen Rindt	Brabham BT26-Repco	2:23.12,600 h

Grand Prix, I, Monza, 8.9.1968
68 x 5,750 km = 391,000 km.
1. Denny Hulme	McLaren M7A-Ford	1:40.14,800 h
2. Johnny Servoz-Gavin	Matra MS10-Ford	1:41.43,200 h
3. Jacky Ickx	Ferrari 312	1:41.43,400 h

Grand Prix, CDN, Mont-Tremblant, 22.9.1968
90 x 4,265 km = 383,850 km.
1. Denny Hulme	McLaren M7A-Ford	2:27.11,200 h
2. Bruce McLaren	McLaren M7A-Ford	-1
3. Pedro Rodriguez	BRM P133	-2

Grand Prix, USA, Watkins Glen, 6.10.1968
108 x 3,701 km = 399,708 km.
1. Jackie Stewart	Matra MS10-Ford	1:59.20,290 h
2. Graham Hill	Lotus 49B-Ford	1:59.44,970 h
3. John Surtees	Honda RA301	-1

Grand Prix, MEX, Mexico City, 3.11.1968
65 x 5,000 km = 325,000 km.
1. Graham Hill	Lotus 49B-Ford	1:56.43,950 h
2. Bruce McLaren	McLaren M7A-Ford	1:58.03,270 h
3. Jackie Oliver	Lotus 49B-Ford	1:58.24,600 h

1968

1. G. Hill	48 P.	1. Lotus-Ford	62 P.
2. J. Stewart	36 P.	2. McLaren-Ford	49 P.
3. D. Hulme	33 P.	3. Matra-Ford	45 P.

1969

Grand Prix, ZA, Kyalami, 1.3.1969
80 x 4,104 km = 328,320 km.
1. Jackie Stewart	Matra MS80-Ford	1:50.39,100 h
2. Graham Hill	Lotus 49B-Ford	1:50.57,900 h
3. Denny Hulme	McLaren M7A-Ford	1:51.10,900 h

Grand Prix, E, Montjuich Park, 4.5.1969
90 x 3,791 km = 341,190 km.
1. Jackie Stewart	Matra MS80-Ford	2:16.53,990 h
2. Bruce McLaren	McLaren M7A-Ford	-2
3. Jean-Pierre Beltoise	Matra MS80-Ford	-3

Grand Prix, MC, Monte Carlo, 18.5.1969
80 x 3,145 km = 251,600 km.
1. Graham Hill	Lotus 49B-Ford	1:56.59,400 h
2. Piers Courage	Brabham BT26-Ford	1:57.16,700 h
3. Jo Siffert	Lotus 49B-Ford	1:57.34,000 h

Grand Prix, NL, Zandvoort, 21.6.1969
90 x 4,193 km = 377,370 km.
1. Jackie Stewart	Matra MS80-Ford	2:06.42,080 h
2. Jo Siffert	Lotus 49B-Ford	2:07.06,600 h
3. Chris Amon	Ferrari 312	2:07.12,590 h

Grand Prix, F, Clermont-Ferrand, 6.7.1969
38 x 8,055 km = 306,090 km.

1. Jackie Stewart	Matra MS80-Ford	1:56.47,400 h
2. Jean-Pierre Beltoise	Matra MS80-Ford	1:57.44,500 h
3. Jacky Ickx	Brabham BT26-Ford	1:57.44,700 h

Grand Prix, GB, Silverstone, 19.7.1969
84 x 4,711 km = 395,724 km.

1. Jackie Stewart	Matra MS80-Ford	1:55.55,600 h
2. Jacky Ickx	Brabham BT26-Ford	-1
3. Bruce McLaren	McLaren M7C-Ford	-1

Grand Prix, D, Nürburgring, 3.8.1969
14 x 22,835 km = 319,690 km.

1. Jacky Ickx	Brabham BT26-Ford	1:49.55,400 h
2. Jackie Stewart	Matra MS80-Ford	1:50.53,100 h
3. Bruce McLaren	McLaren M7C-Ford	1:53.17,000 h

Grand Prix, I, Monza, 7.9.1969
68 x 5,750 km = 391,000 km.

1. Jackie Stewart	Matra MS80-Ford	1:39.11,260 h
2. Jochen Rindt	Lotus 49B-Ford	1:39.11,340 h
3. Jean-Pierre Beltoise	Matra MS80-Ford	1:39.11,430 h

Grand Prix, CDN, Mosport Park, 20.9.1969
90 x 3,957 km = 356,130 km.

1. Jacky Ickx	Brabham BT26-Ford	1:59.25,700 h
2. Jack Brabham	Brabham BT26-Ford	2:00.11,900 h
3. Jochen Rindt	Lotus 49B-Ford	2:00.17,700 h

Grand Prix, USA, Watkins Glen, 5.10.1969
108 x 3,701 km = 399,708 km.

1. Jochen Rindt	Lotus 49B-Ford	1:57.56,840 h
2. Piers Courage	Brabham BT26-Ford	1:58.43,830 h
3. John Surtees	BRM P139	-2

Grand Prix, MEX, Mexico City, 19.10.1969
65 x 5,000 km = 325,000 km.

1. Denny Hulme	McLaren M7A-Ford	1:54.08,800 h
2. Jacky Ickx	Brabham BT26-Ford	1:54.11,360 h
3. Jack Brabham	Brabham BT26-Ford	1:54.47,280 h

1969

1. J. Stewart	63 P.	1. Matra-Ford	66 P.
2. J. Ickx	37 P.	2. Brabham-Ford	49 P.
3. B. McLaren	26 P.	3. Lotus-Ford	47 P.

1970

Grand Prix, ZA, Kyalami, 7.3.1970
80 x 4,104 km = 328,320 km.

1. Jack Brabham	Brabham BT33-Ford	1:49.34,600 h
2. Denny Hulme	McLaren M14A-Ford	1:49.42,700 h
3. Jackie Stewart	March 701-Ford	1:49.51,700 h

Grand Prix, E, Jarama, 19.4.1970
90 x 3,404 km = 306,360 km.

1. Jackie Stewart	March 701-Ford	2:10.58,200 h
2. Bruce McLaren	McLaren M14A-Ford	-1
3. Mario Andretti	March 701-Ford	-1

Grand Prix, MC, Monte Carlo, 10.5.1970
80 x 3,145 km = 251,600 km.

1. Jochen Rindt	Lotus 49C-Ford	1:54.36,600 h
2. Jack Brabham	Brabham BT33-Ford	1:54.59,700 h
3. Henri Pescarolo	Matra-Simca MS120	1:55.28,000 h

Grand Prix, B, Spa-Francorchamps, 7.6.1970
28 x 14,100 km = 394,800 km.

1. Pedro Rodriguez	BRM P153	1:38.09,900 h
2. Chris Amon	March 701-Ford	1:38.11,000 h
3. Jean-Pierre Beltoise	Matra-Simca MS120	1:39.53,600 h

Grand Prix, NL, Zandvoort, 21.6.1970
80 x 4,193 km = 335,440 km.

1. Jochen Rindt	Lotus 72-Ford	1:50.43,410 h
2. Jackie Stewart	March 701-Ford	1:51.13,410 h
3. Jacky Ickx	Ferrari 312B	-1

Grand Prix, F, Clermont-Ferrand, 5.7.1970
38 x 8,055 km = 306,090 km.

1. Jochen Rindt	Lotus 72-Ford	1:55.57,000 h
2. Chris Amon	March 701-Ford	1:56.04,610 h
3. Jack Brabham	Brabham BT33-Ford	1:56.41,830 h

Grand Prix, GB, Brands Hatch, 18.7.1970
80 x 4,265 km = 341,200 km.

1. Jochen Rindt	Lotus 72-Ford	1:57.02,000 h
2. Jack Brabham	Brabham BT33-Ford	1:57.34,900 h
3. Denny Hulme	McLaren M14D-Ford	1:57.56,400 h

Grand Prix, D, Hockenheim, 2.8.1970
50 x 6,789 km = 339,450 km.

1. Jochen Rindt	Lotus 72-Ford	1:42.00,300 h
2. Jacky Ickx	Ferrari 312B	1:42.01,000 h
3. Denny Hulme	McLaren M14A-Ford	1:43.22,100 h

Grand Prix, A, Aring, 16.8.1970
60 x 5,911 km = 354,660 km.

1. Jacky Ickx	Ferrari 312B	1:42.17,320 h
2. Clay Regazzoni	Ferrari 312B	1:42.17,930 h
3. Rolf Stommelen	Brabham BT33-Ford	1:43.45,200 h

Grand Prix, I, Monza, 6.9.1970
68 x 5,750 km = 391,000 km.

1. Clay Regazzoni	Ferrari 312B	1:39.06,880 h
2. Jackie Stewart	March 701-Ford	1:39.12,610 h
3. Jean-Pierre Beltoise	Matra-Simca MS120	1:39.12,680 h

Grand Prix, CDN, Mont Tremblant, 20.9.1970
90 x 4,265 km = 383,850 km.

1. Jacky Ickx	Ferrari 312B	2:21.18,400 h
2. Clay Regazzoni	Ferrari 312B	2:21.33,200 h
3. Chris Amon	March 701-Ford	2:22.16,300 h

Grand Prix, USA, Watkins Glen, 4.10.1970
108 x 3,701 km = 399,708 km.

1. Emerson Fittipaldi	Lotus 72-Ford	1:57.32,790 h
2. Pedro Rodriguez	BRM P153	1:58.09,180 h
3. Reine Wisell	Lotus 72-Ford	1:58.17,960 h

Grand Prix, MEX, Mexico City, 25.10.1970
65 x 5,000 km = 325,000 km.

1. Jacky Ickx	Ferrari 312B	1:53.28,360 h
1. Clay Regazzoni	Ferrari 312B	1:54.13,820 h
1. Denny Hulme	McLaren M14A-Ford	1:54.14,330 h

1970

1. J. Rindt	45 P.	1. Lotus-Ford	59 P.
2. J. Ickx	40 P.	2. Ferrari	52 P.
3. C. Regazzoni	33 P.	3. March-Ford	48 P.

1971

Grand Prix, ZA, Kyalami, 6.3.1971
79 x 4,104 km = 324,216 km.

1. Mario Andretti	Ferrari 312B	1:47.35,500 h
2. Jackie Stewart	Tyrrell 001-Ford	1:47.56,400 h
3. Clay Regazzoni	Ferrari 312B	1:48.09,900 h

Grand Prix, E, Montjuich Park, 18.4.1971
75 x 3,791 km = 284,325 km.

1. Jackie Stewart	Tyrrell 003-Ford	1:49.03,400 h
2. Jacky Ickx	Ferrari 312B	1:49.06,800 h
3. Chris Amon	Matra-Simca MS120B	1:50.01,500 h

Grand Prix, MC, Monte Carlo, 23.5.1971
80 x 3,145 km = 251,600 km.

1. Jackie Stewart	Tyrrell 003-Ford	1:52.21,300 h
2. Ronnie Peterson	March 711-Ford	1:52.46,900 h
3. Jacky Ickx	Ferrari 312B2	1:53.14,600 h

Grand Prix, NL, Zandvoort, 20.6.1971
70 x 4,193 km = 293,510 km.

1. Jacky Ickx	Ferrari 312B2	1:56.20,090 h
2. Pedro Rodriguez	BRM P160	1:56.28,080 h
3. Clay Regazzoni	Ferrari 312B2	-1

Grand Prix, F, Paul Ricard, 4.7.1971
55 x 5,810 km = 319,550 km.

1. Jackie Stewart	Tyrrell 003-Ford	1:46.41,680 h
2. François Cevert	Tyrrell 002-Ford	1:47.09,800 h
3. Emerson Fittipaldi	Lotus 72D-Ford	1:47.15,750 h

Grand Prix, GB, Silverstone, 17.7.1971
68 x 4,711 km = 320,348 km.

1. Jackie Stewart	Tyrrell 003-Ford	1:31.31,500 h
2. Ronnie Peterson	March 711-Ford	1:32.07,600 h
3. Emerson Fittipaldi	Lotus 72D-Ford	1:32.22,000 h

Grand Prix, D, Nürburgring, 1.8.1971
12 x 22,835 km = 274,020 km.

1. Jackie Stewart	Tyrrell 003-Ford	1:29.15,700 h
2. François Cevert	Tyrrell 002-Ford	1:29.45,800 h
3. Clay Regazzoni	Ferrari 312B2	1:29.52,800 h

Grand Prix, A, Aring 15.8.1971
54 x 5,911 km = 319,194 km.

1. Jo Siffert	BRM P160	1:30.23,910 h
2. Emerson Fittipaldi	Lotus 72D-Ford	1:30.28,030 h
3. Tim Schenken	Brabham BT33-Ford	1:30.43,680 h

Grand Prix, I, Monza, 5.9.1971
55 x 5,750 km = 316,250 km.

1. Peter Gethin	BRM P160	1:18.12,600 h
2. Ronnie Peterson	March 711-Ford	1:18.12,610 h
3. François Cevert	Tyrrell 002-Ford	1:18.12,690 h

Grand Prix, CDN, Mosport Park, 19.9.1971
64 x 3,957 km = 253,248 km.

1. Jackie Stewart	Tyrrell 003-Ford	1:55.12,900 h
2. Ronnie Peterson	March 711-Ford	1:55.51,200 h
3. Mark Donohue	McLaren M19A-Ford	1:56.56,700 h

Grand Prix, USA, Watkins Glen, 3.10.1971
59 x 5,435 km = 320,665 km.

1. François Cevert	Tyrrell 002-Ford	1:43.51,991 h
2. Jo Siffert	BRM P160	1:44.32,053 h
3. Ronnie Peterson	March 711-Ford	1:44.36,061 h

1971

1. J. Stewart	62 P.	1. Tyrrell-Ford	73 P.
2. R. Peterson	33 P.	2. BRM	36 P.
3. F. Cevert	26 P.	3. Ferrari/March	33 P.

1972

Grand Prix, RA, Buenos Aires, 23.1.1972
95 x 3,345 km = 317,775 km.

1. Jackie Stewart	Tyrrell 003-Ford	1:57.58,820 h
2. Denny Hulme	McLaren M19A-Ford	1:58.24,780 h
3. Jacky Ickx	Ferrari 312B	1:58.58,210 h

Grand Prix, ZA, Kyalami, 4.3.1972
79 x 4,104 km = 324,216 km.

1. Denny Hulme	McLaren M19A-Ford	1:45.49,100 h
2. Emerson Fittipaldi	Lotus 72D-Ford	1:46.03,200 h
3. Peter Revson	McLaren M19A-Ford	1:46.14,900 h

Grand Prix, E, Jarama, 1.5.1972
90 x 3,404 km = 306,360 km.

1. Emerson Fittipaldi	Lotus 72D-Ford	2:03.41,230 h
2. Jacky Ickx	Ferrari 312B	2:04.00,150 h
3. Clay Regazzoni	Ferrari 312B	-1

Grand Prix, MC, Monte Carlo, 14.5.1972
80 x 3,145 km = 251,600 km.

1. Jean-Pierre Beltoise	BRM P160B	2:26.54,700 h
2. Jacky Ickx	Ferrari 312B	2:27.32,900 h
3. Emerson Fittipaldi	Lotus 72D-Ford	-1

Grand Prix, B, Nivelles, 4.6.1972
85 x 3,724 km = 316,540 km.

1. Emerson Fittipaldi	Lotus 72D-Ford	1:44.06,700 h
2. François Cevert	Tyrrell 002-Ford	1:44.33,300 h
3. Denny Hulme	Mc Laren Mercedes	1:45.04,800 h

Grand Prix, F, Clermont-Ferrand, 2.7.1972
38 x 8,055 km = 306,090 km.

1. Jackie Stewart	Tyrrell 003-Ford	1:52.21,500 h
2. Emerson Fittipaldi	Lotus 72D-Ford	1:52.49,200 h
3. Chris Amon	Matra-Simca MS120D	1:52.53,400 h

Grand Prix, GB, Brands Hatch, 15.7.1972
76 x 4,265 km = 324,140 km

1. Emerson Fittipaldi	Lotus 72D-Ford	1:47.50,200 h
2. Jackie Stewart	Tyrrell 003-Ford	1:47.54,300 h
3. Peter Revson	McLaren M19A-Ford	1:49.02,700 h

Grand Prix, D, Nürburgring, 30.7.1972
14 x 22,835 km = 319,690 km.

1. Jacky Ickx	Ferrari 312B2	1:42.12,300 h
2. Clay Regazzoni	Ferrari 312B2	1:43.00,600 h
3. Ronnie Peterson	March 721G-Ford	1:43.19,000 h

Grand Prix, A, Aring, 13.8.1972
54 x 5,911 km = 319,194 km.

1. Emerson Fittipaldi	Lotus 72D-Ford	1:29.16,660 h
2. Denny Hulme	McLaren M19C-Ford	1:29.17,840 h
3. Peter Revson	McLaren M19C-Ford	1:29.53,190 h

Grand Prix, I, Monza , 10.9.1972
55 x 5,775 km = 317,625 km.

1. Emerson Fittipaldi	Lotus 72D-Ford	1:29.58,400 h
2. Mike Hailwood	Surtees TS9B-Ford	1:30.12,900 h
3. Denny Hulme	McLaren M19C-Ford	1:30.22,200 h

Grand Prix, CDN, Mosport Park , 24.9.1972
80 x 3,957 km = 316,560 km.

1. Jackie Stewart	Tyrrell 005-Ford	1:43.16,900 h
2. Peter Revson	McLaren M19C-Ford	1:44.05,100 h
3. Denny Hulme	McLaren M19C-Ford	1:44.11,500 h

Grand Prix, USA, Watkins Glen, 8.10.1972
59 x 5,435 km = 320,665 km.

1. Jackie Stewart	Tyrrell 005-Ford	1:41.45,354 h
2. François Cevert	Tyrrell 006-Ford	1:42.17,622 h
3. Denny Hulme	McLaren M19C-Ford	1:42.22,882 h

1972

1. E. Fittipaldi	61 P.	1. Lotus-Ford	61 P.
2. J. Stewart	45 P.	2. Tyrrell-Ford	51 P.
3. D. Hulme	39 P.	3. McLaren-Ford	47 P.

1973

Grand Prix, RA, Buenos Aires, 28.1.1973
96 x 3,345 km = 321,180 km.

1. Emerson Fittipaldi	Lotus 72D-Ford	1:56.18,220 h
2. François Cevert	Tyrrell 006-Ford	1:56.22,910 h
3. Jackie Stewart	Tyrrell 005-Ford	1:56.51,410 h

Grand Prix, BR, Interlagos, 11.2.1973
40 x 7,960 km = 318,400 km.

1. Emerson Fittipaldi	Lotus 72D-Ford	1:43.55,600 h
2. Jackie Stewart	Tyrrell 005-Ford	1:44.09,100 h
3. Denny Hulme	McLaren M19C-Ford	1:45.42,000 h

Grand Prix, ZA, Kyalami, 3.3.1973
79 x 4,104 km = 324,216 km.

1. Jackie Stewart	Tyrrell 006-Ford	1:43.11,070 h
2. Peter Revson	McLaren M19C-Ford	1:43.35,620 h
3. Emerson Fittipaldi	Lotus 72D-Ford	1:43.36,130 h

GP 1973 – 1976

Grand Prix, E, Montjuich Park, 29.4.1973
75 x 3,791 km = 284,325 km.

1. Emerson Fittipaldi	Lotus 72D-Ford	1:48.18,700 h
2. François Cevert	Tyrrell 006-Ford	1:49.01,400 h
3. George Follmer	Shadow DN1A-Ford	1:49.31,800 h

Grand Prix, B, Zolder, 20.5.1973
70 x 2,622 km = 183,540 km.

1. Jackie Stewart	Tyrrell 006-Ford	1:42.13,430 h
2. François Cevert	Tyrrell 006-Ford	1:42.45,270 h
3. Emerson Fittipaldi	Lotus 72D-Ford	1:44.16,220 h

Grand Prix, MC, Monte Carlo, 3.6.1973
78 x 3,278 km = 255,684 km.

1. Jackie Stewart	Tyrrell 006-Ford	1:57.44,300 h
2. Emerson Fittipaldi	Lotus 72D-Ford	1:57.45,600 h
3. Ronnie Peterson	Lotus 72D-Ford	– -1

Grand Prix, S, Anderstorp, 17.6.1973
80 x 4,018 km = 321,440 km.

1. Denny Hulme	McLaren M23-Ford	1:56.46,049 h
2. Ronnie Peterson	Lotus 72D-Ford	1:56.50,088 h
3. François Cevert	Tyrrell 006-Ford	1:57.00,716 h

Grand Prix, F, Paul Ricard, 1.7.1973
54 x 5,810 km = 313,740 km.

1. Ronnie Peterson	Lotus 72D-Ford	1:41.36,520 h
2. François Cevert	Tyrrell 006-Ford	1:42.17,440 h
3. Carlos Reutemann	Brabham BT42-Ford	1:42.23,000 h

Grand Prix, GB, Silverstone, 14.7.1973
67 x 4,711 km = 315,607 km.

1. Peter Revson	McLaren M23-Ford	1:29.18,500 h
2. Ronnie Peterson	Lotus 72D-Ford	1:29.21,300 h
3. Denny Hulme	McLaren M23-Ford	1:29.21,500 h

Grand Prix, NL, Zandvoort, 29.7.1973
72 x 4,226 km = 304,272 km.

1. Jackie Stewart	Tyrrell 006-Ford	1:39.12,450 h
2. François Cevert	Tyrrell 006-Ford	1:39.28,280 h
3. James Hunt	March 731-Ford	1:40.15,460 h

Grand Prix, D, Nürburgring, 5.8.1973
14 x 22,835 km = 319,690 km.

1. Jackie Stewart	Tyrrell 006-Ford	1:42.03,000 h
2. François Cevert	Tyrrell 006-Ford	1:42.04,600 h
3. Jacky Ickx	McLaren M23-Ford	1:42.44,200 h

Grand Prix, A, Aring, 19.8.1973
54 x 5,922 km = 319,788 km.

1. Ronnie Peterson	Lotus 72D-Ford	1:28.48,780 h
2. Jackie Stewart	Tyrrell 006-Ford	1:28.57,790 h
3. Carlos Pace	Surtees TS 14A-Ford	1:29.35,420 h

Grand Prix, I, Monza, 9.9.1973
55 x 5,775 km = 317,625 km.

1. Ronnie Peterson	Lotus 72D-Ford	1:29.17,000 h
2. Emerson Fittipaldi	Lotus 72D-Ford	1:29.17,800 h
3. Peter Revson	McLaren M23-Ford	1:29.45,800 h

Grand Prix, CDN, Mosport Park, 23.9.1973
80 x 3,957 km = 316,560 km.

1. Peter Revson	McLaren M23-Ford	1:59.04,083 h
2. Emerson Fittipaldi	Lotus 72D-Ford	1:59.36,817 h
3. Jackie Oliver	Shadow DN1A-Ford	1:59.38,588 h

Grand Prix, USA, Watkins Glen, 7.10.1973
59 x 5,435 km = 320,665 km.

1. Ronnie Peterson	Lotus 72D-Ford	1:41.15,779 h
2. James Hunt	March 731-Ford	1:41.16,467 h
3. Carlos Reutemann	Brabham BT42-Ford	1:41.38,729 h

1973

1. J. Stewart	71 P.	1. Lotus-Ford	92 P.
2. E. Fittipaldi	55 P.	2. Tyrrell-Ford	82 P.
3. R. Peterson	52 P.	3. McLaren-Ford	58 P.

1974

Grand Prix, RA, Buenos Aires, 13.1.1974
53 x 5,968 km = 316,304 km.

1. Denny Hulme	McLaren M23-Ford	1:41.02,010 h
2. Niki Lauda	Ferrari 312B3	1:41.11,280 h
3. Clay Regazzoni	Ferrari 312B3	1:41.22,420 h

Grand Prix, BR, Interlagos, 27.1.1974
32 x 7,960 km = 254,720 km.

1. Emerson Fittipaldi	McLaren M23-Ford	1:24.37,060 h
2. Clay Regazzoni	Ferrari 312B3	1:24.50,630 h
3. Jacky Ickx	Lotus 72D-Ford	-1

Grand Prix, ZA, Kyalymi, 30.3.1974
78 x 4,104 km = 320,112 km.

1. Carlos Reutemann	Brabham BT44-Ford	1:42.40,960 h
2. Jean-Pierre Beltoise	BRM P201	1:43.14,900 h
3. Mike Hailwood	McLaren M23-Ford	1:43.23,120 h

Grand Prix, E, Jarama, 28.4.1974
84 x 3,404 km = 285,936 km.

1. Niki Lauda	Ferrari 312B3	2:00.29,560 h
2. Clay Regazzoni	Ferrari 312B3	2:01.05,170 h
3. Emerson Fittipaldi	McLaren M23-Ford	-1

Grand Prix, B, Nivelles, 12.5.1974
85 x 3,724 km = 316,540 km.

1. Emerson Fittipaldi	McLaren M23-Ford	1:44.20,570 h
2. Niki Lauda	Ferrari 312B3	1:44.20,920 h
3. Jody Scheckter	Tyrrell 007-Ford	1:45.06,180 h

Grand Prix, MC, Monte Carlo, 26.5.1974
78 x 3,278 km = 255,684 km.

1. Ronnie Peterson	Lotus 72E-Ford	1:58.03,700 h
2. Jody Scheckter	Tyrrell 007-Ford	1:58.32,500 h
3. Jean-Pierre Jarier	Shadow DN3A-Ford	1:58.52,600 h

Grand Prix, S, Anderstorp, 9.6.1974
80 x 4,018 km = 321,440 km.

1. Jody Scheckter	Tyrrell 007-Ford	1:58.31,391 h
2. Patrick Depailler	Tyrrell 007-Ford	1:58.31,771 h
3. James Hunt	Hesketh 308-Ford	1:58.34,716 h

Grand Prix, NL, Zandvoort, 23.6.1974
75 x 4,226 km = 316,950 km.

1. Niki Lauda	Ferrari 312B3	1:43.00,350 h
2. Clay Regazzoni	Ferrari 312B3	1:43.08,600 h
3. Emerson Fittipaldi	McLaren M23-Ford	1:43.30,620 h

Grand Prix, F, Dijon-Prenois, 7.7.1974
80 x 3,289 km = 263,11120 km.

1. Ronnie Peterson	Lotus 72E-Ford	1:21.55,020 h
2. Niki Lauda	Ferrari 312B3	1:22.15,380 h
3. Clay Regazzoni	Ferrari 312B3	1:22.22,860 h

Grand Prix, GB, Brands Hatch, 20.7.1974
75 x 4,265 km = 319,875 km.

1. Jody Scheckter	Tyrrell 007-Ford	1:43.02,200 h
2. Emerson Fittipaldi	McLaren M23-Ford	1:43.17,500 h
3. Jacky Ickx	Lotus 72E-Ford	1:44.03,700 h

Grand Prix, D, Nürburgring, 4.8.1974
14 x 22,835 km = 319,690 km.

1. Clay Regazzoni	Ferrari 312B3	1:41.35,000 h
2. Jody Scheckter	Tyrrell 007-Ford	1:42.25,700 h
3. Carlos Reutemann	Brabham BT44-Ford	1:42.58,200 h

Grand Prix, A, Aring, 18.8.1974
54 x 5,911 km = 319,194 km.

1. Carlos Reutemann	Brabham BT44-Ford	1:28.44,720 h
2. Denny Hulme	McLaren M23-Ford	1:29.27,640 h
3. James Hunt	Hesketh 308-Ford	1:29.46,260 h

Grand Prix, I, Monza, 8.9.1974
52 x 5,780 km = 300,560 km.

1. Ronnie Peterson	Lotus 72E-Ford	1:22.56,600 h
2. Emerson Fittipaldi	McLaren M23-Ford	1:22.57,400 h
3. Jody Scheckter	Tyrrell 007-Ford	1:23.21,300 h

Grand Prix, CDN, Mosport Park, 22.9.1974
80 x 3,957 km = 316,560 km.

1. Emerson Fittipaldi	McLaren M23-Ford	1:40.26,136 h
2. Clay Regazzoni	Ferrari 312B3	1:40.39,170 h
3. Ronnie Peterson	Lotus 72E-Ford	1:40.40,630 h

Grand Prix, USA, Watkins Glen, 6.10.1974
59 x 5,435 km = 320,665 km.

1. Carlos Reutemann	Brabham BT44-Ford	1:40.21,439 h
2. Carlos Pace	Brabham BT44-Ford	1:40.32,174 h
3. James Hunt	Hesketh 308-Ford	1:41.31,823 h

1974

1. E. Fittipaldi	55 P.	1. McLaren-Ford	73 P.
2. C. Regazzoni	52 P.	2. Ferrari	65 P.
3. J. Scheckter	45 P.	3. Tyrrell-Ford	52 P.

1975

Grand Prix, RA, Buenos Aires, 12.1.1975
53 x 5,968 km = 316,304 km.

1. Emerson Fittipaldi	McLaren M23-Ford	1:39.26,290 h
2. James Hunt	Hesketh 308-Ford	1:39.32,200 h
3. Carlos Reutemann	Brabham BT44B-Ford	1:39.43,350 h

Grand Prix, BR, Interlagos, 26.1.1975
40 x 7,960 km = 318,400 km.

1. Carlos Pace	Brabham BT44B	1:44.41,170 h
2. Emerson Fittipaldi	McLaren M23-Ford	1:44.46,960 h
3. Jochen Mass	McLaren M23-Ford	1:45.17,830 h

Grand Prix, ZA, Kyalami, 1.3.1975
78 x 4,104 km = 320,112 km.

1. Jody Scheckter	Tyrrell 007-Ford	1:43.16,900 h
2. Carlos Reutemann	Brabham BT44B-Ford	1:43.20,640 h
3. Patrick Depailler	Tyrrell 007-Ford	1:43.33,820 h

Grand Prix, E, Montjuich Park, 27.4.1975.
29 x 3,791 km = 109,939 km.

1. Jochen Mass	McLaren M23-Ford	0:42.53,700 h
2. Jacky Ickx	Lotus 72E-Ford	0:42.54,800 h
3. Carlos Reutemann	Brabham BT44B-Ford	-1

Grand Prix, MC, Monte Carlo, 11.5.1975.
75 x 3,278 km = 245,850 km.

1. Niki Lauda	Ferrari 312T	2:01.21,310 h
2. Emerson Fittipaldi	McLaren M23-Ford	2:01.24,090 h
3. Carlos Pace	Brabham BT44B-Ford	2:01.39,120 h

Grand Prix, B, Zolder, 25.5.1975
70 x 4,262 km = 298,340 km.

1. Niki Lauda	Ferrari 312T	1:43.53,980 h
2. Jody Scheckter	Tyrrell 007-Ford	1:44.13,200 h
3. Carlos Reutemann	Brabham BT44B-Ford	1:44.35,800 h

Grand Prix, Sweden, Anderstorp, 8.6.1975
80 x 4,018 km = 321,440 km.

1. Niki Lauda	Ferrari 312T	1:59.18,319 h
2. Carlos Reutemann	Brabham BT44B-Ford	1:59.24,607 h
3. Clay Regazzoni	Ferrari 312T	1:59.47,414 h

Grand Prix, NL, Zandvoort, 22.6.1975
75 x 4,226 km = 316,950 km.

1. James Hunt	Hesketh 308-Ford	1:46.57,400 h
2. Niki Lauda	Ferrari 312T	1:46.58,460 h
3. Clay Regazzoni	Ferrari 312T	1:47.52,460 h

Grand Prix, F, Paul Ricard, 6.7.1975
54 x 5,810 km = 313,740 km.

1. Niki Lauda	Ferrari 312T	1:40.18,840 h
2. James Hunt	Hesketh 308-Ford	1:40.20,430 h
3. Jochen Mass	McLaren M23-Ford	1:40.21,150 h

Grand Prix, GB, Silverstone, 19.7.1975
56 x 4,719 km = 264,264 km.

1. Emerson Fittipaldi	McLaren M23-Ford	1:22.05,000 h
2. Carlos Pace	Brabham BT44B-Ford	crash
3. Jody Scheckter	Tyrrell 007-Ford	crash

Grand Prix, D, Nürburgring, 3.8.1975
14 x 22,835 km = 319,690 km.

1. Carlos Reutemann	Brabham BT44B-Ford	1:41.14,100 h
2. Jacques Laffite	Williams FW04-Ford	1:42.51,800 h
3. Niki Lauda	Ferrari 312T	1:43.37,400 h

Grand Prix, A, Aring, 17.8.1975
29 x 5,911 km = 171,419 km.

1. Vittorio Brambilla	March 751-Ford	0:57.56,690 h
2. James Hunt	Hesketh 308-Ford	0:58.23,720 h
3. Tom Pryce	Shadow DN5A-Ford	0:58.31,540 h

Grand Prix, I, Monza, 7.9.1975
52 x 5,780 km = 300,560 km.

1. Clay Regazzoni	Ferrari 312T	1:22.42,600 h
2. Emerson Fittipaldi	McLaren M23-Ford	1:22.59,200 h
3. Niki Lauda	Ferrari 312T	1:23.05,800 h

Grand Prix, USA, Watkins Glen, 5.10.1975
59 x 5,435 km = 320,665 km.

1. Niki Lauda	Ferrari 312T	1:42.58,175 h
2. Emerson Fittipaldi	McLaren M23-Ford	1:43.03,118 h
3. Jochen Mass	McLaren M23-Ford	1:43.45,812 h

1975

1. N. Lauda	64,5 P.	1. Ferrari	72,5 P.
2. E. Fittipaldi	45 P.	2. Brabham-Ford	54 P.
3. C. Reutemann	37 P.	3. McLaren-Ford	53 P.

1976

Grand Prix, BR, Interlagos, 25.1.1976
40 x 7,960 km = 318,400 km.

1. Niki Lauda	Ferrari 312T	1:45.16,780 h
2. Patrick Depailler	Tyrrell 007-Ford	1:45.38,250 h
3. Tom Pryce	Shadow DN5B-Ford	1:45.40,620 h

Grand Prix, ZA, Kyalami, 6.3.1976
78 x 4,104 km = 320,112 km.

1. Niki Lauda	Ferrari 312T	1:42.18,400 h
2. James Hunt	McLaren M23-Ford	1:42.19,700 h
3. Jochen Mass	McLaren M23-Ford	1:43.04,300 h

Grand Prix, USA, Long Beach, 28.3.1976
80 x 3,251 km = 260,080 km.

1. Clay Regazzoni	Ferrari 312T	1:53.18,471 h
2. Niki Lauda	Ferrari 312T	1:54.00,885 h
3. Patrick Depailler	Tyrrell 007-Ford	1:54.08,443 h

Grand Prix, E, Jarama, 2.5.1976
75 x 3,404 km = 255,300 km.

1. James Hunt	McLaren 23M-Ford	1:42.20,430 h
2. Niki Lauda	Ferrari 312T	1:42.51,400 h
3. Gunnar Nilsson	Lotus 77-Ford	1:43.08,450 h

Grand Prix, B, Zolder, 16.5.1976
70 x 4,262 km = 298,340 km.
1. Niki Lauda   Ferrari 312T2   1:42.53,230 h
2. Clay Regazzoni   Ferrari 312T2   1:42.56,690 h
3. Jacques Laffite   Ligier JS5-Matra   1:43.28,610 h

Grand Prix, MC, Monte Carlo, 30.5.1976
78 x 3,312 km = 258,336 km.
1. Niki Lauda   Ferrari 312T2   1:59.51,470 h
2. Jody Scheckter   Tyrrell P34-Ford   2:00.02,600 h
3. Patrick Depailler   Tyrrell P34-Ford   2:00.56,310 h

Grand Prix, S, Anderstorp, 13.6.1976
72 x 4,018 km = 289,296 km.
1. Jody Scheckter   Tyrrell P34-Ford   1:46.53,729 h
2. Patrick Depailler   Tyrrell P34-Ford   1:47.13,495 h
3. Niki Lauda   Ferrari 312T2   1:47.27,595 h

Grand Prix, F, Paul Ricard, 18.7.1976
54 x 5,810 km = 313,740 km.
1. James Hunt   McLaren M23-Ford   1:40.58,600 h
2. Patrick Depailler   Tyrrell P34-Ford   1:41.11,300 h
3. John Watson   Penske PC4-Ford   1:41.22,150 h

Grand Prix, GB, Brands Hatch, 18.7.1976
76 x 4,207 km = 319,732 km.
1. Niki Lauda   Ferrari 312T2   1:44.19,660 h
2. Jody Scheckter   Tyrrell P34-Ford   1:44.35,840 h
3. John Watson   Penske PC34-Ford   -1

Grand Prix, D, Nürburgring, 1.8.1976
14 x 22,835 km = 319,690 km.
1. James Hunt   McLaren M23-Ford   1:41.42,700 h
2. Jody Scheckter   Tyrrell P34-Ford   1:42.10,400 h
3. Jochen Mass   McLaren M23-Ford   1:42.35,100 h

Grand Prix, A, Aring, 15.8.1976
54 x 5,910 km = 319,140 km.
1. John Watson   Penske PC34-Ford   1:30.07,860 h
2. Jacques Laffite   Ligier JS5-Ford   1:30.18,650 h
3. Gunnar Nilsson   Lotus 77-Ford   1:30.19,840 h

Grand Prix, NL, Zandvoort, 29.8.1976
75 x 4,226 km = 316,950 km.
1. James Hunt   McLaren M23-Ford   1:44.52,090 h
2. Clay Regazzoni   Ferrari 312T2   1:44.53,010 h
3. Mario Andretti   Lotus 77-Ford   1:44.54,180 h

Grand Prix, I, Monza, 12.9.1976
52 x 5,800 km = 301,600 km.
1. Ronnie Peterson   March 761-Ford   1:30.35,600 h
2. Clay Regazzoni   Ferrari 312T2   1:30.37,900 h
3. Jacques Laffite   Ligier JS5-Matra   1:30.38,600 h

Grand Prix, CDN, Mosport Park , 3.10.1976
80 x 3,957 km = 316,560 km.
1. James Hunt   McLaren M23-Ford   1:40.09,626 h
2. Patrick Depailler   Tyrrell P34-Ford   1:40.15,957 h
3. Mario Andretti   Lotus 77-Ford   1:40.19,992 h

Grand Prix, USA, Watkins Glen, 10.10.1976
59 x 5,435 km = 320,665 km.
1. James Hunt   McLaren M23-Ford   1:42.40,741 h
2. Jody Scheckter   Tyrrell P34-Ford   1:42.48,771 h
3. Niki Lauda   Ferrari 312T2   1:43.43,065 h

Grand Prix, J, Fuji, 24.10.1976
73 x 4,359 km = 318,207 km.
1. Mario Andretti   Lotus 77-Ford   1:43.58,860 h
2. Patrick Depailler   Tyrrell P34-Ford   -1
3. James Hunt   McLaren M23-Ford   -1

1976

1. J. Hunt   69 P.   1. Ferrari   83 P.
2. N. Lauda   68 P.   2. McLaren-Ford   74 P.
3. J. Scheckter   49 P.   3. Tyrrell   71 P.

1977

Grand Prix, RA, Buenos Aires, 9.1.1977
53 x 5,968 km = 316,304 km.
1. Jody Scheckter   Wolf WR1-Ford   1:40.11,190 h
2. Carlos Pace   Brabham BT45-Alfa   1:40.54,430 h
3. Carlos Reutemann   Ferrari 312T2   1:40.57,210 h

Grand Prix, BR, Interlagos, 23.1.1977
40 x 7,960 km = 318,400 km.
1. Carlos Reutemann   Ferrari 312T   1:45.07,720 h
2. James Hunt   McLaren M23-Ford   1:45.18,430 h
3. Niki Lauda   Ferrari 312T2   1:46.55,230 h

Grand Prix, ZA, Kyalami, 5.3.1977
78 x 4,104 km = 320,112 km.
1. Niki Lauda   Ferrari 312T2   1:42.21,600 h
2. Jody Scheckter   Wolf WR1-Ford   1:42.26,800 h
3. Patrick Depailler   Tyrrell P34-Ford   1:42.27,300 h

Grand Prix, USA, Long Beach, 3.4.1977
80 x 3,251 km = 260,080 km.
1. Mario Andretti   Lotus 78-Ford   1:51.35,470 h
2. Niki Lauda   Ferrari 312T2   1:51.36,243 h
3. Jody Scheckter   Wolf WR1-Ford   1:51.40,327 h

Grand Prix, E, Jarama, 8.5.1977
75 x 3,404 km = 255,300 km.
1. Mario Andretti   Lotus 78-Ford   1:42.52,220 h
2. Carlos Reutemann   Ferrari 312T2   1:48.08,070 h
3. Jody Scheckter   Wolf WR1-Ford   1:43.16,730 h

Grand Prix, MC, Monte Carlo, 22.5.1977
76 x 3,312 km = 251,712 km.
1. Niki Lauda   Ferrari 312T2   1:57.52,770 h
2. Jody Scheckter   Wolf WR1-Ford   1:57.53,660 h
3. Carlos Reutemann   Ferrari 312T2   1:58.25,570 h

Grand Prix, B, Zolder, 5.6.1977
70 x 4,262 km = 298,340 km.
1. Gunnar Nilsson   Lotus 78-Ford   1:55.05,710 h
2. Niki Lauda   Ferrari 312T2   1:55.19,900 h
3. Ronnie Peterson   Tyrrell P34-Ford   1:55.25,660 h

Grand Prix, S, Anderstorp, 18.6.1977
72 x 4,018 km = 289,296 km.
1. Jacques Laffite   Ligier JS7-Matra   1:46.55,520 h
2. Jochen Mass   McLaren M23-Ford   1:47.03,969 h
3. Carlos Reutemann   Ferrari 312T2   1:47.09,889 h

Grand Prix, F, Dijon-Prenois, 3.7.1977
80 x 3,800 km = 304,000 km.
1. Mario Andretti   Lotus 78-Ford   1:39.40,130 h
2. John Watson   Brabham BT45-Alfa Ro. 1:39.41,680 h
3. James Hunt   McLaren M26-Ford   1:40.14,000 h

Grand Prix, GB, Silverstone, 16.7.1977
68 x 4,719 km = 320,892 km.
1. James Hunt   McLaren M26-Ford   1:31.46,060 h
2. Niki Lauda   Ferrari 312T2   1:32.04,370 h
3. Gunnar Nilsson   Lotus 78-Ford   1:32.05,630 h

Grand Prix, D, Hockenheim, 31.7.1977
47 x 6,789 km = 319,083 km.
1. Niki Lauda   Ferrari 312T2   1:31.48,620 h
2. Jody Scheckter   Wolf WR2-Ford   1:32.02,950 h
3. Hans-Joachim Stuck Brabham BT45-Alfa Ro. 1:32.09,920 h

Grand Prix, A, Aring, 14.8.1977
54 x 5,942 km = 320,868 km.
1. Alan Jones   Shadow DN8A-Ford   1:37.16,490 h
2. Niki Lauda   Ferrari 312T2   1:37.36,620 h
3. Hans-Joachim Stuck Brabham BT45-Alfa Ro.
1:37.50,990 h

Grand Prix, NL, Zandvoort, 28.8.1977
75 x 4,226 km = 316,950 km.
1. Niki Lauda   Ferrari 312T2   1:41.45,930 h
2. Jacques Laffite   Ligier JS7-Matra   1:41.47,820 h
3. Jody Scheckter   Wolf WR2-Ford   -1

Grand Prix, I, Monza, 11.9.1977
52 x 5,800 km = 301,600 km.
1. Mario Andretti   Lotus 78-Ford   1:27.50,300 h
2. Niki Lauda   Ferrari 312T2   1:28.07,260 h
3. Alan Jones   Shadow DN8A-Ford   1:28.13,930 h

Grand Prix, USA, Watkins Glen, 2.10.1977
59 x 5,435 km = 320,665 km.
1. James Hunt   McLaren M26-Ford   1:58.23,267 h
2. Carlos Pace   Brabham BT45-Alfa   1:58.25,293 h
3. Carlos Reutemann   Ferrari 312T2   1:59.42,146 h

Grand Prix, CDN, Mosport Park, 9.10.1977
80 x 3,957 km = 316,560 km.
1. Jody Scheckter   Wolf WR1-Ford   1:40.00,000 h
2. Patrick Depailler   Tyrrell P34-Ford   1:40.06,770 h
3. Jochen Mass   McLaren M26-Ford   1:40.15,760 h

Grand Prix, J, Fuji, 23.10.1977
73 x 4,359 km = 318,207 km.
1. James Hunt   McLaren M26-Ford   1:31.51,680 h
2. Carlos Reutemann   Ferrari 312T2   1:32.54,130 h
3. Patrick Depailler   Tyrrell P34-Ford   1:32.58,070 h

1977

1. N. Lauda   72 P.   1. Ferrari   95 P.
2. J. Scheckter   55 P.   2. Lotus-Ford   62 P.
3. M. Andretti   47 P.   3. McLaren-Ford   60 P.

1978

Grand Prix, RA, Buenos Aires, 15.1.1978
52 x 5,968 km = 310,336 km.
1. Mario Andretti   Lotus 78-Ford   1:37.04,470 h
2. Niki Lauda   Brabham BT45C-Alfa   1:37.17,680 h
3. Patrick Depailler   Tyrrell 008-Ford   1:37.18,110 h

Grand Prix, BR, Rio de Janeiro, 29.1.1978
63 x 5,031 km = 316,953 km.
1. Carlos Reutemann   Ferrari 312T2   1:49.59,860 h
2. Emerson Fittipaldi Fittipaldi F5A-Ford 1:50.48,990 h
3. Niki Lauda   Brabham BT45C-Alfa   1:50.56,880 h

Grand Prix, ZA, Kyalami, 4.3.1978
78 x 4,104 km = 320,112 km.
1. Ronnie Peterson   Lotus 78-Ford   1:42.15,767 h
2. Patrick Depailler   Tyrrell 008-Ford   1:42.16,233 h
3. John Watson   Brabham BT46-Alfa   1:42.20,209 h

Grand Prix, USA, Long Beach, 2.4.1978
80,5 x 3,251 km = 261,706 km.
1. Carlos Reutemann   Ferrari 312T3   1:52.01,301 h
2. Mario Andretti   Lotus 78-Ford   1:52.12,362 h
3. Patrick Depailler   Tyrrell 008-Ford   1:52.30,252 h

Grand Prix, MC, Monte Carlo, 7.5.1978
75 x 3,312 km = 248,400 km.
1. Patrick Depailler   Tyrrell 008-Ford   1:55.14,660 h
2. Niki Lauda   Brabham BT46-Alfa   1:55.37,110 h
3. Jody Scheckter   Wolf WR1-Ford   1:55.46,950 h

Grand Prix, B, Zolder, 21.5.1978
70 x 4,262 km = 298,340 km.
1. Mario Andretti   Lotus 79-Ford   1:39.52,020 h
2. Ronnie Peterson   Lotus 78-Ford   1:40.01,920 h
3. Carlos Reutemann   Ferrari 312T3   1:40.16,360 h

Grand Prix, E, Jarama, 4.6.1978
75 x 3,404 km = 255,300 km.
1. Mario Andretti   Lotus 79-Ford   1:41.47,060 h
2. Ronnie Peterson   Lotus 79-Ford   1:42.06,620 h
3. Jacques Laffite   Ligier JS9-Matra   1:42.24,300 h

Grand Prix, Sweden, Anderstorp, 17.6.1978
70 x 4,031 km = 282,170 km.
1. Niki Lauda   Brabham BT46B-Alfa   1:41.00,606 h
2. Riccardo Patrese   Arrows FA1-Ford   1:41.34,625 h
3. Ronnie Peterson   Lotus 79-Ford   1:41.34,711 h

Grand Prix, F, Paul Ricard, 2.7.1978
54 x 5,810 km = 313,740 km.
1. Mario Andretti   Lotus 79-Ford   1:38.51,920 h
2. Ronnie Peterson   Lotus 79-Ford   1:38.54,850 h
3. James Hunt   McLaren M26-Ford   1:39.11,720 h

Grand Prix, GB, Brands Hatch, 16.7.1978
76 x 4,207 km = 319,732 km.
1. Carlos Reutemann   Ferrari 312T3   1:42.12,390 h
2. Niki Lauda   Brabham BT46-Alfa   1:42.13,620 h
3. John Watson   Brabham BT46-Alfa   1:42.49,640 h

Grand Prix, D, Hockenheim, 30.7.1978
45 x 6,789 km = 305,505 km.
1. Mario Andretti   Lotus 79-Ford   1:28.00,900 h
2. Jody Scheckter   Wolf WR5-Ford   1:28.16,250 h
3. Jacques Laffite   Ligier JS9-Matra   1:28.28,910 h

Grand Prix, A, Aring, 13.8.1978
54 x 5,942 km = 320,868 km.
1. Ronnie Peterson   Lotus 79-Ford   1:41.21,570 h
2. Patrick Depailler   Tyrrell 008-Ford   1:42.09,010 h
3. Gilles Villeneuve   Ferrari 312T3   1:43.01,330 h

Grand Prix, NL, Zandvoort, 27.8.1978
75 x 4,226 km = 316,950 km.
1. Mario Andretti   Lotus 79-Ford   1:41.04,230 h
2. Ronnie Peterson   Lotus 79-Ford   1:41.04,550 h
3. Niki Lauda   Brabham BT46-Alfa   1:41.16,440 h

Grand Prix, I, Monza, 10.9.1978
40 x 5,800 km = 232,000 km.
1. Niki Lauda   Brabham BT46-Alfa   1:07.04,540 h
2. John Watson   Brabham BT46-Alfa   1:07.06,020 h
3. Carlos Reutemann   Ferrari 312T2   1:07.25,010 h

Grand Prix, USA, Watkins Glen, 1.10.1978
59 x 5,435 km = 320,665 km.
1. Carlos Reutemann   Ferrari 312T2   1:40.48,800 h
2. Alan Jones   Williams FW06-Ford   1:41.08,539 h
3. Jody Scheckter   Wolf WR6-Ford   1:41.34,501 h

Grand Prix, CDN, Montreal, 8.10.1978
70 x 4,500 km = 315,000 km.
1. Gilles Villeneuve   Ferrari 312T3   1:57.49,196 h
2. Jody Scheckter   Wolf WR6-Ford   1:58.02,568 h
3. Carlos Reutemann   Ferrari 312T2   1:58.08,604 h

1978

1. M. Andretti   64 P.   1. Lotus-Ford   86 P.
2. R. Peterson   51 P.   2. Ferrari   58 P.
3. C. Reutemann   48 P.   3. Brabham-Alfa   53 P.

GP 1979 – 1981

1979

Grand Prix, RA, Buenos Aires, 21.1.1979
53 x 5,986 km = 317,258 km.

1. Jacques Laffite	Ligier JS11-Ford	1:36.03,210 h
2. Carlos Reutemann	Lotus 79-Ford	1:36.18,150 h
3. John Watson	McLaren M28-Ford	1:37.32,020 h

Grand Prix, BR, Interlagos, 4.2.1979
40 x 7,874 km = 314,960 km.

1. Jacques Laffite	Ligier JS11-Ford	1:40.09,640 h
2. Patrick Depailler	Ligier JS11-Ford	1:40.14,920 h
3. Carlos Reutemann	Lotus 79-Ford	1:40.53,780 h

Grand Prix, ZA, Kyalami, 3.3.1979
78 x 4,104 km = 320,112 km.

1. Gilles Villeneuve	Ferrari 312 T4	1:41.49,960 h
2. Jody Scheckter	Ferrari 312 T4	1:41.53,380 h
3. Jean-Pierre Jarier	Tyrrell 009-Ford	1:42.12,070 h

Grand Prix, USA-West, Long Beach, 8.4.1979
80,5 x 3,251 km = 261,706 km.

1. Gilles Villeneuve	Ferrari 312 T4	1:50.25,400 h
2. Jody Scheckter	Ferrari 312 T4	1:50.54,780 h
3. Alan Jones	Williams FW06-Ford	1:51.25,090 h

Grand Prix, E, Jarama, 29.4.1979
75 x 3,404 km = 255,300 km.

1. Patrick Depailler	Ligier JS11-Ford	1:39.11,840 h
2. Carlos Reutemann	Lotus 79-Ford	1:39.32,780 h
3. Mario Andretti	Lotus 80-Ford	1:39.39,150 h

Grand Prix, B, Zolder, 13.5.1979
70 x 4,262 km = 298,340 km.

1. Jody Scheckter	Ferrari 312 T4	1:39.59,530 h
2. Jacques Laffite	Ligier JS11-Ford	1:40.14,890 h
3. Didier Pironi	Tyrrell 009-Ford	1:40.34,700 h

Grand Prix, MC, Monte Carlo, 27.5.1979
76 x 3,312 km = 251,712 km.

1. Jody Scheckter	Ferrari 312 T4	1:55.22,480 h
2. Clay Regazzoni	Williams FW07-Ford	1:55.22,920 h
3. Carlos Reutemann	Lotus 79-Ford	1:55.31,050 h

Grand Prix, F, Dijon-Prenois, 1.7.1979
80 x 3,800 km = 304,000 km.

1. Jean-Pierre Jabouille	Renault RE10	1:35.20,420 h
2. Gilles Villeneuve	Ferrari 312 T4	1:35.35,010 h
3. René Arnoux	Renault RE10	1:35.35,250 h

Grand Prix, GB, Silverstone, 14.7.1979
68 x 4,719 km = 320,892 km.

1. Clay Regazzoni	Williams FW07-Ford	1:26.11,170 h
2. René Arnoux	Renault RE10	1:26.35,450 h
3. Jean-Pierre Jarier	Tyrrell 009-Ford	-1

Grand Prix, D, Hockenheim, 29.7.1979
45 x 6,789 km = 305,505 km.

1. Alan Jones	Williams FW07-Ford	1:24.48,830 h
2. Clay Regazzoni	Williams FW07-Ford	1:24.51,740 h
3. Jacques Laffite	Ligier JS11-Ford	1:25.07,220 h

Grand Prix, A, Aring, 12.8.1979
54 x 5,942 km = 320,868 km.

1. Alan Jones	Williams FW07-Ford	1:27.38,010 h
2. Gilles Villeneuve	Ferrari 312 T4	1:28.14,060 h
3. Jacques Laffite	Ligier JS11-Ford	1:28.24,780 h

Grand Prix, NL, Zandvoort, 26.8.1979
75 x 4,226 km = 316,950 km.

1. Alan Jones	Williams FW07-Ford	1:41.19,775 h
2. Jody Scheckter	Ferrari 312 T4	1:41.41,558 h
3. Jacques Laffite	Ligier JS11-Ford	1:42.23,028 h

Grand Prix, I, Monza, 9.9.1979
50 x 5,800 km = 290,000 km.

1. Jody Scheckter	Ferrari 312 T4	1:22.00,220 h
2. Gilles Villeneuve	Ferrari 312 T4	1:22.00,680 h
3. Clay Regazzoni	Williams FW07-Ford	1:22.05,000 h

Grand Prix, CDN, Montreal, 30.9.1979
72 x 4,410 km = 317,520 km.

1. Alan Jones	Williams FW07-Ford	1:52.06,892 h
2. Gilles Villeneuve	Ferrari 312 T4	1:52.07,972 h
3. Clay Regazzoni	Williams FW07-Ford	1:53.20,548 h

Grand Prix, USA, Watkins Glen, 7.10.1979
59 x 5,435 km = 320,665 km.

1. Gilles Villeneuve	Ferrari 312 T4	1:52.17,743 h
2. René Arnoux	Renault RE10	1:53.06,521 h
3. Didier Pironi	Tyrrell 009-Ford	1:53.10,933 h

1979

1. J. Scheckter	51 P.	1. Ferrari	113 P.
2. G. Villeneuve	47 P.	2. Williams-Ford	75 P.
3. A. Jones	40 P.	3. Ligier-Ford	61 P.

1980

Grand Prix, RA, Buenos Aires, 13.1.1980
53 x 5,968 km = 316,304 km.

1. Alan Jones	Williams FW07-Ford	1:43.24,380 h
2. Nelson Piquet	Brabham BT49-Ford	1:43.48,970 h
3. Keke Rosberg	Fittipaldi F7-Ford	1:44.43,020 h

Grand Prix, BR, Interlagos, 27.1.1980
40 x 7,874 km = 314,960 km.

1. René Arnoux	Renault RE20	1:40.01,330 h
2. Elio de Angelis	Lotus 81-Ford	1:40.23,190 h
3. Alan Jones	Williams FW07B-Ford	1:41.07,440 h

Grand Prix, ZA, Kyalami, 1.3.1980
78 x 4,104 km = 320,112 km.

1. René Arnoux	Renault RE20	1:36.52,540 h
2. Jacques Laffite	Ligier JS11/15	1:37.26,610 h
3. Didier Pironi	Ligier JS11/15	1:37.45,030 h

Grand Prix, USA, Long Beach, 30.3.1980
80,5 x 3,251 km = 261,706 km.

1. Nelson Piquet	Brabham BT49-Ford	1:50.18,550 h
2. Riccardo Patrese	Arrows A3-Ford	1:51.07,762 h
3. Emerson Fittipaldi	Fittipaldi F7-Ford	1:51.37,113 h

Grand Prix, B, Zolder, 4.5.1980
72 x 4,262 km = 306,864 km.

1. Didier Pironi	Ligier JS11/15	1:38.46,510 h
2. Alan Jones	Williams FW07B-Ford	1:39.33,880 h
3. Carlos Reutemann	Williams FW07B-Ford	1:40.10,630 h

Grand Prix, MC, Monte Carlo, 18.5.1980
76 x 3,312 km = 251,712 km.

1. Carlos Reutemann	Williams FW07B-Ford	1:55.34,365 h
2. Jacques Laffite	Ligier JS11/15	1:56.47,994 h
3. Nelson Piquet	Brabham BT49-Ford	1:56.52,091 h

Grand Prix, F, Paul Ricard, 29.6.1980
54 x 5,810 km = 313,740 km.

1. Alan Jones	Williams FW07B-Ford	1:32.43,420 h
2. Didier Pironi	Ligier JS11/15	1:33.47,940 h
3. Jacques Laffite	Ligier JS11/15	1:33.13,680 h

Grand Prix, GB, Brands Hatch, 13.7.1980
76 x 4,207 km = 319,732 km.

1. Alan Jones	Williams FW07B-Ford	1:34.49,228 h
2. Nelson Piquet	Brabham BT49-Ford	1:35.00,235 h
3. Carlos Reutemann	Williams FW07B-Ford	1:35.02,513 h

Grand Prix, D, Hockenheim, 10.8.1980
45 x 6,789 km = 305,505 km.

1. Jacques Laffite	Ligier JS11/15	1:22.59,730 h
2. Carlos Reutemann	Williams FW07B-Ford	1:23.02,920 h
3. Alan Jones	Williams FW07B-Ford	1:23.43,260 h

Grand Prix, A, Aring, 17.8.1980
54 x 5,942 km = 320,868 km.

1. Jean-Pierre Jabouille	Renault RE20	1:26.15,730 h
2. Alan Jones	Williams FW07B-Ford	1:26.16,550 h
3. Carlos Reutemann	Williams FW07B-Ford	1:26.35,090 h

Grand Prix, NL, Zandvoort, 31.8.1980
72 x 4,252 km = 306,144 km.

1. Nelson Piquet	Brabham BT49-Ford	1:38.13,830 h
2. René Arnoux	Renault RE20	1:38.26,760 h
3. Jacques Laffite	Ligier JS11/15	1:38.27,260 h

Grand Prix, I, Imola, 14.9.1980
60 x 5,000 km = 300,000 km.

1. Nelson Piquet	Brabham BT49-Ford	1:38.07,520 h
2. Alan Jones	Williams FW07B-Ford	1:38.36,450 h
3. Carlos Reutemann	Williams FW07B-Ford	1:39.21,190 h

Grand Prix, CDN, Montreal, 28.9.1980
70 x 4,410 km = 308,700 km.

1. Alan Jones	Williams FW07B-Ford	1:46.45,530 h
2. Carlos Reutemann	Williams FW07B-Ford	1:47.01,070 h
3. Didier Pironi	Ligier JS11/15	1:47.04,600 h

Grand Prix, USA-East, Watkins Glen, 5.10.1980
59 x 5,435 km = 320,665 km.

1. Alan Jones	Williams FW07B-Ford	1:34.36,050 h
2. Carlos Reutemann	Williams FW07B-Ford	1:34.40,260 h
3. Didier Pironi	Ligier JS 11/15	1:34.48,620 h

1980

1. A. Jones	67 P.	1. Williams-Ford	120 P.
2. N. Piquet	54 P.	2. Ligier-Ford	66 P.
3. C. Reutemann	42 P.	3. Brabham-Ford	55 P.

1981

Grand Prix, USA-West, Long Beach, 15.3.1981
80,5 x 3,251 km = 261,706 km.

1. Alan Jones	Williams FW07C-Ford	1:50.41,330 h
2. Carlos Reutemann	Williams FW07C-Ford	1:50.50,520 h
3. Nelson Piquet	Brabham BT49C-Ford	1:51.16,250 h

Grand Prix, BR, Rio de Janeiro, 29.3.1981
61 x 5,031 km = 306,891 km.

1. Carlos Reutemann	Williams FW07C-Ford	2:00.23,660 h
2. Alan Jones	Williams FW07C-Ford	2:00.28,100 h
3. Riccardo Patrese	Arrows A3-Ford	2:01.26,740 h

Grand Prix, RA, Buenos Aires, 12.4.1981
53 x 5,968 km = 316,304 km.

1. Nelson Piquet	Brabham BT49C-Ford	1:34.32,740 h
2. Carlos Reutemann	Williams FW07C-Ford	1:34.59,350 h
3. Alain Prost	Renault RE20B	1:35.22,720 h

Grand Prix, RSM, Imola, 3.5.1981
60 x 5,040 km = 302,400 km.

1. Nelson Piquet	Brabham BT49C-Ford	1:51.23,970 h
2. Riccardo Patrese	Arrows A3-Ford	1:51.28,550 h
3. Carlos Reutemann	Williams FW07C-Ford	1:51.30,310 h

Grand Prix, B, Zolder, 17.5.1981
54 x 4,262 km = 230,148 km.

1. Carlos Reutemann	Williams FW07C-Ford	1:16.31,610 h
2. Jacques Laffite	Ligier JS17-Matra	1:17.07,670 h
3. Nigel Mansell	Lotus 81-Ford	1:17.15,300 h

Grand Prix, MC, Monte Carlo, 31.5.1981
76 x 3,312 km = 251,712 km.

1. Gilles Villeneuve	Ferrari 126CK	1:54.23,380 h
2. Alan Jones	Williams FW07C-Ford	1:55.03,290 h
3. Jacques Laffite	Ligier JS17-Matra	1:55.52,620 h

Grand Prix, E, Jarama, 21.6.1981
80 x 3,312 km = 264,960 km.

1. Gilles Villeneuve	Ferrari 126CK	1:46.35,010 h
2. Jacques Laffite	Ligier JS17-Matra	1:46.35,230 h
3. John Watson	McLaren MP4/1-Ford	1:46.35,590 h

Grand Prix, F, Dijon-Prenois, 5.7.1981
80 x 3,800 km = 304,000 km.

1. Alain Prost	Renault RE30	1:35.48,130 h
2. John Watson	McLaren MP4/1-Ford	1:35.50,420 h
3. Nelson Piquet	Brabham BT49C-Ford	1:36.12,350 h

Grand Prix, GB, Silverstone, 18.7.1981
68 x 4,719 km = 320,892 km.

1. John Watson	McLaren MP4/1-Ford	1:26.54,800 h
2. Carlos Reutemann	Williams FW07C-Ford	1:27.35,450 h
3. Jacques Laffite	Ligier JS17-Matra	-1

Grand Prix, D, Hockenheim 2.8.1981
45 x 6,789 km = 305,505 km.

1. Nelson Piquet	Brabham BT49C-Ford	1:25.55,600 h
2. Alain Prost	Renault RE30	1:26.07,120 h
3. Jacques Laffite	Ligier JS17-Matra	1:27.00,200 h

Grand Prix, A, Aring, 16.8.1981
53 x 5,942 km = 314,926 km.

1. Jacques Laffite	Ligier JS17-Matra	1:27.36,470 h
2. René Arnoux	Renault RE30	1:27.41,640 h
3. Nelson Piquet	Brabham BT49C-Ford	1:27.43,810 h

Grand Prix, NL, Zandvoort, 30.8.1981
72 x 4,252 km = 306,144 km.

1. Alain Prost	Renault RE30	1:40.22,430 h
2. Nelson Piquet	Brabham BT49C-Ford	1:40.30,670 h
3. Alan Jones	Williams FW07C-Ford	1:40.57,930 h

Grand Prix, I, Monza, 13.9.1981
52 x 5,800 km = 301,600 km.

1. Alain Prost	Renault RE30	1:26.33,897 h
2. Alan Jones	Williams FW07C-Ford	1:26.56,072 h
3. Carlos Reutemann	Williams FW07C-Ford	1:27.24,484 h

Grand Prix, CDN, Montreal, 27.9.1981
63 x 4,410 km = 277,830 km.

1. Jacques Laffite	Ligier JS17-Matra	2:01.25,205 h
2. John Watson	McLaren MP4/1-Ford	2:01.31,438 h
3. Gilles Villeneuve	Ferrari 126CK	2:03.15,480 h

Caesars Palace Grand Prix, Las Vegas, 17.10.1981
75 x 3,650 km = 273,375 km.

1. Alan Jones	Williams FW07C-Ford	1:44.09,077 h
2. Alain Prost	Renault RE30	1:44.29,125 h
3. Bruno Giacomelli	Alfa Romeo 179C	1:44.29,505 h

1981

1. N. Piquet	50 P.	1. Williams-Ford	95 P.
2. C. Reutemann	49 P.	2. Brabham-Ford	61 P.
3. A. Jones	46 P.	3. Renault	54 P.

GP 1982 – 1984

1982

Grand Prix, ZA, Kyalami, 23.1.1982
77 x 4,104 km = 316,008 km.
1. Alain Prost — Renault RE30B — 1:32.08,401 h
2. Carlos Reutemann — Williams FW07C-Ford — 1:32.23,347 h
3. René Arnoux — Renault RE30B — 1:32.36,301 h

Grand Prix, BR, Rio de Janeiro, 21.3.1982
63 x 5,031 km = 316,953 km.
1. Alain Prost — Renault RE30B — 1:44.33,134 h
2. John Watson — McLaren MP4/1B-Ford — 1:44.36,124 h
3. Nigel Mansell — Lotus 91-Ford — 1:45.09,993 h

Grand Prix, USA, Long Beach, 4.4.1982
75,5 x 3,428 km = 258,807 km.
1. Niki Lauda — McLaren MP4/1B-Ford — 1:58.25,318 h
2. Keke Rosberg — Williams FW 07C-Ford — 1:58.39,978 h
3. Riccardo Patrese — Brabham BT49C-Ford — 1:59.44,461 h

Grand Prix, RSM, Imola, 25.4.1982
60 x 5,040 km = 302,400 km.
1. Didier Pironi — Ferrari 126C2 — 1:36.38,887 h
2. Gilles Villeneuve — Ferrari 126C2 — 1:36.39,253 h
3. Michele Alboreto — Tyrrell 011-Ford — 1:37.46,571 h

Grand Prix, B, Zolder, 9.5.1982
70 x 4,262 km = 298,340 km.
1. John Watson — McLaren MP4/1B-Ford — 1:35.41,995 h
2. Keke Rosberg — Williams FW 08-Ford — 1:35.49,263 h
3. Eddie Cheever — Ligier JS17-Matra — -1

Grand Prix, MC, Monte Carlo, 23.5.1982
76 x 3,312 km = 251,712 km.
1. Riccardo Patrese — Brabham BT49D-Ford — 1:54.11,259 h
2. Didier Pironi — Ferrari 126C2 — -1
3. Andrea de Cesaris — Alfa Romeo 182 — -1

Grand Prix, USA, Detroit, 6.6.1982
62 x 4,012 km = 248,744 km.
1. John Watson — McLaren MP4/1B-Ford — 1:58.41,043 h
2. Eddie Cheever — Ligier JS17-Matra — 1:58.56,769 h
3. Didier Pironi — Ferrari 126C2 — 1:59.09,120 h

Grand Prix, CDN, Montreal, 13.6.1982
70 x 4,410 km = 308,700 km.
1. Nelson Piquet — Brabham BT50-BMW — 1:46.39,577 h
2. Riccardo Patrese — Brabham BT49-Ford — 1:46.53,376 h
3. John Watson — McLaren MP4/1B-Ford — 1:47.41,413 h

Grand Prix, NL, Zandvoort, 3.7.1982
72 x 4,252 km = 306,144 km.
1. Didier Pironi — Ferrari 126C2 — 1:38.03,254 h
2. Nelson Piquet — Brabham BT50-BMW — 1:38.24,903 h
3. Keke Rosberg — Williams FW 08-Ford — 1:38.25,619 h

Grand Prix, GB, Brands Hatch, 18.7.1982
76 x 4,207 km = 319,732 km.
1. Niki Lauda — McLaren MP4/1B-Ford — 1:35.33,812 h
2. Didier Pironi — Ferrari 126C2 — 1:35.59,953 h
3. Patrick Tambay — Ferrari 126C2 — 1:36.12,248 h

Grand Prix, F, Paul Ricard, 25.7.1982
54 x 5,810 km = 313,740 km.
1. René Arnoux — Renault RE30B — 1:33.32,217 h
2. Alain Prost — Renault RE30B — 1:33.50,525 h
3. Didier Pironi — Ferrari 126C2 — 1:34.15,345 h

Grand Prix, D, Hockenheim, 8.8.1982
45 x 6,797 km = 305,865 km.
1. Patrick Tambay — Ferrari 126C2 — 1:27.25,178 h
2. René Arnoux — Renault RE30B — 1:27.41,557 h
3. Keke Rosberg — Williams FW 08-Ford — -1

Grand Prix, A, Aring, 15.8.1982
53 x 5,942 km = 314,926 km.
1. Elio de Angelis — Lotus 91-Ford — 1:25.02,212 h
2. Keke Rosberg — Williams FW 08-Ford — 1:25.02,262 h
3. Jacques Laffite — Ligier JS19-Matra — -1

Grand Prix, CH, Dijon-Prenois, 29.8.1982
80 x 3,800 km = 304,000 km.
1. Keke Rosberg — Williams FW 08-Ford — 1:32.41,087 h
2. Alain Prost — Renault RE30B — 1:32.45,529 h
3. Niki Lauda — McLaren MP4/1B-Ford — 1:33.41,430 h

Grand Prix, I, Monza, 12.9.1982
52 x 5,800 km = 301,600 km.
1. René Arnoux — Renault RE30B — 1:22.25,734 h
2. Patrick Tambay — Ferrari 126C2 — 1:22.39,798 h
3. Mario Andretti — Ferrari 126C2 — 1:23.14,186 h

Caesars Palace Grand Prix, Las Vegas, 25.9.1982
75 x 3,650 km = 273,375 km.
1. Michele Alboreto — Tyrrell 011-Ford — 1:41.56,888 h
2. John Watson — McLaren MP4/1B-Ford — 1:42.24,180 h
3. Eddie Cheever — Ligier JS19-Matra — 1:42.53,338 h

1982

1. K. Rosberg	44 P.	1. Ferrari	74 P.
2. D. Pironi	39 P.	2. McLaren-Ford	69 P.
3. J. Watson	39 P.	3. Renault	62 P.

1983

Grand Prix, BR, Rio de Janeiro, 13.3.1983
63 x 5,031 km = 316,953 km.
1. Nelson Piquet — Brabham BT52-BMW — 1:48.27,731 h
2. (Keke Rosberg) — Williams FW08C-Ford
3. Niki Lauda — McLaren MP4/C-Ford — 1:49.19,614 h

Grand Prix, USA-West, Long Beach, 27.3.1983
75 x 3,275 km = 245,625 km.
1. Niki Lauda — McLaren MP4/1C-Ford — 1:53.34,889 h
2. John Watson — McLaren MP4/1C-Ford — 1:54.02,882 h
3. René Arnoux — Ferrari 126C — 1:54.48,527 h

Grand Prix, F, Paul Ricard, 17.4.1983
54 x 5,810 km = 313,740 km.
1. Alain Prost — Renault RE40 — 1:34.13,913 h
2. Nelson Piquet — Brabham BT52-BMW — 1:34.43,633 h
3. Eddie Cheever — Renault RE40 — 1:34.54,145 h

Grand Prix, RSM, Imola, 1.5.1983
60 x 5,040 km = 302,400 km.
1. Patrick Tambay — Ferrari 126C — 1:37.52,460 h
2. Alain Prost — Renault RE40 — 1:38.41,241 h
3. René Arnoux — Ferrari 126C — -1

Grand Prix, MC, Monte Carlo, 15.5.1983
76 x 3,312 km = 251,712 km.
1. Keke Rosberg — Williams FW08C-Ford — 1:56.38,121 h
2. Nelson Piquet — Brabham BT52-BMW — 1:56.56,596 h
3. Alain Prost — Renault RE40 — 1:57.09,487 h

Grand Prix, B, Spa-Francorchamps, 22.5.1983
40 x 6,949 km = 278,620 km.
1. Alain Prost — Renault RE40 — 1:27.11,502 h
2. Patrick Tambay — Ferrari 126C — 1:27.34,684 h
3. Eddie Cheever — Renault RE40 — 1:27.51,271 h

Grand Prix, USA, Detroit, 5.6.1983
60 x 4,023 km = 241,380 km.
1. Michele Alboreto — Tyrrell 011-Ford — 1:50.53,669 h
2. Keke Rosberg — Williams FW08C-Ford — 1:51.01,371 h
3. John Watson — McLaren MP4/1C-Ford — 1:51.02,952 h

Grand Prix, CDN, Montreal, 12.6.1983
70 x 4,410 km = 308,700 km.
1. René Arnoux — Ferrari 126C — 1:48.31,838 h
2. Eddie Cheever — Renault RE40 — 1:49.13,867 h
3. Patrick Tambay — Ferrari 126C — 1:49.24,448 h

Grand Prix, GB, Silverstone, 16.7.1983
67 x 4,719 km = 316,173 km.
1. Alain Prost — Renault RE40 — 1:24.39,780 h
2. Nelson Piquet — Brabham BT52-BMW — 1:24.58,941 h
3. Patrick Tambay — Ferrari 126C — 1:25.06,026 h

Grand Prix, D, Hockenheim, 7.8.1983
45 x 6,797 km = 308,865 km.
1. René Arnoux — Ferrari 126C — 1:27.10,319 h
2. Andre de Cesaris — Alfa Romeo 183T — 1:28.20,971 h
3. Riccardo Patrese — Brabham BT52B-BMW — 1:28.54,412 h

Grand Prix, A, Aring, 14.8.1983
53 x 5,942 km = 314,926 km.
1. Alain Prost — Renault RE40 — 1:24.32,745 h
2. René Arnoux — Ferrari 126C — 1:24.39,580 h
3. Nelson Piquet — Brabham BT52-BMW — 1:25.00,404 h

Grand Prix, NL, Zandvoort, 28.8.1983
72 x 4,252 km = 306,144 km.
1. René Arnoux — Ferrari 126C — 1:38.41,950 h
2. Patrick Tambay — Ferrari 126C — 1:39.02,789 h
3. John Watson — McLaren MP4/1C-Ford — 1:39.25,691 h

Grand Prix, I, Monza, 11.9.1983
52 x 5,800 km = 301,600 km.
1. Nelson Piquet — Brabham BT52-BMW — 1:23.10,880 h
2. René Arnoux — Ferrari 126C — 1:23.21,092 h
3. Eddie Cheever — Renault RE40 — 1:23.29,492 h

Grand Prix, EU, Brands Hatch, 25.9.1983
76 x 4,207 km = 319,732 km.
1. Nelson Piquet — Brabham BT52-BMW — 1:36.45,865 h
2. Alain Prost — Renault RE 40 — 1:36.52,436 h
3. Nigel Mansell — Lotus 94T-Renault — 1:37.16,180 h

Grand Prix, ZA, Kyalami, 5.6.1983
77 x 4,104 km = 316,008 km.
1. Riccardo Patrese — Brabham BT52-BMW — 1:33.25,708 h
2. Andrea de Cesaris — Alfa Romeo 183T — 1:33.37,027 h
3. Nelson Piquet — Brabham BT52-BMW — 1:33.47,677 h

1983

1. N. Piquet	59 P.	1. Ferrari	89 P.
2. A. Prost	57 P.	2. Renault	79 P.
3. R. Arnoux	49 P.	3. Brabham-BMW	72 P.

1984

Grand Prix, BR, Rio de Janeiro, 25.3.1984
61 x 5,031 km = 306,891 km.
1. Alain Prost — McLaren MP4/2-Porsche — 1:42.34,492 h
2. Keke Rosberg — Williams FW 09-Honda — 1:43.15,006 h
3. Elio de Angelis — Lotus 95T-Renault — 1:43.33,620 h

Grand Prix, ZA, Kyalami, 7.4.1984
75 x 4,104 km = 307,800 km.
1. Niki Lauda — McLaren MP4/2-Porsche — 1:29.23,430 h
2. Alain Prost — McLaren MP4/2-Porsche — 1:30.29,380 h
3. Derek Warwick — Renault RE50 — -1

Grand Prix, B, Spa-Francorchamps, 29.4.1984
70 x 4,262 km = 298,340 km.
1. Michele Alboreto — Ferrari 126C4 — 1:36.32,048 h
2. Derek Warwick — Renault RE50 — 1:37.14,434 h
3. René Arnoux — Ferrari 126C4 — 1:37.41,851 h

Grand Prix, RSM, Imola, 6.5.1984
60 x 5,040 km = 302,400 km.
1. Alain Prost — McLaren MP4/2-Porsche — 1:36.53,679 h
2. René Arnoux — Ferrari 126C4 — 1:37.07,095 h
3. Elio de Angelis — Lotus 95T-Renault — -1

Grand Prix, F, Dijon-Prenois, 20.5.1984
79 x 3,887 km = 307,073 km.
1. Niki Lauda — McLaren MP4/2-Porsche — 1:31.11,951 h
2. Patrick Tambay — Renault RE50 — 1:31.19,105 h
3. Nigel Mansell — Lotus 95T-Renault — 1:31.35,920 h

Grand Prix, MC, Monte Carlo, 3.6.1984
31 x 3,312 km = 102,672 km.
1. Alain Prost — McLaren MP4/2-Porsche — 1:01.07,740 h
2. Ayrton Senna — Toleman TG184-Hart — 1:01.15,186 h
3. René Arnoux — Ferrari 126C4 — 1:01.36,817 h

Grand Prix, CDN, Montreal, 17.6.1984
70 x 4,410 km = 308,700 km.
1. Nelson Piquet — Brabham BT53-BMW — 1:46.23,748 h
2. Niki Lauda — McLaren MP4/2-Porsche — 1:46.26,360 h
3. Alain Prost — McLaren MP4/2-Porsche — 1:47.51,780 h

Detroit Grand Prix, Detroit, 24.6.1984
63 x 4,023 km = 253,449 km.
1. Nelson Piquet — Brabham BT53-BMW — 1:55.41,842 h
2. Elio de Angelis — Lotus 95T-Renault — 1:56.14,480 h
3. Teo Fabi — Brabham BT53-BMW — 1:57.08,370 h

Dallas Grand Prix, Dallas, 8.7.1984
67 x 3,901 km = 261,367 km.
1. Keke Rosberg — Williams FW 09-Honda — 2:01.22,617 h
2. René Arnoux — Ferrari 126C4 — 2:01.45,081 h
3. Elio de Angelis — Lotus 95T-Renault — -1

Grand Prix, GB, Brands Hatch, 22.7.1984
71 x 4,207 km = 298,697 km.
1. Niki Lauda — McLaren MP4/2-Porsche — 1:29.28,532 h
2. Derek Warwick — Renault RE50 — 1:30.10,655 h
3. Ayrton Senna — Toleman TG184-Hart — 1:30.31,860 h

Grand Prix, D, Hockenheim, 5.8.1984
44 x 6,797 km = 299,068 km.
1. Alain Prost — McLaren MP4/2-Porsche — 1:24.43,210 h
2. Niki Lauda — McLaren MP4/2-Porsche — 1:24.46,359 h
3. Derek Warwick — Renault RE50 — 1:25.19,633 h

Grand Prix, A, Aring, 19.8.1984
51 x 5,942 km = 303,042 km.
1. Niki Lauda — McLaren MP4/2-Porsche — 1:21.12,851 h
2. Nelson Piquet — Brabham BT53-BMW — 1:21.36,376 h
3. Michele Alboreto — Ferrari 126C4 — 1:22.01,849 h

Grand Prix, NL, Zandvoort, 26.8.1984
71 x 4,252 km = 301,892 km.
1. Alain Prost — McLaren MP4/2-Porsche — 1:37.21,468 h
2. Niki Lauda — McLaren MP4/2-Porsche — 1:37.31,751 h
3. Nigel Mansell — Lotus 95T-Renault — 1:38.38,012 h

Grand Prix, I, Monza, 9.9.1984
51 x 5,800 km = 295,800 km.
1. Niki Lauda — McLaren MP4/2-Porsche — 1:20.29,065 h
2. Michele Alboreto — Ferrari 126C4 — 1:20.53,314 h
3. Riccardo Patrese — Alfa Romeo184T — -1

Grand Prix, EU, Nürburgring, 7.10.1984
67 x 4,542 km = 304,314 km.
1. Alain Prost — McLaren MP4/2-Porsche — 1:35.13,284 h
2. Michele Alboreto — Ferrari 126C4 — 1:35.37,195 h
3. Nelson Piquet — Brabham BT53-BMW — 1:35.38,206 h

Grand Prix, P, Estoril, 21.10.1984
70 x 4,350 km = 304,500 km.
1. Alain Prost — McLaren MP4/2-Porsche — 1:41.11,753 h
2. Niki Lauda — McLaren MP4/2-Porsche — 1:41.25,178 h
3. Ayrton Senna — Toleman TG184-Hart — 1:41.31,795 h

1984

1. N. Lauda	72 P.	1. McLaren-Por.	143,5 P.
2. A. Prost	71,5 P.	2. Ferrari	57,5 P.
3. E. de Angelis	34 P.	3. Lotus-Renault	47 P.

GP 1985 – 1987

1985

Grand Prix, BR, Rio de Janeiro, 7.4.1985
61 x 5,031 km = 306,891 km.
1. Alain Prost   McLaren MP4/2B-Por.   1:41.26,115 h
2. Michele Alboreto   Ferrari156/85   1:41.29,374 h
3. Elio de Angelis   Lotus 97T-Renault   -1

Grand Prix, P, Estoril, 21.4.1985
67 x 4,350 km = 291,450 km.
1. Ayrton Senna   Lotus 97T-Renault   2:00.28,006 h
2. Michele Alboreto   Ferrari156/85   2:01.30,984 h
3. Patrick Tambay   Renault RE60   -1

Grand Prix, RSM, Imola, 5.5.1985
60 x 5,040 km = 302,400 km.
1. Elio de Angelis   Lotus 97T-Renault   1:34.35,955 h
2. Thierry Boutsen   Arrows A8-BMW   -1
3. Patrick Tambay   Renault RE60   -1

Grand Prix, MC, Monte Carlo, 19.5.1985
78 x 3,312 km = 258,336 km.
1. Alain Prost   McLaren MP4/2B-Por.   1:51.58,034 h
2. Michele Alboreto   Ferrari156/85   1:52.05,575 h
3. Elio de Angelis   Lotus 97T-Renault   1:53.25,205 h

Grand Prix, CDN, Montreal, 16.6.1985
70 x 4,410 km = 308,700 km.
1. Michele Alboreto   Ferrari 156/85   1:46.01,813 h
2. Stefan Johansson   Ferrari 156/85   1:46.03,770 h
3. Alain Prost   McLaren MP4/2B-Por.   1:46.06,154 h

Detroit Grand Prix, Detroit, 23.6.1985
63 x 4,023 km = 253,449 km.
1. Keke Rosberg   Williams FW10-Honda 1:55.39,851 h
2. Stefan Johansson   Ferrari 156/85   1:56.37,400 h
3. Michele Alboreto   Ferrari156/85   1:56.43,021 h

Grand Prix, F, Paul Ricard, 7.7.1985
53 x 5,810 km = 307,930 km.
1. Nelson Piquet   Brabham BT54-BMW   1:31.46,266 h
2. Keke Rosberg   Williams FW10-Honda 1:31.52,926 h
3. Alain Prost   McLaren MP4/2B-Por.   1:31.55,551 h

Grand Prix, GB, Silverstone, 21.7.1985
65 x 4,719 km = 306,735 km.
1. Alain Prost   McLaren MP4/2B-Por.   1:18.10,436 h
2. Michele Alboreto   Ferrari156/85   -1
3. Jacques Laffite   Ligier JS25-Renault   -1

Grand Prix, D, Nürburgring, 4.8.1985
67 x 4,542 km = 304,314 km.
1. Michele Alboreto   Ferrari156/85   1:35.31,337 h
2. Alain Prost   McLaren MP4/2B-Por.   1:35.42,998 h
3. Jacques Laffite   Ligier JS25-Renault   1:36.22,491 h

Grand Prix, A, Aring, 18.8.1985
52 x 5,942 km = 308,984 km.
1. Alain Prost   McLaren MP4/2B-Por.   1:20.12,583 h
2. Ayrton Senna   Lotus 97T-Renault   1:20.42,585 h
3. Michele Alboreto   Ferrari156/85   1:20.46,939 h

Grand Prix, NL, Zandvoort, 25.8.1985
70 x 4,252 km = 297,640 km.
1. Niki Lauda   McLaren MP4/2B-Por.   1:32.29,263 h
2. Alain Prost   McLaren MP4/2B-Por.   1:32.29,495 h
3. Ayrton Senna   Lotus 97T-Renault   1:33.17,754 h

Grand Prix, I, Monza, 8.9.1985
51 x 5,800 km = 295,800 km.
1. Alain Prost   McLaren MP4/2B-Por.   1:17.59,451 h
2. Nelson Piquet   Brabham BT54-BMW   1:18.51,086 h
3. Ayrton Senna   Lotus 97T-Renault   1:18.59,841 h

Grand Prix, B, Spa-Francorchamps, 15.9.1985
43 x 6,940 km = 298,420 km.
1. Ayrton Senna   Lotus 97T-Renault   1:34.19,893 h
2. Nigel Mansell   Williams FW10-Honda 1:34.48,315 h
3. Alain Prost   McLaren MP4/2B-Por.   1:35.15,002 h

Grand Prix, EU, Brands Hatch, 6.10.1985
75 x 4,207 km = 315,525 km.
1. Nigel Mansell   Williams FW10-Honda 1:32.58,109 h
2. Ayrton Senna   Lotus 97T-Renault   1:33.19,905 h
3. Keke Rosberg   Williams FW10-Honda 1:33.56,642 h

Grand Prix, ZA, Kyalami, 19.10.1985
75 x 4,104 km = 307,800 km.
1. Nigel Mansell   Williams FW10-Honda 1:28.22,866 h
2. Keke Rosberg   Williams FW10-Honda 1:28.30,438 h
3. Alain Prost   McLaren MP4/2B-Por.   1:30.14,660 h

Grand Prix, AUS, Adelaide, 3.11.1985
82 x 3,778 km = 309,796 km.
1. Keke Rosberg   Williams FW10-Honda 2:00.40,473 h
2. Jacques Laffite   Ligier JS25-Renault   2:01.26,603 h
3. Philippe Streiff   Ligier JS25-Renault   2:02.09,009 h

1985

1. A. Prost	73 P.	1. McLaren-Por.	90 P.
2. M. Alboreto	53 P.	2. Ferrari	82 P.
3. K. Rosberg	40 P.	3. Lotus/Williams	71 P.

1986

Grand Prix, BR, Rio de Janeiro, 23.3.1986
61 x 5,031 km = 306,891 km.
1. Nelson Piquet   Williams FW11-Honda 1:39.32,583 h
2. Ayrton Senna   Lotus 98T-Renault   1:40.07,410 h
3. Jacques Laffite   Ligier JS27-Renault   1:40.32,342 h

Grand Prix, E, Jerez, 13.4.1986
72 x 4,218 km = 303,696 km.
1. Ayrton Senna   Lotus 98T-Renault   1:48.47,735 h
2. Nigel Mansell   Williams FW11-Honda 1:48.47,749 h
3. Alain Prost   McLaren MP4/2C-Por.   1:49.09,287 h

Grand Prix, RSM, Imola, 27.4.1986
60 x 5,040 km = 302,400 km.
1. Alain Prost   McLaren MP4/2C-Por.   1:32.28,408 h
2. Nelson Piquet   Williams FW11-Honda 1:32.36,053 h
3. Gerhard Berger   Benetton B186-BMW   -1

Grand Prix, MC, Monte Carlo, 11.5.1986
78 x 3,328 km = 259,584 km.
1. Alain Prost   McLaren MP4/2C-Por.   1:55.41,060 h
2. Keke Rosberg   McLaren MP4/2C-Por.   1:56.06,082 h
3. Ayrton Senna   Lotus 98T-Renault   1:56.34,706 h

Grand Prix, B, Spa-Francorchamps, 25.5.1986
43 x 6,940 km = 298,420 km.
1. Nigel Mansell   Williams FW11-Honda 1:27.57,925 h
2. Ayrton Senna   Lotus 98T-Renault   1:28.17,752 h
3. Stefan Johansson   Ferrari F186   1:28.24,517 h

Grand Prix, CDN, Montreal, 15.6.1986
69 x 4,410 km = 304,290 km.
1. Nigel Mansell   Williams FW11-Honda 1:42.26,415 h
2. Alain Prost   McLaren MP4/2C-Por.   1:42.47,074 h
3. Nelson Piquet   Williams FW11-Honda 1:43.02,677 h

Grand Prix, USA, Detroit, 22.6.1986
63 x 4,023 km = 253,449 km.
1. Ayrton Senna   Lotus 98T-Renault   1:51.12,847 h
2. Jacques Laffite   Ligier JS27-Renault   1:51.43,864 h
3. Alain Prost   McLaren MP4/2C-Por.   1:51.44,671 h

Grand Prix, F, Paul Ricard, 6.7.1986
80 x 3,813 km = 305,040 km.
1. Nigel Mansell   Williams FW11-Honda 1:37.19,272 h
2. Alain Prost   McLaren MP4/2C-Por.   1:37.36,400 h
3. Nelson Piquet   Williams FW11-Honda 1:37.56,817 h

Grand Prix, GB, Brands Hatch, 13.7.1986
75 x 4,207 km = 315,525 km.
1. Nigel Mansell   Williams FW11-Honda 1:30.38,471 h
2. Nelson Piquet   Williams FW11-Honda 1:30.44,045 h
3. Alain Prost   McLaren MP4/2C-Por.   -1

Grand Prix, D, Hockenheim, 27.7.1986
44 x 6,797 km = 299,068 km.
1. Nelson Piquet   Williams FW11-Honda 1:22.08,263 h
2. Ayrton Senna   Lotus 98T-Renault   1:22.23,700 h
3. Nigel Mansell   Williams FW11-Honda 1:22.52,843 h

Grand Prix, H, Hungaroring, 10.8.1986
76 x 4,014 km = 305,064 km.
1. Nelson Piquet   Williams FW11-Honda 2:00.34,508 h
2. Ayrton Senna   Lotus 98T-Renault   2:00.52,181 h
3. Nigel Mansell   Williams FW11-Honda -1

Grand Prix, A, Aring, 17.8.1986
52 x 5,942 km = 308,984 km.
1. Alain Prost   McLaren MP4/2C-Por.   1:21.22,531 h
2. Michele Alboreto   Ferrari F186   -1
3. Stefan Johansson   Ferrari F186   -2

Grand Prix, I, Monza, 7.9.1986
51 x 5,800 km = 295,800 km.
1. Nelson Piquet   Williams FW11-Honda 1:17.42,889 h
2. Nigel Mansell   Williams FW11-Honda 1:17.52,717 h
3. Stefan Johansson   Ferrari F186   1:18.05,804 h

Grand Prix, P, Estoril, 21.9.1986
70 x 4,350 km = 304,500 km.
1. Nigel Mansell   Williams FW11-Honda 1:37.48,900 h
2. Alain Prost   McLaren MP4/2B-Por.   1:37.29,672 h
3. Nelson Piquet   Williams FW11-Honda 1:38.29,174 h

Grand Prix, MEX, Mexico City, 12.10.1986
68 x 4,421 km = 300,628 km.
1. Gerhard Berger   Benetton B186-BMW   1:33.18,700 h
2. Alain Prost   McLaren MP4/2B-Por.   1:33.44,138 h
3. Ayrton Senna   Lotus 98T-Renault   1:34.11,213 h

Grand Prix, AUS, Adelaide, 26.10.1986
82 x 3,779 km = 309,878 km.
1. Alain Prost   McLaren MP4/2B-Por.   1:54.20,388 h
2. Nelson Piquet   Williams FW11-Honda 1:54.24,593 h
3. Stefan Johansson   Ferrari F186   -1

1986

1. A. Prost	72 P.	1. Williams-Honda	135 P.
2. N. Mansell	70 P.	2. McLaren-Porsche	87 P.
3. N. Piquet	69 P.	3. Lotus-Renault	57 P.

1987

Grand Prix, BR, Rio de Janeiro, 12.4.1987
61 x 5,031 km = 306,891 km.
1. Alain Prost   McLaren MP4/3-Por.   1:39.45,141 h
2. Nelson Piquet   Williams FW11B-Honda 1:40.25,688 h
3. Stefan Johansson   McLaren MP4/3-Por.   1:40.41,899 h

Grand Prix, RSM, Imola, 3.5.1987
59 x 5,040 km = 297,360 km.
1. Nigel Mansell   Williams FW11B-Honda1:31.24,076 h
2. Ayrton Senna   Lotus 99T-Honda   1:31.51,621 h
3. Michele Alboreto   Ferrari F187   1:32.03,220 h

Grand Prix, B, Spa-Francorchamps, 17.5.1987
43 x 6,940 km = 298,420 km.
1. Alain Prost   McLaren MP4/3-Por.   1:27.03,217 h
2. Stefan Johansson   McLaren MP4/3-Por.   1:27.27,981 h
3. Andrea de Cesaris   Brabham BT56-BMW   -1

Grand Prix, MC, Monte Carlo, 31. 5.1987
78 x 3,328 km = 259,584 km.
1. Ayrton Senna   Lotus 99T-Honda   1:57.54,085 h
2. Nelson Piquet   Williams FW11B-Honda1:58.27,297 h
3. Michele Alboreto   Ferrari F187   1:59.06,924 h

Grand Prix, USA, Detroit, 21.6.1987
63 x 4,023 km = 253,449 km.
1. Ayrton Senna   Lotus 99T-Honda   1:50.16,358 h
2. Nelson Piquet   Williams FW11B-Honda1:50.50,177 h
3. Alain Prost   McLaren MP4/3-Por.   1:51.01,685 h

Grand Prix, F, Paul Ricard, 5.7.1987
80 x 3,813 km = 305,040 km.
1. Nigel Mansell   Williams FW11B-Honda1:37.03,839 h
2. Nelson Piquet   Williams FW11B-Honda1:37.11,550 h
3. Alain Prost   McLaren MP4/3-Por.   1:37.59,094 h

Grand Prix, GB, Silverstone, 12./.1987
65 x 4,778 km = 310,570 km.
1. Nigel Mansell   Williams FW11B-Honda1:19.11,780 h
2. Nelson Piquet   Williams FW11B-Honda1:19.13,698 h
3. Ayrton Senna   Lotus 99T-Honda   -1

Grand Prix, D, Hockenheim, 26.7.1987
44 x 6,797 km = 299,068 km.
1. Nelson Piquet   Williams FW11B-Honda1:21.25,091 h
2. Stefan Johansson   McLaren MP4/3-Por.   1:23.04,682 h
3. Ayrton Senna   Lotus 99T-Honda   -1

Grand Prix, H, Hungaroring, 9.8.1987
76 x 4,014 km = 305,064 km.
1. Nelson Piquet   Williams FW11B-Honda1:59.25,793 h
2. Ayrton Senna   Lotus 99T-Honda   2:00.04,520 h
3. Alain Prost   McLaren MP4/3-Por.   2:00.54,249 h

Grand Prix, A, Austriaring, 16.8.1987
52 x 5,942 km = 308,984 km.
1. Nigel Mansell   Williams FW11B-Honda 1:18.44,898 h
2. Nelson Piquet   Williams FW11B-Honda 1:19.40,602 h
3. Teo Fabi   Benetton B187-Ford   -1

Grand Prix, I, Monza, 6.9.1987
50 x 5,800 km = 290,000 km.
1. Nelson Piquet   Williams FW11B-Honda1:14.47,707 h
2. Ayrton Senna   Lotus 99T-Honda   1:14.49,513 h
3. Nigel Mansell   Williams FW11B-Honda1:15.36,743 h

Grand Prix, P, Estoril, 20.9.1987
70 x 4,350 km = 304,500 km.
1. Alain Prost   McLaren MP4/3-Por.   1:37.03,906 h
2. Gerhard Berger   Ferrari F187   1:37.24,399 h
3. Nelson Piquet   Williams FW11B-Honda1:38.07,210 h

Grand Prix, E, Jerez, 27.9.1987
72 x 4,218 km = 303,696 km.
1. Nigel Mansell   Williams FW11B-Honda1:49.12,692 h
2. Alain Prost   McLaren MP4/3-Por.   1:49.34,917 h
3. Stefan Johansson   McLaren MP4/3-Por.   1:49.43,510 h

Grand Prix, MEX, Mexico City, 18.10.1987
63 x 4,421 km = 278,523 km.
1. Nigel Mansell   Williams FW11B-Honda1:26.24,207 h
2. Nelson Piquet   Williams FW11B-Honda1:26.50,383 h
3. Riccardo Patrese   Brabham BT56-BMW   1:27.51,086 h

Grand Prix, J, Suzuka, 1.11.1987
51 x 5,859 km = 298,809 km.
1. Gerhard Berger   Ferrari F187   1:32.58,072 h
2. Ayrton Senna   Lotus 99T-Honda   1:33.15,456 h
3. Stefan Johansson   McLaren MP4/3-Por.   1:33.15,766 h

Grand Prix, AUS, Adelaide, 15.11.1987
82 x 3,779 km = 309,878 km.
1. Gerhard Berger   Ferrari F187   1:52.56,144 h
2. Michele Alboreto   Ferrari F187   1:54.04,028 h
3. Thierry Boutsen   Benetton B187-Ford   -1

1987

1. N. Piquet	73 P.	1. Williams-Honda	137 P.
2. N. Mansell	61 P.	2. McLaren-Porsche	76 P.
3. A. Senna	57 P.	3. Lotus-Honda	64 P.

GP 1988 – 1990

1988

Grand Prix, BR, Rio de Janeiro, 3.4.1988
60 x 5,031 km = 301,860 km.

1. Alain Prost	McLaren MP4/4-Honda	1:36.06,857 h
2. Gerhard Berger	Ferrari F187/88C	1:36.16,730 h
3. Nelson Piquet	Lotus 100T-Honda	1:37.15,438 h

Grand Prix, RSM, Imola, 1.5.1988
60 x 5,040 km = 302,400 km.

1. Ayrton Senna	McLaren MP4/4-Honda	1:32.41,264 h
2. Alain Prost	McLaren MP4/4-Honda	1:32.43,598 h
3. Nelson Piquet	Lotus 100T-Honda	-1

Grand Prix, MC, Monte Carlo, 15.5.1988
78 x 3,328 km = 259,584 km.

1. Alain Prost	McLaren MP4/4-Honda	1:57.17,077 h
2. Gerhard Berger	Ferrari F187/88C	1:57.37,530 h
3. Michele Alboreto	Ferrari F187/88C	1:57.58,306 h

Grand Prix, MEX, Mexico City, 29.5.1988
67 x 4,421 km = 296,207 km.

1. Alain Prost	McLaren MP4/4-Honda	1:30.15,737 h
2. Ayrton Senna	McLaren MP4/4-Honda	1:30.22,841 h
3. Gerhard Berger	Ferrari F187/88C	1:31.13,051 h

Grand Prix, CDN, Montreal, 12.6.1988
69 x 4,390 km = 302,910 km.

1. Ayrton Senna	McLaren MP4/4-Honda	1:39.46,618 h
2. Alain Prost	McLaren MP4/4-Honda	1:39.52,552 h
3. Thierry Boutsen	Benetton B188-Ford	1:40.38,027 h

Grand Prix, USA, Detroit, 19.6.1988
63 x 4,023 km = 253,449 km.

1. Ayrton Senna	McLaren MP4/4-Honda	1:54.56,035 h
2. Alain Prost	McLaren MP4/4-Honda	1:55.34,748 h
3. Thierry Boutsen	Benetton B188-Ford	-1

Grand Prix, F, Paul Ricard, 3.7.1988
80 x 3,813 km = 305,040 km.

1. Alain Prost	McLaren MP4/4-Honda	1:37.37,328 h
2. Ayrton Senna	McLaren MP4/4-Honda	1:38.09,080 h
3. Michele Alboreto	Ferrari F187/88C	1:38.43,833 h

Grand Prix, GB, Silverstone, 10.7.1988
65 x 4,778 km = 310,579 km.

1. Ayrton Senna	McLaren MP4/4-Honda	1:33.16,367 h
2. Nigel Mansell	Williams FW12-Judd	1:33.39,711 h
3. Alessandro Nannini	Benetton B188-Ford	1:34.07,581 h

Grand Prix, D, Hockenheim, 24.7.1988
44 x 6,797 km = 299,068 km.

1. Ayrton Senna	McLaren MP4/4-Honda	1:32.54,188 h
2. Alain Prost	McLaren MP4/4-Honda	1:33.07,797 h
3. Gerhard Berger	Ferrari F187/88C	1:33.46,283 h

Grand Prix, H, Hungaroring, 7.8.1988
76 x 4,014 km = 305,064 km.

1. Ayrton Senna	McLaren MP4/4-Honda	1:57.47,081 h
2. Alain Prost	McLaren MP4/4-Honda	1:57.47,610 h
3. Thierry Boutsen	Benetton B188-Ford	1:58.18,491 h

Grand Prix, B, Spa-Francorchamps, 28.6.1988
43 x 6,940 km = 298,420 km.

1. Ayrton Senna	McLaren MP4/4-Honda	1:28.00,549 h
2. Alain Prost	McLaren MP4/4-Honda	1:28.31,019 h
3. Ivan Capelli	March 881-Judd	1:29.16,317 h

Grand Prix, I, Monza, 11.9.1988
51 x 5,800 km = 295,800 km.

1. Gerhard Berger	Ferrari F187/88C	1:17.39,744 h
2. Michele Alboreto	Ferrari F187/88C	1:17.40,246 h
3. Eddie Cheever	Arrows A10B-BMW	1:18.15,276 h

Grand Prix, P, Estoril, 22.9.1988
70 x 4,350 km = 304,500 km.

1. Alain Prost	McLaren MP4/4-Honda	1:37.40,958 h
2. Ivan Capelli	March 881-Judd	1:37.50,511 h
3. Thierry Boutsen	Benetton B188-Ford	1:38.25,577 h

Grand Prix, E, Jerez, 2.10.1988
72 x 4,218 km = 303,696 km.

1. Alain Prost	McLaren MP4/4-Honda	1:48.43,851 h
2. Nigel Mansell	Williams FW12-Judd	1:49.10,083 h
3. Alessandro Nannini	Benetton B188-Ford	1:49.19,297 h

Grand Prix, J, Suzuka, 30.10.1988
51 x 5,859 km = 298,809 km.

1. Ayrton Senna	McLaren MP4/4-Honda	1:33.26,173 h
2. Alain Prost	McLaren MP4/4-Honda	1:33.39,536 h
3. Thierry Boutsen	Benetton B188-Ford	1:34.02,282 h

Grand Prix, AUS, Adelaide, 13.11.1988
82 x 3,780 km = 309,960 km.

1. Alain Prost	McLaren MP4/4-Honda	1:53.14,676 h
2. Ayrton Senna	McLaren MP4/4-Honda	1:53.51,463 h
3. Nelson Piquet	Lotus 100T-Honda	1:54.02,222 h

1988

1. A. Senna	90 P.	1. McLaren-Honda	99 P.
2. A. Prost	87 P.	2. Ferrari	65 P.
3. G. Berger	41 P.	3. Benetton-Ford	39 P.

1989

Grand Prix, BR, Rio de Janeiro, 26.3.1989
61 x 5,031 km = 306,891 km.

1. Nigel Mansell	Ferrari 640	1:38.58,744 h
2. Alain Prost	McLaren MP4/5-Honda	1:39.06,553 h
3. Mauricio Gugelmin	March 881-Judd	1:39.08,114 h

Grand Prix, RSM, Imola, 23.4.1989
58 x 5,040 km = 292,320 km.

1. Ayrton Senna	McLaren MP4/5-Honda	1:26.51,245 h
2. Alain Prost	McLaren MP4/5-Honda	1:27.31,517 h
3. Alessandro Nannini	Benetton B188-Ford	-1

Grand Prix, MC, Monte Carlo, 7.5.1989
77 x 3,328 km = 256,256 km.

1. Ayrton Senna	McLaren MP4/5-Honda	1:53.33,251 h
2. Alain Prost	McLaren MP4/5-Honda	1:54.25,780 h
3. Stefano Modena	Brabham BT58-Judd	-1

Grand Prix, MEX, Mexico City, 28.5.1989
69 x 4,421 km = 305,049 km.

1. Ayrton Senna	McLaren MP4/5-Honda	1:35.21,431 h
2. Riccardo Patrese	Williams FW12C-Ren.	1:35.36,991 h
3. Michele Alboreto	Tyrrell 018-Ford	1:35.52,685 h

Grand Prix, USA, Phoenix, 4.6.1989
75 x 3,798 km = 284,625 km.

1. Alain Prost	McLaren MP4/5-Honda	2:01.33,133 h
2. Riccardo Patrese	Williams FW12C-Ren.	2:02.12,829 h
3. Eddie Cheever	Arrows A11-Ford	2:02.16,343 h

Grand Prix, CDN, Montreal, 18.6.1989
69 x 4,390 km = 302,910 km.

1. Thierry Boutsen	Williams FW12C-Ren.	2:01.24,073 h
2. Riccardo Patrese	Williams FW12C-Ren.	2:01.54,080 h
3. Andrea de Cesaris	Dallara F189-Ford	2:03.00,722 h

Grand Prix, F, Paul Ricard, 9.7.1989
80 x 3,813 km = 305,040 km.

1. Alain Prost	McLaren MP4/5-Honda	1:38.29,411 h
2. Nigel Mansell	Ferrari 640	1:39.13,428 h
3. Riccardo Patrese	Williams FW12C-Ren.	1:39.36,332 h

Grand Prix, GB, Silverstone, 16.7.1989
64 x 4,780 km = 305,920 km.

1. Alain Prost	McLaren MP4/5-Honda	1:19.22,131 h
2. Nigel Mansell	Ferrari 640	1:19.41,500 h
3. Alessandro Nannini	Benetton B188-Ford	1:20.10,150 h

Grand Prix, D, Hockenheim, 30.7.1989
45 x 6,797 km = 305,865 km.

1. Ayrton Senna	McLaren MP4/5-Honda	1:21.43,302 h
2. Alain Prost	McLaren MP4/5-Honda	1:22.01,453 h
3. Nigel Mansell	Ferrari 640	1:23.06,556 h

Grand Prix, H, Hungaroring, 13.8.1989
77 x 3,968 km = 305,536 km.

1. Nigel Mansell	Ferrari 640	1:49.38,650 h
2. Ayrton Senna	McLaren MP4/5-Honda	1:50.04,617 h
3. Thierry Boutsen	Williams FW12C-Ren.	1:50.17,004 h

Grand Prix, B, Spa-Francorchamps, 27.8.1989
44 x 6,940 km = 305,360 km.

1. Ayrton Senna	McLaren MP4/5-Honda	1:40.54,196 h
2. Alain Prost	McLaren MP4/5-Honda	1:40.55,500 h
3. Nigel Mansell	Ferrari 640	1:40.56,020 h

Grand Prix, I, Monza, 10.9.1989
53 x 5,800 km = 307,400 km.

1. Alain Prost	McLaren MP4/5-Honda	1:19.27,550 h
2. Gerhard Berger	Ferrari 640	1:19.34,876 h
3. Thierry Boutsen	Williams FW12C-Ren.	1:19.42,525 h

Grand Prix, P, Estoril, 24.9.1989
71 x 4,350 km = 308,850 km.

1. Gerhard Berger	Ferrari 640	1:36.48,546 h
2. Alain Prost	McLaren MP4/5-Honda	1:37.21,183 h
3. Stefan Johansson	Onyx ORE1-Ford	1:37.48,871 h

Grand Prix, E, Jerez, 1.10.1989
73 x 4,218 km = 307,914 km.

1. Ayrton Senna	McLaren MP4/5-Honda	1:47.48,264 h
2. Gerhard Berger	Ferrari 640	1:48.15,315 h
3. Alain Prost	McLaren MP4/5-Honda	1:48.42,052 h

Grand Prix, J, Suzuka, 22.10.1989
53 x 5,859 km = 310,527 km.

1. Alessandro Nannini	Benetton B188-Ford	1:35.06,277 h
2. Riccardo Patrese	Williams FW13-Ren.	1:35.18,181 h
3. Thierry Boutsen	Williams FW13-Ren.	1:35.19,723 h

Grand Prix, AUS, Adelaide, 5.11.1989
70 x 3,780 km = 264,600 km.

1. Thierry Boutsen	Williams FW13-Ren.	2:00.17,421 h
2. Alessandro Nannini	Benetton B188-Ford	2:00.46,079 h
3. Riccardo Patrese	Williams FW13-Ren.	2:00.55,104 h

1989

1. A. Prost	76 P.	1. McLaren-Honda	141 P.
2. A. Senna	60 P.	2. Williams-Renault	65 P.
3. R. Patrese	40 P.	3. Ferrari	39 P.

1990

Grand Prix, USA, Phoenix, 11.3.1990
72 x 3,798 km = 273,456 km.

1. Ayrton Senna	McLaren MP4/5B-Honda	1:52.32,829 h
2. Jean Alesi	Tyrrell 018-Ford	1:52.41,514 h
3. Thierry Boutsen	Williams FW13B-Ren.	1:53.26,909 h

Grand Prix, BR, Interlagos, 25.3.1990
71 x 4,325 km = 307,075 km.

1. Alain Prost	Ferrari 641	1:37.21,258 h
2. Gerhard Berger	McLaren MP4/5B-Honda	1:37.34,822 h
3. Ayrton Senna	McLaren MP4/5B-Honda	1:37.58,980 h

Grand Prix, RSM, Imola, 13.5.1990
61 x 5,040 km = 307,440 km.

1. Riccardo Patrese	Williams FW13B-Ren.	1:30.55,478 h
2. Gerhard Berger	McLaren MP4/5B-Honda	1:31.00,595 h
3. Alessandro Nannini	Benetton B190-Ford	1:31.01,718 h

Grand Prix, MC, Monte Carlo, 27.5.1990
78 x 3,328 km = 259,584 km.

1. Ayrton Senna	McLaren MP4/5B-Honda	1:52.46,982 h
2. Jean Alesi	Tyrrell 018-Ford	1:52.48,069 h
3. Gerhard Berger	McLaren MP4/5B-Honda	1:52.49,055 h

Grand Prix, CDN, Montreal, 10.6.1990
70 x 4,390 km = 307,300 km.

1. Ayrton Senna	McLaren MP4/5B-Honda	1:42.56,400 h
2. Nelson Piquet	Benetton B190-Ford	1:43.06,897 h
3. Nigel Mansell	Ferrari 641/2	1:43.09,785 h

Grand Prix, MEX, Mexico City, 24.6.1990
69 x 4,421 km = 305,049 km.

1. Alain Prost	Ferrari 641/2	1:32.35,783 h
2. Nigel Mansell	Ferrari 641/2	1:33.01,134 h
3. Gerhard Berger	McLaren MP4/5B-Honda	1:33.01,313 h

Grand Prix, F, Paul Ricard, 8.7.1990
80 x 3,813 km = 305,040 km.

1. Alain Prost	Ferrari 641/2	1:33.29,606 h
2. Ivan Capelli	Leyton House-Judd 901	1:33.38,232 h
3. Ayrton Senna	McLaren MP4/5B-Honda	1:33.41,212 h

Grand Prix, GB, Silverstone, 15.7.1990
64 x 4,780 km = 305,920 km.

1. Alain Prost	Ferrari 641/2	1:18.30,999 h
2. Thierry Boutsen	Williams FW13B-Ren.	1:19.10,091 h
3. Ayrton Senna	McLaren MP4/5B-Honda	1:19.14,087 h

Grand Prix, D, Hockenheim, 29.7.1990
45 x 6,802 km = 306,090 km.

1. Ayrton Senna	McLaren MP4/5B-Honda	1:20.47,164 h
2. Alessandro Nannini	Benetton B190-Ford	1:20.53,684 h
3. Gerhard Berger	McLaren MP4/5B-Honda	1:20.55,717 h

Grand Prix, H, Hungaroring, 12.8.1990
77 x 3,968 km = 305,536 km.

1. Thierry Boutsen	Williams FW13B-Ren.	1:49.30,597 h
2. Ayrton Senna	McLaren MP4/5B-Honda	1:49.30,885 h
3. Nelson Piquet	Benetton B190-Ford	1:49.58,490 h

Grand Prix, B, Spa-Francorchamps, 25.8.1990
44 x 6,940 km = 305,360 km.

1. Ayrton Senna	McLaren MP4/5B-Honda	1:26.31,997 h
2. Alain Prost	Ferrari 641/2	1:26.35,547 h
3. Gerhard Berger	McLaren MP4/5B-Honda	1:27.00,459 h

Grand Prix, I, Monza, 9.9.1990
53 x 5,800 km = 307,400 km.

1. Ayrton Senna	McLaren MP4/5B-Honda	1:17.57,878 h
2. Alain Prost	Ferrari 641/2	1:18.03,932 h
3. Gerhard Berger	McLaren MP4/5B-Honda	1:18.05,282 h

Grand Prix, P, Estoril, 23.9.1990
61 x 4,350 km = 265,350 km.

1. Nigel Mansell	Ferrari 641/2	1:22.11,014 h
2. Ayrton Senna	McLaren MP4/5B-Honda	1:22.13,822 h
3. Alain Prost	Ferrari 641/2	1:22.15,203 h

Grand Prix, E, Jerez, 30.9.1990
73 x 4,218 km = 307,914 km.

1. Alain Prost	Ferrari 641/2	1:48.01,461 h
2. Nigel Mansell	Ferrari 641/2	1:48.23,525 h
3. Alessandro Nannini	Benetton B190-Ford	1:48.36,335 h

Grand Prix, J, Suzuka, 21.10.1990
53 x 5,859 km = 310,527 km.

1. Nelson Piquet	Benetton B190-Ford	1:34.36,824 h
2. Roberto Moreno	Benetton B190-Ford	1:34.44,047 h
3. Aguri Suzuki	Lola 90-Lamborghini	1:34.59,293 h

Grand Prix, AUS, Adelaide, 4.11.1990
81 x 3,780 km = 306,180 km.

1. Nelson Piquet	Benetton B190-Ford	1:49.44,570 h
2. Nigel Mansell	Ferrari 641/2	1:49.47,690 h
3. Alain Prost	Ferrari 641/2	1:50.21,829 h

1990

1. A. Senna	78 P.	1. McLaren-Honda	121 P.
2. A. Prost	71 P.	2. Ferrari	110 P.
3. G. Berger/N. Piquet	43 P.	3. Benetton-Ford	71 P.

GP 1991 – 1993

1991

Grand Prix, USA, Phoenix, 10.3.1991
81 x 3,721 km = 301,385 km.
1. Ayrton Senna — McLaren MP4/6-Honda 2:00.47,828 h
2. Alain Prost — Ferrari 642 2:01.04,150 h
3. Nelson Piquet — Benetton B190B-Ford 2:01.05,204 h

Grand Prix, BR, Interlagos, 24.3.1991
71 x 4,325 km = 301,401 km.
1. Ayrton Senna — McLaren MP4/6-Honda 1:38.28,128 h
2. Riccardo Patrese — Williams FW14-Renault 1:38.31,119 h
3. Gerhard Berger — McLaren MP4/6-Honda 1:38.35,544 h

Grand Prix, RSM, Imola, 28.4.1991
61 x 5,040 km = 307,440 km.
1. Ayrton Senna — McLaren MP4/6-Honda 1:35.14,750 h
2. Gerhard Berger — McLaren MP4/6-Honda 1:35.16,425 h
3. J. J. Lehto — Dallara F191-Judd -1

Grand Prix, MC, Monte Carlo, 12.5.1991
78 x 3,328 km = 259,584 km.
1. Ayrton Senna — McLaren MP4/6-Honda 1:53.02,334 h
2. Nigel Mansell — Williams FW14-Renault 1:53.20,684 h
3. Jean Alesi — Ferrari 642 1:53.49,789 h

Grand Prix, CDN, Montreal, 2.6.1991
69 x 4,430 km = 305,670 km.
1. Nelson Piquet — Benetton B191-Ford 1:38.51,490 h
2. Stefano Modena — Tyrrell 020-Honda 1:39.23,322 h
3. Riccardo Patrese — Williams FW14-Renault 1:39.33,707 h

Grand Prix, MEX, Mexico City, 16.6.1991
67 x 4,421 km = 296,207 km.
1. Riccardo Patrese — Williams FW14-Renault 1:29.52,205 h
2. Nigel Mansell — Williams FW14-Renault 1:29.53,541 h
3. Ayrton Senna — McLaren MP4/6-Honda 1:30.49,561 h

Grand Prix, F, Magny-Cours, 7.7.1991
72 x 4,271 km = 307,512 km.
1. Nigel Mansell — Williams FW14-Renault 1:38.00,056 h
2. Alain Prost — Ferrari 643 1:38.05,059 h
3. Ayrton Senna — McLaren MP4/6-Honda 1:38.34,990 h

Grand Prix, GB, Silverstone, 14.7.1991
59 x 5,226 km = 308,334 km.
1. Nigel Mansell — Williams FW14-Renault 1:27.35,479 h
2. Gerhard Berger — McLaren MP4/6-Honda 1:28.17,772 h
3. Alain Prost — Ferrari 643 1:28.35,629 h

Grand Prix, D, Hockenheim, 28.7.1991
45 x 6,802 km = 306,090 km.
1. Nigel Mansell — Williams FW14-Renault 1:19.29,661 h
2. Riccardo Patrese — Williams FW14-Renault 1:19.43,440 h
3. Jean Alesi — Ferrari 643 1:19.47,279 h

Grand Prix, H, Hungaroring, 11.8.1991
77 x 3,968 km = 605,536 km.
1. Ayrton Senna — McLaren MP4/6-Honda 1:49.12,796 h
2. Nigel Mansell — Williams FW14-Renault 1:49.17,395 h
3. Riccardo Patrese — Williams FW14-Renault 1:49.28,390 h

Grand Prix, B, Spa-Francorchamps, 25.8.1991
44 x 6,940 km = 305,360 km.
1. Ayrton Senna — McLaren MP4/6-Honda 1:27.17,669 h
2. Gerhard Berger — McLaren MP4/6-Honda 1:27.19,570 h
3. Nelson Piquet — Benetton B191-Ford 1:27.49,845 h

Grand Prix, I, Monza, 8.9.1991
53 x 5,800 km = 307,400 km.
1. Nigel Mansell — Williams FW14-Renault 1:17.54,319 h
2. Ayrton Senna — McLaren MP4/6-Honda 1:18.10,581 h
3. Alain Prost — Ferrari 643 1:18.11,148 h

Grand Prix, P, Estoril, 22.9.1991
71 x 4,350 km = 308,850 km.
1. Riccardo Patrese — Williams FW14-Renault 1:35.42,304 h
2. Ayrton Senna — McLaren MP4/6-Honda 1:36.03,245 h
3. Jean Alesi — Ferrari 643 1:36.35,858 h

Grand Prix, E, Catalunya, 29.9.1991
65 x 4,747 km = 308,555 km.
1. Nigel Mansell — Williams FW14-Renault 1:38.41,541 h
2. Alain Prost — Ferrari 643 1:38.52,872 h
3. Riccardo Patrese — Williams FW14-Renault 1:38.57,450 h

Grand Prix, J, Suzuka, 20.10.1991
53 x 5,864 km = 310,792 km.
1. Gerhard Berger — McLaren MP4/6-Honda 1:32.10,695 h
2. Ayrton Senna — McLaren MP4/6-Honda 1:32.11,039 h
3. Riccardo Patrese — Williams FW14-Renault 1:33.07,426 h

Grand Prix, AUS, Adelaide, 3.11.1991
14 x 3,780 km = 52,920 km.
1. Ayrton Senna — McLaren MP4/6-Honda 0:24.34,899 h
2. Nigel Mansell — Williams FW14-Renault 0:24.36,158 h
3. Gerhard Berger — McLaren MP4/6-Honda 0:24.40,019 h

1991

1. A. Senna	96 P.	1. McLaren-Honda	139 P.
2. N. Mansell	72 P.	2. Williams-Renault	125 P.
3. R. Patrese	53 P.	3. Ferrari	55,5 P.

1992

Grand Prix, ZA, Kyalami, 1.3.1992
72 x 4,261 km = 306,792 km.
1. Nigel Mansell — Williams FW14B-Ren. 1:38.00,056 h
2. Riccardo Patrese — Williams FW14B-Ren. 2:39.29,000 h
3. Ayrton Senna — McLaren MP4/6B-Honda 1:39.34,990 h

Grand Prix, MEX, Mexico City, 22.3.1992
69 x 4,421 km = 305,049 km.
1. Nigel Mansell — Williams FW14B-Ren. 1:31.53,587 h
2. Riccardo Patrese — Williams FW14B-Ren. 1:32.06,558 h
3. Michael Schumacher — Benetton B191B-Ford 1:32.15,016 h

Grand Prix, BR, Interlagos, 5.4.1992
71 x 4,325 km = 307,075 km.
1. Nigel Mansell — Williams FW14B-Ren. 1:36.51,856 h
2. Riccardo Patrese — Williams FW14B-Ren. 1:37.21,186 h
3. Michael Schumacher — Benetton B191B-Ford -1

Grand Prix, E, Catalunya, 3.5.1992
65 x 4,747 km = 308,555 km.
1. Nigel Mansell — Williams FW14B-Ren. 1:56.10,674 h
2. Michael Schumacher — Benetton B191B-Ford 1:56.34,588 h
3. Jean Alesi — Ferrari F92A 1:56.37,136 h

Grand Prix, RSM, Imola, 17.5.1992
60 x 5,040 km = 302,400 km.
1. Nigel Mansell — Williams FW14B-Ren. 1:28.40,927 h
2. Riccardo Patrese — Williams FW14B-Ren. 1:28.50,378 h
3. Ayrton Senna — McLaren MP4/7A-Honda 1:29.29,911 h

Grand Prix, MC, Monte Carlo, 31.5.1992
78 x 3,328 km = 259,584 km.
1. Ayrton Senna — McLaren MP4/7A-Honda 1:50.59,372 h
2. Nigel Mansell — Williams FW14B-Ren. 1:50.59,587 h
3. Riccardo Patrese — Williams FW14B-Ren. 1:51.31,215 h

Grand Prix, CDN, Montreal 14.6.1992
69 x 4,430 km = 305,670 km.
1. Gerhard Berger — McLaren MP4/7A-Honda 1:37.08,299 h
2. Michael Schumacher — Benetton B192-Ford 1:37.20,700 h
3. Jean Alesi — Ferrari F92A 1:38.15,626 h

Grand Prix, F, Magny-Cours, 5.7.1992
69 x 4,250 km = 293,250 km.
1. Nigel Mansell — Williams FW14B-Ren. 1:38.08,459 h
2. Riccardo Patrese — Williams FW14B-Ren. 1:38.54,906 h
3. Martin Brundle — Benetton B192-Ford 1:39.21,038 h

Grand Prix, GB, Silverstone, 12.7.1992
59 x 5,226 km = 308,334 km.
1. Nigel Mansell — Williams FW14B-Ren. 1:25.42,991 h
2. Riccardo Patrese — Williams FW14B-Ren. 1:26.22,085 h
3. Martin Brundle — Benetton B192-Ford 1:26.31,386 h

Grand Prix, D, Hockenheim, 26.7.1992
45 x 6,815 km = 306,675 km.
1. Nigel Mansell — Williams FW14B-Ren. 1:18.22,032 h
2. Ayrton Senna — McLaren MP4/7A-Honda 1:18.26,532 h
3. Michael Schumacher — Benetton B192-Ford 1:18.56,494 h

Grand Prix, H, Hungaroring, 16.8.1992
77 x 3,968 km = 305,536 km.
1. Ayrton Senna — McLaren MP4/7A-Honda 1:46.19,216 h
2. Nigel Mansell — Williams FW14B-Ren. 1:46.59,355 h
3. Gerhard Berger — McLaren MP4/7A-Honda 1:47.09,998 h

Grand Prix, B, Spa-Francorchamps, 30.8.1992
44 x 6,974 km = 306,856 km.
1. Michael Schumacher — Benetton B192-Ford 1:36.10,721 h
2. Nigel Mansell — Williams FW14B-Ren. 1:36.47,316 h
3. Riccardo Patrese — Williams FW14B-Ren. 1:36.54,618 h

Grand Prix, I, Monza, 13.9.1992
53 x 5,800 km = 307,400 km.
1. Ayrton Senna — McLaren MP4/7A-Honda 1:18.15,349 h
2. Martin Brundle — Benetton B192-Ford 1:18.32,399 h
3. Michael Schumacher — Benetton B192-Ford 1:18.39,722 h

Grand Prix, P, Estoril, 27.9.1992
71 x 4,350 km = 308,850 km.
1. Nigel Mansell — Williams FW14B-Ren. 1:34.46,659 h
2. Gerhard Berger — McLaren MP4/7A-Honda 1:35.24,192 h
3. Ayrton Senna — McLaren MP4/7A-Honda -1

Grand Prix, J, Suzuka, 25.10.1992
53 x 5,864 km = 310,792 km.
1. Riccardo Patrese — Williams FW14B-Ren. 1:33.09,553 h
2. Gerhard Berger — McLaren MP4/7A-Honda 1:33.23,282 h
3. Martin Brundle — Benetton B192-Ford 1:34.25,056 h

Grand Prix, AUS, Adelaide, 8.11.1992
81 x 3,780 km = 306,180 km.
1. Gerhard Berger — McLaren MP4/7A-Honda 1:46.54,786 h
2. Michael Schumacher — Benetton B192-Ford 1:46.55,527 h
3. Martin Brundle — Benetton B192-Ford 1:47.48,942 h

1992

1. N. Mansell	108 P.	1. Williams-Renault	164 P.
2. R. Patrese	56 P.	2. McLaren-Honda	99 P.
3. M. Schumacher	53 P.	3. Benetton-Ford	91 P.

1993

Grand Prix, ZA, Kyalami, 14.3.1993
72 x 4,261 km = 306,792 km.
1. Alain Prost — Williams FW15C-Ren. 1:38.45,082 h
2. Ayrton Senna — McLaren MP4/8-Ford 1:40.04,906 h
3. Mark Blundell — Ligier JS39-Renault -1

Grand Prix, BR, Interlagos, 28.3.1993
71 x 4,325 km = 307,075 km.
1. Ayrton Senna — McLaren MP4/8-Ford 1:51.15,485 h
2. Damon Hill — Williams FW15C-Ren. 1:51.32,110 h
3. Michael Schumacher — Benetton B193-Ford 1:52.00,921 h

Grand Prix, EU, Donington Park, 11.4.1993
76 x 4,023 km = 305,748 km.
1. Ayrton Senna — McLaren MP4/8-Ford 1:50.46,570 h
2. Damon Hill — Williams FW15C-Ren. 1:52.09,769 h
3. Alain Prost — Williams FW15C-Ren. -1

Grand Prix, RSM, Imola, 25.4.1993
61 x 5,040 km = 307,440 km.
1. Alain Prost — Williams FW15C-Ren. 1:33.20,413 h
2. Michael Schumacher — Benetton B193-Ford 1:33.52,823 h
3. Martin Brundle — Ligier JS39-Renault -1

Grand Prix, E, Catalunya, 9.5.1993
65 x 4,747 km = 308,555 km.
1. Alain Prost — Williams FW15C-Ren. 1:32.27,685 h
2. Ayrton Senna — McLaren MP4/8-Ford 1:32.44,558 h
3. Michael Schumacher — Benetton B193-Ford 1:32.54,810 h

Grand Prix, MC, Monte Carlo, 23.5.1993
78 x 3,328 km = 259,584 km.
1. Ayrton Senna — McLaren MP4/8-Ford 1:52.10,974 h
2. Damon Hill — Williams FW15C-Ren. 1:53.03,065 h
3. Jean Alesi — Ferrari F93A 1:53.14,309 h

Grand Prix, CDN, Montreal, 13.6.1993
69 x 4,430 km = 305,670 km.
1. Alain Prost — Williams FW15C-Ren. 1:36.41,822 h
2. Michael Schumacher — Benetton B193B-Ford 1:36.56,349 h
3. Damon Hill — Williams FW15C-Ren. 1:37.34,507 h

Grand Prix, F, Magny-Cours, 4.7.1993
72 x 4,250 km = 306,000 km.
1. Alain Prost — Williams FW15C-Ren. 1:38.35,241 h
2. Damon Hill — Williams FW15C-Ren. 1:38.55,583 h
3. Michael Schumacher — Benetton B193B-Ford 1:38.56,450 h

Grand Prix, GB, Silverstone, 11.7.1993
59 x 3,247 km = 191,573 km.
1. Alain Prost — Williams FW15C-Ren. 1:25.38,189 h
2. Michael Schumacher — Benetton B193B-Ford 1:25.45,849 h
3. Riccardo Patrese — Benetton B193B-Ford 1:26.55,671 h

Grand Prix, D, Hockenheim, 25.7.1993
45 x 6,185 km = 306,675 km.
1. Alain Prost — Williams FW15C-Ren. 1:18.40,885 h
2. Michael Schumacher — Benetton B193B-Ford 1:18.57,549 h
3. Mark Blundell — Ligier JS39-Renault 1:19.40,234 h

Grand Prix, H, Hungaroring, 15.8.1993
77 x 3,968 km = 305,536 km.
1. Damon Hill — Williams FW15C-Ren. 1:47.39,098 h
2. Riccardo Patrese — Benetton B193B-Ford 1:48.51,013 h
3. Gerhard Berger — Ferrari F93A 1:48.57,140 h

Grand Prix, B, Spa-Francorchamps, 29.8.1993
44 x 6,974 km = 306,856 km.
1. Damon Hill — Williams FW15C-Ren. 1:24.32,124 h
2. Michael Schumacher — Benetton B193B-Ford 1:24.35,792 h
3. Alain Prost — Williams FW15C-Ren. 1:24.47,112 h

Grand Prix, I, Monza, 12.9.1993
53 x 5,800 km = 307,400 km.
1. Damon Hill — Williams FW15C-Ren. 1:24.32,124 h
2. Jean Alesi — Ferrari F93A 2:39.29,000 h
3. Michael Andretti — McLaren MP4/8-Ford -1

Grand Prix, P, Estoril, 26.9.1993
71 x 4,350 km = 308,850 km.
1. Michael Schumacher — Benetton B193B-Ford 1:32.46,309 h
2. Alain Prost — Williams FW15C-Ren. 1:32.47,291 h
3. Damon Hill — Williams FW15C-Ren. 1:32.54,914 h

Grand Prix, J, Suzuka, 24.10.1993
53 x 5,864 km = 310,792 km.
1. Ayrton Senna — McLaren MP4/8-Ford 1:40.27,912 h
2. Alain Prost — Williams FW15C-Ren. 1:40.39,347 h
3. Mika Häkkinen — McLaren MP4/8-Ford 1:40.54,041 h

Grand Prix, AUS, Adelaide, 7.11.1993
79 x 3,780 km = 298,620 km.
1. Ayrton Senna — McLaren MP4/8-Ford 1:43.27,476 h
2. Alain Prost — Williams FW15C-Ren. 1:43.36,735 h
3. Damon Hill — Williams FW15C-Ren. 1:44.01,378 h

1993

1. Prost	99 P.	1. Williams-Renault	168 P.
2. Senna	73 P.	2. McLaren-Ford	84 P.
3. Hill	69 P.	3. Benetton-Ford	72 P.

1994

Grand Prix, BR, Interlagos, 27.3.1994
71 x 4,325 km = 307,075 km.

1. Michael Schumacher – Benetton B194-Ford – 1:35.38,759 h
2. Damon Hill – Williams FW16-Renault – -1
3. Jean Alesi – Ferrari 412T1 – -1

Pacific Grand Prix, Aida, 17.4.1994
83 x 3,703 km = 307,349 km.

1. Michael Schumacher – Benetton B194-Ford – 1:46.01,693 h
2. Gerhard Berger – Ferrari 412T1 – 1:47.16,993 h
3. Rubens Barrichello – Jordan 194-Hart – -1

Grand Prix, RSM, Imola, 1.5.1994
58 x 5,040 km = 292,320 km.

1. Michael Schumacher – Benetton B194-Ford – 1:28.28,642 h
2. Nicola Larini – Ferrari 412T1 – 1:29.23,584 h
3. Mika Häkkinen – McLaren MP4/9-Peug. – 1:29.39,321 h

Grand Prix, MC, Monte Carlo, 15.5.1994
78 x 3,328 km = 259,584 km.

1. Michael Schumacher – Benetton B194-Ford – 1:49.55,372 h
2. Martin Brundle – McLaren MP4/9-Peug. – 1:50.32,650 h
3. Gerhard Berger – Ferrari 412T1 – 1:51.12,196 h

Grand Prix, E, Catalunya, 29.5.1994
65 x 4,747 km = 308,555 km.

1. Damon Hill – Williams FW16-Renault – 1:36.14,374 h
2. Michael Schumacher – Benetton B194-Ford – 1:36.38,540 h
3. Mark Blundell – Tyrrell 022-Yamaha – 1:37.41,343 h

Grand Prix, CDN, Montreal, 12.6.1994
69 x 4,450 km = 307,050 km.

1. Michael Schumacher – Benetton B194-Ford – 1:44.31,887 h
2. Damon Hill – Williams FW16-Renault – 1:45.11,547 h
3. Jean Alesi – Ferrari 412T1 – 1:45.45,275 h

Grand Prix, F, Magny-Cours, 3.7.1994
72 x 4,250 km = 306,000 km.

1. Michael Schumacher – Benetton B194-Ford – 1:38.35,704 h
2. Damon Hill – Williams FW16-Renault – 1:38.48,346 h
3. Gerhard Berger – Ferrari 412T1B – 1:39.28,469 h

Grand Prix, GB, Silverstone, 10.7.1994
60 x 5,057 km = 303,420 km.

1. Damon Hill – Williams FW16-Renault – 1:30.03,640 h
2. Jean Alesi – Ferrari 412T1B – 1:31.11,768 h
3. Mika Häkkinen – McLaren MP4/9-Peug. – 1:31.44,299 h

Grand Prix, D, Hockenheim, 31.7.1994
45 x 6,823 km = 307,035 km.

1. Gerhard Berger – Ferrari 412T1B – 1:22.37,272 h
2. Olivier Panis – Ligier JS39B-Renault – 1:23.32,051 h
3. Eric Bernard – Ligier JS39B-Renault – 1:23.42,314 h

Grand Prix, H, Hungaroring, 14.8.1994
77 x 3,968 km = 305,536 km.

1. Michael Schumacher – Benetton B194-Ford – 1:48.00,185 h
2. Damon Hill – Williams FW16-Renault – 1:48.21,012 h
3. Jos Verstappen – Benetton B194-Ford – 1:49.10,514 h

Grand Prix, B, Spa-Francorchamps, 28.8.1994
44 x 7,001 km = 308,044 km.

1. Damon Hill – Williams FW16-Renault – 1:28.47,170 h
2. Mika Häkkinen – McLaren MP4/9-Peug. – 1:29.38,551 h
3. Jos Verstappen – Benetton B194-Ford – 1:29.57,623 h

Grand Prix, I, Monza, 11.9.1994
53 x 5,800 km = 307,400 km.

1. Damon Hill – Williams FW16-Renault – 1:18.02,754 h
2. Gerhard Berger – Ferrari 412T1B – 1:18.07,684 h
3. Mika Häkkinen – McLaren MP4/9-Peug. – 1:18.28,394 h

Grand Prix, P, Estoril, 25.9.1994
71 x 4,360 km = 309,560 km.

1. Damon Hill – Williams FW16-Renault – 1:41.10,165 h
2. David Coulthard – Williams FW16-Renault – 1:41.10,768 h
3. Mika Häkkinen – McLaren MP4/9-Peug. – 1:41.30,358 h

Grand Prix, EU, Jerez, 16.10.1994
69 x 4,428 km = 305,532 km.

1. Michael Schumacher – Benetton B194-Ford – 1:40.26,689 h
2. Damon Hill – Williams FW16-Renault – 1:40.51,378 h
3. Mika Häkkinen – McLaren MP4/9-Peug. – 1:41.36,337 h

Grand Prix, J, Suzuka, 6.11.1994
50 x 5,864 km = 293,200 km.

1. Damon Hill – Williams FW16-Renault – 1:55.53,532 h
1. Michael Schumacher – Benetton B194-Ford – 1:55.56,897 h
3. Jean Alesi – Ferrari 412T1B – 1:56.45,577 h

Grand Prix, AUS, Adelaide, 13.11.1994
81 x 3,780 km = 306,180 km.

1. Nigel Mansell – Williams FW16-Renault – 1:47.51,480 h
2. Gerhard Berger – Ferrari 412T1B – 1:47.53,991 h
3. Martin Brundle – McLaren MP4/9-Peug. – 1:48.43,967 h

1994

1. M. Schumacher	92 P.	1. Williams-Renault	118 P.
2. D. Hill	91 P.	2. Benetton-Ford	103 P.
3. G. Berger	41 P.	3. Ferrari	71 P.

1995

Grand Prix, BR, Interlagos, 26.3.1995
71 x 4,325 km = 307,075 km.

1. Michael Schumacher – Benetton B195-Renault – 1:38.34,154 h
2. David Coulthard – Williams FW17-Renault – 1:38.42,214 h
3. Gerhard Berger – Ferrari 412T2 – -1

Grand Prix, RA, Buenos Aires, 9.4.1995
72 x 4,259 km = 306,684 km.

1. Damon Hill – Williams FW17-Renault – 1:53.14,532 h
2. Jean Alesi – Ferrari 412T2 – 1:53.20,939 h
3. Michael Schumacher – Benetton B195-Renault – 1:53.47,908 h

Grand Prix, RSM, Imola, 30.4.1995
63 x 4,892 km = 308,196 km.

1. Damon Hill – Williams FW17-Renault – 1:41.42,552 h
2. Jean Alesi – Ferrari 412T2 – 1:42.01,062 h
3. Gerhard Berger – Ferrari 412T2 – 1:42.25,668 h

Grand Prix, E, Catalunya, 14.5.1995
65 x 4,727 km = 307,225 km.

1. Michael Schumacher – Benetton B195-Renault – 1:34.20,507 h
2. Johnny Herbert – Benetton B195-Renault – 1:35.12,495 h
3. Gerhard Berger – Ferrari 412T2 – 1:35.25,744 h

Grand Prix, MC, Monte Carlo, 28.5.1995
78 x 3,328 km = 259,584 km.

1. Michael Schumacher – Benetton B195-Renault – 1:53.11,258 h
2. Damon Hill – Williams FW17-Renault – 1:53.46,075 h
3. Gerhard Berger – Ferrari 412T2 – 1:54.22,075 h

Grand Prix, CDN, Montreal, 11.6.1995
68 x 4,430 km = 301,240 km.

1. Jean Alesi – Ferrari 412T2 – 1:46.31,333 h
2. Rubens Barrichello – Jordan 195-Peugeot – 1:47.03,020 h
3. Eddie Irvine – Jordan 195-Peugeot – 1:47.04,603 h

Grand Prix, F, Magny-Cours, 2.7.1995
72 x 4,250 km = 306,000 km.

1. Michael Schumacher – Benetton B195-Renault – 1:38.28,429 h
2. Damon Hill – Williams FW17-Renault – 1:38.59,738 h
3. David Coulthard – Williams FW17-Renault – 1:39.31,255 h

Grand Prix, GB, Silverstone, 16.7.1995
61 x 5,057 km = 308,477 km.

1. Johnny Herbert – Benetton B195-Renault – 1:34.35,093 h
2. Jean Alesi – Ferrari 412T2 – 1:34.51,572 h
3. David Coulthard – Williams FW17-Renault – 1:34.58,981 h

Grand Prix, D, Hockenheim, 30.7.1995
45 x 6,823 km = 307,035 km.

1. Michael Schumacher – Benetton B195-Renault – 1:22.56,043 h
2. David Coulthard – Williams FW17-Renault – 1:23.02,031 h
3. Gerhard Berger – Ferrari 412T2 – 1:24.04,140 h

Grand Prix, H, Hungaroring, 13.8.1995
77 x 3,968 km = 305,536 km.

1. Damon Hill – Williams FW17-Renault – 1:46.25,721 h
2. David Coulthard – Williams FW17-Renault – 1:46.59,119 h
3. Gerhard Berger – Ferrari 412T2 – -1

Grand Prix, B, Spa-Francorchamps, 27.8.1995
44 x 6,974 km = 306,856 km.

1. Michael Schumacher – Benetton B195-Renault – 1:36.47,875 h
2. Damon Hill – Williams FW17-Renault – 1:37.07,368 h
3. Martin Brundle – Ligier JS 41 – 1:37.12,873 h

Grand Prix, I, Monza, 10.9.1995
53 x 5,770 km = 305,810 km.

1. Johnny Herbert – Benetton B195-Renault – 1:18.27,961 h
2. Mika Häkkinen – McLaren MP4/10B-Merc. – 1:18.45,695 h
3. Heinz-Harald Frentzen – Sauber C14-Ford – 1:18.52,237 h

Grand Prix, P, Estoril, 24.9.1995
71 x 4,360 km = 309,560 km.

1. David Coulthard – Williams FW17-Renault – 1:41.52,145 h
2. Michael Schumacher – Benetton B195-Renault – 1:41.59,393 h
3. Damon Hill – Williams FW17-Renault – 1:42.14,266 h

Grand Prix, EU, Nürburgring, 1.10.1995
67 x 4,556 km = 305,252 km.

1. Michael Schumacher – Benetton B195-Renault – 1:39.59,044 h
2. Jean Alesi – Ferrari 412T2 – 1:40.01,728 h
3. David Coulthard – Williams FW17-Renault – 1:40.34,426 h

Pacific Grand Prix, Aida, 22.10.1995
83 x 3,703 km = 307,349 km.

1. Michael Schumacher – Benetton B195-Renault – 1:48.49,972 h
2. David Coulthard – Williams FW17-Renault – 1:49.04,892 h
3. Damon Hill – Williams FW17-Renault – 1:49.38,305 h

Grand Prix, J, Suzuka, 29.10.1995
53 x 5,864 km = 310,792 km.

1. Michael Schumacher – Benetton B195-Renault – 1:36.52,930 h
2. Mika Häkkinen – McLarenMP4/10B-Merc. – 1:37.12,267 h
3. Johnny Herbert – Benetton B195-Renault – 1:37.16,734 h

Grand Prix, AUS, Adelaide, 12.11.1995
81 x 3,780 km = 306,180 km.

1. Damon Hill – Williams FW17-Renault – 1:49.38,305 h
2. Olivier Panis – Ligier JS41-Honda – -2
3. Gianni Morbidelli – Footwork FA16-Hart – -2

1995

1. M. Schumacher	102 P.	1. Benetton-Renault	137 P.
2. D. Hill	69 P.	2. Williams-Renault	112 P.
3. D. Coulthard	49 P.	3. Ferrari	73 P.

1996

Grand Prix, AUS, Melbourne, 10.3.1996
58 x 5,302 km = 307,516 km.

1. Damon Hill – Williams FW18-Renault – 1:32.50,491 h
2. Jacques Villeneuve – Williams FW18-Renault – 1:33.28,511 h
3. Eddie Irvine – Ferrari F310 – 1:33.53,062 h

Grand Prix, BR, Interlagos, 31.3.1996
71 x 4,325 km = 307,075 km.

1. Damon Hill – Williams FW18-Renault – 1:49.52,976 h
2. Jean Alesi – Benetton B196-Renault – 1:50.10,958 h
3. Michael Schumacher – Ferrari F310 – -1

Grand Prix, RA, Buenos Aires, 7.4.1996
72 x 4,259 km = 306,648 km.

1. Damon Hill – Williams FW18-Renault – 1:54.55,322 h
2. Jacques Villeneuve – Williams FW18-Renault – 1:55.07,489 h
3. Jean Alesi – Benetton B196-Renault – 1:55.10,076 h

Grand Prix, EU, Nürburgring, 28.4.1996
67 x 4,556 km = 305,252 km.

1. Jacques Villeneuve – Williams FW18-Renault – 1:33.26,473 h
2. Michael Schumacher – Ferrari F310 – 1:33.27,235 h
3. David Coulthard – McLaren MP4/11-Merc. – 1:33.59,307 h

Grand Prix, RSM, Imola, 5.5.1996
63 x 4,892 km = 308,196 km.

1. Damon Hill – Williams FW18-Renault – 1:35.26,156 h
2. Michael Schumacher – Ferrari F310 – 1:35.42,616 h
3. Gerhard Berger – Benetton B196-Renault – 1:36.13,047 h

Grand Prix, MC, Monte Carlo, 19.5.1996
75 x 3,328 km = 249,600 km.

1. Olivier Panis – Ligier JS43-Mugen – 2:00.45,629 h
2. David Coulthard – McLaren MP4/11-Merc. – 2:00.50,457 h
3. Johnny Herbert – Sauber C15-Ford – 2:01.23,132 h

Grand Prix, E, Catalunya, 2.6.1996
65 x 4,727 km = 307,225 km.

1. Michael Schumacher – Ferrari F310 – 1:59.49,307 h
2. Jean Alesi – Benetton B196-Renault – 2:00.34,609 h
3. Jacques Villeneuve – Williams FW18-Renault – 2:00.37,695 h

Grand Prix, CDN, Montreal, 16.6.1996
69 x 4,421 km = 305,049 km.

1. Damon Hill – Williams FW18-Renault – 1:36.03,465 h
2. Jacques Villeneuve – Williams FW18-Renault – 1:36.07,648 h
3. Jean Alesi – Benetton B196-Renault – 1:36.58,121 h

Grand Prix, F, Magny-Cours, 30.6.1996
72 x 4,250 km = 306,000 km.

1. Damon Hill – Williams FW18-Renault – 1:36.28,795 h
2. Jacques Villeneuve – Williams FW18-Renault – 1:36.36,922 h
3. Jean Alesi – Benetton B196-Renault – 1:37.15,237 h

Grand Prix, GB, Silverstone, 14.7.1996
61 x 5,072 km = 309,392 km.

1. Jacques Villeneuve – Williams FW18-Renault – 1:33.00,874 h
2. Gerhard Berger – Benetton B196-Renault – 1:33.19,600 h
3. Mika Häkkinen – McLaren MP4/11B-Merc. – 1:33.51,704 h

Grand Prix, D, Hockenheim, 28.7.1996
45 x 6,823 km = 307,035 km.

1. Damon Hill – Williams FW18-Renault – 1:21.43,417 h
2. Jean Alesi – Benetton B196-Renault – 1:21.54,869 h
3. Jacques Villeneuve – Williams FW18-Renault – 1:22.17,343 h

Grand Prix, H, Hungaroring, 11.8.1996
77 x 3,968 km = 305,536 km.

1. Jacques Villeneuve – Williams FW18-Renault – 1:46.21,143 h
2. Damon Hill – Williams FW18-Renault – 1:46.21,905 h
3. Jean Alesi – Benetton B196-Renault – 1:47.45,346 h

Grand Prix, B, Spa-Francorchamps, 25.8.1996
44 x 6,968 km = 306,592 km.

1. Michael Schumacher – Ferrari F310 – 1:28.15,125 h
2. Jacques Villeneuve – Williams FW18-Renault – 1:28.20,727 h
3. Mika Häkkinen – McLarenMP4/11B-Merc. – 1:28.30,835 h

Grand Prix, I, Monza, 8.9.1996
53 x 5,770 km = 305,810 km.

1. Michael Schumacher – Ferrari F310 – 1:17.43,632 h
2. Jean Alesi – Benetton B196-Renault – 1:18.01,897 h
3. Mika Häkkinen – McLarenMP4/11B-Merc. – 1:18.50,267 h

Grand Prix, P, Estoril, 22.9.1996
70 x 4,360 km = 305,200 km.

1. Jacques Villeneuve – Williams FW18-Renault – 1:40.29,915 h
2. Damon Hill – Williams FW18-Renault – 1:40.42,881 h
3. Michael Schumacher – Ferrari F310 – 1:41.16,680 h

Grand Prix, J, Suzuka, 13.10.1996
52 x 5,864 km = 304,718 km.

1. Damon Hill – Williams FW18-Renault – 1:32.33,791 h
2. Mika Häkkinen – McLarenMP4/11B-Merc. – 1:32.35,674 h
3. Michael Schumacher – Ferrari F310 – 1:32.37,003 h

1996

1. D. Hill	97 P.	1. Williams-Renault	175 P.
2. J. Villeneuve	78 P.	2. Ferrari	70 P.
3. M. Schumacher	59 P.	3. Benetton-Renault	68 P.

GP 1997 – 1999

1997

Grand Prix, AUS, Melbourne, 9.3.1997
58 x 5,302 km = 307,516 km.
1. David Coulthard   McLaren MP4/12A-Mer. 1:30.28,718 h
2. Michael Schumacher   Ferrari F310B   1:30.48,764 h
3. Mika Häkkinen   McLaren MP4/12A-Mer. 1:30.50,895 h

Grand Prix, BR, Interlagos, 30.3.1997
72 x 4,292 km = 309,024 km.
1. Jacques Villeneuve   Williams FW19-Renault 1:36.06,990 h
2. Gerhard Berger   Benetton B197-Renault 1:36.11,180 h
3. Olivier Panis   Prost JS45-Mugen   1:36.22,860 h

Grand Prix, RA, Buenos Aires, 13.4.1997
72 x 4,259 km = 306,648 km.
1. Jacques Villeneuve   Williams FW19-Renault 1:52.01,715 h
2. Eddie Irvine   Ferrari F310B   1:52.02,694 h
3. Ralf Schumacher   Jordan 197-Peugeot   1:52.13,804 h

Grand Prix, RSM, Imola, 27.4.1997
62 x 4,930 km = 305,660 km.
1. Heinz-Harald Frentzen Williams FW19-Renault 1:31.00,673 h
2. Michael Schumacher   Ferrari F310B   1:31.01,910 h
3. Eddie Irvine   Ferrari F310B   1:32.19,016 h

Grand Prix, MC, Monte Carlo, 11.5.1997
62 x 3,367 km = 208,754 km.
1. Michael Schumacher   Ferrari F310B   2:00.05,654 h
2. Rubens Barrichello   Stewart SF1-Ford   2:00.58,960 h
3. Eddie Irvine   Ferrari F310B   2:01.27,762 h

Grand Prix, E, Barcelona, 25.5.1997
64 x 4,728 km = 302,592 km.
1. Jacques Villeneuve   Williams FW19-Renault 1:30.35,896 h
2. Olivier Panis   Prost JS45-Mugen   1:30.41,700 h
3. Jean Alesi   Benetton B197-Renault 1:30.48,430 h

Grand Prix, CDN, Montreal, 15.6.1997
54 x 4,421 km = 238,734 km.
1. Michael Schumacher   Ferrari F310B   1:17.40,646 h
2. Jean Alesi   Benetton B197-Renault 1:17.43,211 h
3. Giancarlo Fisichella Jordan 197-Peugeot   1:17.43,865 h

Grand Prix, F, Magny-Cours, 29.6.1997
72 x 4,250 km = 306,000 km.
1. Michael Schumacher   Ferrari F310B   1:38.50,492 h
2. Heinz-Harald Frentzen Williams FW19-Renault 1:39.14,029 h
3. Eddie Irvine   Ferrari F310B   1:40.05,293 h

Grand Prix, GB, Silverstone, 13.7.1997
59 x 5,140 km = 303,260 km.
1. Jacques Villeneuve   Williams FW19-Renault 1:28.01,665 h
2. Jean Alesi   Benetton B197-Renault 1:28.11,870 h
3. Alexander Wurz   Benetton B197-Renault 1:28.12,961 h

Grand Prix, D, Hockenheim, 27.7.1997
45 x 6,823 km = 307,035 km.
1. Gerhard Berger   Benetton B197-Renault 1:20.59,064 h
2. Michael Schumacher   Ferrari F310B   1:21.16,573 h
3. Mika Häkkinen   McLaren MP4/12A-Mer. 1:21.23,816 h

Grand Prix, H, Hungaroring, 10.8.1997
77 x 3,968 km = 305,536 km.
1. Jacques Villeneuve   Williams FW19-Renault 1:45.47,149 h
2. Damon Hill   Arrows A18-Yamaha   1:45.56,228 h
3. Johnny Herbert   Sauber C16-Petronas   1:46.07,594 h

Grand Prix, B, Spa-Francorchamps, 24.8.1997
44 x 6,968 km = 306,592 km.
1. Michael Schumacher   Ferrari F310B   1:33.46,717 h
2. Giancarlo Fisichella Jordan197-Peugeot   1:34.13,470 h
3. Heinz-Harald Frentzen Williams FW19-Renault 1:34.18,864 h

Grand Prix, I, Monza, 7.9.1997
53 x 5,770 km = 305,810 km.
1. David Coulthard   McLaren MP4/12A-Mer. 1:17.04,609 h
2. Jean Alesi   Benetton B197-Renault 1:17.06,546 h
3. Heinz-Harald Frentzen Williams FW19-Renault 1:17.08,952 h

Grand Prix, A, A1-Ring, 21.9.1997
71 x 4,319 km = 306,649 km.
1. Jacques Villeneuve   Williams FW19-Renault 1:27.35,999 h
2. David Coulthard   McLaren MP4/12A-Mer. 1:27.38,908 h
3. Heinz-Harald Frentzen Williams FW19-Renault 1:27.39,961 h

Grand Prix, L, Nürburgring, 28.9.1997
67 x 4,556 km = 305,252 km.
1. Jacques Villeneuve   Williams FW19-Renault 1:31.27,843 h
2. Jean Alesi   Benetton B197-Renault 1:31.39,613 h
3. Heinz-Harald Frentzen Williams FW19-Renault 1:31.41,323 h

Grand Prix, J, Suzuka, 12.10.1997
53 x 5,864 km = 310,792 km.
1. Michael Schumacher   Ferrari F310B   1:29.48,446 h
2. Heinz-Harald Frentzen Williams FW19-Renault 1:29.49,824 h
3. Eddie Irvine   Ferrari F310B   1:30.14,830 h

Grand Prix, EU, Jerez, 26.10.1997
69 x 4,428 km = 305,532 km.
1. Mika Häkkinen   McLaren MP4/12A-Mer. 1:38.57,771 h
2. David Coulthard   McLaren MP4/12A-Mer. 1:38.59,425 h
3. Jacques Villeneuve   Williams FW19-Renault 1:38.59,574 h

1997

1. J. Villeneuve 81 P.   1. Williams-Renault   123 P.
2. H.-H. Frentzen 42 P.   2. Ferrari   102 P.
3. D. Coulthard   36 P.   3. Benetton-Renault   67 P.

1998

Grand Prix, AUS, Melbourne, 8.3.1998
58 x 5,302 km = 307,516 km.
1. Mika Häkkinen   McLaren MP4/13-Mer. 1:31.45,996 h
2. David Coulthard   McLaren MP4/13-Mer. 1:31.46,698 h
3. Heinz-Harald Frentzen Williams FW20-Meca. 1:31.54,664 h

Grand Prix, BR, Interlagos, 29.3.1998
72 x 4,292 km = 309,024 km.
1. Mika Häkkinen   McLaren MP4/13-Mer. 1:37.11,747 h
2. David Coulthard   McLaren MP4/13-Mer. 1:37.12,849 h
3. Michael Schumacher   Ferrari F300   1:38.12,297 h

Grand Prix, RA, Buenos Aires, 12.4.1998
72 x 4,295 km = 309,240 km.
1. Michael Schumacher   Ferrari F300   1:48.36,175 h
2. Mika Häkkinen   McLaren MP4/13-Mer. 1:48.59,073 h
3. Eddie Irvine   Ferrari F300   1:49.33,920 h

Grand Prix, RSM, Imola, 26.4.1998
62 x 4,930 km = 305,660 km.
1. David Coulthard   McLaren MP4/13-Mer. 1:34.24,593 h
2. Michael Schumacher   Ferrari F300   1:34.29,147 h
3. Eddie Irvine   Ferrari F300   1:35.16,368 h

Grand Prix, E, Catalunya, 10.5.1998
65 x 4,728 km = 307,320 km.
1. Mika Häkkinen   McLaren MP4/13-Mer. 1:33.37,621 h
2. David Coulthard   McLaren MP4/13-Mer. 1:33.47,060 h
3. Michael Schumacher   Ferrari F300   1:34.24,716 h

Grand Prix, MC, Monte Carlo, 24.5.1998
78 x 3,367 km = 262,626 km.
1. Mika Häkkinen   McLaren MP4/13-Mer. 1:51.23,595 h
2. Giancarlo Fisichella Benetton B198-Playl. 1:51.35,070 h
3. Eddie Irvine   Ferrari F300   1:52.04,973 h

Grand Prix, CDN, Montreal, 7.6.1998
69 x 4,421 km = 305,049 km.
1. Michael Schumacher   Ferrari F300   1:40.57,355 h
2. Giancarlo Fisichella Benetton B198-Playl. 1:41.14,017 h
3. Eddie Irvine   Ferrari F300   1:41.57,414 h

Grand Prix, F, Magny-Cours, 28.6.1998
71 x 4,250 km = 301,750 km.
1. Michael Schumacher   Ferrari F300   1:34.45,026 h
2. Eddie Irvine   Ferrari F300   1:35.04,601 h
3. Mika Häkkinen   McLaren MP4/13-Mer. 1:35.04,773 h

Grand Prix, GB, Silverstone, 12.7.1998
60 x 5,140 km = 308,400 km.
1. Michael Schumacher   Ferrari F300   1:47.02,450 h
2. Mika Häkkinen   McLaren MP4/13-Mer. 1:47.24,915 h
3. Eddie Irvine   Ferrari F300   1:47.31,649 h

Grand Prix, A, A1-Ring, 26.7.1998
71 x 4,319 km = 306,649 km.
1. Mika Häkkinen   McLaren MP4/13-Mer. 1:30.44,086 h
2. David Coulthard   McLaren MP4/13-Mer. 1:30.49,375 h
3. Michael Schumacher   Ferrari F300   1:31.23,176 h

Grand Prix, D, Hockenheim, 2.8.1998
45 x 6,823 km = 307,035 km.
1. Mika Häkkinen   McLaren MP4/13-Mer. 1:20.47,984 h
2. David Coulthard   McLaren MP4/13-Mer. 1:20.48,410 h
3. Jacques Villeneuve   Williams FW20-Meca. 1:20.50,561 h

Grand Prix, H, Hungaroring, 16.8.1998
77 x 3,972 km = 305,844 km.
1. Michael Schumacher   Ferrari F300   1:45.25,550 h
2. David Coulthard   McLaren MP4/13-Mer. 1:45.34,983 h
3. Jacques Villeneuve   Williams FW20-Meca. 1:46.09,994 h

Grand Prix, B, Spa-Francorchamps, 30.8.1998
44 x 6,968 km = 306,592 km.
1. Damon Hill   Jordan 198-Mugen   1:43.47,407 h
2. Ralf Schumacher   Jordan 198-Mugen   1:43.48,339 h
3. Jean Alesi   Sauber C17-Petronas 1:43.54,647 h

Grand Prix, I, Monza, 13.9.1998
53 x 5,770 km = 305,810 km.
1. Michael Schumacher   Ferrari F300   1:17.09,672 h
2. Eddie Irvine   Ferrari F300   1:17.47,649 h
3. Ralf Schumacher   Jordan 198-Mugen   1:17.50,824 h

Grand Prix, L, Nürburgring, 27.9.1998
67 x 4,556 km = 305,252 km.
1. Mika Häkkinen   McLaren MP4/13-Mer. 1:32.14,789 h
2. Michael Schumacher   Ferrari F300   1:32.17,000 h
3. David Coulthard   McLaren MP4/13-Mer. 1:32.48,952 h

Grand Prix, J, Suzuka, 1.11.1998
53 x 5,864 km = 310,792 km.
1. Mika Häkkinen   McLaren MP4/13-Mer. 1:27.22,535 h
2. Eddie Irvine   Ferrari F300   1:27.29,026 h
3. David Coulthard   McLaren MP4/13-Mer. 1:27.50,197 h

1998

1. M. Häkkinen   100 P.   1. McLaren-Merc.   156 P.
2. M. Schumacher   86 P.   2. Ferrari   133 P.
3. D. Coulthard   56 P.   3. Williams-Mecachr.   38 P.

1999

Grand Prix, AUS, Melbourne, 7.3.1999
57 x 5,303 km = 302,213 km.
1. Eddie Irvine   Ferrari F399   1:35.01,659 h
2. Heinz-Harald Frentzen Jordan-Mugen-Honda 1:35.02,686 h
3. Ralf Schumacher   Williams FW21-Super. 1:35.08,671 h

Grand Prix, BR, Interlagos, 11.4.1999
72 x 4,292 km = 309,024 km.
1. Mika Häkkinen   McLaren MP4/14-Mer. 1:36.03,785 h
2. Michael Schumacher   Ferrari F399   1:36.08,710 h
3. Heinz-Harald Frentzen Jordan-Mugen-Honda – 1

Grand Prix, RSM, Imola, 2.5.1999
62 x 4,930 km = 305,660 km.
1. Michael Schumacher   Ferrari F399   1:33.44,792 h
2. David Coulthard   McLaren MP4/14-Mer. 1:33.46,057 h
3. Rubens Barrichello   Stewart-Ford SF3   1:33.49,721 h

Grand Prix, MC, Monte Carlo, 16.5.1999
78 x 3,367 km = 262,626 km.
1. Michael Schumacher   Ferrari F399   1:49.31,812 h
2. Eddie Irvine   Ferrari F399   1:50.02,288 h
3. Mika Häkkinen   McLaren MP4/14-Mer. 1:50.09,295 h

Grand Prix, E, Catalunya, 30.5.1999
65 x 4,728 km = 307,320 km.
1. Mika Häkkinen   McLaren MP4/14-Mer. 1:34.13,665 h
2. David Coulthard   McLaren MP4/14-Mer. 1:34.19,903 h
3. Michael Schumacher   Ferrari F399   1:34.24,510 h

Grand Prix, CDN, Montreal, 13.6.1999
69 x 4,421 km = 305,049 km.
1. Mika Häkkinen   McLaren MP4/14-Mer. 1:41.35,727 h
2. Giancarlo Fisichella Benetton B199-Playl. 1:41.36,509 h
3. Eddie Irvine   Ferrari F399   1:41.37,524 h

Grand Prix, F, Magny-Cours, 27.6.1999
72 x 4,250 km = 306,000 km.
1. Heinz-Harald Frentzen Jordan-Mugen-Honda 1:58.24,343 h
2. Mika Häkkinen   McLaren MP4/14-Mer. 1:58.35,435 h
3. Rubens Barrichello   Stewart SF3-Ford   1:59.07,775 h

Grand Prix, GB, Silverstone, 11.7.1999
60 x 5,140 km = 308,400 km.
1. David Coulthard   McLaren MP4/14-Mer. 1:32.30,144 h
2. Eddie Irvine   Ferrari F399   1:32.31,973 h
3. Ralf Schumacher   Williams FW21-Super. 1:32.57,555 h

Grand Prix, A, A1-Ring, 25.7.1999
71 x 4,319 km = 306,649 km.
1. Eddie Irvine   Ferrari F399   1:28.12,438 h
2. David Coulthard   McLaren MP4/14-Mer. 1:28.12,751 h
3. Mika Häkkinen   McLaren MP4/14-Mer. 1:28.34,720 h

Grand Prix, D, Hockenheim, 1.8.1999
45 x 6,823 km = 307,035 km.
1. Eddie Irvine   Ferrari F399   1:21.58,594 h
2. Mika Salo   Ferrari F399   1:21.59,601 h
3. Heinz-Harald Frentzen Jordan-Mugen-Honda 1:22.03,789 h

Grand Prix, H, Hungaroring, 15.8.1999
77 x 3,972 km = 305,844 km.
1. Mika Häkkinen   McLaren MP4/14-Mer. 1:46.23,536 h
2. David Coulthard   McLaren MP4/14-Mer. 1:46.33,242 h
3. Eddie Irvine   Ferrari F399   1:46.50,764 h

Grand Prix, B, Spa-Francorchamps, 29.8.1999
44 x 6,968 km = 306,592 km.
1. David Coulthard   McLaren MP4/14-Mer. 1:25.43,057 h
2. Mika Häkkinen   McLaren MP4/14-Mer. 1:25.53,526 h
3. Heinz-Harald Frentzen Jordan-Mugen-Honda 1:26.16,490 h

Grand Prix, I, Monza, 12.9.1999
53 x 5,770 km = 305,810 km.
1. Heinz-Harald Frentzen Jordan-Mugen-Honda 1:17.02,923 h
2. Ralf Schumacher   Williams FW21-Super. 1:17.06,195 h
3. Mika Salo   Ferrari F399   1:17.14,855 h

Grand Prix, L, Nürburgring, 26.9.1999
66 x 4,556 km = 300,696 km.
1. Johnny Herbert   Stewart SF3-Ford   1:41.54,314 h
2. Jarno Trulli   Prost AP02-Peugeot 1:42.16,933 h
3. Rubens Barrichello   Stewart SF3-Ford   1:42.17,180 h

Grand Prix, MAL, Sepang, 17.10.1999
56 x 5,542 km = 310,352 km.
1. Eddie Irvine   Ferrari F399   1:36.38,494 h
2. Michael Schumacher   Ferrari F399   1:36.39,534 h
3. Mika Häkkinen   McLaren MP4/14-Mer. 1:36.48,237 h

Grand Prix, J, Suzuka, 31.10.1999
53 x 5,864 km = 310,792 km.
1. Mika Häkkinen   McLaren MP4/14-Mer. 1:31.18,785 h
2. Michael Schumacher   Ferrari F399   1:31.23,800 h
3. Eddie Irvine   Ferrari F399   1:32.54,473 h

1999

1. M. Häkkinen   76 P.   1. Ferrari   128 P.
2. E. Irvine   74 P.   2. McLaren-Mercedes   124 P.
3. H.-H. Frentzen 54 P.   3. Jordan-M.-Honda   61 P.